Psychophysical Acting

D1612080

"Being taken step-by-s
concepts of actor train
reading."

Psychophysical Acting i:
on today's actor. Draw
aims to equip actors w
work. Areas of focus ir

- An historical overv
  Stanislavski to the ¡
- Acting as an "energ
  Samuel Beckett, M:
- A system of trainin;
  awareness, dynamic
- Practical applicatio

Psychophysical Acting i:
featuring exercises, pr

Phillip Zarrilli is inte
through Asian martial
of Performance Practi
Reconsidered (2002), *K*
An Introduction (2006,

Psychophysical Acting

An intercultural approach after Stanislavski

Phillip B. Zarrilli

with DVD-ROM by Peter Hulton

Foreword by Eugenio Barba

Routledge
Taylor & Francis Group

LONDON AND NEW YORK

First published 2009 by Routledge
2 Park Square, Milton Park, Abingdon, Oxon OX14 4RN
Simultaneously published in the USA and Canada
by Routledge
711 Third Avenue, New York, NY 10017

Routledge is an imprint of the Taylor & Francis Group, an informa business

© 2009 Phillip B. Zarrilli

Typeset in Interstate and Arno by
The Running Head Limited, Cambridge, www.therunninghead.com

British Library Cataloguing in Publication Data
A catalogue record for this book is available from the British Library

Library of Congress Cataloging in Publication Data
Zarrilli, Phillip B., 1947–
Psychophysical acting: an intercultural approach after Stanislavski / by Phillip B. Zarrilli.
     p.   cm.
Includes bibliographical references and index.
1. Acting.   2. Acting—Psychological aspects.   I. Title.
PN2061.Z37   2008
792.02′8—dc22

                                                                              2008032856

ISBN13: 978–0–415–33457–0 (hb)
ISBN13: 978–0–415–33458–7 (pb)

ISBN10: 0–415–33457–8 (hb)
ISBN10: 0–415–33458–6 (pb)

For Kaite O'Reilly

Contents

List of illustrations and charts   ix

Acknowledgments   xi

Foreword by Eugenio Barba   xiii

A preface in three voices   1

Introduction: a psychophysical approach to acting   7

PART I
What is the actor's work?   11

1   Historical context   13

2   Beginning with the breath   22

3   An enactive approach to acting and embodiment   41

PART II
Work on oneself   61

4   The source traditions: yoga, *kalarippayattu*, and *taiqiquan*   63

5   The psychophysical actor's "I can"   81

6   Exercises for "playing" in-between: structured improvisations   99

PART III
Production case studies   113

7   *The Beckett Project*   115

8   *The Water Station (Mizu No Eki)* by Ōta Shōgo   144

9   *Speaking Stones: Images, voices, fragments . . . from that which comes after*, with text by Kaite O'Reilly and German translation by Frank Heibert   174

10   *4:48 Psychosis* by Sarah Kane   188

11   *Attempts on Her Life* by Martin Crimp   199

Afterword   213

Appendix 1: A. C. Scott and the Asian Experimental
      Theater Program   215

Appendix 2: Yuasa Yasuo's body-scheme   217

Notes   219

Bibliography   235

Index   247

Illustrations and charts

Illustrations

1   The author and Rajashekharan Nayar at the CVN Kalari
    (Thiruvananthapuram) in 1993 practicing with the *otta*   3

2.1 Gurukkal Govindankutty Nayar, of the Thiruvananthapuram, performs
    the lion pose   24

2.2 Demonstration of the extension of breath/energy simultaneously through
    the top of the head and soles of the feet while executing a yoga *asana* 28

2.3 The nine basic states of being/doing (*bhava*) in *kathakali* dance-drama 36

2.4 A rehearsal of the character Hanuman from the play, *The Killing of Lavanasura* 37

3.1 Reader (Phillip Zarrilli) and Listener (Andy Crook) in Samuel Beckett's *Ohio
    Impromptu*   42

3.2 The lion pose from *kalarippayattu*: an intensive training workshop at
    Gardzienice Theatre Association, Poland   53

4.1 Executing the fish pose at the Tyn-y-Parc CVN Kalari/Studio in West Wales 64

4.2 A yoga *asana*   66

4.3 Teaching long staff to a student from Japan at the CVN Kalari,
    Thiruvananthapuram   68

4.4 The author giving massage (*uliccil*) at the Tyn-y-Parc CVN Kalari in Wales 69

4.5 The *cakras* and *nadis* of the subtle body   71

4.6 Yin–yang symbol   74

4.7 Kalamandalam Gopi in the role of King Rugmamgada   79

5.1 Demonstrating hands-on work with the opening breathing exercises at
    Gardzienice Theatre Association, Poland   92

5.2 The flow of energy and movement in the lion pose   95

7.1 Patricia Boyette in *Rockaby*   119

8.1 *The Water Station*: the Girl (Yoo Jeungsook) in Scene 1   145

9.1 *Speaking Stones*, Christian Heuegger in "Footsteps of the Dead"   183

10.1 Lim Sung Mi as Figure in *4:48 Psychosis*, Seoul, Korea, 2008   195
11.1 *(composite)* *Attempts on Her Life*: Scenario 9, "The Threat of International
        Terrorism" (Singapore production, 2007)   207

Charts

1   Three modes of bodymind awareness   33
2   The actor's four embodied modes of experience   52
3   An overview of the psychophysical actor's process   84

Acknowledgments

Thanks to Talia Rodgers, Commissioning Editor at Routledge for her faith in this project; Peter Hulton for his patience, presence, and time; my teachers, especially Gurukkal Govindankutty Nayar, M. P. Sankaran Namboodiri, and A. C. Scott; the actors and directors with whom I have collaborated, especially Patricia Boyette, Andy Crook, and Peader Kirk for work on *The Beckett Project*; Richard Schechner for our early work on *Richard's Lear*; the extraordinary group of international practitioners and students with whom I have been privileged to work, especially Jeungsook Yoo and Klaus Seewald; T. Sasitharan and TTRP; Wlodzimierz Staniewski and Gardzienice Theatre Association; and for the support of the staff and excellent facilities of the Drama Department, Exeter University.

Special thanks to Mr Pocock and the entire staff at the Royal Devon and Exeter Hospital Urology and Oncology Departments for making it possible for me to complete this book and continue my artistic work.

Permissions

Cover Nina Herlitschka
1   Ed Heston
2.1 Phillip Zarrilli
2.2 Przemek Sieraczynski
2.3 Phillip Zarrilli
2.4 Phillip Zarrilli
3.1 Brent Nicastro
3.2 Przemek Sieraczynski
4.1 Phillip Zarrilli
4.2 Photographer unknown
4.3 Photographer unknown
4.4 Kaite O'Reilly
4.5 (a) Print from *The Power of Tantrik Breathing*
      (b) Copy of a nineteenth-century Gujarat manuscript painting
   (c–d) Drawings by Phillip Zarrilli
4.6 Public domain
4.7 Phillip Zarrilli
5.1 Przemek Sieraczynski
5.2 (a) Deborah Proctor
      (b) Phillip Zarrilli
7.1 Brent Nicastro
8.1   Kimberly Tok (courtesy TTRP)
9.1 Nina Herlitschka
10.1 Kim Hyun-Min (courtesy KNUA)
11.1 Choon Hun of PhotoUnique

Website

For up-to-date information about Phillip Zarrilli's work, visit www.phillipzarrilli.com

Arts Archives

ARTS ARCHIVES—an international digital moving image resource for performance practice research—is a Council of Europe-initiated not-for-profit project with copyright held on behalf of the contributors. It is concerned with documenting material which attends closely to the processes and principles at work within performing arts practice in the belief that such insights can contribute to arts development in particular and to an understanding of human experience in general. It was founded and is directed by Peter Hulton (www.arts-archives.org).

Foreword

Eugenio Barba

A landscape made of bridges

This book by Phillip Zarrilli stands on the three arches of a bridge which connects:

1   the traditions of Western and Asian theater;
2   artistic and scientific knowledge;
3   performative work and the work of the performer on his or her inner life.

The author, who belongs to that rare species of scholar/practitioners, emphasizes the relevance of these junctions and the visions that spring from them. He reminds us how, in a direct and indirect way, the experiences of the Great Reform in twentieth-century theater grew out of these interactions.

Around these three main arches the author builds a web of paths and secondary passages, creating a personal and, at times, unpredictable landscape. He progresses through it with a sure step. He has a vast and detailed experience and does not limit himself to simple descriptions. He explains the practical dimensions of the principles on which he throws light, always keeping an eye on the necessity of being useful to those who want to practice theater and are looking for points of departure. This landscape, which is not only made

of bridges, is partially new and therefore both fascinating and valuable for practice.

It is an important book within the teaching context where too often teachers have not chosen their students and students have not chosen their teachers. The book shakes up if not the reality, at least the nostalgia for the transmission of experience based on mutual choice. I hope that the book will circulate both within the academic and professional milieu and among those young people whom nobody professes to teach, while they learn in their own way, often through an intelligent use of misunderstandings.

In art, unfortunately (or luckily), there is nothing that it is absolutely necessary to know, and which therefore is worthy to belong to a teaching syllabus. No true ABC exists. Everyone has his or her own and has to invent his or her own first steps. In art, whenever we find a rule, a principle or an axiom, we are also aware that—in the measure in which it is true—its opposite is also true.

This is not skepticism. It is the reality of which our artistic life and our theatrical common sense are made. In our field, there are no procedures which are good in themselves; there are no absolute rules which are correct, true, and necessary.

Not even openness of mind, the desire for confrontation, and a dialogue between experiences are a value in themselves. Circumstances often push us to think that they are fertile. But it is an illusion. When it comes to artistic practices, whether we like it or not, isolation, an inadequate knowledge of possible alternatives, the absence of comparisons, and exclusive fidelity to one's own forms and conventions work as well as openness of mind, the ability to discuss, and the critical scrutinizing of one's own principles.

We who love dialogue and the wealth of cultural *métissage* and speak of a Eurasian Theatre, recognize that the Western theatrical tradition could very well live without the dialogue with the Asian classical traditions. And vice versa.

It is debatable whether the knowledge of why and how certain things function makes them work better. At times, however much we may regret it, a vague, confused, and superstitious attitude may be as beneficial on a practical level as a scientifically based awareness.

That's why I believe that Zarrilli's book is important. Its correctly scientific apparel in reality conceals an effective ecologist of the mind behind the appearances of a scholar/practitioner.

The landscape made of bridges which this book covers responds to that essential need anyone has who wishes to reflect upon and do theater in our time. It gives density to the way we think about our craft, its techniques, and its practices. It erects a scale of values which is not exclusively reduced to the value of the result. Zarrilli opens a space before and behind theatrical work—training, rehearsals, and performance. It is a vast space of awareness and imagination which allows both the eager beginner and the experienced practitioner to feel they are part of a history, to identify themselves with a system of thought, and to hover between truth and shared necessity.

A preface in three voices

Remember this: all of our acts, even the simplest, which are so familiar to us in everyday life, become strained when we appear [...] before a public [...] That is why it is necessary to correct ourselves and learn again how to walk, move about, sit, or lie down. It is essential to re-educate ourselves to look and see, on the stage, to listen, and to hear.

(Stanislavski 1936: 73)

Meyyu kannakuka: literally, "the body becomes all eyes." A Malayalam folk expression encapsulating that ideal state of embodiment and accomplishment of both the actor and the *kalarippayattu* (Indian martial art) practitioner. When one's "body is all eyes" then like Lord Brahman "the thousand eyed" one is like an animal—able to see, hear, and respond immediately to any stimulus in the immediate environment.

(Phillip Zarrilli)

Psychophysical Acting (book and DVD-ROM) focuses on the relationship between the actor-as-doer and what the actor does. It (re)examines in practice and theory a psychophysical understanding and approach to acting. Drawing on an intercultural set of paradigms and principles, it elaborates and expands upon the assumptions behind the Russian director, actor, and acting teacher Konstantin Stanislavski's innovative use of the compound term "psycho-physical" in the nineteenth century. It re-examines the assumptions we make about both parts of the compound term, "psycho-physical," i.e., the mind, the body, and their relationship. It describes the in-depth process of psychophysical training via Asian martial arts and yoga I have developed since 1976 through which the actor constantly re-educates her bodymind so that one looks and sees, listens and hears anew each time one enters the training studio or stage. It provides an alternative conceptualization and model of the actor's work based not on acting as representation, but on an "energetics" of performance. It explains how energy is activated, how perceptual/sensory awareness is heightened—animal-like—as the body "becomes all eyes," and how both are applied to a variety of dramaturgies.

The first: staying anxious . . . in between

A story is told as much by silence as by speech. Like the white spaces in an etching, such silences render form. But unlike an etching in which the whole is grasped at once, the silence of a story must be understood over time . . . The telling and hearing of a story is not a simple act. The one who tells must reach down into deeper layers of the self, reviving old feelings, reviewing the past. Whatever is retrieved is reworked into a new form, one that narrates events and gives the listener a path through these events that leads to some fragments of wisdom. The one who hears takes the story in, even to a place not visible or conscious to the mind, yet there. In this inner place a story from another life suffers a subtle change. As it enters the memory of the listener it is augmented by reflection, by other memories, and even the body hearing and responding in the moment of the telling. By such transmissions, consciousness is woven.

(Griffin: 1992: 172)

This book and DVD-ROM explore

- the "white spaces" in the etching we call acting;
- the silences that have the potential to render form when we perform;
- one process for inhabiting the silences of this inner space "not visible or conscious to the mind, but there" (Griffin: 1992: 172);
- how in that space the actor's being-in-the-moment resonates with the traces, associations, and/or images called memory, feeling, emotion;
- how embodied consciousness emerges from this inner place with each impulse/action toward a constantly unfolding and unknown horizon;
- how the actor must constantly attune herself to the subtle processes of psychophysiological engagement with the inner vibration and resonance of her energy—manifest in the quality of her embodied awareness;
- how these processes are shared between actors, and with an audience.

What is offered here are not definitive answers, but a way of exploring the questions acting offers us. As Hollis Huston asserts,

The stage is a radical question. The theater appears only when we ask that question and hold the answer in suspense. The theater, if it has a future, belongs to the artists who take the art in their hands and who know the properties of their instrument as you would know the seat of your bicycle. The stage's poetic is terror's anatomy. You must act now, and life or death depends on your choice. If you don't know that actors die, I can show you how to do it.

(Huston 1995: 129, added opening italics)

This publication explores some of the properties of the actor's instrument: the actor's bodymind, awareness, consciousness, and energy. It explores

- how we *might* learn to "act now" on the edge;
- how we might better inhabit this paradoxical place of experience, awareness, and (double/multiple) consciousness;
- how we might actualize an optimal state of not-knowing and surprise.

I invite the reader to question what we do when we are acting, and how we think and talk about acting. As a consequence, this is as much a work of philosophy as of practice—a work that invites us to reconsider the nature of acting and its practice. Some parts of this book and Peter Hulton's DVD-ROM are more poetic in that they leave white spaces to be filled in; some are historical and reflexive; some are pragmatic and descriptive. In its pragmatic sections, this work engages sweating bodyminds in a specific, ongoing process of daily work in the studio. In its theoretical/analytical sections, I invite consideration of the sweating bodymind. *Psychophysical Acting* is a verbal/audio-visual reflection on these problems and possibilities. Its words, still and moving images, and audio reflections do not attempt to fully represent or describe the process I have developed, but rather constitute a complex mosaic which creates its own white spaces for reflection. As Hollis Huston explains,

Only you can think clearly; only you can briefly make a portion of the world make sense; only you can preserve the memory of that moment. These thoughts will not comfort you, but they might make you free. Neither art nor thought is comfortable. I am here to make you nervous. Only when we are anxious, and when we know what to be anxious about, do we have a chance of entering the history of our work.

(Huston 1995: 131)

— ⁓ —

The second: the whole body

"Use the whole body, Zarrilli, your whole body!"

(Gurukkal Govindankutty Nayar, CVN Kalari, 1980)

I will never forget the moment when my first and primary *kalarippayattu* teacher, Gurukkal Govindankutty Nayar of the CVN Kalari (Thiruvananthampuram), shouted at me, "use your whole body!" It was a much needed moment of complete and utter humiliation—and later, of realization. I suspect that anyone who has undergone in-depth training and acted on stage has experienced similar moments—humiliation can be an actor's greatest friend. In the midst of my making every effort to be fully engaged in embodying an exercise as fully and correctly as possible, Govindankutty Nayar had shouted at me to "use your whole body." Of course, at the time I thought I *was* using my entire body. How could I *not* be when on the outside a river of sweat was pouring from my body onto the earth floor, and on the inside I was making such an effort! It *felt* as if I was doing the exercise fully and correctly. What was this "whole body" I was

Figure 1 The author (left) and Rajashekharan Nayar at the CVN Kalari (Thiruvananthapuram) in 1993 practicing a sequence of attacks and defenses with the *otta—kalarippayattu*'s most complex weapon. Advanced practice of *otta* requires each practitioner simultaneously to (1) maintain single-point focus through the opponent's eyes; (2) sustain open awareness of the entire environment; (3) engage and circulate breath/inner-energy throughout the bodymind as well as the weapon; and (4) ensure that the inner-energy is "grounded" through the soles of the feet as they maintain contact with the earth. (Photograph: Ed Heston)

apparently *not* using? I did not yet understand that when he used the term "whole body" he actually meant what I now call bodymind—a deeply felt, resonant inhabitation of the subtle psychophysical dimensions of the body and mind at work together as one in the moment. Engaging the whole body means working with a fully awakened energy coursing through one's entire bodymind. One's awareness is so fully open that one is totally focused within a specific action. Space-time unfolds *through* one's engagement in the actions that constitute one's relationship to the immediate environment in the moment of their performance. At the time I was limited by my then very paltry, partial embodiment of the form, and my incomplete understanding of or ability to articulate the subtler aspects of the body–mind relationship. I had not yet discovered that there was a subtle energy lying within to be awakened and released through every action in which I engaged.

As a young actor and theater director based in Minneapolis in the 1970s, I had been inspired by Antonin Artaud, Jerzy Grotowski, and Eugenio Barba to take my own journey beyond American versions of Stanislavski available to me at the time. That journey took me to Kerala, India in 1976–1977 to study one of the source traditions which had influenced the early work of Grotowski and Barba—*kathakali* dance-drama. I immersed myself fully in the traditional training, undergoing a rigorous regime of eight hours of daily psychophysical training and full-body massage with M. P. Sankaran Namboodiri at the Kerala Kalamandalam—the Kerala State School of the Arts—which Grotowski and Barba had both visited some years earlier. When I encountered the source tradition from which *kathakali's* preliminary body-training exercises and massage were derived—the early twelfth-century yoga-based indigenous martial art, *kalarippayattu*—I was accepted as a student and trained for seven years in Kerala with one of the great masters of the tradition, Gurukkal Govindankutty Nayar (1930–2006).[1]

I am sure that in 1980, from Govindankutty

Nayar's perspective observing me, my bodymind appeared contorted and my energy compressed by effort and that greatest of all villains for the actor—intentionality. I was mistaking the tremendous effort I was exerting in trying to get each action or form into my body for the virtuosity I witnessed when Govindankutty Nayar embodied the same exercise—filling it out with effortless ease with his subtle energy.

From my perspective today, the problem of the actor *not* understanding what it means to inhabit one's "whole body," and therefore *not* being able to access and utilize the type of in-depth bodymind awareness marked by the phrase "use your whole body," remains a common, even banal problem. Intention, effort, and the lack of a more complex understanding of the body–mind relationship continue to be the actor's worst enemies. In an interview, Ryszard Cieslak—the actor whose work with Jerzy Grotowski resulted in luminous performances that have served as a model of the optimal engagement of the actor in his work—observed that

> [An] important thing to remember is that an actor must concentrate on . . . his whole body . . . [J]ust as a musician has to exercise his fingers every day, so an actor has to exercise his body almost to the point of overcoming it, that is, being in complete control of it.
> (Cieslak in Torzecka 1992: 261)

One of Meyerhold's pupils of 1922, Erast Garen, described how when executing the "Shooting a bow" *étude*—one of the main biomechanical exercises—"the movement of the hand affects the whole body" (Braun 1969: 203). For Grotowski and Meyerhold alike their work was devoted to solving how to approach this intractable problem of the actor's "whole body."

My own (often problematic and misguided) struggles to inhabit, experience, and problem-solve my own bodymind in performance informs this publication. At first my body and mind were naïve, inept, and inexperienced strangers. Today, they have become "mature" friends—possessing an often profound and deeply resonant sense of recollection and remembrance. My physical body is inevitably aging, quickly—osteoarthritis in my knees requires constant adjustments in the ways I move and inhabit my bodymind. Our bodyminds do not stand still for us. They can be lazy, recalcitrant, docile, over-energetic, and/or misguided, to list only a few adjectives.

The "problem of the body" is like a virus—it constantly mutates and surprises us. Since our individual bodyminds do not stand still and can be multiple, and since no two bodies, no two selves, no two ensembles, and no two dramaturgies are the same, the tactics I use in the studio and rehearsal room must constantly shift to the ever-changing ways in which the problem of the body is manifest in *this* actor's bodymind, *this* ensemble's collective body, the demands of *this* dramaturgy on the actor's bodyminds at this particular moment. Therefore, the ways I write and think about the actor's bodymind are informed by a pragmatic search for an intelligently informed way of helping actors diagnose and problem-solve their particular form(s) of the "problem of the whole body" as quickly as possible.

The third: acting as enquiry

Perhaps the most important gift and legacy left by Konstantin Stanislavski (1863–1938) was the notion that theater-making is best when it is practiced as an ever-evolving process of constant practical enquiry and reflection in the studio. Enquiry was his obsession and that of many who have followed in his pathway if not his specific footsteps—Michael Chekhov, Meyerhold, Grotowski, and Barba among many others. But this legacy of enquiry in the studio is not just a contemporary Western phenomenon. Take Kan'ami (1333–1384) and especially his son, Zeami (1363–1443), under whose guidance Japanese *noh* evolved into a unique form of Japanese

performance. Zeami not only wrote *noh* dramas, but honed his craft as an actor and teacher, authoring a remarkable set of highly reflexive treatises on the subtle processes of the art of acting that are as important today as when he wrote them. Such practitioners are pedagogues in the best sense of the term—they enter the studio and rehearsal room with a deep passion for discovery, (re)searching the possible ways in which one might attain moments of lucidity about process-in-practice.

This book follows their collective legacy of enquiry by (re)examining the psychophysical processes of the performer—the "pre-expressive" territory that prepares the actor to work on actions and a score, the nature of impulses and physical actions, the inner action concealed within physical actions, and the relationship between bodymind, consciousness, and sensory awareness in the actor's work—in the light of non-Western paradigms and practices. This work questions, and expands upon, earlier articulations of a psychophysical paradigm of acting. It further explores the nature and possibilities of a psychophysical paradigm for understanding and approaching the work of the actor via (re)training the actor's bodymind through Asian martial and meditation arts and insights gained from my long-term encounter with non-Western paradigms and practices of acting—in particular Kerala's martial art, *kalarippayattu*; *hatha-yoga* as taught to me by Dayanidhi and Chandran Gurukkal in Kerala; *taiqiquan*, Wu-style, as taught by A. C. Scott;[2] Japanese *noh* via study with Akira Matsui of the Kita *noh* school; and Kerala's *kathakali* under the guidance of M. P. Sankaran Namboodiri.

Enquiry is a process of exploration born out of intellectual and aesthetic curiosity. *Psychophysical Acting* is not and cannot be "definitive" about either the questions around which the work is organized, or the approach I have taken to solving these questions at certain specific moments. Jean Benedetti explains how toward the end of his career, in 1936, Stanislavski remarked, "'I have created the "system" and I am still revising it'" (Benedetti 1999: 376). Benedetti also reminds us that Stanislavski's findings could not be confined within a set of narrow definitions:

> For Stanislavski, the "system" was never more than an aid to the creative process . . .

A rediscovery of the "system" must begin with the realization that *it is the questions which are important*, the logic of their sequence and the consequent logic of the answers.

> (Benedetti 1999 [1988]: 376, italics added)

Introduction

A psychophysical approach to acting

The work of the contemporary actor

Whether in the US, UK, Europe, Japan, India, Indonesia, Jordan, Singapore, or elsewhere in the world, the work of today's contemporary actor is no longer restricted to playing fully rounded, individual characters such as those authored in the realist plays of Anton Chekhov, Henrik Ibsen, Tennessee Williams, Japanese *shingeki* ("new theater"), etc. Contemporary actors are also expected to perform across a broad spectrum of new, alternative, "post-dramatic" (Lehmann 2006) dramaturgies such as the later plays of Samuel Beckett; Indonesian playwright/director Putu Wijaya's theater of surprise exemplified in his play *Gerr (GEEZ!)* (1981/1986); Sarah Kane's highly poetic, "open" script, *4:48 Psychosis* (Kane 2001); or devised "physical theater."

The psychologically whole character was no longer central to many types of theater after the 1960s, as can be seen in the deconstructive work of the Wooster Group or Robert Wilson's spectacular theater of images in the USA, or the fragmentary thought-provoking, time-based task performances of Forced Entertainment in the UK. In Japan the psychophysical re-creation of Western classics by Suzuki Tadashi's company, and the dynamic *butoh* dance, have dispensed with conventional playing

of characters. What the actor or performer does on stage at the start of the twenty-first century ranges from playing a psychologically realist character to the sequential playing of multiple roles or personae to the enactment of tasks or entry into images without any character implications.

Hans-Thies Lehmann uses the term "post-dramatic" to denote the diverse range of alternative scripted and devised performances produced since the 1970s in which there is no longer a central story/plot or character(s)/subjectivity(ies) forming the center of the theatrical event (2006: 26–27). In "post-dramatic forms of *theatre*, staged text (*if* text is staged) is merely a component with equal rights in a gestic, musical, visual, etc. total composition" (ibid.: 46). Since post-dramatic texts and performances are not necessarily organized around a plot or recognizable individual characters, a variety of alternative "aesthetic logic(s)" (ibid.: 18) inform the structure and type of action, as well as the tasks of the performers.

However important psychology has been to shaping the dramaturgy of realist and naturalist plays from the late nineteenth through the twentieth centuries, conventional realist approaches to acting and/or textual analysis may be inadequate or even inappropriate to the realization of the dramaturgy and acting tasks that constitute an actor's performance score in a post-dramatic text or performance. I argue here that the "psychological" is no longer—if it ever was—a paradigm with sufficient explanatory and/ or practical power and flexibility to fully inform the complexities of the work of the contemporary actor.

This book is intended to help today's actors find appropriate conceptual and practical tools that will allow them to solve the specific acting problems of both conventional "dramatic" as well as "post-dramatic" dramaturgies such as the work of Sarah Kane or Martin Crimp. The psychological is not to be rejected, but considered as one among several conceptual paradigms which can tactically inform *certain specific aspects* of the work of the actor as and when appropriate. Therefore, *Psychophysical Acting* takes a "post-Stanislavskian" approach to acting, i.e., it does *not* reject Stanislavski per se, but rather moves acting theory and practice beyond some of the historical and practical limitations which have informed our understanding of Stanislavski's legacy, especially in the US.

As discussed in Chapter 2, in his attempt to bridge the Western gap between "mind" and "body," the cognitive and sensory realms of our experience, and analysis and embodiment, Stanislavski himself identified the need for a "psychophysical" theory and practice of acting. He therefore drew upon two "new" paradigms and practices to help him solve these intractable problems—Ribot's psychology and Indian yoga. Drawing on newer sciences and in-depth study of non-Western paradigms and practices, the psychophysical approach described in this book provides a set of complementary conceptual and practical tools to help the actor better meet the demands of today's alternative dramaturgies.

Non-Western traditions and the principles that inform them offer an alternative understanding of all the key elements of acting—body, mind, their relationship, emotion, action—and even of acting process. *Psychophysical Acting* is therefore self-consciously intercultural. I draw directly upon non-Western philosophies and practices

in order to freshly (re)consider a psychophysical approach to contemporary acting, East and West. Significantly, with the exception of American method approaches, most of the major theorist/ practitioners of contemporary acting including Stanislavski, Michael Chekhov, Meyerhold, Artaud, Brecht, Grotowski, Barba, Copeau, Tadeusz Kantor, Herbert Blau, Suzuki Tadashi, Yoshi Oida, Ariane Mnouchkine, and Anne Bogart have been influenced in some way by non-Western traditions ranging from Japanese *noh*, Indian yoga or *kathakali* dance-drama, to Beijing opera, among others.

Therefore, the approach to psychophysical acting described here does not begin with psychology or emotion, but rather with work on what Eugenio Barba describes as the "pre-expressive" level of performance (Barba and Savarese 2005: 186–204)—*preparing* the actor's body, mind, sensory awareness/perception, and energy for the expressive work of the actor. Preparation begins with psychophysical training through Asian martial arts and yoga that "attunes" the body and mind and awakens one's inner energy, progresses through a workshop phase in which the actor's awareness and energy are put into free play in structured improvisations, and continues as the actor fine-tunes awareness and energy in response to specific dramaturgies.

Part I reflects on the work of the actor. It considers the underlying philosophical and methodological problems of representationalism and body–mind dualism that vex Western theories and practices of acting. Chapter 1 briefly examines and reconsiders a psychophysical approach to acting from historical and intercultural perspectives. Chapter 2 provides a reflection upon and outline of the type of psychophysical training which prepares the actor's bodymind to be ready for performance. Chapter 3 steps back from the psychophysical approach to acting described here to (re)consider acting and the actor's experience as an enactive phenomenon. This view draws on a variety of newer sciences and methodologies which help us reflect upon the nature and phenomenon of acting and our experience of acting from inside—phenomenology, cognitive science, and anthropological studies of the body, senses, perception, and the environment. Challenging a static representational model, I propose and articulate an enactive account of the actor as perceiver and doer. I argue that acting should be viewed as a set of psychophysical processes by means of which a (theatrical) world is made available in the moment of its appearance and experience for both actors and audiences. The chapter concludes by providing a schematic phenomenological model of the actor's modes of embodied experience and discusses the implications of this view for actor training and process.

Part II, "Work on Oneself," provides an account of the approach to the psychophysical process of acting via Asian martial/meditation arts that I have developed in the training and rehearsal studio over the past thirty years since my first trip to India. Chapter 4 provides a brief account of the source traditions—yoga, *kalarippayattu*, and *taiqiquan*—in cultural context. Chapter 5 discusses how I have organized and transposed key elements and principles of the source traditions into a progressive system for pre-performative training for actors through use of active images, activating phrases, and other methods of opening the actor's sensory awareness, heightening concentration, and directing the actor's focus. Chapter 6 is an account of how these principles and techniques are elaborated and applied to performance problems in a workshop setting via "structured improvisations"—a series of performance-like studio-based exercises I have developed to bridge the possible "gap" between training, principles of training, and performance.

Part III provides a set of in-depth case studies. Each chapter describes and analyzes how, as a director and actor trainer, I have applied this particular psychophysical approach to rehearsals and performances across a wide range of contemporary dramatic and post-dramatic dramaturgies—the later plays of Samuel Beckett, Ōta Shōgo's *The Water Station*, semi-devised physical scores with text by Kaite O'Reilly in *Speaking Stones*, Sarah Kane's *4:48 Psychosis*, and Martin Crimp's *Attempts on Her Life*.

DVD-ROM by Peter Hulton

Peter Hulton's DVD-ROM creates an active dialogue with the book described above. It is an audio-visual "reflection" on the practical training and its application to performance. It includes still images, an interview with the author, interviews and commentaries from actor/performers who have undergone the training process, video footage of the training, as well as its application to selected performances discussed in Part III.

Video footage of training has been selected to demonstrate how techniques, key elements, and principles of training are transmitted to beginners. The training sessions shown are intended to provide insight into the ongoing, *everyday* process of learning rather than virtuosic practice. Occasional footage shows intermediate and more advanced practice. [NOTE: *No individual should attempt to learn or transmit the techniques recorded in this book and DVD-ROM without undergoing proper instruction. The exercises should only be practiced under the guidance of a qualified teacher able to safely guide each individual through the process of learning.*]

As an interactive audio-visual resource, the DVD-ROM stands on its own; therefore, I only occasionally refer the reader to specific locations on the DVD. (The ⦿ DVD-ROM logo/gray "bar" indicates an accompanying section on the DVD-ROM.)

Part I

What is the actor's work?

1

Historical context

The work of Russian actor and theater director Konstantin Stanislavski (1863–1938) revolutionized Western approaches to acting in the late nineteenth and early twentieth centuries. As part of his life-long practical research into the nature and processes of acting, Stanislavski was the first to use the term "psychophysical" (*psikhofizicheskii*) to describe an approach to Western acting focused equally on the actor's psychology and physicality applied to textually based character acting.

When psychology emerged as a separate discipline from philosophy in the nineteenth century, the sciences of mind and the self were often considered separate from the science(s) of the physical body. This split reflected the long-term Western binary dividing mind from body that so problematically crystallized in the mind–body dualism of the seventeenth-century French philosopher René Descartes (1596–1650). Scientists and philosophers who wanted mind and body to be considered in relation to one another, rather than separately, began to use the compound term "psycho-physical" to bridge this gap. As Robert Gordon explains,

> The development of post-Darwinian theories of physiology had produced a new understanding of the nervous system, which rendered obsolete the earlier rhetoric of acting based on a simple use of corporeal and facial signs to express inner feelings. New notions of acting as behavior not only served the Darwinian logic of naturalistic drama appropriately, but also reflected the modern physiological conception of the body as a unified psychophysical organism.
>
> (Gordon 2006: 36)

Stanislavski's use of "psychophysical" in relation to acting was therefore an innovative, if historically limited and not always successful, attempt to problem-solve the relationship between the "psycho" and the "physical" elements of acting. Key elements of Stanislavski's constantly evolving psychophysical approach to acting were drawn from two main sources—the work of psychologist Théodule Armand Ribot (1839–1916) and the limited versions of Indian yoga available to Stanislavski in turn-of-the-century Russia, filtered through the then popular occultism and spiritualism (Wegner 1976: 85–89; Carnicke 1993: 131–145; White 2006: 73). From his early focus on affective memory to his later method of physical actions, Stanislavski always *attempted* to overcome what divided "mind from body, knowledge from feeling, analysis from action" (Benedetti 1982: 66).[1]

> [Ribot's] psychophysical theories [...] state that the mind and body are a unit, and that emotions cannot be experienced without physical sensation [...] As Stanislavski writes in *An Actor Works on Himself, Part I*, "In every physical action there is something of the psychological, and in the psychological, something of the physical."
>
> (Carnicke 1998: 178)

Stanislavski described how the actor's "physical score," once perfected, must go beyond "mechanical execution" to a "deeper" level of experience which "is rounded out with new feeling and . . . become[s], one might say, psychophysical in quality" (1961: 66). In *My Life in Art*, Stanislavski described the actor's optimal state of awareness or concentration as one in which he "reacts not only on his sight and hearing, but on all the rest of his senses. It embraces his mind, his will, his emotions, his body, his memory and his imagination" (1948: 465). Stanislavski's ideal was that "in every *physical action* . . . there is concealed some *inner action*, some feelings" (1961: 228).

What Stanislavski meant by "inner action" and "feelings" were not exclusively informed by Ribot's psychology, but also by Stanislavski's adaptation of yoga exercises, principles, and philosophy.[2] As early as 1906, Stanislavski became interested in yoga (Carnicke 1998: 140). Although his knowledge of yoga was limited and may have been drawn exclusively from books in his library,[3] Stanislavski adapted specific yoga exercises and principles to help attune and heighten the actor's sensory awareness in performance.[4] Arguably the most important material element Stanislavski borrowed from yoga was *prana* (or the Sanskrit compound, *prana-vayu*)—the breath(s), wind, vital energy, or life-force understood to circulate within.[5] Stanislavski provided a fairly accurate description of the movement of *prana* as it is experienced within as follows: "'*Prana* moves, and is experienced like mercury, like a snake, from

your hands to your fingertips, from your thighs to your toes [...] The movement of *prana* creates, in my opinion, inner rhythm'" (Carnicke 1998: 141).

From 1912 in the laboratory setting of the First Studio of the Moscow Art Theatre Stanislavski and/or his artistic and administrative assistant, Leopold Antonovich Sulerzhitsky (1873–1916), utilized exercises clearly drawn from yoga.

First Studio member Vera Soloviova recalls:

> [W]e worked a great deal on concentration. We imagined a circle around us and sent "prana" rays of communication into the space and to each other. Stanislavski said "send the prana there—I want to reach through the tip of my finger—to God—the sky—or, later on, my partner. I believe in my inner energy and I give it out—I spread it."
>
> (White 2006: 79)

Yoga was the basis for Stanislavski's shift in rehearsal methods when he worked on *A Month in the Country*. The actors were requested to "radiate their feelings to communicate the subtext of inner emotions and motivations through eye contact with one another" (Gordon 2006: 47–48). In addition to these specific uses of *prana* for work on concentration, inner action, and the radiation of energy, Stanislavski borrowed from Raja Yoga "the obscure notion of the 'superconscious,' placing it next to the 'subconscious'" (Carnicke 1998: 142).[6]

The Stanislavski legacy

Stanislavski's legacy is profoundly diverse. It is like an aging oak tree—each major branch with its own unique twists, turns, knots, etc.—some of which turn in on themselves. The primary trunk and many of its major branches include those primarily concerned, as was Stanislavski himself, with textually based character acting. Some of these branches were developed by those who studied and/or worked directly with Stanislavski and remained in Russia, such as Maria Osipovna Knebel (1898–1985) or Vasily Osipovich Toporkov

(1889–1970) (Carnicke 1998: 151). Others were developed by those who worked and trained for a while with Stanislavski, but emigrated from Soviet Russia to the West. First among them were Richard Boleslavsky and Maria Ouspenskaya who founded the American Laboratory Theater (1923–1926). Michael Chekhov (1891–1955) founded the Chekhov Theatre Studio at Dartington Hall, UK (1936–1938) and on emigration to the United States further developed his own approach in Ridgefield, Connecticut (1938–1942) and later in Hollywood.[7]

For very different but equally compelling reasons, a historically balanced view of Stanislavski's approach to psychophysical acting has been extremely difficult if not impossible both in Soviet Russia and in the United States. Sharon Carnicke reports how Soviet authorities were so troubled by the idealism of Hindu philosophy informing parts of Stanislavski's work that "censors attacked Stanislavski's interest in yoga," expunged *prana* from the 1938 Russian edition of Stanislavski's acting manual, and emphasized his late method of physical actions while obscuring the importance of symbolism, formalism, and yoga in his work (1998: 144; 1–2).

In the United States the highly problematic English translations of Stanislavski's work by Elizabeth Hapgood (Stanislavski 1936, 1949, 1961),[8] the dominance of American method versions of Stanislavski's approach, and "a Freudian-based, individually oriented ethos [. . .] privileged the psychological techniques of Stanislavski's System over those of the physical" (Carnicke 1998: 1). This early preoccupation in the United States with psychology and the creation of a truthful emotional life for the character meant that, like the Soviet version, the importance of symbolism, formalism, and yoga in Stanislavski's ever-evolving system were also obscured.

In addition to suppressing the influence of yoga and Hindu philosophy on Stanislavski, his attempts to solve the acting problems of alternative forms of new drama, such as the highly static plays of the Belgian symbolist Maurice Maeterlinck (1862–1949), were until recently neglected or forgotten both in Russia and in the US. Inspired by symbolist poetry and the late nineteenth-century European fascination with mysticism and metaphysics, Maeterlinck's plays were written in reaction against historical dramas, drawing-room comedies, as well as emergent naturalism. His plays possess "characters" difficult to situate in a given historical world. Arguably the two most important of Maeterlinck's plays in terms of experimentation with form were his early plays, *The Blind* (1892), first staged in 1892 by French director, Paul Fort, and *The Intruder*, directed by Meyerhold in 1891. In *The Blind* there is "almost no action—just waiting, mounting anxiety, and slow recognition of inevitable death" (Fuchs 1996: 96). *The Blind* and *The Intruder* were notorious at the time as "static theatre" since they placed their "characters" in situations in which there was little if any physical movement.[9]

In 1904 Stanislavski decided that the Moscow Art Theatre would stage three short Maeterlinck plays, including *The Blind*. According to Benedetti, Stanislavski "realized that a new acting technique was necessary for this static drama; however, his own experiments at home in front of a mirror, both vocal and physical, proved unsuccessful" (1999: 152). The production was considered "a failure and Stanislavski was forced to concede the inadequacy of conventional representational methods when faced with the mystical abstractions of the 'new drama'" (Braun 1969: 19). In spite of this failure, Stanislavski remained obsessed with how to successfully stage Maeterlinck's plays (Benedetti 1999: 177); therefore, he began preliminary work on a production of *The Blue Bird* in 1907. After "the longest period of rehearsals the [Moscow Art Theatre] had as yet ever deliberately undertaken" (ibid.: 179), *The Blue Bird* premiered in 1908 and "became Stanislavski's most famous production" (ibid.: 183).

American versions of Stanislavski

When Stanislavski and the Moscow Art Theatre eventually toured America during 1923–1924,

American actors came to know a particular version of Stanislavski based on the realist repertory the company performed and on a series of public lectures about Stanislavski's acting system. While in the US the Moscow Art Theatre performed four plays from their well-established early repertory—Alexei Tolstoy's *Tsar Fiodor*, Maxim Gorky's *The Lower Depths*, and Anton Chekhov's *The Cherry Orchard* and *Three Sisters* (Benedetti 1999: 282–287). There were no performances of Stanislavski's more experimental work, such as Maeterlinck's symbolist plays.

American actors were so curious about Stanislavski's "system" that he gave permission for his former student and assistant on the tour, Richard Boleslavsky, to give a series of six public lectures. At precisely the time when Stanislavski was "placing greater emphasis on physical tasks and physical actions" in the development of his own process, "Boleslavsky stressed the importance of emotion memory, developing the technique beyond Stanislavski's original practice" (Benedetti 1999: 286). The combination of performances from the realist repertory and Boleslavsky's lectures created a distorted and incomplete picture of Stanislavski's directorial interests as well as his approach to acting.

So successful were Boleslavsky's lectures that they were first published in the October 1923 issue of *Theatre Arts Monthly* as "Acting, The First Six Lessons" (Boleslavsky 1949), thus establishing "Boleslavsky's authority as a teacher" of the Stanislavski system in America (Benedetti 1999: 286). Arguably the most influential of those who trained with Boleslavsky and Ouspenskaya at the American Laboratory Theater but never directly with Stanislavski was Lee Strasberg (1901–1982)—the individual most identified with the development of American method acting. Strasberg co-founded the Group Theater (1931–1940) with Harold Clurman and Cheryl Crawford. He focused on developing an actor who "'can create out of himself' . . . To do this the performer must 'appeal to the unconscious and the subconscious'" (Krasner 2000a: 134). Through exercises in "sense memory," the actor "recalls

important events in their life, and then tries to remember only the sensual facets" (ibid.: 132). Exercising one's "affective memory" the actor experiences remembered emotion leading to a release of the actor's emotions on stage (ibid.: 133). Strasberg warned actors that emotion "always should be only *remembered* emotion. An emotion that happens right now spontaneously is out of control—you don't know what's going to happen from it . . ." (ibid.: 136). In spite of such warnings the firm foundation of Stanislavski's system as Strasberg taught it lay in finding "emotional truth" (Smith 1990: 424–425).

Two of many other approaches to Stanislavski-based work in America were created when Stella Adler (1901–1992) and Sanford Meisner (1905–1997)—both of whom were members of the Group Theater and worked with Strasberg—each broke with him in 1934 and 1935 respectively. Adler's 1934 break with Strasberg was prompted by five weeks of work with Stanislavski himself in Paris on a role in *Gentlewoman*.

> What struck Adler most was Stanislavski's insistence on physical action as the basis for building a performance, his rejection of any direct approach to feelings and his abandonment, except as a last resort, of Emotion Memory, which, under the influence of Boleslavsky, had become a feature of Stanislavskian acting in America.
>
> (Benedetti 1999: 351)

Thereafter, Adler wanted the actor's work to be inspired by "the play itself" and not "from the material of one's own personal life" (Krasner 2000a: 141; see also Tom Oppenheim in Bartow 2006: 29–50).

In contrast to Strasberg and Adler, Meisner's approach does not begin with either emotion memory or text. Via his repetition exercise, Meisner emphasized acting as "the reality of doing" (Meisner and Longwell 1987: 16). Meisner removed "emotion, psychology, or 'character' from training" in order to stress the embodiment of impulses via listening as "an act of 'doing'" in the moment (Stinespring 2000: 102–103; see also Durham 2004; Victoria Hart in Bartow 2006: 51–93). For Meisner acting is reacting. The emphasis is on keeping the actor spontaneous. Discoveries are made in the immediacy of impulses and interrelationships built between oneself and others in the moment.

Preoccupation with emotion and the psychological has meant that most American method approaches to work on "the self" and creating a character have been highly susceptible to some form of body–mind dualism. Meisner's emphasis on spontaneity and the reality of "doing" creates a language and approach arguably less prone to dualism than other early American method approaches.

When working on oneself, is the actor working on himself, on himself-as-the-actor, or on both? What aspects of the self are being worked on? At one end of the spectrum is the potential overemphasis on the actor's personal, subjective emotional life. In its most extreme form, acting is reduced to what the actor-as-person feels emotionally in the moment. There is no clear articulation of the distinction between the emotional life of the actor-as-person and that of the character. The result can be self-indulgence to the neglect of the physical side of the acting equation.

When Sherry Dietchman began the process of psychophysical training with me discussed in this book, she astutely observed one of the major problems with her own previous experience of actor training in the United States:

Until I began [this process of psychophysical] training I thought that my focus problems were just mental. The fact that they may be physical as well simply never occurred to me . . . Very often, I think the body is ignored or "cut off" in actor training. Most of my classes emphasized things such as emotional reality, script analysis, substitution, and memory recall. Body training is either kept separate or ignored altogether . . . I wonder what it is in our culture that perpetuates that split. More importantly

. . . I need to find how that separation can be overcome during performance

(Dietchman 1990)

Dietchman's previous experience of training reflects the Euro-American experience of the dichotomy or gap thought to exist between the cognitive (conceptual, formal, or rational) and the bodily (perceptual, material, and emotional). The consequence of this split is that all meaning, logical connection, reasoning, and conceptualization are aligned with mental or rational operations, while perception, imagination, and feeling are aligned with bodily operations (Johnson 1987: xxv).

At the other extreme is an over-intellectualization of the process of creating a character, in which the physical also gets left out. Consider the language Sonia Moore uses in *Training an Actor: The Stanislavski System in Class* (1979). When describing how the actor creates a character Moore gives the impression that the character is an object logically constructed by the mind (psycho-) through textual analysis, and then literally put *into* the physical body in performance. For Moore, the mind is a container—a place where the "emotions" are "stored" (1979: 65) to be re-lived in the act of performance. For Moore, the mind asserts "conscious control" over the body and experience (ibid.: 34). She tells one of her students, "let your body express what you have *in* your mind," (ibid.: 35, emphasis added). She invites the students to take an image *in* mind, and then "make sure that your body expresses it" (ibid.: 37). What is first *in the mind* is then put *into the body*. She instructs people to "think, think and make your body project what is *in* your mind" (ibid.: 42, emphasis added). The mind as a container of images remains separate from the body. Control is provided by what Moore variously calls "thinking," "logic," or "conscious control," i.e., the Cartesian rational mind. It is assumed that whatever is "in the mind" can be transferred into the body. Precisely *how* this transfer from mind to body takes place is never discussed.

When actors are taught to "score" a text by sitting down to map out a set of objectives and/or motivations, this process can unfortunately result in either an over-intellectualization of or an extreme self-consciousness about the acting process.[10] Rather than assimilating the schematic "map" of objectives/motivations into a fully embodied process from which a character emerges for the audience as the actor "plays" actions in the moment, inexperienced actors may take in mind the objective or motivation as they try to put it into the body. When an actor takes an objective or motivation "in mind" he becomes highly self-conscious as he *thinks about* the objective rather than engaging in a psychophysical process of embodiment and inhabitation of the objective-in-action. Sonia Moore never articulates a process by which *bodily action is incarnated or how the body initiates action.*

Moving beyond Stanislavski

From within the Stanislavski lineage, professional actress, author, and teacher Bella Merlin has recently suggested that it is time to move beyond Stanislavski, i.e., beyond the limitations of earlier versions of Stanislavski and into a direct encounter with the late Stanislavski as practiced and taught in Russia. In her three recent books, *The Complete Stanislavski Toolkit* (2007), *Konstantin Stanislavski* (2003), and *Beyond Stanislavski: The Psycho-Physical Approach to Actor Training* (2001) Merlin provides an articulate, no-nonsense, and pragmatic reappraisal of Stanislavski's psychophysical process in light of recent teaching of Stanislavski in Russia and scholarship on postmodern dramatic structure and the historical Stanislavski (Carnicke 1998).

Focusing in particular on Stanislavski's process of "active analysis" developed toward the end of his career, the actor constantly works on her feet through improvisation. The emphasis is "on acting, doing, experiencing, playing" (Merlin 2001: 253). Merlin provides a comprehensive, practical approach to Stanislavski in which there is "no *divide* between body and psychology, but

rather a *continuum*" (ibid.: 27). The optimal state of Merlin's psychophysical actor is helpfully described as one of "constant inner improvisation" (ibid.: 28)—a state in which the actor opens out to, acts within, and responds to the performative environment she inhabits in the moment.

While Stanislavskian-based, Merlin's approach is "catholic" in its openness to other techniques and approaches—whether Michael Chekhov, Grotowski, or Japanese *butoh*. What is important for Merlin is using whatever exercises help the actor (in my language) to "awaken the psychophysical body" and stimulate the actor's active imagination.

(Re)Considering the "psychophysical"

Stanislavski uses the term "psychophysical" with its most obvious and commonplace meaning: "interrelating or existing between the physical and the psychic," or "partaking of both physical and psychical" (*Webster's Third International Dictionary*, 1976: 1833). Certainly the actor's work takes place in this territory between what we in the West think of as the "physical" and the "psychic" or the "outer" and the "inner." But what constitutes each element of this compound? What is the relationship between physical and psychic, outer and inner? Is it possible to develop a language and theory of acting which do not fall prey to our inherent Western body–mind dualism?

"Psycho-," is derived from the Greek *psyche. Psyche* can mean "life, spirit, soul, self" (*Webster's* 1976: 1832). This meaning informs the commonplace contemporary use and understanding of the self as defined by modern psychology—"the science of mind or mental phenomena . . . the science of behavior . . . the mental, attitudinal, motivational, or behavioral characteristics of an individual or of a type, class or group of individuals" (ibid.: 1833).

From the mid-nineteenth through the twentieth century various versions of psychology have come to determine how Westerners usually think and talk about "the self," experience, and one's "inner" life, including the "emotions."[11] As particular assumptions about the "self" and subjectivity have become normative, they appear sufficiently commonplace to hide their historical invention. But as Pfister explains in *Inventing the Psychological*, it is crucial "to reassess the (unhistorical) premise . . . that the psychological is a universal, a 'fixed principle of intelligibility,' a basis—established by psychologists— for the explanation of motivation, character, and behavior" (Pfister and Schnog 1997: 42). Historians, sociologists, psychologists, actors, and theorists of acting alike should "scrutinize and contextualize 'the psychological' itself as a historical category, a phenomenon whose cultural meanings and social significance have altered over time and thus require *explanation*" (Pfister 1997: 42).

The breath or vital energy within

Rather than beginning from a modernist understanding of "psycho" with reference to psychology of the self, I want to argue that conceptually and practically it is more useful for the contemporary actor to begin with a broader understanding of the "inner" territory marked by the original Greek term *psyche*. *Psyche* can also be translated as "the vital principle," comparable to *élan vital* (*Webster's* 1976: 1832), i.e., the enlivening quality of the actor's energy. This meaning of *psyche* is akin to the Greek *psychein* meaning "to breathe, blow" (ibid.) As Joseph Roach explains in his seminal historical study of Western acting, *The Player's Passion* (1993), approaches to acting before the invention of psychology were informed by a variety of paradigms from humoral to vitalist theories, among others.

When taken in this latter sense as "the vital principle" associated with the enlivening, animating, life-giving nature of breath, *psyche* comes very close to the uses and meaning of both the Sanskrit *prana* (or *prana-vayu*) and the Chinese *qi* (Japanese and Korean *ki*). As explained in detail in Chapter 4, *prana* and *qi/ki* are terms

that respectively inform traditional systems of South and East Asian medicine as well as many forms of embodied practice and performance including such well-known genres as Japanese *noh*, *kathakali* dance-drama of Kerala, India, and Beijing opera. These key terms are translated as "breath," "breath of life," "life-force," or "inner energy." As such *prana* and *qi/ki* identify both the material reality of the breath-as-breath, as well as the enlivening quality that can be present as a process of engaging the breath-in-action as a circulating energy. Energy is that which *animates and activates* the actor.

But this animating energy associated with the presence of breath cannot be reduced to the breath per se. It is the breath "plus" something more. The breath as something more is not some sort of diffuse quality, but a material actuality that can be awakened and raised through specific types of training. Once awakened and raised it is qualitatively modulated and shaped for use within specific practices such as traditional medicine (massage, acupressure, etc.), martial arts, meditation, and performance. By undergoing training in specific modes of embodied practice, this energy associated with breath and its accompanying force or power enlivens and quickens one's awareness, heightens one's sensory acuity and perception, and thereby animates and activates the entire bodymind. This inner activity is resonant and therefore "felt."

Prana/qi/ki has specific properties, i.e., it can be strong or weak, dense, thin, etc. Taking one example of many, Chinese performers often state that a good actor must "radiate presence" (*faqi*), while a poor performer would have no presence (*meiyou qi*) (Riley 1997: 206). As detailed later in this book, this inner energy is activated and shaped through training and in rehearsals so that it is constantly available and flows.

In acting, this inner energy takes the form of impulses which initiate action(s) that constitute a performance score. Optimally, the actor's constant flow of *prana/qi/ki* or energy enlivens and qualitatively vibrates or resonates each action as it extends to and is shared with the other actors as well as the audience. The entire performance space is (ideally) suffused with/by the actors' individual and collective energy-in-action. The actor senses and experiences both *the feel* and *the subtle movement* of this energy within *as it is shaped* by the dramaturgy and aesthetic form in the moment of performance. As each action in an actor's performance score extends outward taking shape in kinesthetic and/or verbal form reaching, touching, or vibrating other performers and the audience that action simultaneously *moves within the actor herself.* Inner feeling and outer (physical) form are two sides of the same coin.[12] The actor simultaneously senses the inner feeling of the kinesthetic/verbal form-in-action as it is performed. As Bella Merlin argues, "*inner feeling* and *outer expression* happen at the same time" (2001: 27).

Metaphors marking the presence of an animating energy

It is clear from the discussion above that Stanislavski assumed the presence of an activating energy (*prana*) within the actor that animated form in the shape of character choices. The material reality of energy as *prana* was also central to the development of Michael Chekhov's work on radiation, psychophysical exercises, and psychological gesture where the "aim is to penetrate all the parts of the body with fine [. . .] vibrations" (Chekhov 1991: 43). Liisa Byckling (2005) has argued that

> Chekhov was convinced that the body of an actor must undergo a special kind of development in accordance with the particular requirements of his profession, which is extreme sensitivity of body [sic] to the psychological creative impulses. In his opinion, it could be achieved by psycho-physical exercises [. . .] Quoting Chekhov, "The training of the body is therefore a training in awareness, in learning how to listen to the body, how to be led by it [. . .] Words are so clever, but movement is simpler. Therefore we begin

our work with movement, with psychological gestures, and we let words come on the movement [. . .] The actor's body (shows) the road to emotion."

Chekhov's actor works from body-awareness into and through psychophysical composition. The actor senses and feels the form of the psychological gesture *as he creates and inhabits it.* Building from Chekhov's evocative statement that "the actor imagines with his body," David Zinder provides an extended discussion of how "the imagination is aroused and activated by physical action" (2007: 9; see also Zinder 2002 and Gordon, 2006: 64–71). Zinder's discussion is informed by the much more nuanced understanding we have today of how the body and imagination exist in relationship to one another.

Pursuing his own pathway to in-depth exploration of Stanislavski's method of physical action and the imperative that the actor work on himself, Jerzy Grotowski (1933–1999) practically and theoretically drew on yoga and Hindu philosophy in his search for how the practitioner might actualize an optimal state of bodymind awareness in which one remains "sufficiently flexible and 'empty' to be a pervious channel for the energies" (1995: 129). As discussed in detail in Chapter 4, this state of being/doing is informed by a yogic understanding of the subtle body.

When Vsevolod Meyerhold (1874–1940) broke with Stanislavski, rejected psychology, and developed his own system of psychophysical training, he designed a quasi-scientific system of biomechanics that began from the physical side of the psycho-physical equation with exercises and *études*. Nevertheless, Meyerhold identified the actor's need to possess what is comparable to *prana*—what he called an inner "excitation" but not "ecstasy" (Braun 1969: 200):

> The aim of training [. . .] is to prepare the actor by creating in him a state of "excitability" which can provoke the correct reflex action: the "point of excitability" is like a car whose engine is idling: press the accelerator and the

car "realizes" the action, it moves forward. If the actor is without the "excitability" he is like a car whose ignition is switched off: press its accelerator, and nothing happens.

(Leach 1989: 54)

The engine running within can be felt to vibrate as it idles.

If Meyerhold uses a scientific, mechanistic metaphor to describe the feeling or awareness of what is comparable to *ki/qi/prana-vayu* as it moves within, Etienne Decroux described this dynamic inner movement as follows:

Underneath the stew pot, there's the flame. That's why it boils. That's why the lid lifts off. There must be something underneath. Whatever one says or does, there's something underneath and that something is work. And

work is not agitated movement. It is discipline. It is learning what others have already discovered.

(Decroux 1978: 23)

Whether identified as the idling engine, the flame beneath the stew pot, the inner action that is manifest when one "stands still while not standing still," or in the more culturally specific Asian terminologies as *ki/qi/prana-vayu*, the first point of reference for *psycho-* within the compound term, psycho-physical, is not psychology per se, but rather the actor's complete engagement of her energy, sensory awareness, and perception-in-action in the moment.

Chapter 2 provides an overview of the initial point of departure in this psychophysical process—the breath.

A psychophysical approach to acting explores the "physical" and the "psychic" or the "outer" and "inner." The beginning point is not psychology, but the enlivening quality of the actor's breath as energy (*prana-vayu, qi/ki*). The first concern is with activating and discovering this energy which activates and animates the actor in the moment. The psychophysical approach outlined creates an "energetic theatre," i.e., a "theatre not of meaning but of 'forces, intensities, present affects'" (Jean-François Lyotard, quoted in Lehmann 2006: 37). Here the actor senses and experiences both *the feel* and *the subtle movement* of activating energy within *as it is shaped* by the dramaturgy and aesthetic form in the moment of performance.

2

Beginning with the breath

As long ago as 1973 Robert Benedetti summed up at least one of the goals of "serious actor-training programs" as attempting to help students to discover "stillness at the center" because it "relates to those most fundamental problems of concentration and relaxation" which the actor must actualize on stage (1973: 464, 467). Reflecting on a demonstration performance by Beijing Opera actress Yen Lu Wong, Benedetti noted how the American actor

> often tends to be at the mercy of his own energy because his technique is incapable of encompassing it fully; he has to "work himself up" to high energy levels, while [Yen Lu Wong] carries with [her] a powerful but balanced energy source which [she] taps freely as needed.
>
> (Benedetti 1973: 464)

Yen Lu Wong told Benedetti how throughout her prolonged training period her "main focus was [. . .] on maintaining 'tranquility'"—a state of performance actualization which A. C. Scott summed up as "'standing still while not standing still'" (Benedetti 1973: 463).

(Re)discovering the body and mind through practice

Training the actor to "stand still while not standing still" necessarily means a transformation of the practitioner's relationship to his body and mind in practice, and also of how one conceptualizes the relationship between body and mind. I begin with my own experience of this process of transformation to illustrate the commonplace confusions as well as the idiosyncrasies characteristic of this twofold process. My story takes place between the fields of play on which many American males of my age were enculturated to particular practices and paradigms of the body–mind relationship, and Kerala, South India's *kalaris* or gymnasia-cum-temples and stages where practitioners of *kalarippayattu* and *kathakali* dance-drama are enculturated to a very different understanding and practice of the body–mind relationship.

Before I first traveled to India in 1976 I had very little movement or dance training. My experience of my body was based on a variety of sports: baseball, track, wrestling, basketball, soccer, and (American) football. I assumed that they promoted good health while making me assertive and self-confident. But I also intuitively knew that my high school football training promoted aggressive and potentially violent attitudes and behavior. While being psychophysically shaped by my training in sports, I was philosophically, ethically, and ideologically becoming a pacifist.

But my body remained separate, that is, it would not be "pacified." It had been shaped by a masculine culture of the body which assumed an overarching and directive "will" which, through sheer determination and/or aggression, could shape the body per se, and/or make use of the body to impose that will on someone/something else. Consequently, I unthinkingly forced my body to shape itself to a discipline such as football or soccer, and/or I tried to use that body as a means to an end, that is, for winning. My sports body was the objective or neutral biomedical, physiological body observable from the outside. As my body was a "thing" to be mastered, male culture gave me permission to keep this body sequestered and separate from my beliefs and values. Separate from my biomedical/sports body, I inhabited an *other* body—the personal and private body which was a repository of my feelings. It too existed in a state of tension with my beliefs and ethical values, and also remained separate from my biomedical/sports body.

My (separate) mind was manifest in my will to mastery, in my reflexive consciousness which could watch my sports body from the outside and in my beliefs and values which attempted, through my active will, to impose themselves on either or both bodies. None of these fragmented experiences of my body and mind nor their implicitly dualistic paradigms helped me to inhabit and/or understand either in a way that led me to achieve an integration between them which, at least intellectually, I eventually sought both in performance and in life.

Consequently, when I first went to India in 1976, I was totally unprepared for the psychophysiological experiences I was to undergo. For my first six months I was immersed in studying *kathakali* dance-drama for approximately eight hours of intensive daily training at the Kerala Kalamandalam under M. P. Sankaran Namboodiri.

For an additional three months I began four to six hours of daily training in the closely related martial art, *kalarippayattu*, under Gurukkal Govindankutty Nayar of the CVN Kalari, Thiruvananthapuram.[1]

Over the months and years of observing masters of both *kathakali* and *kalarippayattu*, I began to notice the ease with which they embodied their dynamic arts, manifesting an extraordinary focus and power. In *kathakali* that power is manifest in the full-bodied aesthetically expressive forms through which the actor channels his energy as he realizes each state of being/doing (*bhava*) appropriate to the dramatic context. In *kalarippayattu* that focus and power is manifest not only in performance of the fully embodied forms of exercise but also in the fierce and potentially lethal force of a step, kick, or blow.

When masters of either the dance-drama or martial art performed their complex acrobatic combinations of steps, kicks, jumps, turns, and leaps, as Govindankutty Nayar liked to describe it, they "flowed like a river." At that time, my body did anything *but* flow. The serpentine, graceful, yet powerfully grounded fluidity of movement seemed an unapproachable state of embodiment. My overt physical ineptitude was matched by my equal naivety about how to learn through my body, and how that body was related to my mind. I physically attacked both *kathakali* and *kalarippayattu* exercises. I tried to force the exercises into my body; my body into the forms. I was determined to make myself learn each exercise, no matter how difficult. There in the Indian *kalari* was my Akron, Ohio, Buchtel Griffin high school football coach yelling at me: "Zarrilli, hit him harder. Get up off your ass and let's see you move! And I mean really move this time! Get up and do it again—right, this time!"

Although characteristic of American male sports, this willful, aggressive, assertive approach to one's body-in-training is not restricted to Americans. Many males undergoing training suffer the same problem with the same result—unnecessary tension. Whenever an individual willfully asserts an intention on an action, the body will be full of tension and the mind full of the aggressive attempt to control and assert the will.

Gradually, after years of practice, the relationship of my body and mind in practice and my understanding of that relationship began to alter. When demonstrating the martial art or when acting, I found myself able more consistently to enter a state of readiness and awareness—I no longer attacked the activity or the moment. Rather than being directed to an end or goal, my body and mind were being positively integrated and cultivated for engagement in what I was doing in the present moment. My tensions and inattentions gradually gave way to sensing myself simultaneously as flowing yet power-full, centered yet free, released yet controlled. I was beginning to actualize what Benedetti described as "stillness at my center." I was learning how to "stand still."

Simultaneously, through the long process of repetition of basic forms of practice, I gradually began to sense a shift in the quality of my relationship to my bodymind in exercise or on stage—I was discovering an internal energy which I was gradually able to control and modulate physically and vocally whether in performance or when extending my breath or energy through a weapon when delivering a blow. I was moving from a concern with the physical, external form to awareness of the subtler internal (psycho-) dimension of how to fully embody an action. My body and mind were beginning to become one *in practice*. I was able to enter a state of heightened awareness of and sensitivity to my bodymind and breath in action within, and simultaneously keep my awareness and energy open to the immediate environment. I was beginning to discover how *not* to stand still, while standing still.

I emphasize *beginning* because every day of practice during my initial periods of training in India I watched a master such as Govindankutty Nayar actualize this optimal state of "standing still while not standing still." For example, when he performed the *kalarippayattu* lion pose (Figure 2.1), behind the momentary stasis was a palpable inner fullness reflected in his concentrated gaze and in his readiness to respond—animal-like—to

Figure 2.1 Gurukkal Govindankutty Nayar of the Thiruvananthapuram performs one of CVN Kalari, *kalarippayattu* poses, the lion. Here "the body becomes all eyes." (Photograph: Phillip Zarrilli)

anything that might happen in the immediate environment. Govindankutty Nayar was inhabiting a state in which, like Lord Brahman the thousand-eyed, "the body becomes all eyes" (*meyyu kannakuka*). From my perspective, when the "body is all eyes" one is "standing still yet not standing still." This is the optimal state of readiness that the actor ideally inhabits.

Training toward readiness

When A. C. Scott established the Asian Experimental Theater Program in 1963 and first encountered American actors, he observed how

I was worried by the casual naturalism [American acting students] regarded as acting, impressed by the vitality they needlessly squandered, staggered by their articulate verbosity on the psychological nature of theatre, and dismayed by their fragile concentration span, which manifested itself in a light-hearted attitude toward discipline that seemed to arise from an inability to perceive that a silent actor must still remain a physical presence on both the stage and the rehearsal floor.

(Scott 1993: 52)

Responding to this encounter, Scott began to use *taiqiquan* to train actors "long before the present interest in Asian physical training forms had swept over America" (Scott 1993: 52). Implicit in Scott's use of *taiqiquan* as an actor-training discipline was not only a rejection of American actors' exclusive attention to a psychologically/behaviorally based paradigm of acting, but also an attempt to actualize an alternative psychophysical paradigm.

In this, Scott was inspired by Jacques Copeau, by his own experience of practicing *taiqiquan*, and by the religio-philosophical assumptions which inform such traditional Asian practices. In 1913 Copeau, with Charles Dullin and Louis Jouvet in his troupe of eleven, retired to the French countryside to train and prepare a company and repertoire. For Copeau, training must take place prior to whatever leads to performance. It is a period during which the actor should discover an optimal, psychophysical condition or state of readiness, that is, a state of "repose, calm, relaxation, detente, silence, or simplicity" (Cole and Chinoy 1970: 220) like Benedetti's "stillness at the center." To accomplish this state of motionlessness, Copeau wanted to develop a form of training the actor which was not that of the athlete for whom the body remains an instrument or tool. He wanted a training through which "normally developed bodies [become] capable of adjusting themselves, *giving themselves over* to any action they may undertake." It is a state in which the actor has mastered motionlessness and is *ready* for what comes next. Once a state of motionlessness and readiness has been actualized, actors should begin

all of their work from this state of readiness and not "from an artificial *attitude*, a bodily, mental, or vocal *grimace*." Whatever they do should be done with simplicity in a state of sincerity, that is, "a feeling of calm and power . . . that allows the artist . . . at the same time to be possessed by what he is expressing and to direct its expression" (Cole and Chinoy 1970: 220). So subtle should the actor's training be that he simultaneously develops "an internal state of awareness peculiar to the movement being done." Despite his continuous experiments, Copeau remained dissatisfied with the result: "I do not know how to describe, much less obtain in someone else, that state of good faith, submission, humility, which . . . depends upon . . . proper training" (ibid. 1970: 221). It was Copeau's vision that inspired A. C. Scott to use *taiqiquan* as a form of psychophysical training to help the actor "stand still while not standing still." Copeau and Scott's visions have inspired the psychophysical process described here.

The beginning point: the breath

Drawing on my years of sustained *kalarippayattu* training with Gurukkal Govindankutty Nayar, C. Mohammed Sherif, Sreejayan Gurukkal, Mohamedunni Gurukkal, and Raju Asan, *taiqiquan* training with A. C. Scott, and *hatha yoga* training with Chandran Gurukkal and Dhayanidhi, I have woven together a complementary set of psychophysical disciplines that begins and ends each day of training with a series of simple, breath-control exercises. The training begins with the breath because it offers a psychophysical pathway to the practical attunement of the body and mind. Attentive breathing provides a beginning point toward inhabiting an optimal state of bodymind awareness and readiness in which the "body is all eyes" and one is able to "stand still while not standing still."

Keeping one's external eye focused through a point ahead, and keeping the inner eye focused on tracking inhalations/exhalations to and from the region below the navel is a way of keeping our busy,

---

⦿ DVD-ROM: PREPARATION

Preliminary breath-control exercises

Exercise 1

Stand with the feet at shoulder width, knees unlocked, hands at your sides, keeping the external eye/gaze focused straight ahead, but through the point on which your eyes are focused. Keeping the feet firmly rooted to the ground through the soles of the feet and the external gaze straight ahead, allow the inner eye to focus on the breath. Keeping the mouth closed, follow the path of the breath on the inhalation, tracking its path through the nose, and down, to the region about two to three inches below the navel. As the breath arrives in this region, let it fill out, expanding the diaphragm. Keeping the inner eye focused on the breath, follow the exhalation from below the navel up through the torso, out through the nose, all the time keeping the sense of the breath's connection to the navel region as the diaphragm contracts. Repeat on an inhalation following the breath down, and on an exhalation following the breath back up and out. If there is a distraction, acknowledge it, then bring your attention and focus back to following the in-breath or the out-breath. Sense the moment of initiation of the in-breath, its continuation as it is drawn in and down, and the moment of its completion. Sense the space between this moment of completion of the in-breath, and the moment of initiation of the out-breath. This space between is that place where the potential for impulse and action reside; therefore, *it is the space where acting begins.*

Exercises 2, 3, and 4

While in Exercise 1 the body remains overtly still, in the next three exercises simple movements of the arms/hands are coordinated with each inhalation/exhalation—all the while keeping the external focus fixed on a specific point through which one looks ahead, and keeping the inner eye focused on tracking each inhalation/exhalation to and from the region below the navel. In Exercise 2 the hands/arms are extended but the elbows are not locked. Initially, the extended hands/arms ride an exhalation up to shoulder height. On the ensuing inhalation, the hands/arms open to the outside, coming to a momentary pause point on the completion of the inhalation, and then close back to center or the beginning point on the exhalation. In Exercises 3 and 4 different positions of the arms/hands are coordinated with each inhalation/exhalation.

These breath exercises were taught to me by Sakhav P. V. Mohamedunni Gurukkal of the Navajeevan Kalari Sangham in 1983. In Kerala, one simply does the exercise, imitating the master. There is little if any explanation. As a consequence, it takes years to achieve an optimal state of practice. The instructions and explanation of the inner and outer eye are my own. The instructions help create a bridge that allows the actor to access the potential benefit of the exercises sooner than later.

---

analytical, squirrel-like minds occupied. As early as the fourteenth century Japanese *noh* actor Zeami compared the undisciplined but vibrant energy of the young actor to that of the tree squirrel— exciting but unfocused and uncontrolled (see Nearman 1980). Ideally one does not *think about* the exercise, but by being attentive to the breath and literally following it on its journey inside the bodymind and back up, one is more likely to stay inside the doing. The practitioner enters into

a relationship to the breath through the doing. After several repetitions of these initial breathing exercises, I invite the practitioner to "Imagine that your eyes have literally been relocated to the lower abdomen, approximately two inches below your navel. 'Look' through the point of external focus ahead *from* this place below the navel."

The breath and our attention to it are like the shy bride and bridegroom who must take time to get to know each other.

I then introduce an additional active image that is derived from the unbendable arm exercise taught as part of preliminary Japanese *aikido* training.[2] During the two phases of the exercise, the participant experiences how it feels to use overt muscular strength, as well as intention and one's will-power, to attempt *not* to allow one's extended arm to be bent. This overt muscular

---

The unbendable arm exercise from *aikido*

This exercise is in two parts. In the first part participants use muscular strength as they attempt to keep one of their arms from being bent. In the second part of the exercise, they enter an active image. When using overt muscular strength one uses tension and intention in order to resist having one's arm bent. When using an active image one does not use muscular strength, but the breath and inner energy which together create a different form of strength.

Muscular tension and intention

Participants work in pairs—a doer and a helper. The doer extends the right arm at shoulder height ahead. The helper places one hand just above the elbow, and the other hand on the wrist. (Initially, the doer allows the helper to bend the arm by pressing down at the elbow and up on the wrist so that the helper understands the appropriate directions in which to apply pressure without hurting the doer.) Using muscular strength, and intention/will, the doer should now attempt to resist the helper's attempt to bend the extended arm.

Working with an active image and energy

Standing with the feet at shoulder width, I ask participants to repeat the opening breathing exercise assiduously following the breath with the inner eye on the inhalation down, and on the exhalation back up. I simultaneously invite them to look from the lower abdomen, while keeping an open back awareness, open peripheral awareness through the walls on either side, an open awareness through the head at the top of the spine, and a sense of awareness through the soles of the feet.

Keeping the external eye focus on the horizon through the point ahead, and keeping the inner eye following the breath, enter an active engagement with the following:

"Imagine that there is a clear, calm pool of water located in the lower abdomen two inches below the navel—that point from which you are looking. Imagine that this clear calm pool reaches down . . . through your thighs . . . knees . . . calves . . . and right through the feet and floor to the earth below. This constant, clear pool of water is always present and available to you.

"Imagine that from this clear calm pool, there is a small but continuous stream of water that begins to rise up from the pool . . . up through your lower torso . . . your chest . . . your right shoulder . . . Keep that stream always connected to the pool below, and from the pool downward through your feet . . . it continues to flow through the right shoulder, upper arm, right elbow, forearm, and through the palm and fingertips of the right hand . . . The invisible but continuously flowing stream of water is gushing out through the fingertips now and through the floor . . . Redirect that flow slowly by allowing the arm/hand to rise to shoulder height. The continuous flow of the stream of water is now directly ahead, out through the wall ahead toward the vanishing point on the horizon toward which you are looking."

[The helper is invited to step next to the doer, placing one hand just above the elbow, and the other under the wrist.]

"As the helper places her hands, do not get distracted. Keep following the breath. Keep the image of water flowing constantly out through the fingertips from the clear, calm pool.

"Helpers apply a small amount of pressure . . . more . . . now maximum."

exertion is felt—the muscles quickly tire. In phase two of the exercise the participant uses an active image with no overt muscular resistance. If and when the participant is able to sustain the active image, in the vast majority of instances the helper is unable to bend the doer's arm.

The practitioner's mental engagement in these exercises is as crucial as the attentiveness to the breath. Following the breath with the inner eye, looking from the lower abdomen, and imagining that a continuous, fine stream of water extends from a clear calm pool in the lower body out through the fingertips, or palms of the hands, all provide a means of taming the mind by engaging it in attentive awareness to a specific image/task. They bring the mind into the body, and take the body into our awareness as it engages the image/

task. Gradually, the engagement of the navel region extends along the line of the spine and thereby through the remainder of the body— into the ground through the soles of the feet, out through the arms/hands, up along the spine through the top of the head. In these seemingly simple, almost stationary exercises, one is beginning work on centering, balance, and control of the body so that while it is standing still, it is *not* standing still but internally moving.

Following the preliminary breathing exercises, a complete cycle of daily training lasting approximately three hours includes:

⊙ DVD-ROM: YOGA

- *Hatha yoga* exercises—*suryanamaskar, asanas*, and yoga-stretches (Figure 2.2);

Figure 2.2 Demonstration of the extension of breath/energy simultaneously through the top of the head and soles of the feet while executing a yoga *asana*. As explained in Chapter 4, the simultaneous extension of energy in two directions creates a dynamic opposition from the lower abdomen up and out, and from the lower abdomen out through the feet, thereby "filling" absent or negative space. Intensive workshop at Gardzienice Theatre Association, Poland, May 1999. (Photograph: Przemek Sieraczynski)

- Vocal warm-up—panting, "moming" (a vocal exercise based on Japanese *kyogen*), etc.;

● DVD-ROM: *TAIQIQUAN*

- *Taiqiquan*—short form, Wu style, lasting approximately 20 minutes;

● DVD-ROM: *KALARIPPAYATTU*

Kalarippayattu—poses, steps, kicks, jumps, combined full-body exercise sequences (*meippayattu*), and for very advanced students practice of weapons

The inner circulation of the breath and one's embodied relationship to its circulation introduced in these preliminary exercises is vital to the correct performance and potential benefit of all of the psychophysical exercises that are part of the training.

Daily repetition allows the actor time to explore ever-subtler dimensions of the body, the mind, and their relationship-in-action, i.e., body and mind are gradually being attuned to one another.

The process of training is at first pre-performative. The initial concern is not on the end—on performance per se—but rather on having the actor take the necessary time to work on himself. The self on which one works is not the psychological/behavioral self, but rather the psychophysical self—the experiential/perceiving self constituted in the moment by sensory awareness, perception, and attentiveness to one's bodymind in the act of doing and as responsive to the environment. By staying inside the exercises, by not allowing one's mind to wander from attentiveness to the ever-present breath and yet keeping an open awareness to the environment, the practitioner begins a process of exploring the subtleties of the relationship between the physical and mental/cognitive/perceptual elements woven simultaneously together and at play in embodied work. Japanese philosopher Yuasa Yasuo describes this as a process of "cultivation" (1987: 18), i.e., one is cultivating a certain type of awareness, attentiveness, and perception of the bodymind-in-action and in relation to an environment.

The training takes place in spaces where an appropriate atmosphere for serious training can be maintained. Sufficient time—three to six hours a day initially—is spent in training to allow participants to discover a new awareness of the body–mind relationship in and through time. When appropriate, time is also taken to apply this particular psychophysical paradigm and its embodied principles to structured improvisations, acting problems, and production work.

Using *hatha yoga*, *taiqiquan*, and *kalarippayattu* allows participants to explore three corporeal disciplines each of which requires them to garner and manifest their energy in qualitatively different modes of embodiment and expression. In *hatha yoga*, one is physically still, but one's inner energy is internally active, enlivening the pose. Based on the yoga paradigm, *kalarippayattu* has moments of stasis within sequences that are dynamic and fluid, and manifest tremendous power and energy. While beautiful in its flow, its sequences have sharp, strong, percussive, immediate releases of energy in some of its kicks, jumps, and steps. In contrast, the *taiqiquan* is soft, circular, yet behind that softness is power and a grounded strength. As students progress through the training, the contrast in the quality of energies in these disciplines helps them to begin to understand the potentially rich expressive possibilities open to them through embodied processes of work.

The atmosphere I try to foster in the studio is one of quiet focus on the specific work at hand. Participants are expected to keep focused, concentrated, and completely attentive *in* each moment. I occasionally remind participants:

1 not to space out, zone out, or attempt to relax—rather, their task is, through specificity of focus, to enter a state of concentratedness in the moment which is not energy-less, but energy-full or energized;
2 not to push or attempt to find some mystical or spiritual something in what they are doing, that is, they are to assume that what they find will come out of the specificity of their embodied relationship to the exercise in the moment of its performance;

3   not to work so hard at attempting to find or keep focus that they are distracted by their trying, to allow themselves to acknowledge distractions but learn how to discipline their (naturally) wandering attention by bringing it back to a specific point of focus and breath;

4   that they are engaged in a long-term process which they are likely to find at times frustrating and boring in its repetition, and therefore should not expect immediate, earth-shattering, and/or constant discoveries, that is, they must be patient and work with and through time;

5   that this work is not for me, their teacher, but for themselves, and therefore they must begin from the first day to become their own teachers, that is, to internalize the discipline which my outside eye and comments at first call to their attention. Such attention to the focused and concentrated deployment of their (energized) bodies in space through time must become intuitive.

Training through repetition of forms can too easily become empty and habitual—like the mind-less way in which some people work out in a sports center through repetition of exercises while watching television or listening to the radio. The mind can be elsewhere while the body is being exercised and toned.

Psychophysical training through repetition of embodied forms cannot be allowed to become empty or habitual! The actor must commit him/herself fully to training as an ongoing process of self-definition. As Eugenio Barba explains:

> Training does not teach how to act, how to be clever, does not prepare one for creation. Training is a process of self-definition, a process of self-discipline which manifests itself indissolubly through physical reactions. It is not the exercise in itself that counts—for example, bending or somersaults—but the individual's justification for his [sic] own work, a justification which, although perhaps banal or difficult to explain through words, is physiologically perceptible, evident to the observer. This approach, this personal justification decides the meaning of the training, the surpassing of the particular exercises which, in reality, are stereotyped gymnastic movements.
>
> This inner necessity determines the quality of the energy which allows work without a pause, without noticing tiredness, continuing even when exhausted and at the very moment going forward without surrendering. This is the self-discipline of which I spoke.
>
> (Barba 1972: 47)

This process of *self*-definition and personal justification can never end—the practitioner must constantly (re)discover the self in and through the training with *each* repetition.

As with any new experience, the first few sessions are often interesting and intriguing; however, participants can become confused or have doubts about the applicability to acting of their repetitious practice of psychophysiological exercises. As one participant observed, "For the longest time I had difficulty imaging how the discipline work could be directly applied to my acting!" In part I attribute these doubts and confusions to the assumptions some actors bring with them about what acting is or is not, about the relationship (or lack thereof) between themselves, acting, and embodiment, as well as a lack of experience and clarity about how training *through the body* relates to acting.

Richard Schechner calls our attention to "the whole performance sequence, that is, a seven phase progression stretching from training to workshops, rehearsals, warm-ups, performance, cool-down, and aftermath" (1985: 16). For many young actors, their first experiences in the theater are with the rehearsal process, that is, one is cast in a specific role for which there are lines to learn, rehearsals to attend, and then performances. Unlike dance, gymnastics, or playing a musical instrument, one is not required to go through any bodily training before auditioning and rehearsing. If would-be actors have had training in the United States, until recently it was usually of the method or Stanislavskian-based kind. In the UK young actors are exposed to many more types of training processes, but may not have had sustained in-depth training in a particular discipline. Consequently, with the exception of those few individuals who may have been in programs where Suzuki training, for example, is offered, many young actors have little experience or understanding of the difference between a preparatory form of in-body training and rehearsals, at least as Copeau and more recently Schechner have defined them: "Rehearsal is a way of setting an exact sequence of events. Preparations are a constant state of training so that when a situation arises one will be ready to 'do something appropriate'" (Schechner 1976: 222).

Consequently, intensive body training must first awaken in the participant an awareness of the body which has been missing from his or her experience and understanding of the acting process. Dora Lanier explains why this separation of preparation from rehearsal was important for her as she worked through the psychophysical training described here: "When I'm in training I can work specifically on each psychophysiological exercise and there is no need to solve specific [acting/dramatic] problems, whereas in rehearsals you have to solve all these problems [of interpretation and choices] to get on stage." But, as Blau reminds us, in Euro-American theater one is always "working against time" (Reinelt and Roach 1992: 443). As much as it can be, training should be a time out to "work against time." This time is intended as a space in which the participant begins to discover an alternative relationship *to* time *through the body*. Since participants enter the training process predisposed to work against time, that is, filled with the necessity of getting to a T H E R E (somewhere), it is at first difficult to encourage them to settle their bodies and minds into not trying to get there, to staying in the here and now.

Some actors are in such a rush! Another former student, Brooke Nustad, explains how she gradually arrived at a realization of the importance of allowing herself the time to focus:

The idea of focusing the "inner eye" on the breath made sense to me, but it wasn't as easy as I thought. Because I had never spent so much time concentrating on my body before, it took a lot of effort. This was a surprise to me. I guess I thought that these things would "happen" to me just by being in the class. Therein was my next obstacle . . . I started trying to make [things] happen. Instead of . . . concentrating on my breath, I began to think with every move, "How does this make me feel? Am I changing? Is there progress?" . . . At some point . . . I finally gave up the "trying," and that's when I actually made some progress. I stopped pushing so hard, and it helped. This made me realize that the same applies to acting. When I keep on task without pushing what I'm doing, I do a better job.

Through repetition and practice the actor optimally begins to develop a new relationship to one's body and mind, and their relationship. The bodymind becomes singular as one engages fully one's awareness in what one is doing as it is done. One begins to discover a state of calm and repose as well as a heightened sense of awareness of the body-in-action. Copeau was precise about the type of embodied awareness that training should develop in the actor: "What is needed is that *within them every moment be accompanied by an internal state of awareness peculiar to the movement being done*" (Cole and Chinoy 1970: emphasis added). With each repetition of each exercise, for the nth time, there is this subtle "something more" that can be found in one's relationship to movement/action. It is repetition per se which leads one, eventually, to the possibility of re-cognize-ing oneself and one's bodymind relationship through exercise.

Copeau's vision of training shares several important basic assumptions with training in Asian martial arts and yoga. The act of embodiment is present as a mind-aspect ("an internal state of awareness"), and that *progressive development* of such an awareness comes *through the process of corporeal training per se*. These ideas reject Cartesian body–mind dualism, assuming instead that the bodymind is an integrated whole. As David Edward Shaner explains,

> Phenomenologically speaking, one can never experience an independent mind or body ... "Mind-aspects" and "body-aspects" have been abstracted so frequently that there is a tendency to believe that these terms have exact independent experiential correlates ... Although there may be mind-aspects and body-aspects within all lived experience, the presence of either one includes experientially the presence of the other. This relationship may be described as being "polar" rather than "dual" because mind and body require each other as a necessary condition for being what they are. The relationship is symbiotic.
>
> (Shaner 1985: 42–43)

Consequently, Shaner refers to the "presence of both aspects in all experience as 'bodymind'" (1985: 45).

Shaner differentiates between three modes of bodymind awareness (Chart 1). At one end of the spectrum is the type of "reflexive, discursive consciousness" (1985: 48)—third-order bodymind awareness in which the kinesthetic dimension is least evident. In this mode of consciousness we are using the right side of our brain to analyze a mathematical problem, solve a puzzle, or score an acting script. We can become completely absorbed in thinking about something and momentarily forget we have a body. As I write this sentence I am exercising propositional, analytical knowledge in order to communicate about the complex processes of training, acting, etc. I am obviously not *doing* acting, but writing about and helping the reader think about the phenomenon of acting as an embodied process. We are both using third-order awareness as we write and/or read. Analysis and understanding of a specific dramatic text is of course an important part of preparing to play a specific role; however, analysis and/or scoring are forms of preparation for approaching the embodiment of a role.

At the other end of the spectrum from propositional forms of knowledge is first-order bodymind awareness, which is pre-reflective. Imagine that you are out for a walk in the woods. You are not intent on going anywhere specific. There is nothing specific on your mind. You are simply walking, and in a state of being open, listening to the environment. Our lived experience in this state is at its most naive, natural, or innocent. There is no intentionality in our walking, thinking, doing. In this state "one might suggest that we think with our body and act with our mind and vice versa" (1985: 46).

Second-order bodymind awareness is also pre-reflective, but with a difference. This is that optimal state of being/doing one accomplishes through assiduous modes of embodied practice such as martial arts, yoga, or acting. It is a non-intentional state of "presencing" (Shaner 1985: 52–53) in which the "horizon is a gestalt" of possibilities. This horizon of possibilities is the structure of a martial arts sequence, a yoga pose, or the acting score developed in rehearsals. At first an exercise or action may be filled with intentionality—we are *trying* to do it rather than simply doing it. Through practice or rehearsals as we gradually expand our awareness and perception, the exercise or score becomes known to us and our "intentions are neutralized" (ibid.: 53). In second-order awareness, both bodily tensions and mental intentions therefore recede into the background. "Tensions and intentions are like mud put into a clear stream ... They dam the flow of presencing and muddy one's awareness ... When tensions and intentions are neutralized, one's responsiveness to the situation may be immediate" (ibid.).

In second-order bodymind awareness one also "thinks with the body and acts with the mind" but one does so while embodying the structure or form within which one acts. In performance, our consciousness/awareness is polar, i.e., it moves un-selfconsciously between bodily and perceptual elements within the structured activity. Throughout this book I will use the term "bodymind" as synonymous with psychophysical to mark the polar nature of this relationship

Chart 1: Three modes of bodymind awareness

Phenomenologist David Edward Shaner differentiates between three modes of bodymind awareness (1985: 48–54). (The chart has been adapted and expanded from Lorraine Sutherland (2007: 31) informed by Zarrilli 2001.)

First-order	Second-order	Third-order
Pre-reflective	*Pre-reflective*	*Reflective/reflexive*
First-order awareness is pre-reflective. It is that mode of experience *prior* to intentional experience. It is direct awareness of the bodymind within the horizon as a whole. In this state nothing is privileged.	Second-order awareness is also pre-reflective. Bodymind awareness is secondary to that toward which one primarily attends. One is not thinking about, but one attends to. This is the most primordial form of intentionality. This is the optimal state of being/doing when practicing martial arts, or yoga, playing a musical instrument, or acting.	This is reflexive discursive consciousness in which there are many vectors or foci for our attention. This type of awareness is necessary for reflection and analysis such as scoring an acting text for beats, or an attempt to understand and explain a complex action.
No intentionality	*Assiduous* Assiduous practice renders second-order bodymind awareness.	*Most intentionality*
	Knowledge of "how" Developed *through* active engagement in doing.	*Knowledge "about"* Propositional, reflexive knowledge about what one does. Meta-theoretical knowledge such as writing this book or reflecting on one's practice of acting.

Note: Many Asian traditions and classical texts emphasize that the modes of knowing most valued are those other than reasoned, propositional, theoretical knowledge. One such mode of coming to know is affective knowledge learned through assiduous, embodied practices. As a consequence, "knowing how" is often the most admired form of knowledge. In South Asian yoga, Buddhist, and Taoist traditions, and therefore in the martial and performing arts, practical "know how" is preferred to propositional knowledge. "Such knowledge is often not articulated in words or propositions. . . . [T]he kind of knowledge implicit in an effortless practical mastery . . . would only be obstructed, or even lost, by the adept's fruitless attempt to regiment it into a systematic theory" (Cooper 2003: 64).

between the perceptual and bodily based aspects of second-order awareness.

Actualizing a state in which one "thinks with the body and acts with the mind" is precisely what Copeau hoped corporeal training would accomplish, and what training through the martial arts and yoga has the potential to accomplish. In Asian disciplines of practice, as in Copeau's vision, it is assumed that one accomplishes this state progressively through time. As Yuasa Yasuo asserts, such a view "starts from the experiential assumption that the mind–body modality changes

Non-Western philosophical systems and their related disciplines of practice have long recognized that "the mind–body issue is not simply a theoretical speculation but it is originally a practical, lived experience (*taiken*), involving the mustering of one's whole mind and body. The theoretical is only a reflection of this lived experience" (Yuasa 1987: 18). Except for the phenomenological movement, the Western philosophical tradition has always asked, what is the relationship between the mind and the body? In contrast, Eastern body–mind theories begin by asking, "How does the relationship between the mind and body *come to be* (through cultivation)? Or What does it *become?*" (Yuasa 1987: 18).

through training of the mind and body by means of cultivation (*shugyo*) or training (*keiko*)" (Yuasa 1987: 18, emphasis added). When practicing psychophysical exercises like yoga, *kalarippayattu*, and *taiqiquan*, under the watchful tutelage of a master teacher, we assume that there will be a progressive alteration and refinement in the body–mind relationship which is different from the normative, everyday body–mind relationship. As we have seen, such practice begins with the external body and progresses from the outside inward toward realization of an ever more subtle and refined relationship in practice. Speaking about Zeami's theory of acting in the *Kadensho*, Yuasa explains how "art cannot be mastered merely through the conceptual understanding, but must be acquired, as it were, through one's body. In other words, it is a bodily acquisition by means of a long, cumulative, difficult training (*keiko*)" (1987: 104–105).

Toward actualizing an alternative, psychophysiological paradigm of acting through the body

But what, precisely, is acquired or brought to accomplishment through long-term bodily based training? First, to be accomplished is to acquire a

certain type and quality of relationship between the doer and the done. The accomplished practitioner is one who has achieved and is able to manifest *in practice* a heightened and focused (internal and external) relationship to specific acts: the object of meditation for the practitioner of meditation, the target for the martial practitioner, and the tasks within the actor's performance score. Although the specific discourses used to explain the qualities and nature of this relationship are culture-, genre-, and period-specific, there is the shared belief that practice is palpable, visceral, physiologically based, and felt. From the practitioner's perspective, especially powerful is the link between the breath and the body-in-motion. It is assumed that correct practice is observable to the outside eye trained to read the signs of its presence.

Consequently, theorists of acting working from a corporeally based process of training and traditional Asian bodily based systems of martial arts and actor training share remarkably similar descriptions of the psychophysiology of practice, all of which are written from the participant's point of view, that is, from inside the experience of one's relationship to the body in practice. Copeau said that the actor must develop an "internal knowledge of the passions he expresses" and an ability "to modulate the intensity of his dramatic expression" (Cole and Chinoy 1970: 219). He expected this ability of internal modulation of expression to be accomplished by practicing

appropriate exercises so that he may learn [the difference between] neutral motionlessness [and] expressive motionlessness . . . He will be made to experiment so that he can learn how, in various cases, the internal attitude, the physiological state . . . will be different.
(Cole and Chinoy 1970: 222)

In a similar vein to Copeau's description of this phenomenon as a palpable "physiological state," theater visionary Antonin Artaud called for actors to become "crude empiricists" and to examine the "material aspect" of the expressive possibilities of their bodyminds. Artaud postulated that the actor, through breath control, would be able to place the breath in specific locations in the body in order to cause psychophysiological vibrations which would "increase the internal density and volume of his feeling" and "provoke . . . spontaneous reappearance of life" (Cole and Chinoy 1970: 236, 239). Artaud assumed that these emotional states have "organic bases" locatable in the actor's body; therefore, "for every feeling, every mental action, every leap of human emotion there is a corresponding breath which is appropriate to it" (ibid.: 236). The actor's task is to develop an "affective musculature which corresponds to the physical localizations of feelings" (ibid.: 235), that is, the actor must cultivate the "emotion in his body" (ibid.: 239) by training the breath. As the actor becomes able to localize control of the breath, he will be able voluntarily to "apportion it out in states of contraction and release," thereby serving as a "springboard for the emanation of a feeling" (ibid.: 238). Once trained, "with the whetted edge of breath the actor carves out his character" (ibid.: 237).

Artaud was never able to develop a psychophysical technique actualizing this vision of the actor as an "athlete of the heart." Among actors who openly display Artaud's vision of an "affective musculature" controlled by manipulating the breath, perhaps the best known is the *kathakali* actor-dancer who literally wears his emotional states in his bodymind.

An example of the psychophysical Asian actor at work: *kathakali* dance-drama

The most obvious dimension of the *kathakali* actor's expressive power is his instantaneous ability to embody nine basic facial expressions (*navarasas*) or emotional states—the erotic, comic, pathos, anger/fury, the heroic, fear, disgust, wonder, and at-onement (Zarrilli 2000a: 78) (Figure 2.3; see next page). The actor-dancer learns how to embody and enliven each of these states of being/doing through long-term training of the breath (*prana-vayu*)—that inner energy or

life-force assumed to be present and available for circulation/manipulation within.

As I have explained in detail elsewhere (Zarrilli 2000: 65–97), when performing *kathakali*'s basic states of being/doing, the actor's breath animates not only the particular facial expression to which the audience's attention is drawn, but simultaneously enlivens and activates the actor's entire body as it assumes a dynamic posture appropriate to the particular emotional state. For example, when performing the erotic state (*rati bhava*, Figure 2.3a) the actor animates his external facial mask via this specific breathing pattern:

> Beginning with a long, slow and sustained in-breath, the eyebrows move slowly up and down. The eyelids are held open half-way on a quick catch breath, and when the object of pleasure or love is seen (a lotus flower, one's lover, etc.), the eyelids quickly open wide on an in-breath, as the corners of the mouth are pulled up and back, responding to the object of pleasure.

Throughout this process the breathing is deep and connected through the *entire* bodymind via the root of the navel (*nabhi mula*), that is, it is not shallow chest breathing, nor is the activity of the breath only in the face. The characteristic breath pattern associated with the erotic sentiment is slow, long, sustained in-breaths with which the object of love or pleasure is literally taken-in, that is, the sight, form, etc. of the lotus or the beloved is breathed in. The accomplished realization of any of the basic expressive states occurs when the mature, virtuosic actor's entire psychophysiology is engaged in this dynamic and intricate process. There is the external form—the appropriate engagement of the facial mask—and the internal dynamic that animates the form—the enlivening action of the *prana-vayu*. At the periphery of his awareness, the *kathakali* actor senses or feels the form as it is animated and as it takes shape. He fully embodies the erotic state with his entire bodymind. He *is* that state of being/doing at the moment it is brought to actualization.

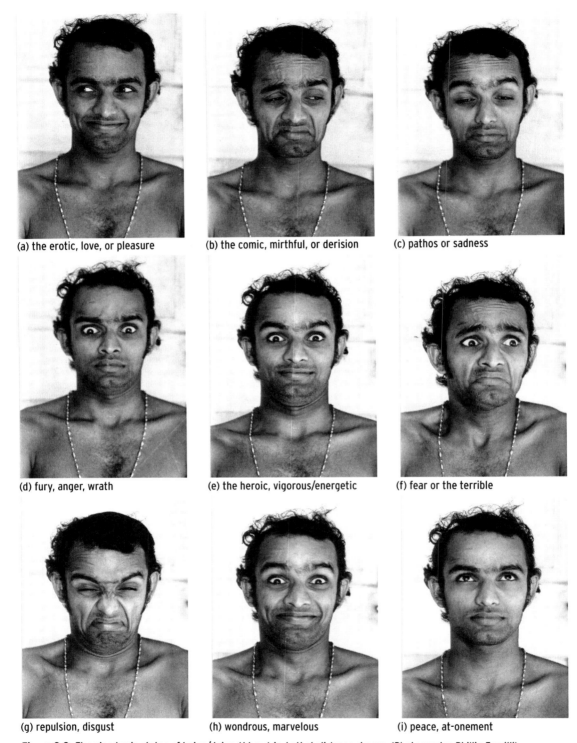

(a) the erotic, love, or pleasure

(b) the comic, mirthful, or derision

(c) pathos or sadness

(d) fury, anger, wrath

(e) the heroic, vigorous/energetic

(f) fear or the terrible

(g) repulsion, disgust

(h) wondrous, marvelous

(i) peace, at-onement

Figure 2.3 The nine basic states of being/doing (*bhava*) in *kathakali* dance-drama. (Photographs: Phillip Zarrilli)

Kathakali's understanding of the psychophysiology of performance is based on indigenous concepts of medicine and physiology—in India this understanding is derived from the physiology of the traditional system of medicine (Ayurveda) as well as from a yogic understanding of the subtle body. Therefore, the *kathakali* actor, yoga practitioner, and *kalarippayattu* martial artist all make two assumptions about their practice: (1) that the *vāyu* (breath/energy/life-force) is spread throughout the body and (2) that control of the breath is an implicit part of the training. It is by repetition of daily exercises that the breath is eventually controlled. Students are instructed to breathe only through their nose, and not the mouth—a simple instruction which, when adhered to along with maintenance of correct spinal alignment when performing a variety of exercises, develops breathing which originates at the root of the navel.

Correct instruction also comes from the hands-on manipulation of the student's body by the teacher. As *kathakali* teacher M. P. Sankaran Namboodiri explains, "Without a verbal word of instruction the teacher may, by pointing to or pressing certain parts of the body, make the student understand where the breath/energy should be held or released." When a student assumes *kathakali*'s basic position with the feet planted firmly apart, toes gripping the earth, it creates a dynamic set of internally felt oppositional forces as the energy is pushed down from the navel through the feet/toes into the earth (Figure 2.4), while it simultaneously pushes up through the spine/torso, thereby supporting and enlivening the upper body, face, hands/arms.

This centered groundedness is behind all aspects of *kathakali* performance including delivery of elaborate hand-gestures (*mudrā*). In performance, actors "speak" with their hands/arms through a complete and complex sign-language. Psychophysiologically, each gesture originates in the region of the root of the navel (*nābhi mūla*) as the breath/energy extends outward through the gesture, optimally giving it full expressivity

Figure 2.4 A rehearsal of the character Hanuman from the play, *The Killing of Lavanasura*: the triangle illustrates the dynamic, oppositional triangulation of energy created between the lower abdominal region (the root of the navel) and the floor. Energy extends from the lower abdomen through the feet, creating a dynamic inner psychophysical connection to the embodied form. (Photograph: Phillip Zarrilli)

appropriate to the dramatic moment. Finally, it should be noted that *kathakali* teachers, when teaching some of the basic facial expressions, occasionally instruct students specifically to "push the breath/energy" *into* a certain part of the face, for example the lower lids, in order to create the psychophysiologically dynamic quality necessary to actualize fully a state of being/doing—in this case, *krodha bhāva*, or the furious sentiment (Figure 2.3d).

When compared to *kathakali*'s dynamic mode of displaying the emotions openly in codified facial expressions, supported by a dynamic and fully expressive body, the *noh* theater seems to epitomize a form in which the actor must literally stand still. But, behind the surface stillness, the master actor is not standing still. Commenting on Zeami's treatises on *noh* acting, Mark Nearman clearly explains how Zeami's understanding of the effects of an actor's performance is based on a physiological vibratory theory of performance (1982–1983). Therefore, implicit in the training of the *noh* actor is the necessity that he be able to modulate his internal energy/breath (ki/qi) in order to create the effects used in creating a character. Nearman explains how

> the emotions that the portrayed character appears to experience and that are attributed by some spectators to the actor's personal feelings are seen by Zeami to be the product of the trained actor's use of his voice, particularly through the manipulation of the tonal properties of speech . . . However real these "emotions" or the character may appear to a spectator, they are not truly identical with the personal feelings of the actor. The actor's focus is upon creating these effects. Thus, he cannot permit himself to respond emotionally to his own performance in the same way as the spectator would respond.
>
> (Nearman 1984a: 44)

Nearman goes on to explain that "Zeami's term for this vocally created feeling is *onkan*, 'tonal [or vibratory] feeling'" (1984a: 44), that is, "character . . . arises from the relation of the actor's use of his voice and body to the ambience in which the character appears to exist" (1984a: 46; see also Zeami 1984: 74). Paralleling Nearman's careful exegesis of Zeami's texts, Junko Berberich (1985) has called attention to the palpably dynamic physical tensions that the *noh* actor generates when he moves, which create the vibratory affects that Nearman discusses, and which form the basis for the "not standing still" which is behind the actor's surface quietude.

The physicalization of thought: the optimal state of the actor's awareness

In finding a means to overcome the separation between the mind and body, a psychophysiological understanding and practice of acting make available to the actor an alternative to the too often cognitively based model of the psychological/behavioral creation of the character. Practice of disciplines such as *taiqiquan*, *kalarippayattu*, and yoga allows actors to discover the breath-in-the-body and, through acting exercises, to apply this qualitative body-awareness to performance. Working toward mastery of embodied forms, when combined with the ability to fix and focus both the gaze and the mind, frees the practitioner from "consciousness about," allowing the actor instead to enter into a state of concentratedness informed by the performer's relationship to his or her breath, its circulation through the body, and the deployment of this energy and focus through the body into the performance space. Training in intensive psychophysical disciplines which cultivate the bodymind empowers the actor with a means of making *embodied* acting choices, and not simply choices that remain empty mind-full intentions.

As discussed earlier, it is not that reflective consciousness does not have its place in acting. Copeau clearly differentiated between the nature of the actor's cognitive engagement in preparing a role and performing that role, between what Shaner describes as third- and second-order consciousness (1985). In contrast to first-order bodymind awareness which is a "pre-reflective neutral consciousness in which there is no intentionality," second-order consciousness is "pre-reflective, assiduous consciousness as exemplified by an athlete during intense competition or a musical artist during performance," while third-order consciousness is the "reflective discursive consciousness" (Shaner 1985: 48).

In workshops or rehearsals, one approach to characterization is for the actor to use third-order "reflective discursive consciousness" to direct an interpretive choice suitable for each dramatic moment. This is traditional "table work" in terms of textual and/or character analysis. Another approach, evident, for example, in Michael Chekhov's (1991) concept of "psychological gesture," is to make use of second-order pre-reflective consciousness as one explores the possibilities of physicalizing the role. As argued in detail in Chapter 3, in both these cases when the performer actually performs, what had been the object of preparation "ceases to be an object of study," and the physical/kinesthetic becomes the enactive point for the actor in each action/task in his score.

Copeau helpfully defined the relationship between the performer and the performed as a state in which the performer simultaneously "directs [the passions] but . . . is possessed by them" (Cole and Chinoy 1970: 219). Copeau recognizes the optimal state of performance as a gestalt. The performance score created during the preparatory period may of course use the type of third- and second-order modes of analysis/consciousness discussed above. But in performance all such preparation becomes intuitively present as it informs the structuring of the actor's score. Such preparatory work is present to the actor, but (usually) remains at the periphery of one's primary focus or mode of consciousness. Occasionally of course, such choices or decisions may be intentionally displayed or shown. Whether one is showing or hiding one's artistry, each action in a performance score contains its own specific horizon or set of possibilities for its realization by the actor.

The actor trained through psychophysical disciplines learns to direct the passions as he or she learns to control the breath. Yuasa's research on the body and body–mind relationship eventually led him to describe the practitioner who develops an experiential sensitivity to the internal circulation of ki (breath/energy) as a ki-sensitive person whose psychophysiological awareness he describes as "a self-grasping sensation of one's body, that is, as an awareness of the whole of one's body" (Nagatomo, 1992b: 60). Yuasa asserts that the ki-sensitive person, through disciplines such as the martial arts, has activated "a mediating system that links the mind and the body" (ibid.: 59), thereby

overcoming Descartes's mind–body dichotomy. For Yuasa the internal flow of ki-energy brings into awareness what he calls the "emotion–instinct circuit." The individual who actualizes an intuitive awareness of ki-energy and is able to channel this energy throughout the body is able to control and extend it out from the body, whether through vocal or physical action or into active images.

How unimaginatively we have conceived of the imagination. Under the influence of Cartesian dualism, the imagination is too often considered to be simply an image conceived of as something in the mind. From the points of view of Yuasa and phenomenology, imagining is a psychophysiological act of the entire bodymind. For the actor, to actualize an image, such as visualizing the seagull in Chekhov's play by the same name, means much more than seeing the gull projected onto the screen of one's mind. The actor trained through the body, who has begun to actualize ki-sensitivity, should be able intuitively to actualize a full-bodied connection to that image which is palpable through the actor's body— from the soles of the feet through the eyes to the top of the head. This is what Barba described as a distillation of "patterns of energy which [are] applied to the way of conceiving or composing a dramatic action" (1985a: 15). This is the "physical aspect to thought" which is the counterpart of "thinking with the body," both of which are essential for the actor if he or she is to be a complete artist capable of creating thoughts with the body.

Herbert Blau, who used taiqiquan in working with his company, KRAKEN, comments on how actors engaged in this type of psychophysiological work which is intended to "physicalize thought" must take their engagement in that work beyond "mere experience."

Thus, now, doing nothing but breathing (and taking time, take time). You are living in your breathing. Stop. Think. You are dying in your breathing. Stop. Think. You are living in your dying, dying in your living. (Take time, breathing.) Stop. Show. The doing without showing is mere experience. The showing is critical, what makes it theater. What makes it show (by nothing but breathing) is the radiance of inner conviction, the growing consciousness that it must be seen, what would make the word come even if there were no breath.

(Blau 1982a: 86)

The actor who is unable openly to *display* his or her art while fully engaged in making it is prone to repeating the fundamental ideological mistake that Artaud made by conflating into some imagined real the palpably present, physiologically based vibratory feelings that one experiences while acting and the actor's own personal emotions. What differentiates Blau's as well as the Asian actor's understanding of embodiment is that, as Zeami makes clear, in the moment of performance the actor so fully embodies the tasks of his performance score that he modulates the intensity of his or her breath/energy through the body for the *artistic* purposes of the moment, that is, to create aesthetic effects for an audience, and not to make him/herself feel good.

This takes me back to Scott's observation about the excess energy of American actors and their confusions over the nature of their relationship to themselves in creating their art. The messiness of the young actors' problems is locked up as much in their conceptions of acting as in their inability to unlock their bodyminds for creative artistry. However, the possibilities of disciplined training through the body, so easy to articulate here, are only grudgingly actualized by the most patient and dedicated students who refuse to lose themselves in the discipline from which they can find so much. As Blau put it, the wholly trained actor perches "on the edge of a breath, looking" (1982a: 86).

Toward actualizing a psychophysiological paradigm of acting

At the most advanced level of *kalarippayattu* training, the practitioner sits in a basic yoga position with legs crossed—full or half lotus. As

the practitioner settles into this position, he begins to follow his breath. Keeping his eyes open, and his awareness open to the space around him, he then takes into his mind's eye himself performing a specific sequence. Little if any overt action is visible; however, behind that apparent inaction is the blazing flame of an active, inner, vibratory perceptivity. An inner necessity informs this psychophysical task. The practitioner's entire bodymind is doing the exercise even as he does *not* literally perform it with his physical body.

When the actor's body is rendered virtually immovable in playing many of Samuel Beckett's plays or in the achingly slow movement required for Ōta Shōgo's *The Water Station*, the requirement that an inner necessity of action/task be embodied quickly becomes apparent to the actor. Being "on the edge of a breath" captures the moments of necessary suspension always present in acting as the actor rides the breath/thought/action— that moment where the possibility of failure is palpable. It is that moment of possible failure where the perceiving consciousness (or action) bodies forth because it must. Performance "on the edge" requires of the actor an unremitting attention to engaging what Blau calls "the necessary"—the consciousness that each task in an actor's score must be seen, i.e., "what would make the word come even if there were no breath" (Blau 1982a: 86).

Blau describes the acting required in Beckett's plays as "realism in extremis. Which is to say that the realistic vision, its methodology, is taken about as far inside as it can go, interiorized so intensely that it seems to occur at the nerve ends" (1994: 53). The actor's presence is dilated, decocted, or compressed into an intensity that might "blow the lid off." It is precisely the requirement for simplicity, dilation, and compression that can be so useful to actors in learning how to "stand still while not standing still." Parts II and III elaborate precisely how work on "the necessary" is developed in daily training (Chapter 5), and then applied to structured improvisations (Chapter 6) and specific dramaturgies in performance (Chapters 7–11).

3

An enactive approach to acting and embodiment[1]

Theories and meta-theories of acting

This chapter steps back from the particular psychophysical approach to actor training and acting that is the primary focus of this book in order to examine acting more generally as a phenomenon. In *Acting (Re)Considered* I argued that

> Every time an actor performs, he or she implicitly enacts a "theory" of acting—a set of assumptions about the conventions and style which guide his or her performance, the structure of actions which he or she performs, the shape that those actions take (as a character, role, or sequence of actions as in some performance art), and the relationship to the audience.
>
> (Zarrilli 2002a: 3)

Informing any theory of acting is an historically and culturally variable set of assumptions about the body, mind, their relationship, the nature of the self, the inner experience of what the actor does—often called emotion or feeling—and the relationship between the actor and spectator. Specific practices of acting and their attendant theories are invented and sustained to actualize (one or more) aesthetic form(s) within a specific performance context. Studio-based discourses are developed to provide

shortcuts and/or cues into a process of actualizing a particular mode of embodiment or inhabitation of action within an aesthetic form. One of the major problems with contemporary theories of and approaches to Western acting is that they often do not differentiate between the actor's preliminary work in constructing a particular type of performance, such as a psychologically real or believable character, and the embodied phenomenon of acting per se.

In his book *The Purpose of Playing: Modern Acting Theories in Perspective*, Robert Gordon identifies six major approaches to contemporary Western acting in the new millennium:

1 realistic approaches to characterization: psychological truth;
2 the actor as scenographic instrument: performance as artifice;
3 improvisation and games: theater-making as play;
4 performance as political praxis: acting as rehearsal for change;
5 exploration of self and the other: acting as personal encounter;
6 performance as cultural exchange: playing one's otherness.

(Gordon 2006: 6)

Using this "taxonomy of categories," Gordon discusses many of the major theorist/practitioners of twentieth-century Western theater—Stanislavski, Michael Chekhov, Strasberg, Craig, Meyerhold, Copeau, Saint-Denis, Spolin, Brecht, Boal, Artaud, Grotowski, Brook, Barba, among others—in order to "enable the reader to grasp the dialectical relationship between major traditions of performance" (2006: 5). Gordon argues that each practitioner/theorist "proposes a different solution" to the underlying phenomenon of the cultivation of expressive form (ibid.). This book proposes a seventh category for Gordon's taxonomy—*Performance as psychophysiological process: the embodiment and shaping of energy.*

Implicit in all these approaches to acting are meta-theoretical questions, i.e., principles or perspectives which invite us to step back from and to reflect more generally on the nature, practice, and phenomenon of acting. Meta-theoretical questions about acting are not only raised by specific acting theories/approaches, but by the increasingly diverse range of post-dramatic alternative scripted and devised dramaturgies/performances produced since the 1970s, as well as perspectives drawn from a convergence of new/er sciences and the implications of these new perspectives on how we think and talk about acting.

Drawing on recent developments in phenomenology, cognitive science, and anthropological ecology, this chapter explores an enactive approach to a meta-theoretical understanding of acting as a phenomenon. In contrast to a representational or mimetic meta-theory of acting that is constructed from the position of the outside observer to the process/phenomenon of acting, this chapter articulates a theory and practice of acting from the perspective of the actor as enactor/doer from inside.[2]

I begin with a brief discussion of the problem of acting Reader and Listener in Samuel Beckett's post-dramatic text, *Ohio Impromptu* (premiere, 1981).

The account I provide below is constructed from my perspective as an actor inside the performance while on tour in the US with

Figure 3.1 Reader (Phillip Zarrilli) and Listener (Andy Crook) in Samuel Beckett's *Ohio Impromptu*. As Reader reads the story from the pages of the well-worn book, the two figures sit motionless throughout most of the performance "as though turned to stone" (Beckett 1984: 287). (Photograph: Brent Nicastro)

The Beckett Project. From this position inside performance, I summarize the problem of the actor's body. I then elaborate in detail how an enactive approach to acting views the actor as a skilled practitioner—a sentient being able to be, to do, to respond, and to imagine in (theatrical) environments. In the final section of the chapter I elaborate a model of the actor's embodied modes of experience. The implications of this view of acting are briefly explored in a concluding discussion and throughout the remainder of this book.

What I describe, as best I can, in the text box opposite, is how as a stage actor I simultaneously

Beckett's *Ohio Impromptu*

Two figures—Reader and Listener—are identically dressed in long black coats with long white hair (Figure 3.1). They are seated as mirror images at a 4' × 8' white table with "head[s] bowed proper on right hand[s]" (Beckett 1984: 285). Open before reader on the table is a "worn volume" and a single wide-brimmed black hat. As Reader reads the story, the two figures sit "motionless" throughout most of the performance "as though turned to stone" (ibid.: 287). Reader reads the text "without colour," i.e., without the typical vocal contours that characterize everyday conversation. Listener listens. Physical actions are minimal. Listener knocks on the resonant wooden table when he wishes Reader to stop and repeat a phrase, or when he wishes the reading to continue. When the story is complete, the last page turned, and the book closed, after a final knock Reader and Listener gradually raise their heads to look into one another's eyes.

Performing Reader in Beckett's *Ohio Impromptu*

September 15, 2006, the Gilbert Hemsley Theatre, Madison, Wisconsin. Tonight is the first of eight performances of *The Beckett Project*. We have just received our five-minute call for *Ohio Impromptu*. Andy Crook (Listener) and I (Reader) leave our dressing room, mirror images of one another in our long black coats, black trousers, and long white wigs. Since we have not yet taken our places within the specific on-stage environment Beckett envisaged for *Ohio Impromptu*, anyone encountering us backstage as we walk down the short corridor into the theater would find us laughable—are we a pair of daft Goths who have wandered in off the street, or perhaps we have arrived over a month early for Madison's infamous Hallowe'en street party?

Entering the theater we double-check the placement of our straight-backed white chairs, check with the house manager about how much time we have until they want to open the doors and let the audience enter. "Three minutes." We take our seats at the 4' x 8' white table. Andy and I settle into our chairs. As Reader I am situated to Andy's right, and as Listener he is to my left. I begin my final personal preparations. I check my placement on the chair, sensing the feel of the chair against my thighs and buttocks. I arrange and rearrange my long black coat so that it is not caught up beneath me. I let my awareness open through the soles of my feet—sensing their relationship to the floor, and sensing the relationship between my lower abdomen and the soles of my feet.

"Two minutes." I double-check the precise placement of the book on the table before me. Following up on our earlier vocal warm-up, I place the palm of my right hand on my sternum and repeat a set of strong, resonant vocal pulses—"ha, ha, ha, ha"—in a pitch that vibrates my sternum. With my external focus directed outward through the theater, my voice "sounds" both my body and the space. Andy and I settle into our identical physical positions under the watchful eye of our acting colleague, Patricia Boyette. As each of our right hands frames our foreheads, she ensures that from the audience's perspective we do indeed look identical. Patricia makes any final adjustments to this nearly still-life image we will inhabit for fifteen to seventeen minutes, lowering a knuckle of a finger for one of us and ensuring a wisp of hair is not loose. In the final few moments before the house is open and the audience enters, I "sound" the text by seeing if I hit the chest resonator at the correct pitch on the opening line, "Little is left to tell . . ." I sense the act of articulation of the "t" and "tt"s in the line as my tongue hits the back of my teeth, waking up my mouth, filling my body.

My attention shifts to my breath. I follow my in-breath as it slowly drops in and down to my lower abdomen. Keeping my primary attention on my in-breath and out-breath, I open my auditory awareness to Andy about three feet to my left . . . Listening for his breath. I open my awareness further beyond Andy to the periphery, out through the top of my head toward the back of the theater, and behind me. We are "ready." Patricia gives the house manager the all clear. The doors are opened, and the audience, chatting as they enter, are like a wall of energy and sound moving into the space. Their sound passes through me. I am aware of it, but not distracted by it. My sensory awareness and attention are not singular, but multiple—taking in my breathing as it begins to synchronize with Andy's. Now, we are breathing together . . . in . . . and out . . . as one. Our awareness is open to each other. My awareness simultaneously takes in the audience . . . reaching toward the back row of the space and the rustling presences there. They begin to sit, and settle. I sense the heat of the lengthy lighting cue as its warmth begins to touch my hands and as the brightness of the light hits the table and illuminates the text before me. The audience further settles.

I am perched on the edge of speech, sensing the potential words in my mouth, sensing the touch of the page of the book on the table with my left hand, and the touch of the weight of my forehead against my thumb and first two fingers. Following my breath, when I sense the lighting cue is at its full warmth and intensity, and that the audience has indeed fully settled and the last cough has been coughed, the first line of the text unexpectedly comes out of my mouth riding a breath on a pitch with little color but that nevertheless resonates in my sternum: "Little is left to tell . . . In a last attempt . . ." The sharp, resonant sound of knuckles hitting the surface of the table stops my reading. I follow my breath, sensing its synchronization with Andy's, inhabiting with that breath this space-time between us.

Just as my sensory/perceptual awareness is open, my imagination is also open. As I read the opening line, associations momentarily present themselves to me at the periphery of my consciousness/awareness. Usually there is a sense of an impending end . . . the end of *this* particular reading of the story—there is only one page left to turn in this book . . . the end of a life—my father's . . . my mother's . . . my own . . . ?

inhabit, act within, and respond as a sentient, perceptual being to the very specific (theatrical) environment that constitutes the *mise-en-scène* of Beckett's *Ohio Impromptu*. As Reader, the actions I initiate—reading the text, turning a page, closing the book—and my responses to stimuli—my reading of the first line or Andy's knock—are specific to the play's dramaturgy as actualized in this theater on this day. Precisely when does his knock with the knuckles of his left hand stop my reading of the text? Ideally, I never know. By being perceptually responsive to Andy's actual presence in this environment my reading is stopped by his knock as/when it happens in each performance. The word or part of a word that is interrupted differs every night. Precisely what my imagination will conjure in response to that first line, "Little is left to tell," I do not know with absolute precision. What is imaginatively conjured has not been reduced to a single possibility, but rather falls within a range of appropriate possibilities triggered by my engagement with reading/hearing the sentence at the moment of its saying/hearing.

Andy Crook and I are not abstract constructs, but rather specific persons acting, i.e., sensing,

perceiving, and imagining as living human organisms in the moment to each other and to the environment. In this view, acting may be defined as that psychophysiological process by means of which a (theatrical) world is made available at the moment of its appearance/experience for both the actors and audience. However pedestrian, the above description of acting in *Ohio Impromptu* is intended to provide some idea of just how complex the embodied phenomenon and experience of acting is at the moment it takes place. Although any such account can never completely describe the phenomenon of acting in all its complexities, following philosopher Alva Noë I have tried to "catch experience in the act of making the world available" (2004: 176).

The problem of the body and body–mind dualism

As discussed in the first two chapters, contemporary theories and accounts of acting and of Western psychological realism in particular, are susceptible to body–mind dualism because they often assume a static, essentialist model when representing acting. If body–mind dualism remains a problem, how are we to think and talk about the body, mind, and their relationship in acting? Several complementary methodological tools are used to address the body–mind relationship in acting in this chapter—the post-Merleau-Ponty phenomenology of Alva Noë (2004), Drew Leder (1990), Shigenori Nagatomo (1992a, 1992b), and Yuasa Yasuo (1987, 1993);[3] the philosophical linguistics of George Lakoff and Mark Johnson (1999, 1980; Johnson 1987) which reconsider the foundational role of embodiment and experience in linguistic/cognitive formations; cognitive science as developed in the work of Francisco Varela and associates (1991) and James Austin (1998); and an ecological approach to perception developed by social anthropologist Tim Ingold (2000).

My discussion builds on the earlier uses of phenomenology in the analysis of theater. Previous studies by Stanton Garner (1994), Alice Rayner (1994), Bruce Wilshire (1982), and Bert O. States (1971) have contributed much to our understanding of the theatrical event, and redressed the critical disappearance of the (lived) body and embodiment in the creation of meaning and experience within the theatrical event. As in my account of *Ohio Impromptu* above, what differentiates this account from earlier studies is my focus on the livedness of the actor's modes of embodiment, perception, and experience from the actor's perspective inside training and performance, and my discussion of the implications of this view of acting for the preparation of the actor.[4]

Beginning in the seventeenth century, Western philosophers came to identify the body as a physical object much like other material objects—as having certain anatomical and functional properties that could be characterized as following certain scientific principles. Among those systematically challenging this understanding of the body during the 1960s, a series of three books by Maurice Merleau-Ponty—*Phenomenology of Perception* (1962), *The Primacy of Perception* (1964), and *The Visible and the Invisible* (1968)—marked a paradigmatic shift in Western thinking about the role of the body in the constitution of experience when he raised the fundamental philosophical problem of the body's role (or lack thereof) in constituting experience. Merleau-Ponty critiqued the hitherto static, objective nature of most representations of the body and experience:

> [T]hinking which looks on from above, and thinks of the object-in-general must return to the "there is" which underlies it; to the site, the soil of the sensible and opened world such as it is in our life and for our body—not that possible body which we may legitimately think of as an information machine but that actual body I call mine, this sentinel standing quietly at the command of my words and acts.
> (Merleau-Ponty 1964: 160–161)

Rejecting the exclusive assumption of the natural sciences and modern psychology that treated the physical body (*Körper*) as a thing, object, instrument, or machine under the command and control of an all-knowing mind, and thereby challenging the Cartesian *cogito*, Merleau-Ponty (re)claimed the centrality of the lived body (*Leib*) and embodied experience as the very means and medium through which the world comes into being and is experienced. He demanded an account of the "actual body I call mine," that is, the body as "an experienced phenomenon . . . in the immediacy of its lived concreteness," and "not as a representable object . . . for the abstractive gaze" (Schrag 1969: 130). He thereby rejected mind–body dualism, and (re)claimed the centrality of the body and embodied experience as the locus for "experience as it is lived in a deepening awareness" (Levine 1985: 62). For Merleau-Ponty, the focus of philosophical inquiry shifted from "I think" to an examination of the "I can" of the body, i.e., sight and movement as modes of entering into inter-sensory relationships with objects, or the world (1964: 87). Dermot Moran summarizes Merleau-Ponty's contribution as undoubtedly producing "the most detailed example of the manner in which phenomenology can interact with the sciences and the arts to provide a descriptive account of the nature of human bodily being-in-the-world" (2000: 434).

Acting as a process of "I can": an enactive view[5]

When Merleau-Ponty shifted from an examination of "I think" to the "I can" of the body, he laid the philosophical foundation for a more processual account of how our relationship to the worlds we inhabit is constituted by our inter-sensory and inter-subjective engagement with those worlds. The actor, like other skilled practitioners, ideally gains the ability to inhabit a particular world of the "I can." Among other scholars, Francisco Varela and his associates have argued for viewing experience and its relationship to cognition as processual—a view which challenges a static, essentialist, representational model:

> We propose as a name the term enactive to emphasize the growing conviction that cognition is not the representation of a pregiven world by a pregiven mind but is rather the enactment of a world and a mind on the basis of a history of the variety of actions that a being in the world performs. The enactive approach takes seriously, then, the philosophical critique of the idea that the mind is a mirror of nature.
>
> (1991: 9)

Implicit in Merleau-Ponty's theory of the body as an "I can" is a theory of perception. Western philosophy has long viewed perception and action as distinct. As Maximilian de Gaynesford explains,

> On this old view, the mind receives sensory information from its environment, information which is then given structure by various cognitive processes and fed into the motor cortex to produce action. This view seems erroneous for numerous neurophysiological,

behavioural and philosophical reasons. We should, instead, treat perception and action as constitutively interdependent.

> (2003: 25)

One of the first to challenge the old view of perception and to argue for perception and action as interdependent was psychologist James Gibson. In his seminal 1979 book, *The Ecological Approach to Visual Perception*, Gibson challenged the common view among psychologists at the time which assumed that we constructed representations of the world around us in our brains/heads. Anthropological ecologist Tim Ingold explains how psychologists in the 1960s and 1970s assumed that

> the mind got to work on the raw material of experience, consisting of sensations of light, sound, pressure on the skin, and so on, organizing it into an internal model which, in turn, could serve as a guide to subsequent action. The mind, then, was conceived as a kind of data-processing device, akin to a digital computer, and the problem for the psychologist was to figure out how it worked.
>
> (2000: 3)

Gibson took a radically different approach. He rejected the notion first developed by Descartes that the mind is a separate organ that operates on the data the bodily senses provide. Gibson argued that

> Perception [. . .] is not the achievement of a mind in a body, but of the organism as a whole in its environment, and is tantamount to the organism's own exploratory movement through the world. If mind is anywhere, then, it is not "inside the head" rather than "out there" in the world. To the contrary, it is immanent in the network of sensory pathways that are set up by virtue of the perceiver's immersion in his or her environment.
>
> (Ingold 2000: 3)

One proponent of this new view of the interdependence of perception and action is philosopher Alva Noë. Noë draws on the earlier work of Gibson, phenomenology, and cognitive science to further develop an enactive approach to perception and perceptual experience. Noë's thesis is that "perceiving is a way of acting. Perception is not something that happens to us, or in us. It is something we do . . . the world makes itself available to the perceiver through physical movement and interaction" (2004: 1). If perception is not something that unfolds in the brain, neither is it like the sense of sight which makes it seem as if we are passive to the world. Noë argues that perception is like the sense of touch.

> [T]he content of perception is not like the content of a picture. In particular, the detailed world is not given to consciousness all at once in the way detail is contained in a picture. In vision, as in touch, we gain perceptual content by active inquiry and exploration.
>
> (2004: 33)

Perception is active and relational.

Paralleling Noë's perspective, anthropologist Tim Ingold takes an "ecological approach to perception" in which the sentient, perceiving person is considered an organism like other organisms (2000: 3). Ingold invites us to consider what happens when we think of ourselves as a "living thing" existing in relation to one or more environments. "[A] relational view of the organism" conceives of the human being "not as a composite entity made up of separable but complementary parts, such as body, mind, and culture, but rather as a singular locus of creative growth within a continually unfolding field of relationships" (Ingold 2000: 4–5). For Ingold the "whole-organism-in-its-environment" is not a bounded entity, but rather is constituted by an ongoing "*process* in real time: a process, that is, of growth or development" (ibid.: 19–20). This process of growth or development consists of the acquisition of perceptual skills. For Ingold the

notion of skills incorporates, but should not be reduced to, bodily based skills; rather, perceptual skills are "the capabilities of action and perception of the whole organic being (indissolubly mind and body) situated in a richly structured environment" (ibid.: 5).

Indeed, the content of our perceptual experience is acquired through bodily skills that we come to possess. "*What we perceive* is determined by *what we do* (or what we know how to do; it is determined by what we are *ready* to do . . . [W]e *enact* our perceptual experience; we act it out." (Noë 2004: 1). The enactive approach is therefore counterintuitive in that it rejects the overly simplistic view of an input and output model where "perception is input from the world to mind, action is output from mind to world, thought is the mediating process" (Noë 2004: 3). As discussed in Chapter 2, this overly simplistic input–output model is too often assumed in conventional, textually based acting where the actor analyses and scores a script (input), and then acts the score (output). Rather than this computer model of perception and the mind, perception is "a kind of skillful activity on the part of the animal as a whole" (Noë 2004: 2).

Noë and Ingold both argue that it is impossible to divorce perception, action, and thought. Rather "all perception . . . is intrinsically active. Perceptual experience acquires content thanks to the perceiver's skillful activity," and "all perception is intrinsically thoughtful" (Noë 2004: 3). Therefore, to perceive "is *not merely to have sensations*, or to receive sensory impressions, it is to have sensations that one understands" (ibid.: 33, emphasis added). For the actor/doer as a sentient perceiver on stage, perception should not be reduced to merely having subjective feelings. Perception occurs when we experience sensations sufficiently that make a certain sort of sense to us, i.e., we understand that the sensations we experience are constitutive in some way.

Noë discusses two main types of understanding, though there is no sharp distinction to be made between them— sensorimotor understanding and conceptual understanding (2004: 33). Genuine perceptual experience does not just depend on the type and quality of stimulation we receive, but rather is constituted by our use or exercise of sensorimotor knowledge. "For mere sensory stimulation to constitute perceptual experience—that is, for it to have genuine world-presenting content— the perceiver must possess and make use of *sensorimotor knowledge*" (ibid.: 10). Perceptual knowledge is therefore practical knowledge, i.e., one knows how. Over time one gains a "practical grasp of the way sensory stimulation varies as the perceiver moves" (ibid.: 12). We develop a battery or repertoire of sensorimotor skills and ways of being attentive which are the foundation for our perceptual encounter with the world. At the simplest level, possessing sensorimotor knowledge allows us, for example, to grasp our spatial relationship to things. This is a form of practice, not theoretical or propositional knowledge. Whether in the domain of vision or in touch "spatial properties present themselves to us as 'permanent possibilities of movement'" (ibid.: 99).

At the more complex level of non-ordinary modes of skillful embodied practice, there is an ever subtler shape or feel that is intrinsic to specific bodily based activities such as the practice of *kalarippayattu*, *taiqiquan*, or yoga, or when performing a well-rehearsed performance score. The shape and feel of a practice are not derived from or intrinsic to the sensations per se, but rather are gained from what becomes an implicit sensory, embodied knowledge of the organization and structure of sensation-in-action. As Noë explains, "the shape is made available thanks to the way in which your sensations co-vary or would co-vary with actual or possible movements" (Noë 2004: 15). As one learns a specific form of movement, such as *kalarippayattu*'s elephant pose or the opening moves of short-form *taiqiquan*, both the pattern and the optimal quality of one's relationship to the repetition of each form constitute what Noë describes as a form of sensorimotor knowledge.

The implications of an enactive view for acting

When we construct an acting score during rehearsals, as for *Ohio Impromptu*, the score constitutes a form of embodied, sensorimotor knowledge for the actor. From my perspective as the actor playing Reader, my kinesthetic knowledge of the score consists of the feel of my body in the chair as Reader, the feel of the fingers of my left hand as they touch the pages of the book before me, or the feel of the words in my mouth when reading aloud the opening line, "Little is left to tell." These forms of perceptual knowledge are not present somewhere in my brain, but rather, the content of this (past) perceptual experience is virtually present to me, the actor, as available. I make adjustments in the moment as necessary. The form or structure of the acting score is available for inhabitation at the moment we initiate entry into embodying/ expressing each action in the score. The structure/ form is available as a horizon of possibilities. Noë explains how

> I experience the world as present even when the detail is hidden from view . . . My experience of all that detail consists in my knowing that I have access to it all, and in the fact that I do in fact have this access.
> (Noë 2004: 67)

When one initiates a form of movement, or enacting an acting score, one's relationship to each specific repetition of that same form or structure is similar, yet different. Optimally, in the present moment of doing one does not think about the form/structure or draw upon some mental representation of it or try to reproduce the experience of the last repetition; rather, one *enters a certain relationship* to the form/structure in the present moment of doing through one's cultivated perceptual/sensory awareness. As one learns to inhabit a form or structure of action, one is gradually attuned to an ever-subtler experience of one's relationship to that structure.

Experience is always of a field, with structure, and you can never comprehend the whole field in a single act of consciousness. Something always remains present, but out of view . . . Qualities are available in experience as possibilities, as potentialities, but not as givens.

(Noë 2004: 135)

Therefore, experience is a process of engaging the dynamic possibilities of the particular form or structure as it happens. As one continues to repeat a particular form or structure over time, a larger field of experience accumulates as an expanding field of possibilities. Ideally one is able to improvise within this larger field of possibilities for movement/action.

Expanding on Gibson's ecological approach to visual perception noted above, Noë argues that to perceive within any specific environment is for an animal to perceive the affordances offered by that environment: "When you see a tree, you not only directly perceive a tree, but you directly perceive something up which you can climb." In other words, when we perceive, "we perceive in an idiom of possibility for movement" (Noë 2004: 105). Such affordances are specific to a particular animal within a particular environment, and are also skill-relative. Over time our experience of specific practices such as the skilled playing of a sport or acting acquires content in terms of the possibilities for action.

The actor engaged in certain forms of training builds a repertoire of sensorimotor skills which afford various possibilities of action within the theatrical environment. There is the potential affordance available within the forms of training per se in terms of its generation of a particular kind of awareness or the raising of one's energy; however, the forms also exist with a second set of affordances—those for application, i.e., how one might apply one's energy/awareness to various performance structures or dramaturgies.

As one gains practical mastery of a particular sensory modality and awareness, this practical mastery constitutes a form of "perceptual content" that is "available to experience" (Noë 2004: 119). Here thought and experience are

not (dualistically) separate domains but rather continuous. The sensorimotor skills one develops are themselves "cognitively basic" or "proto-conceptual" (ibid.: 183–184). Perception therefore becomes "a *way of thinking* about the world because it is '*directed* toward' and therefore *about* the world" (ibid.: 189). In the act of perception we enter into a relationship. The perceiver is always active within an environment. As Gibson first argued, there is a gradual symbiotic development or "*perceptual attunement* between animal and environment. Because of this attunement, animals (as embodied wholes . . .) are directly sensitive to the features of the world that afford the animal opportunities for action" (ibid.: 21).

If we consider the actor as a gestalt—a human animal inhabiting a specific performance environment such as Andy Crook and I as Listener and Reader in *Ohio Impromptu*—then the training that actors undertake should provide them with a practical, experiential means of attuning their perceptual awareness so that they are able to be immediately responsive and sensitive to the performance environment shaped by a particular dramaturgy. This type of preparation must take place on two levels—the preparation of the actor's perceptual awareness necessary for any/all performance environments, and the preparation of the actor's perceptual awareness specific to a particular performance environment shaped by each specific dramaturgy and the need of each specific performance score. The attunement of the actor's perceptual awareness should ideally provide a heightened, non-ordinary ability to inhabit one's bodymind and stay sensorially and perceptually alert in the moment to the acting tasks at hand, such as *Ohio Impromptu*.

An actor's performance score is a structure that is available to the actor as a certain range of possibilities based on the aesthetic logic of a particular dramaturgy. The details of this score are not present to our experience as a representation, but as a set of accessible possibilities for realization or actualization. We bring the sensorimotor knowledge accumulated in training and rehearsal to bear on the actual experience of enacting the score. In the moment of enactment we are utilizing our perceptual/sensory experience and cumulative embodied knowledge as skillful exploration in the moment of the specific theatrical world or environment created during the rehearsal process.

To summarize my argument thus far, human perception is enactive, relational, and specific to an environment. I have considered a meta-theory of acting not in terms of how the actor constructs a character or how the actor makes a performance believable, but rather in terms of the phenomenon of acting viewed from the perspective of the actor-as-(human) doer/enactor inside the performance of an acting score. Stage acting may therefore productively be considered as one among many extra-daily skilled modes of embodied practice requiring the performer to develop a heightened attunement of sensory and perceptual awareness of a certain sort in order to be fully responsive to theatrical environments and dramaturgies. According to this alternative paradigm or meta-theory, it may be more useful to consider acting in terms of its dynamic energetics than in terms of representation. Rather, it implies an "'energetic theater'"—a "theater not of meaning but of 'forces, intensities, present affects'" (Lyotard, quoted in Lehmann 2006: 37; see also Hornby 1992: 10 and Pavis 2003: 95ff). Meaning and representation may present themselves to the viewer or critic of a performance, but they are a result of the actor's immediate and appropriate deployment of her energy in the act of performance and the spectator's experience of that performance. In this view the actor practically negotiates interior and exterior via perception-in-action in response to an environment. As Eugenio Barba has observed, the actor-as-perceiver/doer ideally undergoes training that allows one's bodymind to become like an animal, ready "to leap and act" (2005: 197). Chapters 4–6 will specifically explore how training through martial arts and yoga further attunes the actor's sensory and perceptual awareness and energy, animal-like, toward extra-daily engagement of acting tasks. In the second part of this chapter, I turn from a meta-theoretical consideration of acting to the more specific consideration of the

lived embodiment and experience of perception and awareness from the actor's position inside performance.

Toward a model of the actor's embodied modes of experience

We organize the world we encounter into significant gestalts, but the body I call mine is not *a* body, or *the* body. Rather my body is constituted in the process of embodying the several bodies that I encounter—my body as experienced in everyday, habitual activities, and my body as experienced in extra-daily activities such as acting, ballet, or training in psychophysical disciplines. This notion of embodiment as a process of experiential encounters opens up the body not as a single object, and "carries us past the inveterate tendency to reify what we are trying to think and understand and engage" (Levine 1999: 128). As Stanton Garner points out, "embodiedness is subject to modification and transformation, multiple and varying modes of disclosure, and . . . the forms of ambiguity that characterize the phenomenal realm represent experience in flux, oscillating within and between modes of perceptual orientation" (1994: 51).

Drew Leder's post-Merleau-Ponty account probes one of the most vexing problems of the body—corporeal absence, i.e., the "question of why the body, as a ground of experience . . . tends to recede from direct experience" (1990: 1) and thereby becomes absent to us. Leder provides an extensive account of the modes of bodily absence characteristic of our two everyday bodies—the surface and recessive bodies. Given my focus on the contemporary actor's modes of bodily being-in-the-world, I build upon Leder's account by proposing two additional extra-daily modes of embodiment, experience, and absence characteristic of acting:

- an aesthetic inner bodymind discovered and shaped through long-term, extra-daily modes of practice such as yoga, martial arts, and other in-

depth forms of psychophysical training, and
- an aesthetic outer body constituted by the actions/tasks of the actor's performance score—that body offered for the abstractive gaze of the spectator.

I supplement my discussion of Leder by drawing upon Japanese philosopher Yuasa Yasuo's (1987) complementary analysis of body schema, *ki*-energy, and awareness (Appendix 2).

A fundamental paradox: "the absent body"

Drawing upon, but attempting to address some of the inadequacies in Merleau-Ponty's phenomeno-logical account of the everyday experience of the body, Drew Leder's *The Absent Body* addresses a fundamental problem and paradox:[6]

> While in one sense the body is the most abiding and inescapable presence in our lives, it is also essentially characterized by absence. That is, one's own body is rarely the thematic object of experience. When reading a book or lost in thought, my own bodily state may be the farthest thing from my awareness. I experientially dwell in a world of ideas, paying little heed to my physical sensations or posture.
> (Leder 1990: 1)

Such forgetfulness is not "restricted to moments of higher-level cognition," but equally characterizes our engagement in activities such as sports, physical labor, or the performing arts—dance, acting, live performance, etc. When "engaged in a fierce sport, muscles flexed and responsive to the slightest movements of my opponent . . . it is precisely upon this opponent, this game, that my attention dwells, not on my own embodiment" (Leder 1990: 1). Stanislavski recognized this forgetfulness of the body as a fundamental problem in both acting and everyday life:

> When a man is completely dominated by passion, involved in it with his whole being, he forgets his physical objectives, he executes them mechanically, oblivious to them. In real life we are often oblivious of what we are doing—walking, ringing a bell, opening a door, greeting someone or other. All this is done largely in an unconscious way.
> (1961: 6)

How are we to account for this bodily absence in everyday life and in acting? For Leder, the lived body (*Leib*) is not a homogeneous thing, but rather "a complex harmony of different regions, each operating according to indigenous principles and incorporating different parts of the world into its space" (1990: 2). Leder provides a lengthy description of two modes of embodiment through which our everyday experience is usually constituted—the *surface body* and the *recessive body* (Chart 2, see overleaf), each of which is characterized by its own mode of bodily absence.

The ecstatic surface body

We inter-subjectively engage the world around us through our sensorimotor *surface body*, for example, when we use a hand to explore, touch, or relate to the world. This body encompasses the most prominent functions which shape our experiential field, such as the power of the gaze. The basic stance of the surface body *vis-à-vis* the world it encounters is ecstatic in that the senses open out to the world. This is the body of "flesh." Leder's use of "flesh" and "ecstatic" to describe the surface body is descriptive as well as metaphorical.

Unless disturbed or interrupted in some way, our experience is usually characterized by a certain degree of ongoing spatio-temporal continuity. "My eyes can scan a visual world that is without sudden gaps or crevices. If I abandon one sense, perhaps closing my eyes, the other senses help to maintain the continuity of the world" (Leder 1990: 42). Physiologically, the surface body is characterized primarily by *exteroception*, i.e., the outer-directed five senses open us out to the external world, usually "without immediate emotional response"

Chart 2: The actor's four embodied modes of experience

This chart provides an overview of the four embodied modes of experience that collectively constitute the actor's experience of performance. The first two bodies (surface and recessive) are based on Leder's study. The third and fourth bodies (aesthetic inner and outer) are my own contribution.

First body	Second body	Third body	Fourth body
surface body	recessive body	aesthetic inner bodymind	aesthetic outer body (the body constituted by actions/tasks in performance, i.e., the character in drama, offered for the gaze of the audience)
sensorimotor	visceral	subtle	fictive
Stance in relation to the world			
ecstatic	recessive	hidden/then ecstatic in practice	once created as score then ecstatic or recessive
Fundamental direction			
outward	inward	once awakened: outward/inward as a dialectic	once created as score, that to and from which one acts
Mode of disappearance			
focal and background disappearance	depth disappearance recedes	absent once cultivated	absent once created
		Modes of disappearance are both focal/background and recessive	
Mode of perception			
exteroception (plus proprioception)	interoception	attentiveness to exteroception, proprioception, interoception	"as if"
Mode of operation/awareness			
that from which I exist in the world	the inner depths	that through which I may heighten or cultivate my relationship to subtle modes of interiority and/or the world (voluntary)	that through which I appear to act in "a world"
Mediated/marked primarily by			
"flesh"	"blood"	"breath"	"appearance"

Note: Also drawing upon Merleau-Ponty, Japanese philosopher Yuasa Yasuo in his *Ki Shugyo Shintai* (*The Body, Self-Cultivation, and Ki-Energy* (1993)) proposes his own version of a "body-scheme" in order to describe and analyze the dynamic lived relationship between "the lived and living body" (Nagatomo 1992a: 49). See Appendix 2.

(ibid.: 43). However, the lived body

always constitutes a nullpoint in the world I inhabit. No matter where I physically move, and even in the midst of motion, my body retains the status of an absolute "here" around which all "theres" are arrayed . . . Precisely as the center point from which the perceptual field radiates, the perceptual organ remains an absence or nullity in the midst of the perceived.

(Leder 1990: 13)

Given that the body constitutes a nullpoint in our perceptual field, we experience *from* the body, and the sensory world "involves a constant reference to our possibilities of active response" (Leder 1990: 18). It is precisely in the ecstatic nature of our corporeality that the body is forgotten, i.e., "the body conceals itself precisely in the act of revealing what is Other" (ibid.: 22). This primordial absence is correlative with the very fact of being present in/to the world we experience. "The surface body tends to disappear from thematic awareness precisely because it is that *from* which I exist in the world," i.e., "my organs of perception and motility are themselves transparent at the moment of use" (ibid.: 53). When we fix our visual focus "upon that which lies spatially and temporally ahead, the back of the body is comparatively forgotten. It is absorbed in background disappearance" (ibid.: 29).

This commonplace disappearance of our surface body is made possible in part by the operation of a second mode of perception—*proprioception*—the "sense of balance, position,

Figure 3.2 The lion pose from *kalarippayattu*: an intensive training workshop at Gardzienice Theatre Association, Poland, May 1999, led by the author in the center forward position. When learning the lion pose, students are taught to keep the heels of the two feet in line with one another, with the external gaze ahead, hands crossed right over left, hips forward, and spine lengthened. As this is a beginning workshop, not all the participants yet display the fully correct form. For some the heels are not fully in line, or the hips are displaced slightly to the right so that they are not fully centered. Eventually, as one attunes the body toward correct practice, the internal eye is keeping an awareness and link to the negative space from the lower abdomen down through the rear foot and into/through the floor, along the lengthened spinal column to the space behind, and out through the two palms to the periphery both right and left. (Photograph: Przemek Sieraczynski)

and muscular tension, provided by receptors in muscles, joints, tendons, and the inner ear" (Leder 1990: 39). Proprioception allows our surface body to adjust our limbs, muscles, etc. appropriately to any motor task; therefore, we do not usually have to think about how to walk up a set of steps.

The sensorimotor repertoire of the lived body is in a constant state of transformation most evident when learning a new skill. Skill acquisition is at first extrinsic where one acts "*to* the skill qua thematized goal" (Leder 1990: 31). For example, when first learning the lion pose (Figure 3.2) in the Indian martial art, *kalarippayattu*, a beginner must learn how to assume the pose correctly by placing one foot facing forward, and the other foot at ninety degrees while keeping the two heels in line with one another, the knees directly above the feet providing support, the external focus ahead, and the spine lengthened. Skill acquisition is often at first characterized by a volitional shift of attention prompted either by a teacher's instruction to, for example, "check the alignment of the heels" or a self-conscious shift of one's attention to check one's own alignment. The "to" over time becomes the "from," as one acquires skill in taking the lion pose and moving to and from it. What was extrinsic becomes intrinsic and intuitive. The practitioner has *incorporated* the lion pose and its steps to the point of mastery in which s/he can now act on and operate in the world *from* a place of knowing how to move to and from the lion pose. The individual's proprioceptive sense allows one to make subtle, minor adjustments to the very act of placing the foot without thematizing the adjustment, i.e., one's bodymind intuitively adjusts as one moves. In this sense, the body disappears.

The "recessive" visceral body

The second body Leder describes is the *recessive body*, i.e., the deep, inner, visceral body of corporeal depths which in physical terms includes the mass of internal organs and processes enveloped by the body surface, such as digestion and sensations such as hunger. Physiologically,

our experience of our internal viscera and organs is characterized by *interoception*. Compared to the surface body, "interoception does not share the multidimensionality of exteroception" (Leder 1990: 40). Leder provides the example of taking a bite of an apple which, before swallowing, is experienced through sight, touch, smell, and taste. But once swallowed, "these possibilities are swallowed up as well" (ibid.: 39). Except for the occasional and often unpleasant evidence of digestive activity or dysfunction, "the incorporation of an object into visceral space involves its withdrawal from exteroceptive experience" (ibid.: 39). The withdrawal of the visceral body is a form of "depth disappearance" in that the viscera are "part of the body which we do *not* use to perceive or act upon the world in a direct sense" (ibid.: 53). Lacking the specificity of the surface body, visceral sensations are therefore often vague and anonymous—we experience this body as recessive, i.e., going or falling into the background. Characterized by its recession, the visceral body is therefore much more difficult to thematize. This is the (metaphorical) body of blood, suggesting that depth dimension of experience "beneath the surface flesh" (ibid.: 66), and suggesting our temporal emergence into life at the moment of birth.

The normative disappearance of both surface and recessive bodies is reversed when we experience pain or dysfunction. In pain, sensory intensification in the body demands direct thematization (Leder 1990: 77ff). Pain is an affective call which has the quality of compulsion, i.e., the pain seizes and constricts our attention. I must act now *to* the body to relieve the discomfort. If I begin to lose my balance when walking up a set of steps at home or on stage, my proprioceptive sense thematizes the dysfunction in my normally good balance, and I automatically attempt to regain my balance before falling. In both cases I involuntarily act toward the body, not from it.

Our everyday experience of the lived body is a constant intermingling and exchange of flesh and blood, i.e., "we form one organic/perceptual circuit" inhabiting the surface/recessive body(ies) as a gestalt which moves between ecstatic and recessive states—projecting out into the world and falling back. The body's disappearance and absence thereby mark our "ceaseless relation to the world" and our immediate environment (Leder 1990: 160). Leder's account concludes that the lived body's ecstatic and recessive nature provides an "ambiguous set of possibilities and tendencies that take on definite shape only within a cultural context" (ibid.: 151). The West has tended to valorize "immaterial reason," and this dissociation of mind from body has encouraged us to "abandon sensorimotor awareness for abstracted mathematical or linguistic forms" in contrast to more positive modes of cultivating the types of bodily awareness often required of the actor/performer (ibid.: 153).

The aesthetic inner bodymind

Since my focus is in constructing a phenomenological analysis and practically useful account of the lived body which takes into consideration not only the everyday surface and recessive bodies, but also the non-ordinary, extra-daily lived body, I propose adding to the surface and recessive bodies an equally important (third) mode of awareness and experience—the aesthetic inner bodymind. This body is that realm of extra-daily perception and experience associated with long-term, in-depth engagement in certain psychophysical practices or training regimes—yoga, the martial arts, *butoh*, acting/performing per se, or similar forms of embodied practice which engage the physical body and attention (mind) in cultivating and attuning both to subtle levels of experience and awareness. This process of cultivation and attunement is aesthetic in that it is non-ordinary, takes place over time, and allows for a shift in one's experience of the body and mind aspects from their gross separation, marked by the body's constant disappearance, to a much subtler, dialectical engagement of body-in-mind and mind-in-body. It is, therefore, marked as aesthetic since experience is gradually refined to ever-subtler

levels of awareness, and inner since this mode of experience begins with an exploration from within as the awareness learns to explore the body.

As an example, let us consider the well-documented paradigm of the bodymind developed in Indian yoga and the closely related Indian martial art, *kalarippayattu*, where a subtle level of inner awareness is often accessed through attentiveness to the breath. In contrast to the involuntary, everyday modes of disappearance and absence, or the sudden attention given to the body in pain, these positive, voluntary modes of refined self-presencing allow the practitioner to explore realms of embodiment which, while always bound by certain phenomenal constraints, nevertheless allow one to (re)negotiate the terms and quality of engagement of the lived bodymind in its encounter with itself in the world—at least during optimal moments of psychophysical practice or engagement.[7]

Chapter 4 describes in more detail how, at first, this subtle inner bodymind is hidden, unknown, and therefore fundamentally absent from experience. Since this bodymind and mode of experience is not necessary for the survival of the everyday body, it is understood to lie dormant within, available only to and through certain modes of psychophysical practice that engage the awareness. When an individual undergoes assiduous practice of particular embodied disciplines like yoga and related martial arts, this body has the potential to be awakened, i.e., this mode of experience and perception through the body is opened and can become available to the experience of the practitioner as the bodymind. To awaken the subtle inner bodymind, one must first attend directly to a particular embodied activity.

While practicing yoga and the martial arts such attentiveness is often achieved by means of focusing on the breath. This inner body is therefore literally as well as metaphorically marked by the breath—the inner circulation of wind/energy/life-force identified in non-Western paradigms of the body as *prana* or *prana-vayu* in India, in Chinese practices as *qi*, and in Japanese as *ki*. For Buddhists and Hindus, this inner bodymind is fully mapped as the "subtle body" of yoga where the breath or life-force travels along channels (*nadi*) and activates wheels (*chakras*) along the line of the spine.[8] For Chinese Taoists this mode of inner experience of the viscera is pictured "as centers along greater and lesser pathways for the circulation of *qi*" (Leder 1990: 182).

Over long-term practice the result is that one's experience of body and mind aspects of experience can be fundamentally altered, i.e., an inner subtle bodymind is revealed, and can be cultivated aesthetically through specific practices. Once awakened, this bodymind or mode of awareness becomes ecstatic, it begins to vibrate/resonate and therefore move. In workshops, *butoh* performer Fran Barbe has described this as the "sparkling body," thereby marking the vibrating sensation generated by inner activity. Given its ecstatic, sparkling quality, it can be directed inward and/or outward through one's practice. The ecstatic nature of this inner experience is often manifest in non-Western paradigms as extremely subtle vibrations and/or heat. It can operate *from* the body, *to* the interior of the body, or between the "from" and the "to." In some disciplines, especially inwardly directed forms of meditation intended to take the practitioner away from engagement with the everyday world and away from the body toward renunciation or self-transcendence, the direction is inward, and the body therefore intentionally recedes. These modes of practice are ecstatically recessive. But in other disciplines, especially martial arts or those modes of meditation intended to enliven and alter one's encounter with the immediate environment, the direction is outward toward this encounter with the environment and world as one meets it. It is in these outwardly oriented practices that one's stance ecstatically modulates between the inner and outer, the to-the-body and from-the-body—the inner/depth core, and the outer world one encounters.

Of all the processes of the recessive visceral body, respiration—the act of breathing which involves surface exchanges several times each minute—is the most susceptible of our visceral processes to intentional control. Our breathing responds instantaneously to shifts in emotion; therefore, "breathing is 'based in existence more than any other physiological function'" (Leder 1990: 183). It is through the breath that the aesthetic inner body reaches and touches both the surface body of exteroception, and also the depth ("blood") body of our inner recesses.

The fundamental state of absence of this third, aesthetic inner bodymind is witnessed in our everyday relationship to breathing. The act of breathing, like other visceral domains, normally disappears unless a particular physical condition such as a heart problem, or a non-normative mode of exertion such as climbing 200 stairs quickly, calls our attention to difficulties or pain in breathing. Alternatively, focusing our attention in and on the act of breathing in a particular way, and in relation to the body, provides one means by which to work against the recessive disappearance of the breath in order to cultivate the breath and our inner awareness toward a heightened, ecstatic state of engagement in a particular practice and/or in relation to a world. For example, some masters of the Indian martial art, *kalarippayattu*, teach simple breathing exercises at the beginning of training. As described briefly in Chapter 2, individuals stand with feet at shoulder width, external gaze fixed on and through a point ahead at eye level. I instruct practitioners to keep the mouth closed, and to breathe through the nose, simultaneously (and literally) following with their inner eye the breathe as it travels in and down along the line of the spine down to the lower abdominal region about two inches below the navel (in Sanskrit, the root of the navel, *nabhi mula*; in Chinese, *dantian*). Sensing the completion of the in-breath, and keeping the inner eye fixed on the breath, on the exhalation the practitioner follows the breath on its journey back up and out through the nose. The practitioner's attention is directed simultaneously outward with the external eye, and inward and down with the inner eye.

Japanese philosopher Yuasa Yasuo discusses how it is "possible to correct the modality of the mind by correcting the modality of the body" through the use of breathing exercises (Nagatomo 1992: 56).

> Physiologically, the respiratory organ is regulated and controlled by the autonomic nerves and motor-nerves; the respiratory organ has an ambiguous character of being linked both to the voluntary and involuntary muscles. This means that one can consciously control the rhythm and pattern of breathing, and in turn affect the physiological functions governed by the autonomic nervous system.
>
> (Nagatomo 1992: 56)

The experiential circuit developed through such practices is the "unconscious quasi-body" that corresponds to the *ki*-meridian system or network beneath the skin covering the entire body that is used by practitioners of acupuncture (Nagatomo 1992, *passim*). It is roughly equivalent to the subtle body of yoga.

Such attentive breathing can gradually shift one's awareness to the breath in the here and now as it traverses its way to the visceral depths of the body below the navel. Eventually with long-term practice the sensory awareness of following the breath can be extended from the lower abdomen downward through the lower body and out through the soles of the feet, up through the torso along the line of the spine and out the top of the head, and out through the arms/hands/fingers or palms as the inner wind or energy travels through the body. It is a process of what Yuasa Yasuo calls developing "*ki*-awareness" (Nagatomo 1992, *passim*). Although it is normal for a beginner to at first space out or experience the mind wandering away from staying attentive to the simple task of following the breath to and from the lower abdomen—keeping the eyes in the gut—over long-term practice such attentiveness to breath works against the normative disappearance of the body.

Although I have focused here on the example of the subtle body of yoga and *kalarippayattu* because this particular interior map of the subtle

body has been well documented ethnographically, the existence of an aesthetic inner bodymind marked by this particular map is not, I would argue, exclusive to these particular practices. Rather, numerous modes of traditional as well as contemporary actor/dancer training such as Japanese *noh*, LeCoq, Meyerhold's biomechanics, Grotowski-based work, *butoh*, Suzuki training, *kathakali* dance-drama, etc., provide practitioners with modes of deep, assiduous training in which the practitioner has the potential to develop an aesthetic inner bodymind. Each particular cultural, historical, or artistic/pedagogical practice over time develops a version of this aesthetic inner bodymind. The mature practitioner ideally develops the ability to voluntarily thematize the body through use of the breath so that one stays [more] present in the moment of practice. Although this type of self-presencing experience is not one of the primary, everyday "ways in which most of us live out the body" (Leder 1990: 153), for the actor, martial artist, or meditator, such attention to bodily activity itself is practically cultivated through long-term training and/or through long-term experience onstage where one is able to attain a non-ordinary, optimal inner awareness to be deployed to the tasks that constitute one's practice. Immersion in an ongoing psychophysical process allows the practitioner to explore, on a subtle level, the sense of experience/awareness of what one is doing as it is being done, i.e., the vibratory quality of one's relationship to the acting task in relation to the environment one inhabits.

To summarize the discussion thus far, one's experience of the gestalt body-as-a-whole is usually within the context of experiential disappearance; however, for the individual practicing some type of psychophysical discipline or through long-term embodied practice, the experience of surface and recessive bodies can be enhanced and modulated by the gradual awakening and attunement of a third, inner aesthetic inner bodymind toward heightened perceptual awareness.

The aesthetic outer body

In performance, the actor enacts a specific performance score—that set of actions/tasks that constitutes the aesthetic outer body offered for the abstractive gaze of the spectator—often read and experienced as character in a conventional drama.[9] The actor's body, therefore, is dually present for the objective gaze and/or experience of an audience, and as a site of experience for the actor. The actor's body is a site through which representation as well as experience are generated for both self and other. As an actor, one undergoes an experience that is one's own, and is therefore constitutive of one's being-in-the-world, and simultaneously constitutes a (theatrical) world for the other. Stanton Garner describes this as the "irreducible twinness of a field that is—from all points—simultaneously inhabited and seen" (1994: 51). For spectators attending the enactment of a drama, this fourth body is conventionally read and experienced as a particular character. For spectators attending a non-dramatic performance such as a Japanese *butoh* performance, this fourth fictive body is present, not as a character but as the living/human vehicle through which potential experience and/or meaning are generated.

During performance, the actor ideally embodies, attends to, and inhabits an experiential field structured by the set of actions/tasks immediately at-hand. Whether based on an authored text, or the structure of an improvisatory exercise, these actions/tasks constitute the performance score. The actor embodies/inhabits these tasks/actions by dynamically shaping one's energy, attention, and awareness to the qualities and constraints of the aesthetic form and dramaturgy informing the score. For the actor operating at virtuosic levels, once the score is created during workshops/rehearsals, it presents itself to the actor as potentially both ecstatic and recessive. The score is that to and/or from which the actor's performance moves, modulates, and oscillates. As a construction the score is fictive in that it is absent until it is created, rehearsed, and bodied forth in performance. Once created and present for the actor as a score

the modes of disappearance are both focal/background, and recessive.

For the actor enacting the score, perception operates between exteroception, proprioception, and interoception. That is, the actor makes adjustments as necessary to/with/for the immediate demands of the four bodies. Ideally the actor thematizes the score as it unfolds, inhabiting as fully as possible each action within the score, and linking each action as its moment of enactment arrives. However, as in the description of *Ohio Impromptu*, constant adjustments must be made to and within the moment of enactment—to one's balance, to the action of another actor, to a cough or a laugh from the audience, etc. The experiential field of the actor is, as Garner explains, "subject to ambiguity and oscillation. At the center of this ambiguity is the tension between inside and outside" (1994: 51). The actor, therefore, operates with a dual consciousness in a process of constant modulation of the four bodies with all their ambiguities and tendencies, always ideally thematizing the unfolding score. The actor is inhabiting and embodying a score through which he appears to act in a world or environment. The actor's breath appears to be the character's breath, i.e., the actor's breath both is his own, and simultaneously is the breath of the character.

The actor's bodymind as a gestalt

For the actor-as-self, the "organic/perceptual circuit" experience knits together all of the bodies as a whole or a gestalt within which there is constant, dialectic movement between ecstatic and recessive states with respect to each of the bodies (Leder 1990: 160). None of these bodies is settled or absolute, they are in a constant state of ambiguity. Therefore, the actor's lived experience within the world of performance engages a constant dialectic between and among these four bodies or experiential circuits. Like Noë, Japanese philosopher Yuasa Yasuo calls this kind of knowledge "somatic"—"knowledge gained *through the body*" and not "knowledge of the body."

Such knowledge may be contrasted with "intellectual" knowledge. Intellectual knowledge is that mode of cognition which results from objectifying a given object, which propositionally takes a subject-predicate form, and which divorces the somaticity of the knower from "the mind" of the knower. For these reasons, intellectual knowledge circumscribes its object; it is incapable of becoming one with the object. Somatic knowledge in its immediate, everyday occurrence lacks this objectification. There is a "feeling-judgment" operative in somatic knowledge. In feeling-judgment, "knowing that" and "feeling that" are one and the same in the constitutive momentum of forming a judgment. In this experience, there is an attunement of mind and body, of "I" and other, and of human nature qua microcosm and physical nature qua macrocosm.

(Nagatomo 1992: 63)

Optimally, in heightened extra-daily activities such as performance, the surface and recessive bodies recede further into the background, but of course are always present. The lived bodymind is a gestalt that is present as an intersecting, intertwining, chiasm of multiple bodies.

The actor's body as the chiasmatic body

The notion that the experience of the lived body may best be described as a chiasm—braiding, intertwining, or criss-crossing—originated with Merleau-Ponty's early description of the intertwining that characterizes the body's fundamental relationship to the world through the surface body (1968, *passim*). In the model proposed here, the chiasmic nature of experience as a braiding and intertwining is more complexly elaborated in the modulation of the four modes of bodily experience described above—the ecstatic surface, the depth/visceral recessive, the subtle inner bodies, and the fictive body of the actor's score. Leder's analysis adds to Merleau-Ponty's

earlier work the dimension of depth or verticality associated with our deep, visceral experience (1990: 62–63). Such verticality is most evident in the voluntary modes of psychophysical practice that awaken experience through the subtle, inner bodymind. When one exercises the bodymind through the various forms of yoga or martial arts practice, one is understood to be braiding, interweaving, or tying knots within the inner body. As the practitioner repeats over and over again a form like the *kalarippayattu* lion pose, the practitioner moves from one lion into another by sliding the rear foot along the earth and inside through the center (or lower abdomen) before sliding the foot forward. When performed correctly with the hips forward and a lengthened spine, the repetitious action of bringing the foot/leg in (to one's center), and then out (from the center) constitutes a form of churning or knotting which exercises the lower abdominal region. This action creates a constant opposition—the type of opposition we experience when we tie a tight knot in a rope, pulling with our two hands on both ends of the rope simultaneously in opposite directions to tighten the knot. Here the results of long-term exercise of the body-as-chiasm can be manifest as a grounding energy circulated out from the lower abdomen, through the feet (the ends of the rope), along the spine, and available to/in the hands (the ends of the rope). In this model, acting/performance begins as a dynamic deployment of one's inner energy in relation to the tasks/actions of a performance score. *How* that dynamic energy is shaped depends, of course, on the dramaturgy and *mise-en-scène* within which it is being deployed.

In such heightened modes of psychophysical practice, one is able to experience a "bidirectional incorporation" where "the boundaries between inner and outer . . . become more porous" (Leder 1990: 165). The lower abdominal region is the activated inner depth to and from which one's attentive thematization of the body can travel along the line of the spine outward through the rear foot, out the top of the head, through the palms. Within a South Asian paradigm, one's ability to engage in and encounter the world is ideally heightened and attuned to the point where "the body becomes all eyes"—the actor's perceptual/sensory awareness is so attuned that one is able to respond, animal-like, to the (theatrical) environment.

The chiasmic model of experience and embodiment outlined here points not to a mode of subjectivity that is unitary in its self-presencing, but rather, the operation of subjectivity as a constantly shifting *tactical improvisation* modulating betwixt and between one's bodymind and its modes of engaging its own deployment in the score (physical and textual) during training and performance. As should be clear from the initial discussion of the opening of *Ohio Impromptu*, one is in a constant process of making adjustments to one's presence and/or absence in relation to the bodies as they encounter *this particular* moment of enactment of a score. Each of these bodies might be thought of as a circuit of experience. Within the phenomenological model explored here, the actor's complex subjectivity is never settled or fixed within *a* present or *a* body, but rather is continuously engaged in a process of its own play with the "to-s and from-s" which are characteristic of each mode or circuit of embodiment/experience. The structure of the actor's score provides the actor with one set of tasks or actions to be played, i.e., to be corporeally engaged with and through one's bodymind.

Concluding discussion

Understanding how absent our body can become to us points to the necessity of having practical strategies for enhancing the cultivation of work on impulse, action, and the type of bodily based awareness in which absent or negative space is inhabited during performance. The specific discursive and practical strategies I have developed to address the problem of the absent body through training in Asian martial arts and yoga are specifically discussed in the next chapter. The discussion of practice in Chapters 4–6 explores practical ways through which the actor's body-as-a-whole can voluntarily thematize and thereby better inhabit the bodymind in space and through time so that it does not disappear but remains present to us. What happens when one looks from behind or maintains an active awareness of the soles of the feet as one part of the dialectic of the bodies-in-performance? These, of course, are open-ended questions of how to apply the principles underlying this approach to specific dramaturgies, and to which I return throughout Parts II–III.

Part II

Work on oneself

4

The source traditions

Yoga, *kalarippayattu*, and *taiqiquan*

You should wash the floor of the *kalari* with your sweat.
Kalarippayattu is 80 percent mental and only the remainder is physical.

(Gurukkal C. V. Govindankutty Nayar)

It is 1983, at the CVN Kalari in Thiruvananthapuram, Kerala. I arrive for training at 6 a.m. After wrapping and securing my *lengoti* (loin-cloth) and entering the *kalari* to pay respects to the deities, along with Sathyan, Rajasekharan, Hari, Peter, et al., I apply *gingely* (sesame) oil to my body before beginning the training. Everyone in the *kalari* begins to warm-up on his own—performing a variety of kicks, poses, steps, and jumps that are part of body preparation. By the time another hour has passed, I have completed four full body-exercise sequences. Now, with Peter as my partner I repeat *tanjamppayattu*—one of *kalarippayattu*'s most exhausting sequences which includes numerous repetitions of the lion pose as one moves forward and backward across the space with lion steps. I stand at the student's end of the *kalari* (to the east). Sweat streams down my body. So copious is the sweat that a pool of muddy water is forming where I stand. Today, like other days, I too have begun to wash the floor of the *kalari* with my sweat.

Another day. Another year. With the body-memory of my five to six hours of intensive training and sweating body still very much present to me, in one of my many evening discussions with Gurukkal Govindankutty Nayar, he explains one of the paradoxes of in-depth practice of this yoga-based martial art: "*Kalarippayattu* is 80 percent mental and only the remainder is physical."

In Chapters 4 and 5 we encounter the whole body in the studio—the sweating, material bodymind. Even when the actor-as-doer is physically still and the body is not literally sweating, the mind and inner energy are optimally *always in motion* and therefore one is always sweating. Sweat is not only the 20 percent physical, but encompasses the 80 percent mental that lies behind the obvious physical. The 80 percent mental dimension of sweat is the subtle domain of inner activation, i.e., the flame of an active, inner, vibratory perceptivity and engagement. When the actor sweats it signals the actor's optimal engagement of energy, sensory awareness, and perception when heightened, open, and dynamically shaped by a specific dramaturgy.

Antonin Artaud described the psychophysical actor as "crude empiricist" (Artaud 1970). The practice of yoga, *kalarippayattu*, and *taiqiquan* is one means by which the primary empirical, material elements of the psychophysical actor's art are discovered and then attuned. The psychophysical exercises begin with the body and move both inward toward subtle realms of experience and feeling, and outward to meet the environment. They are a form of empirical as well

Figure 4.1 Executing the fish pose at the Tyn-y-Parc CVN Kalari/Studio in West Wales. The *kalari* is located in a quiet, rural environment near the Irish Sea and, as in Kerala, has an earthen floor to absorb sweat and oil. From left to right: Heidi Love, Soledad Garre-Rubio, Jo Shapland, and Klaus Seewald. (Photograph: Phillip Zarrilli)

as (meta)physical (re)search. This (re)search is *not* undertaken by the side of our brain which engages propositional, analytical thought, but by the bodymind together as they become one in and through daily practice. Because the beginning exercises are repeatable structures in which, as Grotowski observes, "every element has its logical place, technically necessary," they are a means to "work on oneself" (1995: 130) in the psychophysical sense. The logic of each structure is revealed in and through guided practice. Chapters 4 and 5 together explain the logic implicit within those structures. In this chapter I focus on the logic of the source traditions within the Indian and Chinese cultural contexts.[1]

Within each specific Asian culture, modes of embodied practice—martial arts, meditation techniques, traditional medical practices such as massage, and the performing arts—were woven into the fabric of daily life and thought, and were therefore in constant interaction with one another. Chinese and Indian martial arts were village practices. Children learned from an early age. Local martial artists were those who also practiced massage, bone setting, physical therapies, and (especially in China) herbal medicine. The interchange between and among traditional embodied practices is also witnessed in the fact that many of the best-known traditional Asian performing arts have been directly influenced by indigenous martial arts. The Chinese martial arts have informed the styles of movement and stage combat distinctive to Beijing Opera. *Kalarippayattu* was the immediate precursor of

Kerala's *kathakali* dance-drama. Japanese martial arts have directly influenced both *noh* and *kabuki*.

Most significantly, a common set of principles, assumptions, and paradigms of the body, the mind, their relationship, and emotion inform the various modes of embodied practice unique to each culture. Embodied practices were not separate from the development of philosophical thought; rather, practices such as yoga and Buddhist meditation contributed to and were shaped by the development of ever-changing religio-philosophical systems of thought as they traveled from South Asia to Southeast Asia, China, Korea, and Japan.

I briefly examine each of the three practices which I have organized into a systematic daily training for the actor—yoga, *kalarippayattu*, and *taiqiquan*. I conclude the chapter by considering how Asian perspectives on the body, the mind, their relationship, and emotion might help us better conceptualize the psychophysical approach to contemporary acting discussed in Chapters 5–6.

Yoga and *kalarippayattu* in the South Asian context

The specific term "yoga" is derived from the Sanskrit root, *yuj*, meaning "to yoke or join or fasten . . . make ready, prepare, arrange, fit out . . . accomplish" (Monier-Williams 1963: 855–856). Yoga encompasses any ascetic, meditational, or psychophysiological technique which achieves a binding, uniting, or bringing together of the bodymind. A wide variety of yogic pathways developed historically in South Asia including *karma yoga* or the law of universal causality; *maya yoga* or a process of liberating oneself from cosmic illusion; *nirvana yoga* or a process of growing beyond illusion to attain at-onement with absolute reality; and *hatha yoga* or specific techniques of psychophysiological practice. Classical *hatha yoga* includes repetition of breath-control exercises, forms/postures (*asana*), combined with restraints/constraints on diet and behavior. These practices are understood to act

on both the physical body (*sthula sarira*) and the subtle body (*suksma sarira*) most often identified with Kundalini-Tantric yoga. Problematically, popular use and understanding of the term "yoga" in the West today usually associates its practices exclusively with one or more of the many forms of *hatha yoga*, often practiced for relaxation in our busy, hurried, and stressful cosmopolitan lives.

As early as the Rig Veda (1200 BCE) ascetic practices (*tapas*) are mentioned.[2] By the time of composition of the Upanishads (c. 600–300 BCE), specific methods for experiencing non-ordinary, higher states of consciousness and control of the self were well developed. The earliest use of the specific term "yoga" is in the *Katha Upanisad* where the term means "the steady control of the senses, which, along with the cessation of mental activity, leads to the supreme state" (Flood 1996: 95).

Philosophical assumptions informing yoga vary widely, and range from monist (all is one) to dualist (all is two) to atomist (all is many) (White, 1996: 16). Yoga's psycho-physical/spiritual practices have therefore never been "confined to any particular sectarian affiliation or social form" (Flood 1996: 94).[3] As a consequence, both yoga philosophy and yogic practices are ubiquitous throughout South Asia and inform all modes of embodied practice including Indian wrestling (Alter 1992) and martial arts, as well as the visual, plastic, and performing arts.

From the earliest stages of its development, yoga developed as a practical pathway toward the transformation of consciousness (and thereby self) and spiritual release (*moksa*) through renunciation by withdrawal from the world and the cycles of rebirth. Some yogic pathways provide a systematic attempt to control both the wayward body and the potentially overwhelming senses/ emotions that can create disequilibrium in daily life. Rigorous practice therefore can lead to a sense of detachment (*vairagya*) through which the *yogin* withdraws completely from daily life and its activities, and is understood to achieve a state of *kalalita* where he transcends time.

However, yoga philosophy and its practices

Figure 4.2 Executing a yoga *asana*: the torso is rotated around the vertical spinal axis extending from the base of the spine through the top of the head. While executing the *asana*, I invite the doer to "keep residual awareness of the right palm in contact with the floor, and through the forward foot." (Photographer unknown)

expected to bring pleasure and aesthetic joy both to the diverse gods of the Hindu pantheon and to those one was serving and entertaining.

In contrast to the classical yoga practitioner-as-renunciant who withdraws from everyday life, for martial artists and performers yogic practices do not lead to renunciation and/or disengagement from daily life. Rather as the practitioner engages in yoga-based psychophysical practices, the ego becomes quiet and the emotions calm. One is better able to act within their respective socio-cultural domain while still in the world. The martial or performing artist who practices yoga-based psychophysical techniques does so to transcend personal limitations to better act rather than withdraw from the world. In the South Asian context, later in life, when one's duties and social obligations have been fulfilled, the individual might choose to become a renunciant and follow the radical, ideal pattern of the yogi who withdraws from life.

Kalarippayattu and the yogic paradigm

Kalarippayattu is a specific, regional martial art indigenous to the southwest coastal region of South Asia known as Kerala State today.[4] It dates in something like its present form from at least the twelfth century, although like other regional martial arts such as Manipur's distinctive *thang-ta*, it has roots in Indian antiquity. The earliest Indian forms of martial practices were collectively known as Dhanur Veda (the science of archery) since bow and arrow were considered the supreme weapon, while bare-hand combat was the least desirable form of fighting.

Dhanur Veda was highly regarded and considered one of the eighteen traditional branches of knowledge. Its principles and practices are known to us from the stories embedded in the early epic literature (*Mahabharata* and *Ramayana*), and most comprehensively from the earliest extant Dhanur Vedic text—a collection of chapters (249–252) in an encyclopedic text known as the *Agni Purana* which dates from the eighth

have also always informed and/or been directly adapted by non-renunciants as well, i.e., those who keep both feet firmly in the spatio-temporal world. Traditionally this included India's martial castes (*ksatriyas*) who served as rulers and/or those martial artists and warriors in the service of rulers, and a wide variety of artists—actors, dancers, musicians, painters, and sculptors. Rulers, martial artists, and performing and plastic artists had to live and act very much in and upon the world and/or its social order. Rulers and *ksatriyas* were required to govern, maintain the cosmic order mirrored in the microcosm of worldly kingdoms, and be able to use well-honed martial skills to maintain order. Artists and performers were century (Pant 1978: 3–5). The yogic paradigm is a leitmotif throughout the text suggesting how the martial artist achieves a state of superior mental accomplishment. Practice is circumscribed by ritual. The archer "gird[s] up his loins"; after he has "collected himself" he ties in place his quiver; he places an arrow on the string after "his mind [is] divested of all cares and anxieties" (M. N. Dutt Shastri 1967: 897). When the archer has become so well practiced that he "knows the procedure," he "fix[es] his mind on the target" before releasing the arrow (Gangadharan 1985: 648). The consummate martial master progresses from training in basic body postures, through mastery of specific techniques, to attaining single-point focus, to ever-subtler aspects of mental (psychophysiological) accomplishment:

> Having learned all these ways, one who knows the system of *karma-yoga* [associated with this practice] should perform this way of doing things with his mind, eyes, and inner vision since one who knows [this] yoga will conquer even the god of death (Yama) [...] Having acquired control of the hands, mind, and vision, and become accomplished in target practice, then [through this] you will achieve disciplined accomplishment (*siddhi*).
>
> (Dasgupta 1993)

The trajectory of practice outlined above is clearly informed by the yogic paradigm of divestment of anything personal or extraneous from attaining a heightened, non-ordinary state of psychophysical accomplishment—a state in which the practitioner is self-controlled, mentally calm, inhabits one-point concentration, and accesses powers for use in combat.

The body(ies) in *kalarippayattu* practice

Like the early Dhanur Vedic tradition, *kalarippayattu* is practically and conceptually informed by yoga, as well as Ayurveda. Just as the *hatha yoga* practitioner begins by learning basic postures (*asana*) and breathing exercises, so the *kalarippayattu* practitioner at first tames both body and mind via poses, body exercises, and breath-control exercises. A traditional Muslim *kalarippayattu* master told me, "he who wants to become a master must possess complete knowledge of the body." Possessing "complete knowledge of the body" traditionally meant gaining knowledge of three different bodies of practice: (1) the fluid body of humors and saps, (2) the body composed of bones, muscles, and the vulnerable vital junctures or spots (*marmmam*) of the body, and (3) the subtle, interior body associated with the practice of yoga. The first two bodies are based on Ayurveda, and together constitute the external physical body (*sthula-sarira*). The third—the subtle, interior body (*suksma-sarira*)—is understood to be encased within the physical body. While each body has its own conceptual and practical history, they are experienced by the practitioner as a gestalt—as a whole and as one's own.

For the martial artist, complete knowledge of the body begins with the physical or gross body (*sthula-sarira*) as it is experienced through practice of exercises and breathing exercises, and receipt of massage. Together they are considered body preparation (*meyyorukkam*). The exercises include a vast array of poses, steps, jumps, kicks, and leg exercises performed in increasingly complex combinations back and forth across the *kalari* floor. Collectively, they are considered a body art (*meiabhyasam*). Individual body exercise sequences (*meippayattu*) are taught one-by-one, and every student masters simple forms before moving on to more complex and difficult sequences. Most important is mastery of basic poses (*vadivu*), named after animals, and comparable to the basic postures (*asana*) of yoga; and mastery of steps (*cuvadu*) by which one moves to and from poses. *Kalarippayattu* forms incorporate both straight line and circular movements. Some *kalarippayattu* forms and sequences are based on yoga, such as the *kalari vanakkam* which is probably derived from the salutation to the sun (*surya namaskaar*).

Figure 4.3 Teaching long staff to a student from Japan at the CVN Kalari, Thiruvananthapuram. Use of the staff introduces students to extension of energy. (Photographer unknown)

At first the exercises are "that which is external," but as the forms come correct the practitioner should begin to manifest physical, mental, and behavioral signs (*lakshana*) indicating change. Like the practice of *hatha yoga*, eventually the exercises become "that which is internal" (*andarikamayatu*). At first the practitioner must overcome the physical limitations of the gross, physical body, stretching muscles to enable the body to assume difficult forms, removing mental distractions, and beginning to actualize one-point focus (*ekagrata*). Observe the focus of Gurukkal Govindankutty Nayar in Figure 2.1 (p. 24). Only when the student reaches a sufficient state of psychophysical development is he introduced to a vast array of weapons beginning with the long staff (Figure 4.3) and progressing through the short

stick, the dagger, the *otta* (a unique curved stick; see Figure 1, p. 3), sword and shield, spear, mace, and spear versus sword and shield.

Vigorous practice is undertaken in the cool monsoon period. Practitioners apply oil to the body before exercise, observe yogic restrictions, and receive an annual, extremely deep oil massage (*uliccil*) (Figure 4.4) of the entire body. Using his feet as he holds onto ropes suspended from the ceiling and occasionally the hands, the master massages the student's entire body daily over a fifteen-day period. The intensive exercises, the production of sweat through the pores of the oiled surface of the skin, and the deep massage are understood to stimulate all forms of the wind humor to course through the body. The massage cleanses and purifies the physical and subtle

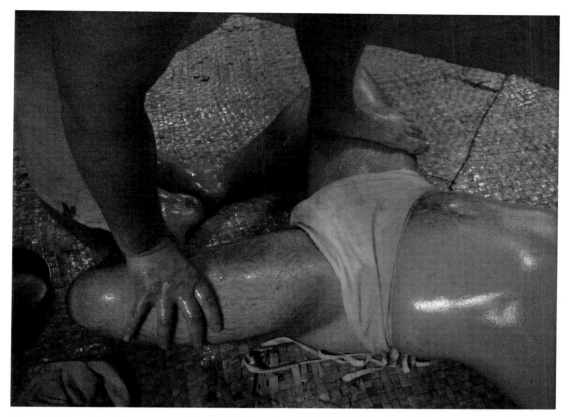

Figure 4.4 The author giving massage (*uliccil*) at the Tyn-y-Parc CVN Kalari in Wales. Special oil is applied to the entire body so that massage strokes are deep as they work on both the physical and subtle bodies. (Photograph: Kaite O'Reilly)

bodies. Long-term practice enhances the ability to endure fatigue through balancing the three bodily humors, and to acquire internal and external ease of movement and bodymind fluidity so that, as one master said, you are "flowing (*olukku*) like a river."

Making the body flow and positively affecting the fluid body of humors and saps and the subtle, interior, yogic body occurs only as the student learns to assume the correct position of the basic forms and techniques of practice. But what constitutes correct practice? Kallada Balakrishnan explains how "Each movement, step, and pose [and weapon] has its own 'inner life' (*bhava*) which must be exhibited when practicing *kalarippayattu*." *Bhava* is a term commonly used to refer to the actor's psychophysiological embodiment of a character's states of being/doing

(emotions) in the popular *kathakali* dance-drama of Kerala (see Zarrilli 2000a: 159–174). Gurukkal Govindankutty Nayar compared the process of the martial artist's process of "becoming one" with the "original qualities" of the forms of practice with that of the *kathakali* actor "becoming" his role. "Take the role of Duryodhana. He lives that part by becoming it." For the *kathakali* actor "becoming the character" is a psychophysical process in which the actor controls and circulates his inner energy (*prana-vayu*) into and through the stylized and codified forms he has come to embody and thereby uses to create the character. Just as the actor becomes the character by embodying the various states of being/doing required by the dramatic context of the play, so the martial artist "becomes one with the original qualities" of a pose or movement. The inner life of each movement is assumed to be present as the seed of the form, implanted by the master during each first lesson. The practitioner himself does not create the benefits or powers which are eventually realized through practice of a discipline; rather, practice itself is a means of cultivating or bringing such powers "to their maximum efficiency" (Varenne 1976: 134).

This gradual discovery of a form and its application reflects the general cultural assumption that long-term practice of psychophysical exercises cultivates a certain form of bodymind awareness. As the *Bhagavad-Gita* (4.38) explains, "he who attains perfection through the practice of yoga *discovers of his own accord, with time*, the brahman present in his soul" (Varenne 1976: 58, italics mine). The *Amritabindu Upanisad* provides the following account of how knowledge is already present in the bodymind, but hidden and then discovered through practice:

> And knowledge is hidden in the depth of each individual
> just as in milk
> the butter we cannot see is hidden;
> this is why the wise practitioner
> must carry out a churning operation within himself,
> employing his own mind without respite as the churning agent.
>
> (Varenne 1976: 59)

Through psychophysical exercises, one churns the bodymind. This churning cultivates and actualizes its hidden *bhava*—manifest as an awakening and sharpening of one's energy, awareness, focus, etc.

Becoming one with the inner life of a *kalarippayattu* pose means that the practitioner embodies the qualities of the animal for which each pose is named, and manifests this quality in his practice. The life of the animal is assumed to be there in the form. If one is unable to achieve such oneness, then the martial form becomes nothing or loses its actuality. The potential power (*sakti*) in a form may never be awakened or realized.

The subtle body and the vital energy

As a yoga-in-motion, correct practice of *kalarippayattu* exercises tames and purifies the external body as it balances the three humors, makes the mind quiet, and calms one's personal emotions. Eventually the practitioner should begin to discover the subtle body (*suksma sarira*) most often identified with Kundalini/Tantric yoga (Figure 4.5). For martial practitioners this discovery is essential to embodying power (*sakti*) to be used in fighting and giving healing massage therapies.

The subtle body refers to the ideational construct assumed by many South Indians to identify and articulate the psycho-spiritual experiences of the yogi, martial artist, and the pilgrim/devotee. It maps the experiential landscape encountered when one practices a psychophysiological discipline. The map of this landscape allows the practitioner to make sense of the psychophysiological effects of practice on his bodymind as practice reshapes his experience.

The physical and subtle bodies are *not absolute categories*. They are fluid conceptual and practical counterparts. Specific parts of the subtle body are thought to correspond to specific places in the physical body. These are analogous/homologous correspondences and are never exact (Varenne 1976: 155). The two are so fundamentally related that what affects one body is understood to affect the other.

Although physical and subtle bodies are integrally related, the concept and specific inner alchemy of the subtle body historically developed separately from Ayurveda as part of ascetic and yogic practice (Eliade 1958: 234; Filliozat 1964: 234) and appears fully developed after about the eighth century CE in the *Yoga Upanisad* and *Tantra*. The essential elements of the subtle body usually identified in these texts, as well as in *kalarippayattu* versions of the subtle body, include structural elements, wheels, and centers (*cakra*), channels (*nadi*), and dynamic elements, vital or vibrative energy or wind (*prana*, *vayu*, or *prana-vayu*) and the cosmic energy (*kundalini* or *sakti*) sleeping coiled within the lowest center.

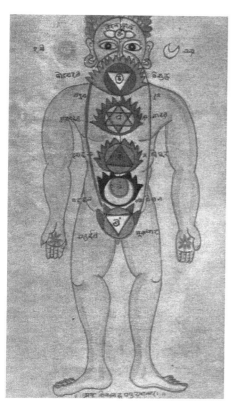

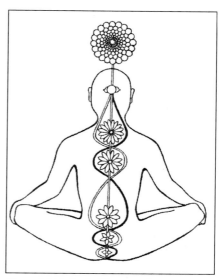

Figure 4.5(a)
The *cakras* of the subtle body. Each *cakra* is represented by a flower with petals. The number of petals indicates the respective frequency of vibration once a *cakra* is activated. The lowest *cakra* has the smallest number of petals and least vibration, while the *cakra* located at the top of the spine has most. (Print from *The Power of Tantrik Breathing*)

Figure 4.5(c) Seated figure: a simple representation of the *cakras* with their petals and the two main *nadis* (*ida* and *pingala*) that intertwine and join the *cakras* along the spine.

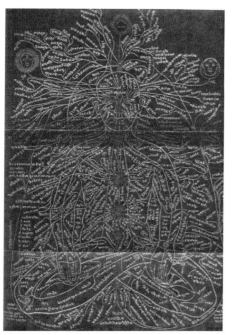

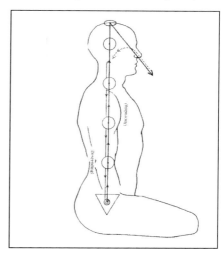

Figure 4.5(b)
The *nadis* (channels) of the subtle body spread throughout the body "like veins through a pipal leaf." (Copy of a nineteenth-century Gujarat manuscript painting)

Figure 4.5(d) Kneeling figure (side view): a representation of the descending and ascending breath as it moves through the nadis and reaches the *cakras* arrayed along the line of the spine. As the breath is taken in on an inhalation it descends all the way to the root of the navel (*nabhi mula*) and lowest *cakra*, and then ascends on the exhalation upward—optimally all the way through the top of the head as it travels out through the nose. (Drawings: Phillip Zarrilli)

Through the channels or conduits (*nadi*) flows the vital energy or inner wind. The channels usually range in number from ten to fourteen. Of the three most important channels two (*ida* and *pingala*) reach from the lower end of the spinal column (*muladhra cakra*) to the left and right nostrils. Between and intertwined with them is the central channel (*susumna-nadi*). It too originates at the root of the spinal column and stretches to the top of the head. All the channels originate at the lower end of the spinal column and form an intricate network through the body linking *muladhara-cakra* with the various limbs and sense organs.

The wheels or centers (*cakra*) number from five to eight and take the form of a stylized lotus (*padma*). They are arrayed vertically from the base of the spine (along the corresponding central *susumna nadi*) up to and through increasingly refined and more subtle centers. These centers are places within the subtle body where latent functions, often represented as half-opened buds, await the invigorating exercise of the internal energy. The number of petals indicates the respective frequency of vibration once a *cakra* is activated.

Traditional *kalarippayattu* masters who interpret practice using this paradigm agree that the subtle body is gradually revealed as the student (1) develops one-point focus (*ekagrata*), (2) corrects the forms of practice so that the inner energy circulates along the spine and throughout the body while practicing forms, and (3) develops proper breath control so that the inner energy/wind circulates correctly. As in yoga practice, when forms come correct then, as the *Siva Samhita* (III.90) explains, "the vital airs of the practitioner at once become completely equable, and flow harmoniously through the body" (Vasu 1975: 39).

When the simple breathing exercises (*swasam*) taught to me by Mohammedunni Gurukkal are performed correctly, "your mind is simply on what you are doing. There is a grip or power at the base of the navel (*nabhi mula*) at the full point of inhalation." During vigorous practice sustained breathing is maintained so that there is a constant gripping (*piduttam*) which comes naturally to the lower abdomen. This is where the traditional loin cloth (*kacca; lengoti*) is securely wrapped and tied to hold in the life-force.

For the martial artist (or the actor!) simply mimicking an external form is never enough to attain inner actualization or awakening. Gurukkal Govindankutty Nayar explains how practice too often "lacks something. It is lacking that spark or life (*jivan*) that makes this a real and full practice." Exercises can be a mere shell if the internal wind or energy is not manifest behind the form. Only when the wind/life-force/vital energy (*prana-vayu*) is awakened and spread throughout the bodymind, thereby enlivening both, is the full benefit of such practice actualized. As Gurukkal Govindankutty Nayar explained to me one day:

> Who am I? My hands, legs, nose, etc.? Who am I? My hands, legs, breast? That, all of these, is *prana*. Just to close your eyes—that is one *prana*. Yawning is another *prana*. Therefore, life itself (*jivan*) is *prana*.[5]

Actualizing free circulation of the vital energy (*prana-vayu*) within allows the practitioner to dynamically release and shape this energy for healing therapies and/or for concentrated attack in fighting. As the vital energy is released, circulates within, and is shaped/channeled through training exercises, through the palms when using a weapon or giving massage, or through the feet, there is a felt, experiential quality to the flow of *prana-vayu*. Optimally, the *kalarippayattu* practitioner attains a state in which the bodymind has "become all eyes"—the practitioner is able to utilize his energy and heightened awareness to respond in the moment to the immediate environment, animal-like. The bodymind is fully and constantly energized as and when it moves.

Taiqiquan in the Chinese context[6]

Taiqiquan is described by its advocates as "gentle wind, fine rain" [. . .] Movements are slow, smooth, rounded, flowing and gentle, with no perceptible hesitation between movements and postures [. . .] Ground contact must be maintained. One moves with the center of gravity well under the body which generates a feeling of strength and graceful movements [. . . I]n combat the *taiqiquan* artist becomes a formidable opponent who is able to unleash a constant stream of martial combinations, counter and movement.

(Wong 1978: 58–59)

The principles and practices known and taught today as *taiqiquan* derive from a rich elixir of religion, philosophy, mythology, and history. Along with *hsing-i* and *baqua*,[7] *taiqiquan* is usually identified as one of the three primary internal or soft (*nei-chia*) martial practices as a complement to the external or hard (*wai-chia*) practices. These are not exclusive categories, but rather descriptive terms which provide a general sense of the type of skills developed and the way a particular martial art is organized. Outer skills were developed via exercises for physical conditioning such as callisthenics, weight training, isometric exercises, holding deep stances, and aerobic/anaerobic methods such running, hill-climbing, etc. External systems often emphasize use of force against force. Inner skills focus especially on the development of *qi*—the vital life-force or internal energy assumed to circulate throughout the body. Internal systems emphasize give and take, constant change, and circularity. Most Chinese martial practices combine elements of both the external and internal.[8]

Conflicting theories exist on the origin of *taiqiquan* as a specific martial arts practice. Chronologically arranged, these theories include its invention and subsequent development during the T'ang dynasty (618–907) into four schools; its invention during a dream by a Taoist priest during the Yuan dynasty (1279–1368); its invention during the Ming dynasty (1368–1654) by the Ch'en family in Honan Province; and finally the theory that while the original founder of *taiqiquan* is not known to us, its practice was developed by Wang Tsung-yueh of Shansi Province during the Ch'ine-lung period (1736–1795) of the Ch'ing

dynasty (Draeger and Smith 1980: 35; see also Wong 1978: 59). Whatever the veracity of these vastly different histories of *taiqiquan*, the result was the emergence of four main historical lineages of practice: Ch'en, Yang, Wu, and Sun.[9] All four lineages practice form training—a set of either long or short forms. Each is a continuous choreography of approximately thirty-seven basic movements elaborated into 108 movements taking between fifteen and forty-five minutes to perform. The basic forms are taught within temples or the private homes of a master, and at advanced levels practitioners learn to use sword, knife, and staff.

The principles and practice of *taiqiquan* are informed by Taoist practices dating from the third and fourth centuries CE, with additional influences from neo-Confucianism, Zen (Ch'an) Buddhism, and to some degree Indian yoga (see Wong 1978: 33). The Tao ultimately cannot be defined and has no doctrine. It means "way" or the movement of the universe, but it is not itself that whole. Rather "Tao is flux, transformation, process ('way') of alternation and principles of cyclical time: 'Nameless, it is the origin of Heaven and Earth named, it is the Mother of the Ten Thousand Beings' (*Tao-te ching*, chapter 1)" (Schipper 1993: 4).

The name *taiqiquan* has been translated as the "supreme ultimate," "a cosmological concept meaning 'grand terminus'" (Wong 1978: 61), and "boxing of the Highest Ultimate" (Schipper 1993: 137–138). The yin–yang symbol (Figure 4.6) used to represent *taiqiquan* dates to as early as a 3,000-year-old metal urn. Yin and yang are complementary opposites constituting between them an interactive whole. The complete outer circle is the cosmos within which there is an eternal, complementary give-and-take motion (the curved line) between dark (yin) and light (yang), soft and hard, yielding and active, feminine and masculine, death and life. The small circle of dark in light, and light in dark reveals the fact that within yin there is yang, and within yang is yin.

Their complementary opposition exists in everything and their alternation is the first

Figure 4.6 Yin–yang symbol: dark/black represents yin and light/white represents yang—two complementary opposites in a constant process of transformation.

law of Chinese cosmology: when yin reaches its apex, it changes into yang, and vice-versa. This movement of transformation is ceaseless, spontaneous, moving through phases which, like phenomena themselves, participate in more and more elaborate cycles.

(Schipper 1993: 35)

Practicing *taiqiquan* is one of many means to experiencing the complementary movement of the cosmos within. Its practice is a means of obtaining and maintaining health by establishing equilibrium between the yin and yang elements, i.e., a means of "Keeping the One" (Schipper 1993: 139). Wang Tsung-yueh's fifteenth-century treatise explains how "*Taiqi* as the ultimate form arises out of [. . .] the Formless. It is the origin of movement and quietude, and the mother of Yin and Yang. In movement it opens, in quietude it closes" (quoted in Wong 1978: 61).

James I. Wong explains how practicing *taiqi* allows the individual "to transcend the polarized duality, to transform energy, to realize one's true nature (Tao)" (1978: 61). Eliminating all hindrances one optimally reaches a state of "no-mindedness"

(*wu-hsin*). Yuasa Yasuo explains that this state of "no-mind" (Japanese *mushin*) is "a state of self-forgetfulness, in which consciousness of oneself as the subject of bodily movement disappears and becomes the movement itself" (1993: 27).

Attaining internal equilibrium through practice of *taiqiquan* and the closely associated practices of *qigong* is accomplished through gaining use of *qi*—breath, energy, air, the enlivening vital force. *Qigong* literally means "exercises of the vital breath." Taoist breathing techniques are similar to those of yoga (Wong 1978: 33–35). As understood in Chinese philosophy, metaphysics, and medicine, *qi* is the psychophysical material, animating force of both life itself and the universe. It permeates everything. In Chinese culture it is not necessary to conceptualize *qi*; rather, what is important is to functionally perceive and understand what it does. *Qi* is neither matter nor energy, but rather "matter on the verge of becoming energy, or energy at the point of materializing" (Kaptchuk 1983: 35), i.e., it is a "thing" as well as a "form of energy" (Kennedy and Guo 2005: 27).

Qi animates all movement, i.e., gross physical activity such as walking, the involuntary movement of the heart, the act of eating, or the generation of thought. *Qi* can be dense, as in rocks and earth, or ethereal as in one's thoughts. In Chinese medicine *qi* is read according to its manifest qualities, i.e., it may be strong or weak, etc. If *qi* is out of balance, one is ill. Within the body *qi* is understood to be in constant motion: entering, leaving, ascending, or descending (Kaptchuk 1983: 37; see also Needham 1954, and Huard and Wong 1977).

For the Chinese philosopher Mencius, Heaven and Earth are both understood to be composed of *qi*—Heaven is refined while the earthly remains gross. Mencius describes the "superior person" as one who cultivates "a flood-like *qi* within" and thereby is "not leadenly rooted in the world of material desire" (Cooper 2003: 72). Such persons are able to create a balance between themselves and the cosmos.

The reservoir of this vital force lies in the abdomen just below the navel (the *dantian*). It is the central point from which *qi* is manifest. *Qi* is understood to flow throughout the body via an invisible network of channels known as *jing-luo* (see Kaptchuk 1983: 77–114). Often identified as the meridians, this network connects the interior of the body to the exterior. Acupuncture is understood to operate on the basis of stimulating points via the surface of the body that affect the flow of *qi* inside the body. Classical Chinese medical theory recognizes 365 acupuncture points located on the surface meridians. Over 2,000 points have been identified; however, most acupunturists make use of 150 points (Kaptchuk 1983: 80).

The meridian system is understood to regulate the balance between yin and yang in the body. Yuasa Yasuo explains that

> The substance of the unknown energy *ki* is not within our [present] understanding. It is a flow of a certain kind of energy unique to the living organism which circulates in the body, although it is uncertain yet what generates such a function. To be more specific, when the flow of *ki* is examined psychologically it can be perceived as an extraordinary sensation, as a lived body's self-grasping sensation . . . Furthermore, when it is seen physiologically, it can be detected on the surface of the skin which is the boundary wall between the body and the external world.
>
> (in Nagatomo 1992b: 70)

Qi can be cultivated through specific forms of movement and/or meditation. *Neikong* (internal work) "means the use of internal exercises to bring control, harmony, and awareness to the mind and body" (Liao 2000: 27). Taoist meditation is a form of "kneading medicine"—a metaphorical expression for the meditator's ability to develop *qi* (Yuasa 1993: 204). Practice of *taiqiquan* is also understood to internally cultivate *qi*. It does so via an even pattern of inhalation and exhalation while in constant motion—the give and take of complementarity, of up with down, out, and in, of balance and counter-balance in the flow and transition from one moment to the next.

"Practiced with regularity, these preliminary exercises are a way of setting the body to music" (Schipper 1993: 139).

One of the most vivid, subtle descriptions of correct *taiqiquan* is that offered by master Chang San-Feng, dating from approximately 1200 CE. This archaic text encapsulates the underlying psychophysical principles informing *taiqiquan* practice:

> Once you begin to move, the entire body must be light and limber. Each part of your body should be connected to every other part [. . .] The internal energy should be extended, vibrated like the beat of a drum. The spirit should be condensed in toward the center of your body [. . .] When performing *taiqi* it should be perfect; allow no defect. The form should be smooth with no unevenness, and continuous, allowing no interruptions [. . .] The internal energy, *qi*, roots at the feet, then transfers through the legs and is controlled from the waist, moving eventually through the back to the arms and fingertips [. . .] When transferring the *qi* from your feet to your waist, your body must operate as if all the parts were one; this allows you to move forward and backward freely with control of balance and position. Failure to do this causes loss of control of the entire body system. The only cure for such a problem is an examination of the stance. [. . .] Application of these principles promotes the flowing *taiqi* movement in any direction: forward, backward, right side, and left side [. . .] In all of this, you must emphasize the use of mind in controlling your movements, rather than the mere use of the external muscles. You should also follow the *taiqi* principle of opposites: when you move upward, the mind must be aware of down; when moving forward, the mind also thinks of moving back; when shifting to the left side, the mind should simultaneously notice the right side—so that if the mind is going up, it is also going down [. . .] When the entire body is integrated with all parts connected together, it becomes a vast

connection of positive and negative energy units. Each positive and negative unit of energy should be connected to every other unit and permit no interruption among them.

(Liao 2000: 87–93)

In master Chang San-Feng's text, the Chinese term *hsin* has been translated as mind. While the translation is technically correct, in the context above his use of mind in the phrase "when you move upward, the mind must be aware of down" does *not* refer to analytical, propositional, third-order, "reflective discursive consciousness" (Shaner 1985: 48). Rather, mind refers to the cognitive/mental element present when the practitioner fully engages second-order bodymind awareness while in movement. As discussed in Chapter 3, during optimal performance the practitioner's active, perceptual awareness encompasses this principle of opposites. In the opening move of Wu-style *taiqiquan*, as the hands and arms are moving upward the mind is going down or filling the absent space vacated by the hands and arms. Long-term training in *taiqiquan*, *kalarippayattu*, and yoga allows the practitioner to develop the bodymind's perceptual awareness to a point in which one literally "thinks with the body and acts with the mind." This is the optimal state of "no-mind" where all intentionality disappears.

Asian perspectives on mind, body, and emotion

I discussed earlier how the problem of Western dualistic thinking creates problems for the actor. Acting is either too easily over-intellectualized or becomes overly subjective. This is due to our compartmentalization of mind, body, and emotion. It is commonplace to assume that mind is an absolute organ or category separate from the body or our feelings and emotions. We often assume that a thought is something taking place in the head or that emotions are irrational. While certain intellectual processes can and do seem to occur in our heads, and while experiencing an extreme emotional state such as an unexpected

bereavement can be personally debilitating or lead to seemingly irrational behavior, to separate mental processes from the body and our feeling/emotional world or vice versa, is highly problematic from the perspective of understanding acting process.

Asian perspectives on mind, body, and emotion can therefore be quite useful in reconsidering how we think about mind, body, emotion, and their relationship—especially when engaged in an embodied practice. Philosopher David Cooper explains that

> The Chinese word usually translated as "mind"—*hsin*—can also mean "heart"; in fact, though, it fuses both concepts, and might be better translated as "heart-mind" or "the thinking heart." What this indicated is the absence of the dichotomy, familiar in the Western tradition, between the mind as the "organ" of knowledge and the "heart" as the centre of mere passion and subjective feeling, between the "cognitive" and the "affective."
>
> (Cooper 2003: 63)

Likewise, the Japanese *shin* means the "mind/heart" (Yuasa 1993: 70). The Japanese reading of the Chinese character *xin* as *kokoro* may be translated "mind," but the term also "embraces the affective dimension of the heart" (ibid.: 204). Therefore, the term can be understood as "consciousness" itself (ibid.: 70) as it is deployed in a kinesthetic practice.

In South Asia there are two Sanskrit terms usually translated as "mind." The first, *mana* (*manasa*), actually

> means both mind and heart, as well as mood, feeling, mental state, memory, desire, attachment, interest, attention, devotion, and decision. These terms do not have a single referent in English, and must be understood through clusters of explicit and implicit meanings . . . [T]he terms for emotion and thought, mind and heart are not opposed.
>
> (McDaniel 1995: 43)

Another Sanskrit term, *cittam*, means thinking, mind, intelligence, will, heart. When used in relation to martial arts, yoga, or acting, both *mana* and *cittam* are understood as consciousness, awareness, or the act of directing one's attention. It assumes one's complete mental engagement in a practice. The "80 percent mental" of *kalarippayattu* and the wise yoga practitioner's mind which serves as the churning agent within describe an individual's awareness that is completely engaged in embodied practice. The "mental" is not a thought in the head, but an operation of the mind-in-the-body.

Let us consider one example of how Asian actors psychophysically actualize the inner emotional world of a character. In Chapter 2, I provided a brief description of how for the *kathakali* actor/dancer their inner energy (*vayu*) is spread all over the body and is then shaped to animate hand and facial gestures in order to actualize specific states of being/doing (*bhava*). As an example of how the *kathakali* actor embodies these states, let us take an example from the play, *King Nala's Victory* (*Nalacaritam*), *First Day* by Unnayi Variyar (*c.* 1675–1716). At one moment in this most famous play in the *kathakali* repertory the actor playing the male hero, Nala, embodies the following verse as it is being sung by the on-stage vocalists: "Having heard [the sage] Narada's words, and the words of other travellers, Nala's mind, already immersed in thinking about Damayanti, became pained by his longing for her" (Varryar, 1975: 213).

In performance, this verse is rather simply enacted and does not employ *kathakali*'s highly codified language of hand gestures used to deliver first-person lines; however, it requires the actor's consummate skill in interior acting as he subtly embodies *cinta bhava*—a state of being/doing best translated as reflecting. Nala's active state of reflection is about his love for the beautiful heroine of the play, Damayanti—an act which causes him pain because he is unsure whether his budding love for her will be assuaged.

Working within the sense of appropriateness (*aucitya bodham*) to the dramatic context when played by a refined heroic male character in green (*pacca*) make-up, the actor first assumes a physical attitude of thoughtful reflection. Nala's state is subtly conveyed to the audience through the actor's use of his eyes and facial expressions, both of which are infused with the emotional resonance of the moment through the actor's subtle and skillful use of his breath (*prana-vayu*). At the culminating point in the Malayalam verse and as the on-stage vocalist slowly sings, "it happened, his mind was pained by sorrow," on a quick catch-breath the actor moves his right hand to his chest as his eyes look up at the sky, and then, slowly following the trajectory of the gradual exhalation of his breath, his eyes trace a line downward toward the ground as he heaves a deep sigh, and his facial expression assumes a pained sorrow (*soka bhava*). Although the audience's primary attention is on the actor's face, the actor's art is to allow the animating breath to enliven his entire bodymind with sorrow. The actor's psychophysical score engages his entire bodymind as he moves from reflection to sorrow which causes pain.

The actor playing Nala lingers thoughtfully on his beloved, taking sufficient time to psychophysically elaborate Nala's inner mental state. For the actor playing Nala, embodying the state of reflection (*cinta bhava*) necessarily involves psychophysiologically moving through the progression from reflection to sorrow (*soka bhava*) to feeling the pain caused by sorrow. The amount of time it takes for the actor to psychophysically elaborate a line like the above is much longer than the real time it would take to either speak the line or behaviorally enact it.

The actor's bodymind is the vehicle for the audience's experience. Connoisseurs in an audience who know the story and Nala's state of mind are able to taste and relish Nala's act of reflection and the resulting pain he suffers. The audience thereby has an experience of *rasa*—Nala's reflective state of mind which gives way to sorrow aesthetically resonates within the audience.

The progression from reflection to sorrow to pain exemplifies the fact that the *kathakali* actor's performance score is constituted as he embodies a sequential set of states of being/doing (*bhava*) which bring the text to life. The actor's ability to fully embody each state begins with the preliminary exercises drawn from *kalarippayattu* that attune the actor's bodymind. The full embodiment of each state is realized as the actor specifically directs his external gaze while delivering hand and facial gestures, and simultaneously engages his inner eye (attention, or perceiving consciousness in-the-moment) as well as breath/energy (*prana-vayu*) in what he is doing. As connoisseur G. S. Warrier explained to me in an interview,

> You get the entire emotion on the face. Then the actor practices what is called concentrating the thought there, and gives it wind (*vayu*). It's one of the great secrets of acting . . . It gives nervous control.

For the actor, concentrating the thought obviously does *not* mean third-order, propositional thought as a mental act; rather, it is the felt dimension of concentrating the mind-in-reflection on his beloved that is manifest in the performative moment.

For the actor-qua-actor who plays Nala his own thought/consciousness/awareness (*cittam*) is active as he plays the role of Nala in this state of reflection (*cittam*). It is not a thought in the actor's head. The actor concentrates his thought (consciousness/awareness) by engaging both his breath and his field of visual/mental focus in and through what he is doing in each moment. As the actor playing Nala moves his right hand to his chest and as his external focus goes upward, he is not thinking about or mentally reflecting upon either his own (actorly) state or condition of sorrow or that of the character; rather, sorrow is that *emergent state* that results from his full, active, embodied engagement in real time of his inner energy/breath (*prana-vayu*) in focusing his gaze and placing his hand. From the *kathakali* actor's perspective, his felt sense of this state of sorrow is not the same as one's personal experience of sorrow in everyday life. They may have similarities, but they are not the same.

The English word "focus" does not do justice to the actor's fully embodied engagement in this psychophysical action. The actor is not looking at something and bringing his eyes into focus in a scientific sense; rather, looking is a manifestation of a fully embodied inner state of engagement of both the physical and subtle bodies discussed earlier in this chapter. In this example, nervous control is the actor's felt sense of the movement of

---

🔘 **DVD-ROM:** *KATAKHALI* SCENE

King Rugmamgada's Law

A second example of the *kathakali* actor at work is from the play *King Rugmamgada's Law*. The main character, King Rugmamgada, faces a dramatic dilemma. The goddess Mohini has demanded that as a king he fulfill a vow of honor which requires that he cut off his son's head with the sword representing his power as king. The dramatic high point of a production is the moment when the actor playing Rugmamgada psychophysically embodies/enacts in quick succession the character's inner conflict between three heightened states of being/doing—anger at the goddess Mohini who has demanded that he cut off his son's head, pathos over the loss of his son whom he must sacrifice, and the heroic state of kingship represented by his sword which requires that he keep a vow. The actor's lengthy psychophysical training allows him to switch from embodying one state to another in succession. The scene culminates when Rugmamgada—hitherto unable to bring himself to cut off his son's head—loosens his hair and enters a state of transformative fury which allows him to transcend the limitations of his human feelings for his son. Dancing out this fury, just as he is about to cut off his son's head, Lord Vishnu intervenes. Thankful for Lord Vishnu's divine intervention, Rugmamgada falls at his feet. (For a full translation of the play and an account of the performance, see Zarrilli 1990: 159–174.)

Figure 4.7 Kalamandalam Gopi in the role of King Rugmamgada: the moment of transformative fury in which he has loosened his hair and is about to cut off his son's head with the sword representing kingship. (Photograph: Phillip Zarrilli)

prana-vayu within as it is psychophysically shaped and moduled into sorrow. The actor's embodiment of sorrow allows the audience to have their own aesthetic experience of the character's emotional state of sorrow.

To summarize, the *kathakali* actor's performance score is a complex set of psychophysiological states (*bhava*) sequentially embodied and animated via the actor's attentiveness, awareness, and inner energy (*prana-vayu*). The actor's *manasa* (mind/attention/heart) elaborates each emotional state of being/doing (*bhava*) that constitutes the score. In this sense, the actor undergoing in-depth psychophysical training such as *kathakali* learns to direct his passions as he or she learns to control and shape his breath and thereby his energy.

The psychophysical actor's relationship to the

> ### The psychophysical actor's performance score
>
> The psychophysical actor's performance score is a complex set of psychophysiological states of being/doing sequentially embodied and animated via the direction of the actor's energy and attention. Simultaneously the actor's perception and awareness remain open. The actor's inner energy is shaped as appropriate to the aesthetic form and dramaturgy of each specific performance score.

performance score could be described as in the box above.

In an embodied, psychophysical approach to acting, the mind-aspect of performance refers to the engagement of the actor's focus and awareness to tasks within the score, as well as to the felt vibration/engagement that arises when the actor is assiduously focused and concentrated with her entire bodymind while inhabiting each specific psychophysiological state of being/doing within the score. The actor experiences and is aware of this felt dimension. Training in traditional disciplines such as yoga, *kalarippayattu*, and *taiqiquan* cultivates and provides access to what Yuasa Yasuo calls an "*inner world*" (Yuasa Yasuo: 1993) not defined or actualized through psychology, but rather, as in the example of both *King Nala's Law* and *King Rugmamgada's Law*, by the circulation and shaping of energy and awareness.

5

The psychophysical actor's "I can"

[Asian] martial arts use concrete physiological processes to destroy the automatisms of daily life and to create another quality of energy in the body . . . [A]ll Asiatic martial arts show a decided body ready to leap and to act. This attitude . . . [takes] the form of extra-daily technique, of the position of an animal ready to attack or defend itself.

(Barba 1991: 197)

In my work with actors, yoga, *kalarippayattu*, and *taiqiquan* are practiced not as an end per se, but a means to an end—a continuous exploration of the underlying dynamics and principles of the energetics of acting. There is no place in my studio for mindless repetition of physical exercises to tone or tune up the body. Exercising the body without the full engagement of mind, i.e., without engaging one's full sensory, perceptual awareness, and focus, is pointless. Better to go to the gym or health-club for a work-out. As Suzuki Tadashi explains, "any time an actor thinks he is merely exercising or training his muscles, he is cheating himself. These are *acting* disciplines [. . .] That's why I don't call them exercises [. . . P]hysical fitness teachers don't go on the stage. We do" (Brandon 1978: 36). The language, active images, and metaphors through which I teach, coach, and direct actors provide the bridge that opens the actor's bodymind psychophysically inward into the feeling of aesthetic form, as well as outward to others and the (theatrical) environment.

Identifying and transposing key elements and principles for acting

As discussed in the previous chapter, traditional training in Asian disciplines often begins in childhood. Through long-term embodied practice, psycho-dynamic elements and principles are experienced and made available for use within that practice. Elements and principles such as energy (*ki/qi/prana-vayu*) associated with breath or the yogic subtle body are interpreted and explained, if at all, by a master using indigenous paradigms. Identifying and discussing these elements and principles are usually unnecessary in traditional Asian practice. Mastery is defined by the degree of virtuosity of practice, and not by the ability to explain what one does.

While these traditional paradigms continue to inform practice in Asia today, recent shifts in context and in the application of a particular training must be taken into account. The rapid spread of global cosmopolitanism has reached rural villages. Emphasis on getting a modern education means that many young people do not have the time to devote hours to a traditional training. Influenced by contemporary popular cinema and television, youth in Kerala may be more likely to train in a popular street-fighting style of East Asian kung fu rather than *kalarippayattu*. Many people seldom if ever experience traditional performing arts like *kathakali* or Beijing Opera. Especially in post-(British) colonial countries such as India and Singapore, those raised in cosmopolitan areas often receive their education in part or in full through English. They are as likely to receive Western biomedical care as traditional Ayurvedic care. Throughout Asia these and numerous other factors influence the degree to which indigenous paradigms inform life today. As a consequence, when I work with contemporary actors in/from Asia, many have had little if any exposure to their traditional arts and/or the psychophysical elements and principles embedded within them.

For those few who *have* trained in a traditional art like *kathakali*, just like the Western ballet dancer who wishes to move from ballet into acting/performance, a shift is necessary in order to apply what has been learned from the traditional training to a new form of artistic practice. While I was training and directing actors for the Theatre Training and Research Programme (TTRP) in Singapore in 2007 (see Chapter 11: *Attempts on Her Life*), one member of the ensemble, Sajeev Purushothama Kurup, had undergone six years of traditional full-time professional training in *kathakali* in Kerala. After several years performing, he chose to (re)train at TTRP in order to gain the additional tools necessary to become a contemporary actor/performer. His journey has necessarily involved an attempt to learn how to bring what he had absorbed from his traditional training to the unique problems of contemporary acting.[1]

But this is neither easy nor obvious. Applying what the actor learns through traditional trainings alone is not a simple process of synthesis. When the contemporary actor trains in non-Western psychophysical disciplines there is a necessary process of transposing the underlying psycho-dynamic elements and principles into a new key. To transpose means to put or place something into a different context, style, or manner of expression. If a clarinettist wishes to play a piece of piano music on the clarinet, the music must be transposed. Likewise, elements, principles, and dynamic qualities of any form of psychophysical training must be contextualized so that they are accessible and immediately useful to the contemporary actor.

Moving from *kalarippayattu* to *kathakali*, or *taiqiquan* to Beijing opera requires a shift in a single key as one transposes bodymind preparation within a martial art to a traditional form of acting within the same cultural context. Transposing from *kalarippayattu, taiqiquan*, and yoga to contemporary acting requires a triple process—moving from a martial/meditation art to performance, from an Asian to a cosmopolitan context, and from teaching children to training adults.

In the acting studio, I am *not* teaching *kalarippayattu, taiqiquan,* or yoga as traditional disciplines in a specific Asian cultural context. While some of those who train with me become virtuosic in these arts, the goal of training is not to make all who train with me expert martial artists! I am training actors to act. These disciplines are a vehicle to this end, and not necessarily an end in itself. Therefore, as I teach these disciplines side-by-side, key elements and principles in the process of training must be rendered immediately useful for the contemporary actor. Drawing on traditional paradigms, I utilize images and key-phrases to coach those doing the training toward the type of attunement and awareness necessary for acting. As Grotowski explains, psychophysical disciplines are one way of working on the self in a psychophysical sense:

> One cannot work on oneself . . . if one is not inside something which is structured and can be repeated, which has a beginning, a middle and an end, something in which every element has its logical place, technically necessary.
>
> (Grotowski 1995: 130)

In the remainder of this chapter and in Chapter 6, I step back from the culturally specific understanding of the trainings discussed above in order to identify and discuss how key elements and principles common to traditional systems of training are transposed for use with contemporary actors.

The optimal state of the psychophysical actor's "I can"

Over the past thirty plus years I have identified six primary psycho-dynamic elements and/or principles common to psychophysical systems of training. Through assiduous training, these elements and principles are evident in accomplished practice:[2]

1 Awakening energy: through attentive breathing, the practitioner gradually awakens, discovers, and then is able to circulate the energy (*ki/qi/prana-vayu*) that lies within. Once activated, inner energy becomes available. It is often experienced as a subtle form of inner vibration or resonance. Once activated it can be qualitatively heightened, directed, and shaped as one embodies a practice.
2 Attunement: through psychophysical exercise, the practitioner attunes body and mind into a gestalt or whole. As body and mind are attuned to one another the practitioner achieves a psychophysical state beyond dualism.
3 Heightening awareness: during the process of attunement, one's perceptual/sensory awareness is opened both inward and simultaneously outward toward the environment and others in the environment.
4 Attending to: as concentration and awareness are heightened, one is able to attend to specific actions/tasks assiduously with one's primary focus.
5 Doing and being done: at optimal virtuosic levels of performance, one does the action/task while simultaneously being done by the action/task. The actor plays the acting score but is simultaneously played by the score. The dancer dances but is danced by the dance. Distinctions disappear. One is what one does, even as one is able to adjust as one does.
6 Inhabiting dual/multiple consciousness: while attending to a specific task/action with a fully embodied primary focus and awareness, one simultaneously is able to keep an open perceptual awareness, i.e., one possesses an active dual/multiple consciousness. The actor or martial artist is able to stay on task or in action while making adjustments as necessary to others, the activity, the audience, etc. in the moment. As explained in Chapters 2 and 3, the movement between dual and multiple tasks and awareness is experienced as polar and chiasmatic—an interweaving or intertwining.

In the accomplished actor all elements/principles are manifest as a gestalt—a whole. This is the actor's optimal "I can." Chart 3 overleaf and the detailed commentary that follows provide an overview of how these elements and principles emerge in the actual process of ongoing psychophysical training. The four-phase process begins with training, moves toward performance, takes place in performance, and then returns to the ongoing process of training.

———

Phase I: training

1. The preliminary psychophysical training is at first a form of preparation of the bodymind
The preliminary training is pre-performative. It is intended initially as work on oneself. At first the physical body must be prepared as new exercises or forms are learned, and therefore new muscles are stretched. Unfamiliar systems of movement require patience as one adjusts to ever-subtler levels of balance necessary to assume and perform particular movements. At the earliest stages the mind often speaks to the body, trying to tell it what to do when. But through daily practice of the exercises, and especially through the concentrated use of breath in relation to movement and use of images to engage the mind, one eventually begins to experience the body and mind as related and

---

Chart 3: An overview of the psychophysical actor's process

Phase I: Training

1. The psychophysical training prepares both body and mind for integration as the bodymind, i.e., as a gestalt.

2. Preparation of the bodymind begins to awaken one's hitherto dormant inner energy.

3. Continuous training cultivates the body–mind relationship, i.e., there is a gradual and progressive attunement and sensitization of one's awareness.

▼

4. Attunement and sensitization of awareness open one's ability to sense and feel deeply. This begins with the feeling of form absorbed from the training exercises. As an actor one becomes more available to the resonance or feeling of what one does in the moment, i.e., one is more emotionally available.

Phase II: From training to performance

1. As one is attuned, energized, and opened, the actor learns how to shape, modulate, and deploy energy and awareness according to the demands of specific aesthetic forms and dramaturgies.

2. For each specific performance the actor develops a specific psychophysical performance score.

▼

Phase III: In performance

1. Drawing on the psychophysical training and its principles, the actor prepares and attunes the bodymind/ awareness for the specific performance.

▼

Phase IV: Back to training (Phase I)

2. The actor returns to the ongoing process of developing an ever-subtler awareness by returning to the psychophysical process of training.

▼

Continued psychophysical training provides further, subtler integration of the bodymind as a gestalt. As a consequence, one optimally becomes more open and available as an actor.

---

therefore as one circuit rather than two separate often warring entities. Within this inner circuit of the bodymind a nuanced sense emerges that there might be something there, moving within as the breath, traveling. Once discovered and sensed, the presence of the energy-in-the-breath within becomes more consistently present and moves as the bodymind moves.

One of the most important parts of this process of embodied learning is work on balance and centering. A. C. Scott explains that through practice of *taiqiquan*

with the slow, precisely controlled sequences of the . . . forms, the practitioner becomes conscious of the contrasting elements working together in the total, effective transference of energy. There is a *direct, sensory realization of each movement and gesture* through this complete transition, which eventually leads to a sharpened sense of timing and the expressive nuances of silence necessary in realizing that internal rhythm marking the difference between style and mediocrity on the stage. The relationship between the performer and his body becomes manifest in the process of articulation, which stimulates awareness of the anticipatory moment preceding change—what Jacques Copeau so tellingly described as "that expressive stillness which contains the embryo of the action to follow." A quality which, when realized, marks all the difference between a good and mediocre performer.

(Scott 1993: 55, italics added)

But the preliminary training is not simply a preparation of the physical body, i.e., a toning-up or warm-up of the body to engage in a sports activity. It is the beginning of a process of discovering an alternative bodymind which is then attuned. This is the psychophysical body as a gestalt of mind and body as one. Japanese philosopher Ickikawa describes this as the "subject-body" (Nagatomo 1992b: 6)—that body "not capable of reduction to either the physical or the mental."

> [W]e live it from within, grasping it immediately. This body is the basis (*kitai*) for our action, penetrating through a bright horizon of consciousness [...] to an [...] horizon. It is always present in front of, or rather with us. In spite of this, or because of this, it in itself remains without being brought to awareness. In this sense, we should say that we do not have the body, but we are the body.
> (quoted in Nagatomo 1992b: 6)

The aim is psychophysical integration—reaching an alternative state in which body–mind dualism is transcended. In this process of attunement, how one relates to both the internal and external worlds and to the relationship between is altered.

Shigenori Nagatomo has distinguished between three different types or degrees of psychophysical integration (1992b: 184).

The first type is the normative, everyday relationship between the mind and the body which is experienced as dualistic. Inherent in our daily experience of body and mind as separate is an underlying tension. In *kalarippayattu* training, when an individual first tries to perform an

exercise, he usually begins by using the right side of the brain to figure out whether the feet, back, etc. are in the correct position. The mind is attempting to figure out how to do something with the body and attempts to command it. The result is that there is no flow. There is tension. Similarly in acting, when an actor *tries* to put an action into the body rather than *doing the action unthinkingly*. Here there is little to no psychophysical integration.

An intermediate stage of integration is when an individual de-conditions this dualistic relationship via psychophysical training. Body and mind are gradually de-tensed, and a flow is discovered within.

In the third stage of attunement, one achieves a fully "non-tensional state" (Nagatomo 1992b: 184). Mind and body are experienced not as separate but as a single system of co-synthesis. Actions are experienced as having both mind-aspects and body-aspects, and not as one or the other. As the degree of one's somatic knowledge is refined, one obtains a gradually subtler or higher degree of psychophysical integration, or attunement within the body–mind relationship. Rather than sensing an opposition between body–mind, internal–external, self–object, self–other, there is a co-synthesis between each of these binaries.

When we reach a high level of attunement and co-synthesis, we enter into an inter-subjective relationship *between* self and object, or self and other. Ultimately, the goal of personal attunement would be to achieve a fully non-tensional state within oneself as a person.

2. Preparation leads to an awakening of energy
What is being awakened within is one's inner energy—the quickening, enlivening force of life materially present in the breath, i.e., *prana-vayu*, *qi/ki*. This inner energy is like a seed that lies dormant within us which, once germinated, can grow through proper nurturing and cultivation. One's inner energy is awakened via work on the lower abdominal area. By psychophysically exercising this center, we can awaken energy and

let it travel throughout the bodymind. Especially important is enlivening the energy/awareness along the line of the spine—the central axis of the bodymind. The exercises cultivate the flow of *ki-*energy as an awareness from the abdominal center, through the feet, palms/fingertips, top of the head, etc. As it moves and flows one senses *ki-*energy animating and/or vibrating physical, vocal, and mental activity.

While I emphasize the elements noted above—constant engagement of the lower abdominal region and activation of energy-as-breath—like Jerzy Grotowski I do *not* emphasize or make use of all elements of the map of the yogic subtle body. There is a potential problem with getting too specific in the use of the yogic map, especially with regard to the channels (*nadi*) and wheels (*cakras*). Getting too specific can mislead the practitioner if one attempts to manipulate or engineer awareness according to some predetermined idea about what the experience or reality of a particular relationship to a moment of practice might or might not be. This can lead to introversion and an overly subjective introspection. Grotowski explained how in his own explorations of yoga and similar disciplines:

> [W]e avoid as much as possible to verbalize the questions of the centers of energy which we can locate in the body [. . .] Do they belong to the biological domain or to one that is more complex? The best known are the centers according to the yoga tradition, those called *cakras*. It is clear that one can in a precise way discover the presence of centers of energy in the body: from those that are most clearly linked to biological survival, then sexual impulses, etc., to centers that are more and more complex (or, should one say, more subtle?). And if this is felt as a corporal topography, one can clearly draw up a map. But here there is a new danger: if one starts to manipulate the centers (centers in the sense close to the Hindu *cakras*), one begins to transform a natural process into a kind of engineering, which is a catastrophe. It becomes

a form, a cliché. [. . .] If all this is verbalized, there is also a danger of manipulating the sensations which one can artificially create in different places of the body.

> (Grotowski 1992)

Like Grotowski, I use a terminology that is precise, but not so fixed as to lead the practitioner into the trap of intention.

Caution

If and when you have a predetermined idea of what it is you can or should be doing, feeling, or experiencing, your relationship to what you are doing will not be totally in the moment. Your relationship to a task or action will be tainted by an intention or an idea. You will not be inhabiting the bodymind and energy simply and clearly—as fully available . . . here . . . now.

Eventually, with sustained practice, one begins to sense how energy/awareness can be moved and shaped, how it communes as it moves. What is the feel of this energy and its movement within? How is this energy sent outward, and how does it establish our relationship to the environment around us? Following Yuasa Yasuo, I define one's awakening to this inner energy circulating within as the development of *ki-*awareness, i.e., one becomes aware that *ki* is present and can travel within, as well as outward through the bodymind into the environment.

Yoga, *kalarippayattu*, and *taiqiquan* activate, attune, and sensitize actors so that they are better able to work at an optimal level as a gestalt—a whole in which the bodymind acts and responds in the moment. Given a specific acting score and aesthetic form, the actor's bodymind optimally is acting/responding as simply, clearly, and efficiently as possible. One should never expend unnecessary energy. There should be no unnecessary tension or intentionality in any action or task. The actor's bodymind has "become all eyes," i.e., the flame of (invisible) energy has been attuned and is lit underneath, burning as the actor plays the performance score.

Activation refers to the awakening and attuning of the subtle, vibratory energy within that connects each of us as individuals to the tasks and actions we perform in an acting score. Sensitizing the actor is a process of gradual attunement of the body and mind, and an opening of our energy, awareness, and feeling to the flow of actions/tasks within a score.

> The practitioner begins to discover that energy does *not* equal effort, as in more energy or "give me more." Too often an attempt to animate or energize fails because of the *intention* in the effort. What is important is reaching a level at which one is activated. One releases energy as appropriate to the task.

There is also an awakening to the impulses that shape actions. From within the psychophysical gestalt, the origin of impulses and their resulting actions is *not* the will or the ego. Even when shaped as part of a score or structure, such as a martial arts sequence or acting score, impulses and actions generated from the bodymind gestalt are not characterized by *intentionality*. They are one's own, i.e., they are generated by the bodymind as a whole. But this sense of the gestalt as a whole is not part of our everyday mode of being/doing. It is only possible through cultivation and therefore remains invisible until actualized. The consequence is intellectual skepticism toward the existence of any such alternate body–mind relationship or the experience/actions generated by and through it.

3. The continuous process of training is a means of cultivation, i.e., it leads to attunement, decoction, sensitization, and deployment of ki-energy
Once *ki* is discovered, it can gradually be cultivated. There are three complementary ways in which this process of cultivation becomes manifest

to the practitioner: (1) One is gradually able to attune oneself in ever-subtler ways to *ki* within. As this process of attunement becomes subtler, one is better able to modulate *ki* as it moves within the bodymind. (2) Simultaneously, one begins to be able to deploy *ki* and *ki*-awareness in relation to the immediate environment, i.e., one deploys and modulates *ki* as one moves and in relation to objects and/or people within the environment. In the ongoing training *ki* is deployed through form exercises, and eventually to weapons such as the staff. (3) Simultaneously, this process of attunement can also be described as one of decoction. If one trains assiduously, one's *ki*-energy is constantly being cooked. In this process anything non-essential is taken away.[3] Like a perfume or medicine being prepared through a process of boiling and cooking over and again, *ki* itself and one's awareness of the presence of *ki* is manifest and shows itself in an ever subtler, more condensed state for modulation and deployment. Energy/awareness are quickened.

Through the structured improvisations discussed in Chapter 6, the actor's energy is attuned to sensory awareness and the feeling tone of the dramatic—especially in exercises where the actor is told he cannot. This creates an inner felt vibration that is feeling-full. Tadeusz Kantor described *psyche* as the "supersensuous" aspect of the actor's presence when fully inhabiting with one's entire bodymind "the force called 'imagination'" (1993: 264). The actor's imagination here is active and reactive at the same time. It is not passive. One enters into a psychophysiological relationship with one's entire bodymind and perceptual awareness as one inhabits a certain state of being/doing. The actor's bodymind is attuned to a supersensuous ability to activate and engage.

During psychophysical practice, stray, wandering thoughts and distractions as well as the emotions are cleared and/or calmed. This is one of the major differences between Western sports and psychophysical methods of cultivation. Practicing a sport does not usually involve affect or working with what Yuasa Yasuo calls "the emotion–instinct circuit" (see Appendix 2). One of the goals of psychophysical self-cultivation is "'control(ling) the patterns of emotional response,' or more broadly, the function of the emotion–instinct circuit" (Nagatomo 1992b: 66). What does "controlling emotions" mean? Yuasa does "not mean an exercise of conscious will to suppress emotions" as suggested by Kant; rather, it is a process that "works on the third emotion–instinct circuit" (ibid.: 67). Through repeated psychophysical exercises, there is no conscious or willful attempt to stop one feeling emotions and thereby control them. Rather, the process is one of modulating the effect and affect of feeling as it happens in the bodymind.

In active forms of moving meditation such as the martial arts, mind and *ki*-energy are brought into congruence or accord with each other (Nagatomo 1992b: 73). Yuasa explains how

> The mind appropriates the flow of *ki*-energy through its feeling-awareness. That is, *ki*-energy is not the function which the ordinary, everyday consciousness can perceive, but is a new function which the consciousness (mind) becomes gradually capable of perceiving.
> (Nagatomo 1992b: 73)

In the optimal state of development, there is a degree of heightened awareness and attunement where the bodymind and affect could be said to vibrate. When this occurs, the result is a oneness of body and mind. Throughout this process of cultivation, *ki*-energy and awareness are nurtured for simultaneous deployment within the bodymind and in relation to the environment.[4]

Phase II: from training to performance

4. With energy awakened in pre-performative training, it is essential that the underlying principles and techniques be transposed toward performance, i.e., the actor/performer must learn how to modulate, shape, and deploy one's energy in order to practically solve aesthetic and dramaturgical problems

It is not enough to simply engage some form of psychophysical training. Rather, what is essential is that the principles and techniques absorbed from a form of pre-performative training be transposed into pragmatically useful tools that help the actor/performer solve specific problems of aesthetic form and dramaturgy. In this part of the process actors learn how to shape and modulate their inner energy and awareness to the demands of specific dramaturgies and acting tasks through structured improvisations. This process is explained in detail below.

5. Applying the pre-performative training to a specific performance project requires the actor to develop a specific psychophysical performance score
As discussed in detail in Part III, the principles and techniques of training must always be transposed within the workshop/rehearsal space in order to address the specific problems of the actor's score within a production. Within Beckett's later plays the psychophysical performance score is tightly structured with little variation. When actors play multiple roles (as in *Speaking Stones*, Chapter 9) their performance score as a whole is constituted by mini-scores specific to each particular scene.

Phase III: in performance

6. Once a complete psychophysical score has been prepared, the actor utilizes the pre-performative training and its principles as immediate preparation for each performance, and as a set of psychophysical sensory awareness tools to tweak the performance of the score in the moment of each performance
From the pre-performative training, a selection of psychophysical exercises allow both individual and ensemble to attune themselves individually and as a group in relation so the theatrical environment immediately prior to a performance. While in performance the training in sensory awareness allows the actor to deploy and modulate one's energy within the moment as necessary to each particular performance.

As suggested in Chapter 3, the actor's bodymind consciousness and awareness operate chiasmatically as a gestalt in the moment of performance. The performance score structures tasks and actions that direct the actor's primary modes of attending to.

Phase IV: back to training (Phase I)

Awakening and cultivation are fundamental processes of engagement directed both within as well as outward to the environment. They are never finished or complete. The ongoing process of practice provides one with the possibility of continuing to return over and again to the beginning and therefore to the (re)discovery of the simplicity of one's engagement in simple psychophysical tasks. The process could be compared to one of gardening. The training is a form of fertilization that enriches the soil. It is only after actors have applied this process to at least two quite different problems of aesthetic form or two different dramaturgies that they begin to understand how necessary it is to always begin at the beginning.

—

Toward awareness and activation

In order to transpose and make more immediately useful the key elements and principles embedded in the traditional training, I have developed a set of complementary teaching/coaching strategies that help attune and activate the actor from the moment they begin the training:

1   active images;
2   inhabiting the space between . . . on the cusp;
3   activating phrases and residual awareness;
4   hands-on work;
5   energy vectors;
6   opening auditory awareness.

These strategies are like the different surfaces of a prism—each offers a unique but mutually complementary point of view and/or point of entry into the same process. I use these six strategies to help the practitioner develop bodymind awareness as a gestalt so that the body is not absent but constantly present to us. The actor must develop a non-ordinary, extra-daily bodymind that is totally open in the moment.

In Chapter 3 I discussed the fact that when we fix our visual focus "upon that which lies spatially and temporally ahead, the back of the body is comparatively forgotten. It is absorbed in background disappearance" (Leder 1990: 29). Let us return to the example of the *kalarippayattu* lion pose. When learning the lion pose, the external gaze is directed ahead. As a consequence the back of the body and the space behind usually disappear from awareness. The strategies outlined below help the practitioner to more fully engage absent or negative space through the skin and with an open, wider awareness. They engage the mental element of the bodymind as a gestalt, taking the practitioner beyond the simple habitual repetition of a physical form. The images and verbal cues introduced below and in the DVD-ROM assist the practitioner to inhabit an open, attentive awareness which engages the entire bodymind in the moment.

Active images

From the moment I introduce the beginning breathing exercises, I make use of three important **active images**:

- placing the eyes in the lower abdomen (*dantian*) so that wherever the external gaze is directed, one is looking from/within the bodymind as a whole;
- having an active inner eye that literally follows the in-breath down and the out-breath back up;
- extending *ki*-energy as a thin stream of water to and from the lower *dantian*.

Active images

Active images are not static pictures. One does not look at a specific image. Rather, they are active in that each provides a simple but clear point of entry into *developing and sustaining a relationship to the exercises while doing them*. When fully engaging an active image, the mind does not wander, but is active as one enters and embodies the image. Rather than thinking about an image or end-gaining, when embodying the image the doer enters a relationship to the image and exercise that actively engages both mind and body as one. Active images thereby help awaken and activate energy and awareness while doing the exercises.

Each image engages the mental (awareness) element within the bodymind as a gestalt. Optimally one moves and is moved by/within the image. The image is not separate from the doer. The doer becomes one with and *is* the image as it acts.

Inhabiting the space between . . . on the cusp

Following each in-breath and out-breath with the inner eye sensitizes the bodymind to the nuances of the space between in- and out-breath. Action is given birth on the cusp of an in/out-breath, from the space between. In the *Kakyo* Zeami refers to this space between as that "place where nothing is done," i.e., the "intervals between . . . things" (Zeami 2006: 140). This space between is that place/moment where impulse originates, and therefore where transitions in an acting score are given birth. The actor here learns how to do nothing. One inhabits the space between with "no-mind"—a concentrated, full-attentive bodymind.

When you have reached the level of "no-mind," your concentrated mind will be hidden even from yourself, thus binding everything that

comes before or after to these intervals of "doing nothing." This refers precisely to the intuitive power that binds all skills together with the concentrated mind.

(Zeami 2006: 141)

Activating phrases and residual awareness: keeping the body present to us and filling absent space

Another strategy to help open and sensitize the practitioner's inner and outer awareness is the use of side-coaching through *short activating phrases* and/or verbal prompts to utilize one's *residual awareness*. Once practitioners have gained sufficient experience with the basic forms, I often use side-coaching as the group repeats a particular exercise or form. For example, while the group is doing a repetition of the *taiqiquan*, I instruct them at specific moments in the ongoing sequence of forms to "open the awareness . . ."

- "to the periphery, through the walls"
- "to the space behind"
- "through the sole of the right foot as it slides along the surface of the floor"
- "through the top of the head," etc.

These short phrases help to open and activate the practitioner's *secondary awarenesses* both through the body and out into/through the environment—the ceiling, floor, and walls of the space in which one is exercising. When doing specific exercises, such as the *kalarippayattu* lion pose (Figure 3.2, p. 53), I invite the practitioner to feel the sole of the foot as it travels along the floor, or sense the line of the spine as you open your back awareness. These simple instructions invite the practitioner to engage tactile awareness through the surface of the skin—a mode of sensory experience too often neglected in acting.

The lower abdominal, visceral region is that place to and from which the intertwining extensions of attention/awareness are circulated. This enhances the chiasmatic nature of one's relationship to self and environment in the process of engaging both. This can easily be seen in yoga *asanas* as well.

Coaching participants to "open the back awareness" or "open awareness through the feet" (or palms) invites an opening of one's secondary awareness to the negative or absent space furthest away from the point of external focus. The space behind or on the periphery or above can and should be as fully inhabited as the place of the gaze ahead. Optimally one looks from behind, one sees from and through one's feet, keeping an awareness of the feet as the foot moves along the surface of the floor. As the gestalt of the bodymind-as-a-whole expands beyond the surface and recessive bodies to include the feeling of the form such as the lion pose, it is possible for the actor to voluntarily thematize both the body and space around and behind the body which usually disappears from our awareness.

Tactile awareness *through the skin*

The feel of the sole of the foot on the floor (Figure 3.2, p. 53) or the palm (Figure 4.2, p. 66) as *ki*-energy extends through foot or palm from lower *dantian* begins to awaken and attune the practitioner to *tactile sensation*—the potential for awareness *through the skin*. Similarly, opening the awareness through the back along the spine activates a tactile sensation of the space behind.

Enhancing secondary modes of awareness such as tactile sensation through the feet or along the back and to the space behind complement the primary point of focus/awareness in the gaze directed ahead through the space. Utilizing secondary awareness prevents the practitioner from over-determining or over-directing the external focus so that one's wider awareness is never closed down. The development of secondary awareness as part of the training is essential to acting process so that the actor learns how to stay on task—focused upon and performing a specific action—while simultaneously staying

open with secondary awareness to the theatrical environment, including the audience.

In addition, I constantly remind practitioners to make use of what I call residual awareness when repeating the form training. As one gains sufficient experience with the exercises, each specific form has its own specific kinesthetic/energetic feeling—such as the feel of the energy extending through the feet as they move through lion steps.

Residual awareness

Residual awareness is the trace, resonance, and/or feel of one's kinesthetic/energetic relationship to each specific form in action. This relationship is kinesthetic (in/from the body) and energetic (filled out by *ki*-energy as appropriate to the form).

Keeping residual awareness as one moves from one form to another means that each subsequent form is influenced by the feel of the form before it, and thereby is linked both kinesthetically and energetically to the entire sequence of forms. For example, in doing *this* specific repetition of the opening *taiqiquan* movement in this moment, the practitioner engages the feeling of each form in the moment as it happens, and in resonance with the body's recollection of being/doing of the form for the *n*th time. It is the open play between primary and secondary bodymind awareness that characterizes the shift in a practitioner from normative, everyday modes of awareness to a more open, heightened virtuosic one in which "the body becomes all eyes."

My teaching of *taiqi* is equally informed by this process of filling empty space. As noted above, I ask practitioners to keep a residual awareness of the space vacated with each shift of external focus. This fundamental principle of filling empty space with one's *ki*-energy/awareness as space is evacuated is underscored by the principle of opposites noted in Chang San-Feng's early *taiqi* text quoted earlier in this chapter, i.e.:

when you move upward, the mind must be aware of down; when moving forward, the mind also thinks of moving back; when shifting to the left side, the mind should simultaneously notice the right side—so that if the mind is going up, it is also going down.

(Liao 2000: 92)

The result of assiduous attention to filling empty/absent space is the knitting together of internal and external awareness into a finely textured fabric of embodied consciousness/awareness. Chang San-Feng explains that "When the entire body is integrated with all parts connected together, it becomes a vast connection of positive and negative energy units. Each positive and negative unit of energy should be connected to every other unit and permit no interruption among them" (Liao 2000: 93). As discussed in Chapter 6, this description of optimal consciousness/awareness could just as well describe acting Beckett as doing *taiqiquan.*

In phenomenological terms, this process of attunement over time leads to a dialectical thematizing of the "to" and the "from," or a heightening of one's embodied awareness of movement as one moves. Deane Juan explains how tactile, bodily based sensation can provide "'two streams of information . . . one that gives me impressions about the object [of touch], and another that gives me impressions about the body part that is doing the contacting and its relationship to the rest of me" (in Don Hanlon Johnson 1995: 375).

Hands-on work

The process of sensitizing the actor's bodymind to the correct form and to the movement of *ki*-energy within a form is enhanced through the use of hands-on work. Working in pairs, one partner is designated as the doer, and the other as the helper. I instruct the helpers in how and where to place a hand or fingertip on the doer in order to check that the form is becoming more correct, to enhance the feeling of the form, and/or to enhance the sense

of the flow of energy while doing the form. For example, while working on the opening breathing exercises, the doer guides the helper's fingertips to the location of center (*dantian*) about two inches below her navel (Figure 5.1). Once the helper's fingertips are in place and applying a fair amount of pressure, the doer is invited to "relocate your eyes" to the lower *dantian* while looking ahead. Each of the three preliminary breathing exercises is then performed. The doer tracks with the internal eye the journey of the in-breath down to lower *dantian* and back up, and is invited to keep an "open head awareness" especially on the exhalation. Placing the fingers on the lower *dantian* helps the doer become sensitized to the feel of the breath moving to and from this center.

Figure 5.1 Demonstrating hands-on work with the opening breathing exercises at Gardzienice Theatre Association, Poland. (Photograph: Przemek Sieraczynski)

● DVD-ROM: *KALARIPPAYATTU* LION POSE

I utilize hands-on work while practicing the *kalarippayattu* poses, such as the lion. As noted earlier, correct practice of the lion pose engages a constantly lengthened spine. When awakened, *ki*-energy travels along the spine. While the doer performs lion steps, sliding a foot forward along the floor, the helper slides her hand from the top of the spine at the nape of the neck down along the lengthened spine to the base of the spine. I call this "petting the lion." This hands-on process optimally helps the doer open her back awareness while keeping the external eye directed ahead, and peripheral awareness open. The feeling of the lion form is enhanced as the tactile awareness of both the back and spinal line is further opened, and as the energy is generated and regenerated as it opens outward to the environment as each step is taken.

Another form of hands-on work with the lion is when partners perform the lion opposite each other. With their external gaze fixed on the partner's eyes, I instruct the pairs of partners to move forward or backward with lion steps. As they do so, they look into the other's eyes from the lower *dantian*, and open their peripheral awareness. Then the helper becomes the doer, and the doer the helper. The helper places her right fingertips on the palm of the doer's right hand. The doer is invited to utilize the image of the small stream of water coming out through the palm from the lower abdomen—with the pool of water reaching all the way down through the feet and thereby through the floor. The doer then takes lion steps forward and backward while (optimally) keeping the *ki*-energy flowing through the right palm as it is shaped by the image of the flowing stream of water. The helper eventually is able to sense (1) if there is a gap in the optimally constant flow of energy; (2) if the doer is pushing or putting intentionality into the palm; or (3) if the doer's *ki*-energy is not available or present in the palm.

Hands-on work emphasizes a further opening of one's tactile awareness through the skin. The feel of the touch on the palms of the hands, the feel of a hand on one's back as it tracks the energetic connection while in movement both help to create a heightened kinesthetic memory that further opens sensory, tactile awareness. The feel of a movement over time becomes subtler, fuller, more dynamic and heightened.

As *ki*-energy is awakened and one's awareness activated and opened, this process affects what Yuasa Yasuo calls the "emotion–instinct circuit" within use (Appendix 2). *Ki*-energy cannot be reduced to emotion, but it generates a heightened sensory awareness and therefore can be understood to be available in aesthetic forms to resonate with affect. The "feeling of form" is present to us even if one is not experiencing a basic emotion caused by an external stimulus.

Energy vectors and inter-subjectivity in training

A fourth important strategy I utilize is introducing the principle of **energy vectors.** Early in the training this dynamic principle is difficult to grasp.

Energy vectors

An energy vector may be defined as a palpable sense that a certain magnitude, quantity, and quality of energy extends outward in a line from an individual, thereby connecting that individual to and through the space and/or to one or more individuals in that space. When a practitioner has sufficiently awakened *ki*-energy, then multiple energy vectors may simultaneously radiate at once—connecting that individual outward to the environment, as well as back inside the bodymind.

I use several simple aids to help discover the presence of energy vectors. Similar to the hands-on partner work with the lion noted above, I also have partners work with a long piece of cloth about six inches wide. This cloth is tied tightly around the lower *dantian*. The doer assumes the lion position, while the helper firmly grasps the cloth and applies a fair amount of resistance/

tension while holding the cloth. The doer is instructed as follows:

> Put your eyes in the lower *dantian*—that place to and from which the cloth extends. Keeping external focus ahead, open your awareness through your feet. As you slide the right foot forward into the line, open the awareness in the left foot. Keep the knees open as you take the lion steps. When you move backward move to and from the center with energy extending constantly through the vector ahead and simultaneously down through your feet. Keep an open back awareness.

The cloth makes literal the notion of there being a vector of energy that extends from the individual's center (*dantian*) outward toward a vanishing point (ahead) in space, or to and through a partner.

Optimally, the practitioner radiates energy vectors in all directions. Like a sunburst an individual is surrounded by dynamic vectors of energy that radiate from the center (*dantian*) in all directions. Once the exercise with the cloth literalizes the vector ahead, lion steps are performed without the cloth to see if one is able to keep the heightened sense of the connection to the horizontal energy vector ahead.

In my discussion of hands-on practice above, I discussed doing the lion with partners. This partnering exercise also helps make palpable the presence of the horizontal energy vector. As soon as two individuals take position in the lion opposite one another, they open their external point of awareness to and through the partner's eyes. Direct eye contact with the partner opposite opens between them a vector of energy—a palpable sense that a certain magnitude, quantity, and quality of energy are being shared between them.

Once awakened, energy and the vectors through which it travels are not simply straight lines. Energy can move in any direction—straight, curving, looping, or in undulating, wave-like patterns. Allowing energy to move in any direction is crucial to a psychophysical approach to acting.

In order to understand how energy vectors shape and create a dynamic relationship to movement, let us take the full lion pose as it is performed when doing a full *kalarippayattu* body exercise sequence. Figure 5.2 illustrates the sequence of movements which collectively constitute the full lion pose performed in the CVN style (Thiruvananthapuram). It is dynamic. Notice how firm and natural is the lengthened line of the spine. This is even the case with the initial left kick when the left big toe is extended upward. The correct practice of this complete form originates from the center in the lower abdomen (technically here the *nabhi mula*). As demonstrated in Figure 5.2b, the power and strength of the form is generated in the dynamic oppositional energy present within the form. As the left big toe, foot, and leg extend outward and upward (Figure 5.2a), the right knee is slightly bent and energy is generated down through the right foot into the ground simultaneously as the left big toe extends up and out in a powerful release of energy. Similarly, as the practitioner moves into the final position, there is a gripping in the lower abdomen that creates an oppositional force—outward and forward from the center along the line of the spine and through the arms, hands, eyes, and back downward through the right foot into and through the earth. The body forms a solid triangle (Figure 5.2b): the base of the triangle (B) is the ground point of downward oppositional/energy; the tip (A) of the triangle is the point of outward energy; the spinal column is the central axis and line of the triangle (A–B). The movement to/from the lower abdomen is the energized life-force that creates the practitioner's dynamic relationship to the form. The flow of energy here is an undulating, wave-like motion. It crosses straight line vectors: the straight line from the lower abdomen ahead through one's initial point of external gaze, through/under the ground, and along the diagonal line of the spine. The energy and power used to attack or defend is made available precisely as this undulating, wave-like energy crosses the straight-line vectors.

Energy vectors are extremely important as they provide an invisible but palpable connection

Figure 5.2 The flow of energy and movement in the lion pose: (*a*) With hands/arms crossed over the chest and ready, the movement originates in the center at the root of the navel. The leg is kicked up—energy flowing out through the knee, the foot, extending up to forehead level with the big toe extended. The leg then descends along the line of the body, the energy flow returning to center, as the foot is placed forward in a step. The firmly planted left foot provides the base from which one executes a small, leonine-like jump as the hands are extended behind the body, and above the head. Landing from the jump the energy is recycled and drawn into the center as the final position (*b*) is assumed, hands in front of the chest. This opposition creates the triangle which is the lion pose's solid base and source of strength. Note the central axis of the spine along the long line of the triangle. The spinal column and the interior "subtle channel" of the body is thought to be the central axis through which the vital energy flows. (Photographs: (*a*) Deborah Proctor, (*b*) Phillip Zarrilli)

between two or more individuals. In the lion-partnering exercise described above, the two partners move as if one—sharing the energy in the space between them. This opening of space between begins to attune and activate actors to each other *inter-subjectively*. So important is this opening of awareness and energy to others that within the first day or two of beginning the psychophysical training, I introduce partnering practice with the balancing exercise. The external gaze is focused through the other as one looks from the lower *dantian*. The two partners share their energy/awareness as they initiate, continue, and bring to completion each of the two parts of the exercise.

One's consciousness, awareness, and *ki*-energy are deployed and adjusted in the moment inter-subjectively between and amongst everything

in the environment. One's relationship to the other(s) in the environment can and should never be over-determined. One should optimally remain constantly open in the process of inter-subjective engagement (see overleaf).

● DVD-ROM: *KALARIPPAYATTU— TRAINING WITH STICKS*

Those who go on to advanced *kalarippayattu* training with me are introduced to weapons—first the long staff (*kettukari*). As soon as an individual picks up a staff, there is a process of exchanging energy in the inter-subjective space between us. The staff demands practical use of vectors of energy. Articulating vectors of energy helps the practitioner understand how dynamic energy

---

Inter-subjectivity: what is "between"

Psychophysical training must focus not only on oneself as doer, but equally should engage each individual in a training that is inter-subjective. In this inter-subjective space "between," one begins to attune one's bodymind to whatever is "other"—the performance score/text, the other actors, the audience, props, and objects within the environment, etc. One engages whatever is "other" as both a "to" and a "from"—that to which and that from which one acts and reacts. There is a constant dialectical, inter-subjective engagement of the "to" and "from" in performance.

---

is created when using a weapon. Whenever one faces another with or without a weapon (Figure 1, p. 3 and Figure 4.3, p. 68) between the lower abdominal area of both there exists an invisible energy vector. A second vector is manifest along the spine line of each practitioner. It reaches from the lower abdomen out through the top of the head. The diagonal vector is mirrored in the line of the staff (Figure 4.3) when it is first placed in the hands. When a weapon like the staff is manipulated, the power of a particular hit toward the opponent's temple, ankle, ribs, head, etc. is generated when the weapon crosses or criss-crosses an energy vector. It is the inherent opposition of an embodied, psychophysically connected energy moving in two directions that creates power. Power in use of a weapon does not come from overtly exerting force.

Training in staff is extremely beneficial in that it demands that each individual confront their often unarticulated preconceptions about taking up what is perceived as a weapon in their hands. For the vast majority of people I have trained, as soon as they pick up a staff, they forget completely that they have a body and have been working on bodymind awareness. All their focus/attention goes into the staff as they tend to over-focus by pushing with the weapon, or are afraid to release and make use of the energy they have discovered

moving within. Some people will attempt to hit at the opponent *with* the staff rather than allowing the flow of energy *into/through* the staff. I constantly remind individuals to make use of the awareness on which we have worked—especially behind, to the sides, through the feet, etc. Training with weapons further sensitizes and awakens the palms and hands to the potential for tactile, energetic engagement with objects in acting.

Since many actors with whom I work do not train long enough to begin working with the staff as a weapon, I introduce a non-martial exercise with the staff in partnering work. This exercise introduces actors to vectors of energy and tactile awareness of the hands as they hold the staff. The exercise builds from the inter-subjective energy exchange developed while performing the lion pose with partners. Working with the staff, the principle of an exchange of energy is put into free play as the stick literally joins partners. They begin by standing opposite each other in the lion. I place the staff between the partners' right palms with the tip of the staff supported by the energy flowing from lower *dantian* through the palm.

> Allow yourself to make use of the active use of the image of water flowing through your right palm. Place your eyes in the lower *dantian*, and sense the connection from lower *dantian* out through the right shoulder and arm through the right palm. At the beginning keep your external gaze focused through the eyes of your partner. Gradually allow the energy flowing through the staff between you to move without ever knowing where it will move. As that energy begins to move between you, see where it takes you. Do not know where you will be moving. Keep the energy connected from lower *dantian* down through your feet as you move, and keep a very open peripheral awareness . . . Come to a "pause" point, but sustain the dynamic quality of the energetic connection between you whatever position you are in at the moment . . . Continue . . .

Once we have played this partnering exercise

long enough for the energetic connection to be maintained, I begin to change the rules of engagement. The staff can change hands so it is not always just held in the right hand, but moves freely as necessary from right to left. The tempo-rhythm of the exchange becomes quite free, as does the use of space. We eventually play a version in which, rather than having direct visual focus on the partner, they *cannot* focus on the other. Their only connection to the other is the energetic connection to the staff, and their peripheral/back awareness. Finally, I take away the staff, and ask partners to slowly melt into an everyday position, and move actively/reactively to/from the partner. This exercise moves our work into the territory of acting—addressed fully in Chapter 6 and Part III.

Opening auditory awareness to oneself and others

As participants progress with the training, I eventually attempt to move them toward opening their auditory awareness through the ears. This is perhaps the subtlest of the awarenesses on which we work during the training. I invite this awareness to be opened inward by inviting participants to "listen to your own breath"—even if it is not sounding. "Hear the movement of the in-breath as it moves downward . . . as it moves upward." I then invite everyone in the group to

> open your auditory awareness not just to yourself and your own breath, but also to each other. Using both your peripheral and back awareness, as well as opening your ears, "take in" everyone else in the space so that you are moving as one.

This invitation opens inter-subjective awareness not just to a partner, but to the group as a whole. Breathing together . . . in . . . and out . . . and in . . . and out . . . the entire group should, eventually, begin to move as one with no outside prompting or coaching. The sharing of breath-as-energy becomes palpable in the studio if and when everyone in the studio is taking equal

responsibility for inhabiting fully their bodymind awareness, and sharing that awareness generously with all the others in the space. One's awareness opens inward and outward simultaneously, and one begins to make constant subtle adjustments as there is a constant non-verbal dialogue between and among the group as a whole. No one initiates an exercise; all move as one.

Concluding discussion

All of the above strategies attempt to avoid the tendency for form training to become empty and habitual. I am constantly coaching those who train with me toward taking responsibility for developing and maintaining the open, alert awareness that can be developed through these trainings. Practicing these disciplines is not in the end about simply getting the external *form correct*! Yes, working toward correct form is important; however, form training *only* makes sense if and when one's sensory awareness and the feeling of each form both opens one within to ever-subtler levels and nuances, and radiates outward into a relationship with the immediate environment.

Through these complementary strategies, the practitioner gradually internalizes for herself a state of fuller attentiveness—within which she is "physically alert, physically prepared" (Hamilton 2000: 27) to respond or react to . . . something. Learning to attend to with the bodymind creates an additional mode and quality of self-presencing within the relationship between oneself and what is being attended to. Acting requires attunement to the subtler qualities and modes of such fully embodied acts of awareness when attending to both self and others (actors). It also requires the ability to sustain a fully engaged bodymind relationship between one moment and the next. This active state of awareness is not restricted to the visual mode of awareness, but is a rendering of the practitioner into a state of bodymind readiness to respond through the entire range of senses to the environment—visual, tactile, auditory, and even taste. It is the engagement of both surface and depth bodies in the voluntary process of exercise that renders the possibility of open engagement to the depths within, and to the world outside the body. Eugenio Barba usefully describes this optimal bodymind awareness as "the bridge which joins the physical and mental bank . . . the river of creative process"—the actor's body and mind are "dilated" (1985: 14–15).

Voluntary thematization of the bodymind as a whole allows the actor to focus attention in the embodied act of realizing each moment and action in a performance score. If the actor's attention drops out, the actor fails to maintain the type of awareness that will be sufficient to allow one to stay in communication with fellow actors, and/or to attract the audience's attention. A gap in the fully embodied attentiveness of the actor leads to a gap in the audience's attention. The actor's self-presencing engagement is therefore a to–from both for himself and for others. In this optimal state, embodied knowledge becomes tacit, i.e., the "I can" is now second nature. "How" is no longer a question, but has been fully incorporated and acquired.

6

Exercises for "playing" in-between

Structured improvisations

Playing implies trust, and belongs to the potential space between.

(Winnicott 1989: 51)

This chapter discusses how the principles and techniques of psychophysical training are initially transposed and applied to acting. As described in Chapters 4 and 5, the optimal state of readiness is one of pure and open spontaneity. Like the martial artist, the actor's bodymind becomes "all eyes." The actor's bodymind is activated so that she is able to "play" freely in the moment between as she acts and reacts to and within the immediate environment. Learning how to inhabit this place/space/state between begins with the breathing exercises as one explores this place of suspension between the in- and out-breaths. Although both the martial artist and actor know a training sequence or acting score because each has been well rehearsed, the individual ideally embodies that sequence or score with a state of innocence, naivety, or not-knowing. Activated, one enters an accomplished state of being "at play."

Psychotherapist D. W. Winnicott provides insight into this optimal state of play as a space between. For Winnicott playing is universal. But what is important about play for babies is that it "is immensely exciting . . . [because it] is always the precarious interplay of personal psychic reality and the experience of control of actual objects" (1989: 47). Play therefore

implies trust, and belongs to the potential space between . . . [P]laying involves the body [. . . P]laying is essentially satisfying . . . Playing is inherently exciting and precarious. This characteristic derives not from instinctual arousal but from the precariousness that belongs to the interplay . . . [between] that which is subjective . . . and that which is . . . perceived.

(1989: 51–52)

Winnicott argues that it is "perhaps only in playing" that both child and adult can be "free to be creative" (1989: 53). Winnicott locates playing neither in "inner psychic reality" located "in the mind or in the belly or in the head somewhere within the bounds of the individual's personality," nor in "what is called external reality . . . located outside those bounds" (ibid.). Developmentally, Winnicott locates the origins of what he means by play in the "potential space between the mother and baby" (ibid.); therefore, an optimal state of play dialectically engages the space *between* self and score, character and character, actor and audience. Playing is manifest when we engage moments of transition, in the dialectically open interplay between . . . (ibid.: 64). As Andrew Quick observes, "play, it would seem, also keeps the I at bay" (2006: 160).

The beginning actor's commonplace problems of anticipation, pushing, not listening, inattention, etc. are all manifestations of not entering fully into a state of being at play in the moment. The structured improvisations explained in this chapter provide a point of entry into the actor's inhabitation and experience of this state of play in-between.

Structured improvisations: from psychophysical exercises toward performance

Structured improvisations are a set of very simple psychophysical tasks organized into increasingly complex rule-based structures played in a workshop setting. The most essential elements cultivated in psychophysical training—*ki*/sensory awareness, energy, and attention—are applied to these tasks. They provide a bridge between the ongoing pre-performative training and performance. Freed from any concern with technique or form by the workshop setting, key elements, and principles of training are put into play within structures that are, in essence, mini-performances. One acts without "acting."

"Acting" is in quotation marks because the point of entry into each structured improvisation is the same as in the daily psychophysical training. Both begin with attentiveness to the breath and the embodied awareness that arises when one is attentive to the breath. The actor attentively engages his bodymind in each simple psychophysical task while keeping an open *ki*/sensory awareness. In pre-performative training, the *ki*/sensory awareness and energy aroused are heightened but neutral in that they have not been shaped or resonated with dramatic structures. In these exercises awareness and energy resonate and radiate within and outward with the feeling of (dramatic) forms that take shape as "acting." Engaging with simple task-based structures, the actor begins to more explicitly explore the nature of impulse and action as they are shaped into what looks like, and indeed constitutes, performance. The tasks and structures become increasingly

complex and layered as I introduce desire into the instructions—a desire to look, hear, touch, move, speak, etc. As the actor's subtle awareness is attuned and enhanced, to the observer watching the performance of a structure what emerges are all the elements that constitute acting—behavior, character, and relationships. The actor begins to act "without [trying to] act."

The process of bridging training to performance is devising specific structured improvisations that help the actor solve the problems of a specific dramaturgy. Energy and vibration are shaped into inner states of being/doing by a particular aesthetic logic. From the spectator's perspective, the character emerges from the actor's fully embodied engagement in psychophysical tasks in the moment.

The rules for each structure are specific. They require the actor to deploy and shape *ki*/sensory awareness and focus/attention in specific ways in the moment. Each structure is "played" by inhabiting attention/perception/awareness in the moment without intention and without thinking about the rules. The actor ideally begins to "play" (unthinkingly) within each structure

- not knowing when there will be a shift in awareness or focus/attention;
- discovering experientially what it feels like to inhabit a psychophysical score without pre-meditation.

What is essential in "playing" a structure is to work simply within its rules and thereby to be open to perceptual experience and discovery *as they take place*.

At work on structured improvisations

In the remainder of this chapter I move between first- and third-person voices, providing a description of the exercises, addressing the reader directly as actor/doer in the studio, or stepping back momentarily from the process for reflection.

Getting started

Each workshop session begins with repetition of the three beginning breath-control exercises, and the opening two moves of the *taiqiquan* sequence. These initial exercises re-settle, focus, and ground the participant to be ready. At the first session with any group, I introduce the reduction exercise. Once introduced, this is repeated as necessary. The reduction exercise is followed by introducing the first and simplest structured improvisation. More complex structures follow. When I introduce each new exercise or element the entire group participates. Then the group is divided into two, one half of the group observes while the other half participates.

Repetition of opening *taiqiquan* and breathing

Spread out throughout the studio space, facing in any direction rather than towards me as during the daily training. Standing with feet at shoulder width, repeat three cycles of the opening breath-control exercise, keeping your internal eye focused on the in-breath and out-breath. Check your awareness: above, behind along the back, of the soles of the feet, to the periphery. Sense the completion of the final out-breath, and on the impulse of the next exhalation allow the arms to come to shoulder height, and repeat three cycles of both the second and third breath-control exercises.

When you come to a point of stasis in the space between, when the impulse of the next inhalation comes, allow your arms to ride the breath in the opening *taiqiquan* move, and on the exhalation allow the arms to ride the breath back to their beginning place beside you. Repeat two more cycles of the opening *taiqi* moves.

● DVD-ROM: REDUCTION AND SHIFTING FOCUS

The reduction exercise

The dynamic principle of psychophysical reduction has been utilized for centuries. The earliest description of the fundamental principle informing the exercise is Zeami's *Kakyo*:

> 'Work the mind ten-tenths, work the body seven-tenths' means that after [the student has learned to] perform according to his teacher's instructions the thrusting of a hand and the moving of a foot [appropriate] to what he is studying and has completely mastered these [mechanical] parts, he [then] holds the gesturing hand back a little, inside, from the mind, by not working [his body] so [intensely as] his mind.
>
> (Nearman 1982: 350)

For Zeami the actor's subtle inner work (the mind) constantly modulates *ki* in action. This inner work continues at 100 percent while what the actor shows (the body) to the audience is held back slightly or reduced. This process creates a psychophysically dynamic inner relationship to action.

Although I knew about this principle from reading Zeami's texts, the first practical demonstration of reduction I witnessed was Eugenio Barba's version conducted with several masters of Asian disciplines at the 1986 International School for Theatre Anthropology (ISTA) in Holstebro, Denmark. My version is a slight adaptation of Barba's.

> When we begin, while staying attentive to the in- and out-breath, repeat the opening two moves of the *taiqiquan* sequence. When performing the *taiqi* you are working 100 percent outside and 100 percent inside. The outside or external form is what is visible to the outside eye of the observer, i.e., the arms as they come to shoulder height, the line of energy through the wrist on the way up, and the

arc of the arms as they return to their beginning place with energy down through the wrist.

The internal is constituted by three key elements: *ki*-energy, *ki*/sensory awareness, and your use of focus, i.e., the external gaze directed ahead, the inner eye following the breath, and the awareness of your relationship to the spatial surround. Keeping your inner engagement at 100 percent—following your breath, keeping the point of external focus, coordinating movement with the half-breath, and sensing the space between each half-breath—and without changing the shape and arc of the outer/external form, I will ask you to reduce the external form—what is visible to the outside eye—by a specific percentage, such as 75 percent, 50 percent, 25 percent, etc.

On the impulse of the next inhalation, reduce the external form by 50 percent . . . On completion of the exhalation, repeat this reduction once again by 50 percent, all the while keeping the 100 percent inside of your relationship to the form.

Come to a pause point on completion of the exhalation and stay attentive to my instructions while still following your breath with your inner eye. Keep the point of external focus ahead. During the next cycle of repetition of the two opening *taiqi* moves, I will ask you to reduce the external form by a different percentage . . . Through two cycles reduce the form by 10 percent, leaving 90 percent visible to the outside eye . . . Now by 75 percent leaving only 25 percent . . . Now by 90 percent leaving only 10 percent . . . Now by 99 percent leaving only 1 percent. Keep your inner awareness and attention to breath, focus, etc. operating at 100 percent.

As explained in Zeami's treatise, while doing this type of exercise "If the student does not maintain the inner level of intensity, but simply reduces the size of his gestures, the resultant movement will appear weak" (Nearman 1982: 351). The experience of reducing or withholding some part of the external form usually produces a heightened inner-sensory awareness of one's *ki*-energy and its relationship to physical action. The further the action is reduced toward 1 percent, the greater the intensity of one's relationship to whatever remains of the original movement. Heidi Love explained her experience of the exercise as follows:

> Phillip instructed the group to reduce the external action to 1% while stressing, "keep active in your listening and awareness." While observing, I found the intensity and dynamic of this almost "still" movement electrifying [. . .] Subsequently, when I was engaged in doing the structure reduced to 1%, my ability to remain fully engaged through my "open" awareness helped me to activate and extend my own "energy in space."
>
> (Love 2005)

Heidi's experience of the movement as "electrifying" reflects her heightened experience of *ki*-energy while doing the exercise. This is typical. The reduction operates like a *ki*-energy dimmer switch. The actor experiences how much more energy is available within. This is often a surprise because intensity of feeling is often equated with emotion. As in the training, there is nothing emotional generating the intensity of energy experienced here. Experiences such as this help the actor understand how the intensity of one's inner experience should not be confused with forced emotion. As Mark Nearman explains in his commentary on Zeami's *Kakyo*, experiencing the principle of reduction "safeguards the student from falling into the error of confusing intensity in performance with an uninhibited display of emotion that dissipates the actor's energy and makes him appear crude and excessive" (1982: 350–351).

Once assimilated, the actor should be able to apply this principle to acting in any context, i.e., always working psychophysically at 100 percent with energy, attention, and awareness while simplifying/reducing what is shown outside. The result is acting with restraint but without sacrificing inner intensity.

Creating psychophysical scores and reduction

This exercise utilizes the basic principle and dynamic of reducing an external form while maintaining the inner activation that arises from form. For this exercise I ask everyone to select three different specific forms from *kalarippayattu*, yoga, or *taiqiquan*. One individual might select to link the elephant from *kalarippayattu*, the opening *taiqi* move, and conclude by placing the hands/palms together at the chest in the movement which begins the sun salutation (*surya namaskaar*). The three forms selected are psychophysically linked to one another by the breath and awareness—looking from lower *dantian*. This creates a short three-form psychophysical score which can be repeated over and over again. Then I ask everyone to reduce this score by at least 90 percent or more so that an outside observer cannot identify the forms selected. In its reduced form the score is rehearsed and re-rehearsed until it appears everyday. When necessary the full 100 percent set of forms should be repeated to ensure that the feeling of the inner action of each form is present in the reduced version of the score.

This exercise is not introduced until those training have had sufficient experience to inhabit the forms unthinkingly. In their reduced form, one should be able to inhabit the internal feel and action of each form as it resonates within. The inner feeling of the form activates the doer. These small scores are then performed individually over and again, and then as a dialogue between two individuals as an improvisation. This simple exercise frees the practitioner from thinking of form training as restrictive. The forms learned in training should be a resource for activation of energy, awareness, and attention.

Beginning structures

The first structures introduced build directly from the actor's experience of coordination of breath with movement and shifting external focus on the impulse of a half-breath—especially evident in *taiqiquan*, yoga, and the *kalari vanakkam*.

Stand with your feet at shoulder width. As in training, throughout this exercise continue to follow your in- and out-breath with your inner eye while keeping an open awareness. When I ask you to begin, on the impulse of each half-breath, i.e., each inhalation or exhalation, allow the impulse of the breath to move one of your arms somewhere, and simultaneously allow your external eye to focus somewhere on the hand or arm that is put into play. Do not anticipate which hand or arm will be put into play, and do not anticipate where your external focus will go. Discover which hand/arm moves, and where your focus goes as it happens. After the initial breath/movement, sense its completion at the end of each cycle of half-breath. On the impulse of the next half-breath, the same hand/arm that initially moved moves somewhere else and your external focus simultaneously shifts to another place on that hand/arm. And so on, allowing the one hand/arm in play to move on each subsequent half-breath accompanied by the shift in external focus. Keeping your external gaze ahead, drop in to your awareness and breath . . . And . . . on the impulse of the next inhalation put one hand/arm into play, taking your external gaze from ahead to a specific place on that hand/arm.

Additional structures are added, such as the following:

As in the first structure, standing with your feet at shoulder width, the rules are as follows: the external focus shifts on each half-breath, but may be on either hand or arm, i.e., both hands/arms are in play. There is no overt movement of the body through space, but there may be residual movement of the body as you shift the primary point of external focus.

With the feet still at shoulder width, the focus shifts on each half-breath to any point on your body you can see, i.e., not your back.

As the group "plays" each structure, I side-coach participants as they work. I provide feedback, inviting them to keep an open awareness of their back and the space behind, or of the peripheral awareness, the top of their head, etc.

> As you continue to work within the structure, if/as your hand comes closer to your face, it will be more difficult to keep an open awareness of the environment. Whenever you encounter "close focus," keep the full-body awareness open . . .
>
> As you shift your direct external focus from one point to another, keep a residual awareness of the point from which you have just shifted your focus. Connect with your residual awareness one moment to the next. As you complete each half-breath, and then initiate the next movement/shift of focus, do not cut off the awareness of where you have just been—what you have just seen, or sensed in that previous moment. Weave one moment into the next with your breath/awareness.

The principle of residual awareness

One of the most important principles of psychophysical acting is residual awareness. As the point to which one attends shifts, primary attention is directed to the new point, but one must nevertheless maintain a residual/ secondary awareness of the feel and quality of one's relationship to the previous moment. It is so very easy to cut off one moment from the next! Keeping residual awareness allows the actor to psychophysically connect one moment to the next.

Residual awareness is clearly part of the training process described in Chapters 4 and 5. Being able to maintain residual awareness allows the actor to weave together psychophysical tasks and actions into a set of connected sensory relationships. The actor initially engages these structures as one does *taiqiquan*, allowing one's *ki*-energy to be the invisible weaver. The web is spun but there is no visible weaver.

Crucially, the energy deployed in performance is not always relational and seamless. Some dramaturgies, aesthetics, or acting scores require the actor to cut off one's energy/attention/ awareness from one moment to the next, or step out as the actor shifts performance registers. The actor-qua-actor must first develop the ability to inhabit a heightened, seamless, relational deployment of one's energy so that he can then *choose* to cut off, displace, or separate that energy/ awareness from one moment to the next *as an acting choice*.

I side-coach actors while playing structures, emphasizing one or more of the rules as necessary in order to keep their *ki*/sensory awareness animated and open within the structure, and in order to allow them to make discoveries about how this work is about being simple. As players learn to inhabit the structures within these rules, some are relaxed. For example, at later stages the external focus does not have to shift on each half-breath.

● DVD-ROM: IMPROVISATION ARISING FROM *TAIQIQUAN*

Seated structures

After the first few rounds are played standing, we begin a series of structures with everyone seated in chairs arranged in a single row across the room. Having the actors seated early in this process is extremely useful. Being seated ensures that the possibilities for movement are initially kept relatively simple. This allows the actor to experience the process of inhabiting one's relationship to breath and the initiation of simple movements such as looking at one's hand, a slight turn of the head, etc.

> Take a seat on the front of your chair with your feet firmly making contact with the floor. Allow your arms to be at your sides. In this seated position we will begin with two cycles of the opening *taiqiquan* moves. Keeping an open awareness through your feet into the floor,

Basic rules guiding beginning work with structured improvisations

When first working on structured improvisations the following rules guide work within each structure:

- external focus shifts on each half-breath
- external focus is at first always directed to a specific point
- let the impulse of the half-breath move both the body and external focus according to the rules of each structure
- when the impulse comes, the focus goes from one point to another, and does not travel or take in anything else until it reaches the next point (other forms of focus are introduced later)
- keep an embodied, open spatial awareness beyond the primary point of focus above, behind, to the periphery, and through the feet
- the internal eye follows each half-breath—down on inhalation to lower abdomen, and up on exhalation
- work simply and without premeditation, allowing the impulse of each half-breath to initiate each action and change of external focus
- keep active and inhabit the space between inhalation and exhalation, i.e., sense the completion of the previous breath/impulse, and after the sense of completion, the impulse of the next half-breath comes
- when using close focus, ensure that your awareness/energy extends beyond the specific point of focus
- each shift of focus/movement must be sensed through the entire bodymind, even if there is no overt movement in all parts of the body
- as you move from one point of focus to another, keep a residual awareness and therefore a connection to the moment/location/place of awareness from before so that each new impulse/action is connected to the next, and the next, etc. As you move through the structures, you do not need to keep the same rhythm, i.e., the amount of time that the breath takes can and should shift and change, sometimes being sustained, and sometimes taking much less time.

behind you, above you, and to the periphery, on the next inhalation, begin . . . up through the wrists, allowing the arms to come up to shoulder height . . . and on the exhalation, down through the wrists, allowing the arms to come back to your sides . . . and repeat again . . . Come to a pause point and stay active in your listening . . . Open your awareness to all the other players seated to your right and left . . . Keeping this open awareness of each other, when everyone is ready . . . and without me cuing you when to begin, perform two complete cycles of the opening *taiqi* moves together as one . . . Come to a pause point and stay active in your listening . . . Sensing your relationship to your body and the spatial surround from the repetition of the *taiqi*, and keeping the sense of your relationship to your feet, allow yourself to assume any physical position in the chair as long as you keep one foot touching the floor to keep you grounded . . . Double-check that in this position you are looking from your gut, and that you are keeping the animated sense of your spine line . . .

In whatever position you've assumed, take your external focus through a point directly ahead, in front of you . . . Keep following your breath with your inner eye . . . For the initial structure we will use the same rules as the first standing structure. When I say, "begin," on the impulse of the half-breath put one hand into play and allow your external focus to travel directly to a specific place on that hand/arm . . . On each subsequent half-breath, allow the hand/arm to move somewhere else, even a subtle shift is enough, and allow the external focus to move to another point, keeping a residual awareness of the place from which the focus has moved . . . "Begin" . . .

After playing one or two rounds of this very simple structure to ensure that everyone understands the basic rules while seated and has begun to sense how animated the entire bodymind can be while seated, I begin to elaborate slightly more complex structures. Each new round of play is initiated by the seated opening *taiqi*.

Taking any seated position with one foot touching the floor, in the next structure you will shift your external point of focus on each half-breath between the point directly ahead, and somewhere on your right palm . . . As you work between these two points, allow your physical position to shift with the impulse of the breath . . . It is not necessary to shift physically, but allow yourself to explore that possibility . . . Keep the residual awareness of the last point whenever the external focus shifts . . . What is that residue? . . . Come to a pause point and stay active in your listening . . . We will now add a third point: focusing either on your right palm, the right palm of one of the other players, or straight ahead . . . On the impulse of the next half-breath, "begin" . . . Keep an open back awareness, and open peripheral awareness . . . Wherever your external focus, extend your peripheral awareness to all the other players . . . Keep the internal eye following the breath to *dantian* . . . Keep residual awareness of the point you've just left . . .

At this phase in the process, the three points of awareness can be endlessly changed. For example, the focus might shift between

1   your right hand or right foot, and another player's right hand or right foot;
2   between a point directly ahead, a door to the player's right, and a point approximately two feet on the floor in front of you;
3   your right hand, one of the other player's

right hands, or the face of one of the the other players.

By limiting the points of focus in the first example above to parts of player's bodies, the playing begins to create a set of relationships between and among the players. The second example emphasizes the players' relationship to the spatial environment. A major shift in the type and quality of playing occurs in the third example when one of the three points is the face of another player. Since the focus continues to shift on each half-breath, none of the players know if or when they will or will not actually make eye contact with another player. Side-coaching players when they make face-to-face contact is crucial:

Keep simple . . . Do not try to be clever . . . Do not impose or project attitudes . . . See what you discover . . . and keep a residual awarness of where you just looked as you shift focus . . . Carry what was there into the next point . . .

Observation and reflection are as important as doing. After watching each other work, I invite responses to each step of the process from the perspective of "inside as a doer" and that of "outside as observer/spectator." I invite observations from the outside on "what attracts or sustains your attention?" Invariably comments are offered about being attracted to the performance of a structure when one is "being simple," "not anticipating," "not pushing, "not showing attitude," or manifesting a "full awareness."

Each structure has no predetermined meaning, narrative, or conclusion. However, as the structures become more complex and when played with full psychophysical engagement in each task, from the spectator's position, structures begin to take on the quality of drama, i.e., relationships appear, comparisons are made, associations and meaning arise, and stories materialize. But the actors are not acting with motivations or objectives. Rather, they are absorbed in and attentive to breath, movement, and weaving together psychophysical structures with a fully embodied awareness in the moment. They are open to each moment as they play. They do not know what is next. For some actors in this process, a moment of realization occurs: it is crucial to simply be available in the moment with one's entire bodymind.

Increasingly complex structures are built by adding additional points of external focus, or creating a more complex dynamic relationship by juxtaposing three types of points. With all participants seated in a row, I place one empty chair about six feet from the entire group, facing them. One set of points of focus with which to begin work with the chair include: the empty chair, a place on the floor approximately two feet in front of each player, or one of the other players' faces. Once the actors have been put into play, a certain dynamic is created by the juxtaposition of the three points—external focus that is slightly down, focus on an empty chair, and focus on another player's face. The dynamic created in one group's playing of this structure may be different from another's, so rather than characterizing it, I simply point to the fact that more dynamic possibilities for associations are available in this set of points of focus than in many previous sets. This is intentional because the process is intended to work from the more neutral use of vectors of energy in martial arts and yoga toward and into what we usually identify as drama—qualities of energy/engagement shaped into relationships-in-action.

Double/multiple consciousness or awareness in structured improvisations

While playing a structure, the actors are expected to work with a double consciousness or awareness. The actor-as-doer remains primarily attentive within the rules of the structure, but simultaneously deploys and maintains a fully embodied awareness in relation to the environment. While remaining attentive to the in- or out-breath, and while allowing the focus to shift on each half-breath to a new external point, one remains secondarily attentive to their bodymind in the environment by sensing the space behind through one's back, above through the top of the head, the floor through the soles of the feet, or the periphery. At first I constantly side-coach—reminding the actors to keep attentive to the structure but to simultaneously check and inhabit the sensory surround. With repetition and practice, the type of chiasmatic awareness described in Chapter 3 begins to manifest itself as one plays.

Introducing a desire

The next stage of the process is the introduction of desire into playing some of the same structures discussed thus far. One example follows:

Using the following three points of external focus—directly ahead, one of the other actors' faces, or the empty chair ahead—add the desire to get up and go sit in the empty chair. This desire should be constant. Wherever your point of external focus, the desire to go and sit in the empty chair must be present. You should sense that desire with each impulse, and each shift of the half-breath, but you are not allowed to act on that desire. However strong this desire to go and sit in the empty chair, you cannot move. With your initial point of focus ahead, on the next inhalation, begin . . .

Allow that desire to be stronger . . . and even stronger . . . Be careful not to *point to* the desire. Sense it on the cusp of the breath . . . in your feet . . . in the space behind . . . Come to a pause point and stay active in your listening. We are going to add yet another element the structure. With the next impulse of the half-breath, sensing that desire to move to the chair, act on that desire, but STOP! You cannot move there. You must stay where you are no matter how strong that desire!

The principle of introducing a desire, but denying the actor the possibility of externally acting on the desire, is a further refinement of Zeami's notion of withholding or reduction. In terms of *ki*-awareness, the psychophysical act of stopping an action once initiated by a strong impulse to move creates an extremely strong inner psychodynamic relationship. So much is happening inside the actor that it vibrates and resonates the actor's entire bodymind, and creates interest for the spectator. In the *Kakyo* Zeami elaborates how central this principle of reduction is to the process of acting:

> This [principle] should certainly not be limited [only] to the physical [aspects of] movements. When [the actor] uses greater reserve in the working of his body than [he does in the work of] his mind even [when it comes] to his use of body for expressing [emotional] behavior, his body will [then] become [for the spectator] the causal agent [for interpretation] and the spirit [of the character portrayed] will become the effect, [with the result that] there will be a feeling of interest [generated in the audience].
>
> (Nearman 1982: 350)

Energetically so much is happening inside the actor that it attracts the attention of the audience. Crucially, the actor's experience of the intensity of desire produces an extraordinary amount of feeling. The feeling is generated by the actor's fully embodied attention to and awareness of the task, while keeping an open kinesthetic awareness.

As with the basic structures, there is an endless number of desires that can be introduced into the process. What is crucial is that each desire set in motion is simply stated, task-specific, and clear. Feeling is the result of putting a task-specific desire into play in the moment.

As the group gains experience with playing structures, I begin to loosen some of the rules, especially the necessity that the external focus shift on each half-breath. When I introduce this change, I emphasize the fact that any time there is a shift in external focus it should ride a half-breath. When the rule of half-breath shifting of external focus is relaxed, I carefully observe the players to catch

out anyone that begins to become self-indulgent or anticipate. The purpose now becomes to trust taking time as one stays in the moment, "playing" in relation to . . . and in between one moment and the next.

Introducing objects

A whole new realm and quality of playing is usually opened up when I introduce objects into structured improvisations. I will elaborate one progressive structure I often use with objects. I ask each actor to bring to the studio an object that has some specific personal use or association attached to it. It can be anything—a utilitarian object such as the water bottle an individual uses daily and carries all the time, a scarf, a watch, a signed baseball, a particular hat, etc. It need not be something that has sentimental value attached to it. It is best if the object is not overwrought with personal memories. I set up a large table or set of tables around which all the actors take a seat.

> Place each of your objects on the table in front of you. After the opening unison *taiqi*, take any physical position in your chair. Your points of focus are either your object, or one of the other players' objects, shifting focus on each half-breath. When we begin, you may touch your own object, but you cannot touch any of the other players' objects.

After playing a round or two with the entire group and their objects, we divide into two groups. One group sits behind a large table with their objects on the table, facing the others who are now observers.

> Your points of focus this time include your own object, one of the other players' objects, or one of the players' faces. Allow the focus, for now, to shift on each half-breath. You may touch your own object, but not another player's object.

After playing the structure through several rounds, I add the "desire to touch another player's object, but you cannot actually touch it." The playing usually becomes even more dynamic when "desire to touch" is introduced. I coach players through allowing the intensity of the desire to be stronger, but always also side-coach individuals to keep an open awareness and not to become over-determined in their focus on any object.

From the outside, the "objects on a table" structure starts to take on the intensity of a poker game. Who will make a move when? Who desires which object? Who is looking at my object? Who wants my object? The result from the outside is often comedic as relationships around objects and desires form and dissolve. Because this structure is usually played with high dynamic intensity, but has a light quality, it is extremely useful for helping actors understand that laughter is produced by staying on task and being specific and simple.

The structure is then further loosened. Players are allowed, on an impulse, to trade objects. One cannot simply take another's object. There must be an unspoken agreement, on a particular impulse, to exchange.

Adding text: the desire to speak

Yet another layer is added when I invite the playing of a structure to include the desire to speak. This desire may be added to any structure, such as the "objects on a table" structure, or the "chair in front of a group" structure. When added, I side-coach as follows:

> As you continue to play the structure, if the desire to speak comes to you on a particular impulse, allow yourself to feel the shape of that word or phrase in your mouth, but do not actually speak . . . What word or words come to you . . .? What is the "feel" of those words, of that phrase . . .? Sense the desire to speak in your feet . . . from your *dantian* . . .

Eventually, I invite the players to speak, but when first allowed to do so, they may only vocalize one word, then three, and then a complete phrase.

● DVD-ROM: IMPROVISATION ON JEAN GENET'S *THE MAIDS*

Inventing structured improvisations: *The Maids*

The final stage is to invent structures that address the specific needs and dynamics of a particular dramaturgy. To introduce this process, I briefly discuss how and why I have developed structures for working on Jean Genet's *The Maids*. Additional examples are provided in the production case studies in Part III.

I have long been fascinated by Genet's *The Maids* both as a director and in terms of the tremendous acting challenges offered by the roles of Madame and her two maids, Claire and Solange. I have worked on the play in intensive workshops and have directed it four times because actors are "at play" within realistic roles within a dramaturgy and aesthetic that puts what is real into play.[1] As Jean-Paul Sartre explains, in *The Maids* "the real is something melting [. . .] reabsorbed when touched" (1954: 31). "Reality" and the appearance of reality are put into play.

Acting is therefore central to *The Maids* in two ways. Sociologist Erving Goffman has analyzed how each of us performs or acts one or more roles in everyday life. Maids and airline stewardesses are two of the most obvious examples of social roles that require those in the roles to act the part whenever they are in the public eye. Rules and conventions constrain the playing of those social roles and the type of behavior one is allowed to manifest in public. Behind the exterior performance of the social role, the individual playing the role is experiencing a variety of feelings in relation to the performance of the social role. But these personal feelings must remain suppressed until the individual has gone off stage—such as when the maids are either in the kitchen or their garret.

In Genet's play, whenever Madame is away, the two sisters "take the stage" to play the ceremony they have created. They take turns playing the role of Madame, or the role of Madame's maid as played by their sister. Claire and Solange construct their own versions of the role of Madame based on observing Madame playing this social role. Each bases their playing the maid to Madame on observations of their sister. Each of the characters therefore plays not only herself, but also at least one other role. Madame constructs herself as a gesture, but now her gestures are even grander as she plays out the fantasy of departing with Monsieur, the criminal. Claire and Solange are the most complex. They move between four performance registers—Claire as Claire with her sister backstage in the kitchen/garret, Claire-as-Claire-the-maid when serving Madame, Claire-as-Madame, and Claire-as-Solange-the-maid serving Solange playing Madame.

The ceremony, like acting, is a game which is always the same, but different. Claire and Solange always play it to the hilt. In each round of the ceremony, which of Madame's dresses will be chosen? Whose turn is it to insult whom? What insults will be given? What new element will each of the two role-players invent or improvise in *this* moment of playing? Are they really about to kill Madame? Toward the end of *The Maids*, when the game is to be played for the last time, the game is deadly. Or is it? Does Claire really drink the poisoned tea? The actors must play the game with a sense of its potentially deadly consequences. Acting any of the three roles in *The Maids* requires each actor to enter a state of being at-play in the moment. The actor cannot know a choice before it happens. Change, a shift in tactics, and surprise are at the heart of the actor's work in *The Maids*. Especially for Claire and Solange, who will get the best of whom? Playing *The Maids* requires actors to be on the edge . . . between one moment and the next, between one role and the other . . . in a state of "not-knowing."[2]

In the structured improvisations I have devised for preliminary work on *The Maids*, I put into psychophysical "play" the underlying tension between appearance and reality that informs the play. A series of dynamic questions arise that are explored through these structures:

- What are the boundaries, if any, between the role and character, between self and other—especially for Solange and Claire in relation to each other and to Madame?
- What kind of symbiotic dynamic exists between Claire and Solange, the two maids and Madame, or in the way each plays Madame?
- What is the logic and structure of power with the games that are played?
- What is the dynamic nature of the ecstatic state of playing these transgressive power games?
- Ultimately, who is stronger? Claire or Solange?

These open-ended questions and specific passages from Genet's text are the beginning point for creating structures that psychophysically explore the dynamic quality of the characters' relationships-in-action. I provide an explanation of only the first of many structures that are played either in a workshop setting, or when working with a cast during the initial stage of rehearsals.

The Madame–maid dynamic

To begin exploring the Madame–maid dynamic, those playing Madame sit in chairs at a (dressing) table. Behind each Madame stands a Solange. (In the next round, this will be Claire.) In front of each Madame is an imaginary mirror.[3] Madame's task is to prepare herself for a visit to Monsieur; however, she keeps her focus on herself and her preparations—not on Monsieur. Madame's external focus shifts between and among the following: gazing and taking in either her general visage and look in the mirror, examining some specific aspect of her look such as an eyebrow, eyelash, a cheek-bone, her mouth, or one of the objects on her dressing-table such as a lipstick, comb, hairbrush, etc.

Solange stands with her palms clasped together in front at her waist, or held behind her back. Solange possesses the desire *not to be present*. She has the very strong desire to turn away and leave the room, but she cannot. She *must be here*, present to Madame. While in Madame's presence Solange's external gaze must be indirect. She is not supposed to look directly at Madame in the mirror. Her external gaze is therefore directed slightly down to the right or left.

Madame's initial focus is in the mirror, head slightly turned to right or left, as she gazes at herself. Solange's gaze is slightly down right, or left. On the next half-breath, begin to play the structure.

Keep your focus direct. Possess a sense of "ownership" of yourself, your look, the objects before you . . . the entire environment. It is *your* environment. Madames: when you gaze at yourself, inhabit the sense of, "I am beautiful" on a long sustained in- or out-breath. Sense the presence of the figure behind you, but do not directly notice or give attention to her . . . You are what is important. You are present to yourself, for yourself . . . She is invisible to you . . . unless and until you wish to give her visibility . . . When you sense her, let the awareness of her pass through you. It is not important . . . Heighten the sensitivity in your fingertips, palms . . . Allow this heightened sensitivity to come from your *dantian* . . . allow each moment of touch—of your objects, your lips, an eyebrow—to vibrate you.

Solange(s): keep your gaze high enough to allow yourself to sense and see what Madame is doing. Whenever she touches herself, such as her lips with a fingertip, the desire to leave is even stronger. Allow your in-breaths and out-breaths to be short and shallow. Your breath feels tight and short. Have an even stronger desire to leave each time she touches herself . . . Allow yourself to begin to physically act on that desire, but it must be interrupted . . . You cannot leave . . . Catch a glimpse of Madame in the mirror . . . Does she see you? . . . If/when you sense her gaze on you, you must smile . . . smile through the desire to leave . . . Sense this desire to leave in your throat . . . Allow the saliva to gather in your mouth . . . Sense the distaste of the saliva gathered there . . . Your desire to leave . . . You must maintain the small smile through the distaste . . .

For the actors playing Solange in this structure, psychophysically the distaste of the saliva in the mouth creates an inner dynamic tension with the necessity of smiling through this distaste.

When we play the same structure with Claire as Madame's maid, the inner dynamic for Claire is in complete contrast to Solange. Claire stands behind Madame with hands clasped, as did Solange.

Although you are not supposed to look at Madame, you have the very strong desire to catch a glimpse of Madame—to admire and enjoy her beauty. When you do catch a glimpse of her in the mirror, or of her possessions on the table before her, you prolong and enjoy each moment . . . When she touches herself, you sense that her fingertips are yours . . . Vicariously sense each moment, and allow that touch to show itself with a slight smile . . . When you see her, you see/sense yourself as her.

The same structure is next played by Claire and Solange as each takes a turn playing Madame. When Claire or Solange plays Madame, Madame must be played with the additional layer of a set of quotation marks. The quotation marks must be played with psychophysical subtlety. When Claire and Solange play each other as the "maid" to their sister's "Madame," they do so with their sister's psychophysical score.

When Claire plays Madame she enjoys each moment—and tastes it as such in her mouth. Her mouth is Madame's mouth. Her fingertips are Madame's fingertips. It is a privilege to inhabit her every gesture and her skin. But at a moment's notice, the sense of ecstatic pleasure she tastes in her mouth at each moment of playing Madame can turn to loathing and disgust—"I can't stand my hands, my black stockings, my hair."

As we play structures between the Claires and Solanges, which of the two is stronger? What is the moment when one is, for this moment at least, dominant? How does this dominance manifest itself in the gaze and in one's psychophysical energy dynamic? What is the psychophysical feel of these shifts within at the moment of change?

Concluding commentary

Structured improvisations create a bridge between the heightened *ki*/sensory awareness developed in the pre-performative training and performance. Playing structures based on a specific dramaturgy shape the actor's awareness and energy according to the particular psychophysical dynamics of that dramaturgy. In *The Maids* the psychophysical dynamic is specifically shaped by the unique qualities of each of the three characters, and the contours of the character's journey within the play. For Claire and Solange, every transformation is a transgression, and every transgression is a transformation. It is a territory where (for Solange) a "spurt of saliva" becomes a "spray of diamonds." The playing of structured improvisations prepares the actors for "playing" this constantly shifting dramatic terrain. As we shall see throughout Part III, other structured improvisations prepare actors for playing alternative dramaturgies.

Part III

Production case studies

Introduction

Part III is a series of in-depth case studies documenting and analyzing how the psychophysical approach to acting outlined in earlier chapters is applied to specific problems of the actor's dramaturgy in performance. What do I mean by the "actor's dramaturgy"? The term "dramaturgy" refers to how the actor's tasks are composed, structured, and shaped during the rehearsal period into a repeatable performance score that constitutes the fictive body available for the audience's experience in performance—the fourth among the actor's modes of embodiment discussed in Chapter 3. The actor's performance score is shaped by the aesthetic logic of the text and the production per se as it evolves in rehearsals.

When working with a text, I begin by analyzing the overall aesthetic logic as it might be realized within a specific *mise-en-scène*. I identify specific structural units and their requirements within the aesthetic logic as the whole. I then develop (1) an overall strategy for the period of devising/workshopping/rehearsing, (2) the acting tasks that will constitute and create each major structure or unit of action within the performance score, and (3) the actor's point and mode of entry into embodying each task, i.e., *how* the actor

approaches each specific task. My directorial goals are twofold:

- to find a means of activating each actor as an individual through psychophysical processes and images that constantly engage that actor's bodymind, energy, awareness, and the sensation/feeling of form; and
- to find a means of activating the actors intersubjectively as an ensemble so that they are being active/reactive in the moment for each other.

The production's aesthetic logic guides the overall dramaturgy, style, and tempo-rhythm. All these are shaped to create a specific experience for the audience. Post-dramatic productions often require the actor to develop a performance score that has multiple dramaturgies—each requiring a different approach to and point of entry into its acting tasks. Today's actor may be expected to shift instantaneously from one mode of inhabitation to another—not unlike the instantaneous shifts from embodying one emotional state to another evidenced in the acting of David Garrick or the *kathakali* actor. These shifts are not driven by a consistent, causal, developmental character-based logic, but rather by alternative aesthetic logics.

The case studies included here range across a broad spectrum of dramaturgies. According to the specific aesthetic logic of each production, I utilized everything from realist acting to the engagement of the actor in non-character based, *butoh*-like tasks and image-based performance work. Each chapter begins with an introduction to the specific text and production, discusses the context within which the production was realized, describes the problems of the actor's dramaturgy specific to the aesthetic logic of the production, and analyzes specific examples of how these problems were addressed in rehearsal and/or performance. When available, actors with whom I have worked reflect on how they applied the psychophysical training to acting tasks.

The Beckett Project (Chapter 7), *The Water Station* (Chapter 8), and *Speaking Stones* (Chapter 9) were fully realized, publicly licensed professional productions played for the general public. *4:48 Psychosis* (Chapter 10) and *Attempts on Her Life* (Chapter 11) both had two manifestations—the first as an exercise within a laboratory/pedagogical setting, and the second as fully licensed publicly performed productions for the general public.

7

The Beckett Project

Thought of everything? . . . Forgotten nothing?

(from *Eh Joe*; Beckett 1984: 202)

As we well know, it's the simple that complicates.

(Blau 1982a: 85)

Introduction

If in-depth psychophysical training takes one to the "edge of a breath" where thought takes shape as impulse/action—a place where one "stands still while not standing still," Beckett's plays take the actor to this same place "between" where meanings, associations, and experiences are left open for the audience. The Chinese philosopher Lao Tsu might have called this "the space between heaven and earth."

Both the actor's work and Beckett's plays inhabit this state or place "between." Herbert Blau describes this place between as one that "stink[s] most of mortality" (1982a: 83). The "stink of mortality" derives from both Beckett's contrapuntal turns of thought, and the often excruciatingly difficult process of embodiment required of the actor in his plays. One way of describing these demands is that the actor's bodymind is precariously counterpoised and counterbalanced "on the edge of a breath" (ibid.: 86). Acting Beckett highlights those moments of necessary suspension always present in acting, as the actor rides the breath/thought/action—that moment of absolute exposure where the possibility of failure is palpable. It is in that moment of possible failure that perceiving

consciousness (or action) bodies forth because it must. Beckett and Blau require of the actor an unremitting attention to engaging "the necessary"—the "consciousness that it *must* be seen, what would make the word come even if there were no breath" (ibid.: 86).

What Beckett's plays demand of the actor is not the creation of characters nor the realization of conventional dramatic action, but an embodied actualization of thought as perceiving consciousness in action as it happens (unthinkingly) in the moment. Beckett makes special demands on the actor—an attentiveness to an indeterminate necessary—actions and words whose meanings cannot be foreclosed. Jonathan Kalb argues that a poetics of Beckett performance should follow the simple standard that "ambiguity [is] . . . a positive performance value" (1989: 48). This ambiguity is part of the structure and content of Beckett's plays, of their musicality where there is no realist progression to a narrative or character-based conclusion. Discussing the indeterminacy of Beckett, Blau cites the example of *Footfalls*:

> What I was always moved by in Beckett . . . was a certain manic fitfulness of mind, as in the iterations of *Footfalls*: "it all, it all." Where you could virtually bite your tongue over the

painful indeterminacy of that (w)hole in it. It all, it all. What's the referent?

(Blau 1994: 59)

The iterative ambiguity of Beckett's plays challenges conventional dramatic modes of representation and meaning. Any attempt to reduce these inherent ambiguities by trying to determine *a* meaning, and any attempt to use conventional representational character acting to actualize the potential in a Beckett play is likely to produce a pedestrian result and not provide the audience with the unique experience offered by Beckett's plays. When Billie Whitelaw, the critically acclaimed actress who either premiered or played a number of Beckett's most important female roles in London—*Not I*, *Footfalls*, *Eh Joe*, *Happy Days*, *Play*, *Rockaby*—began rehearsals for the English premiere of *Play* at the Old Vic in 1964, she realized that Beckett's plays "were working with a totally new set of rules" (1995: 82) which had little if anything to do "with normal characterization or psychology" (ibid.: 76).[1]

Actors cannot act ambiguity; however, they *can* define, embody, and enact a precise set of psychophysically charged and energized actions for which there is no conclusive single referent for themselves *or* for the audience. The iterative ambiguity of Beckett's plays can thereby become a palpable experience for an audience—actualized when actors simplify and hone psychophysical actions to a point where nothing extraneous exists. As Tom Stoppard astutely observes,

> Historically, people had assumed that in order to have a valid theatrical event you had to have *x*. Beckett did it with *x* minus 5. And it was intensely theatrical. He's now doing it with *x* minus 25 [...] He changes the ground rules.
> (in Knowlson and Knowlson 2006: 283–284)

Beckett's later, shorter plays reduce overt on-stage action to a minimum—as close to zero as possible.[2]

Why Beckett?

The practical and intellectual challenges an actor faces when confronted by the new rules and iterative ambiguity of Beckett's stripped-down plays captured my attention in the early 1990s, and have preoccupied me ever since. As carefully crafted as the genres of traditional Asian theater to which I have long been exposed, Beckett's scores, in my view, do not so much inhibit the actor's creativity but aptly challenge it, requiring the work of the contemporary actor to be as precise as that of Japanese *noh*. With Beckett and *noh* "you can't cut corners" (Whitelaw, in Knowlson and Knowlson 2006: 174–175). When a psychophysical energetic approach is applied to the stringent requirements of Beckett's plays, the actor can discover tremendous freedom in actualizing their formal limitations.

While Director of the Asian Experimental Theater Program, I began working regularly with Beckett's non-verbal physical score, *Act Without Words I*, as an in-class exercise. *Act Without Words I* offers a practical lesson in how difficult it is for the actor to actualize that now hackneyed expression, less is more, i.e., how to strip away *anything* unnecessary. *Act Without Words I* appears simple since it is a series of specific stage directions, beginning as follows:

> The man is flung backwards on stage from right wing. He falls, gets up immediately, dusts himself, turns aside, reflects.
> Whistle from right wing.
> He reflects, goes out right.
> Immediately flung back on stage he falls, gets up immediately, dusts himself, turns aside, reflects.
> Whistle from left wing.
> He reflects, goes out left.
> Immediately flung back on stage he falls, gets up immediately, dusts himself, turns aside, reflects.
> Whistle from left wing.
> He reflects, goes towards left wing, hesitates, thinks better of it, halts, turns aside, reflects.
> (Beckett 1984: 43)

Beckett offers no indication of why the man is flung on stage or who has "flung" him. The actor playing the man "is flung." Having been "flung" onto the stage, he "falls." Having fallen and finding himself on the floor, he "gets up immediately." Having gotten up from the fall, he "dusts." Having dusted he "turns aside," and then "reflects."

The initial act of being flung sets in motion a series of related actions. But the challenge is *not* to work on a subtext that determines *a* reason or motivation that answers who, what, and why one is flung. Rather, the actor inhabits perceiving consciousness/awareness, responding to whatever happens as it happens in the immediate (theatrical) environment. The unseen force that propagates whatever happens is the environment as it acts on the protagonist/actor. The actor's task is to respond to each stimulus that directly acts upon him (flung) or in response to what is done to him (falls after being flung; dusts after falling). The actor must inhabit a state of unknowing innocence.

Working on *Act Without Words I*, there is no character to fall back on, no habits or dialogue on which the actor can rely. The score is exposing for anyone who attempts it. Anticipation and intention are readily evident. It is a master class in the chiseled-down simplicity that playing Beckett requires, and that *should* inform all acting and performance work.

Beckett's acting scores simplify action by paring away all that is extraneous to the moment. They confront the actor with the problem of how to be simple, i.e., how to inhabit and fill out a score by shaping the intensities of one's energy/awareness in the moment without premeditation. Stanislavski perceptively explained one problem with such simplicity long before Beckett composed his unique body of work,

> When you want to be simple, all you think about is being simple and not the basic tasks of the role or the play and so you begin to act being simple. What you get are clichés of being simple, the worst clichés of all.
> (quoted in Benedetti 1999: 218)

The degree and specific types of simplicity Beckett demands are particularly difficult to achieve. Each play is a complex, architectural structure textured like a snowflake with its own contours, edges, gaps, and silences. The actor's inner energy and awareness modulate and play a score by psychophysically linking one action to the next.

Psychophysically inhabiting a score gives rise to associations of varying intensity. If the actor predetermines an action by making realistic, motivational choice about why the protagonist has been flung, such a choice shows itself as a form of predetermined intentionality. The *necessary indeterminacy* of what might have caused anything will be over-determined. The actor denies himself the possibility of discovery and realization in the moment, and denies the audience the potential enjoyment of witnessing the actor's discovery as it happens.

Playing Beckett requires the actor to let go of one's confidence in realist textual analysis and concentrate on inhabiting a simple physical and/or vocal score.[3] The actor must find an alternative approach to action which, while specific, decided, and sedimented, possesses neither a psychological nor an emotional conclusion. In playing Beckett the actor is always challenged to enter a state of play where every action is unpremeditated and unknowing.

For actors who expect to ask questions about motivation or meaning, letting go of the psychological can be experienced as disorienting. When working on *Play*, Billie Whitelaw recalls that she "had no idea what [the play] *meant*" (1995: 76), nor did she think that it was necessary to reach such an understanding. However, in contrast to Whitelaw her fellow actors

> Rosemary Harris and Robert Stephens naturally wanted to know more about the characters they played, the meaning of the piece, and why the man had left his wife, and what sort of pre-history the mistress had, etc. I somehow felt this wasn't what mattered. The excitement would come from the musicality of the piece, rather than the story-telling.

I wasn't the least bothered by the lack of characterization or psychology.

(1995: 76)

When American, Stanislavskian-trained Peder Melhuse worked with me on Beckett's plays in 1994–1995,

> I was free to spend my energy and attention on my relationship to movement instead of some psychologically motivated cause or effect. I found, too, that playing with the borders of ambiguity was empowering. If I almost reacted with "color" I would play on that borderline that Beckett seems to inhabit . . . [These experiences] taught me to explore the borders of purgatory and all the meanings of that word. It taught me to do nothing until compelled to.
> (Journal, 1995)

Beckett's inherent interpretive indeterminacy can produce in the actor a palpable (and positive!) form of terror as the actor faces this unknown present in the performative moment. Creating as simple a score as possible, the actor enters the terror of the present working totally "within the moment." This experience of simplification can help one discover "the cleansing action of a true craft," i.e., "an attitude of reverence toward the moment, letting it happen rather than making it happen . . . relinquishing oneself, getting out of the way" (Blau 1982a: 123–124).

When acting Beckett one encounters philosophy and metaphysics—not in the head, but through the perceiving bodymind. Space and time open out, often devoid of the comfortable familiarity of props, scenery, and the type of realist dialogue that make obvious sense of behavior. The encounter is full of the unsaid and unknown, not in a psychological, but a perceptual, existential, and/or metaphysical sense. Each step, gesture, word, or phrase must be taken on its own terms and progressively linked to the next moment through one's use of energy, breath, and perception without reference to a settled psychological or behavioral choice.

Architecture and musicality in Beckett's scores

Given Beckett's life-long fascination with art and architecture, it is not surprising how meticulously Beckett delineates each precise and sparse image in his plays. Lawrence Held has observed how

> Sam's liking of the spaces between the houses said something about his writing: the spaces he allows between the bits of dialogue, the spaces between the bits of the set, even the spaces between the characters (also the characters and the set, the characters and the audience), which are as much a part of the characters as their own corporeal existence.
> (in Knowlson and Knowlson 2006: 206)

When directing his own plays, Beckett concentrated "on the 'picture,' working to get the stage image as close as possible to what he had in mind" (Haynes and Knowlson 2003: 43). James Knowlson has argued that Beckett should be considered an "important visual artist" in his own right (ibid.).

So minimal is the action in some of Beckett's stage pictures—*Play* (1963), *Eh Joe* (1966), *Not I* (1972), *A Piece of Monologue* (1979), *Rockaby* (1981), *Ohio Impromptu* (1981)—that they are virtually single image, still-life paintings. In *Play* the heads of two women and the man between them protrude from "three identical grey urns" (Beckett 1984: 147). The three heads face "undeviatingly front throughout . . . so lost to age and aspect as to seem almost part of urns" (ibid.). In a sea of black, either a single spotlight illuminates in turn each crumbling face which is "lost to age," or in choral sections a trio of spotlights illuminates all three faces simultaneously. In *Not I* the actress playing Mouth is immobilized and invisible—seemingly suspended and hovering in a sea of black, seven to eight feet above the stage floor—except for her moving mouth with its red lips, white teeth, and pink gums/tongue lit by a single tightly focused spotlight. Mouth is attended by a dimly lit Auditor who bears witness by the raising and lowering of

Figure 7.1 Patricia Boyette in *Rockaby*. (Photograph: Brent Nicastro)

the arms on three occasions. In *Ohio Impromptu* two male figures, Reader and Listener, appear "as alike in appearance as possible" in their long black coats and long white hair seated in two identical white chairs at the 4′ × 8′ white table, "bowed head[s] propped on right hand[s]" (ibid.: 285; Figure 3.1, p. 42). In *Rockaby* we discover a "prematurely old" woman sitting in a rocking-chair facing front downstage with "unkempt grey hair. Huge eyes in white expressionless face. White hands holding end of armrests" (ibid.: 275; Figure 7.1). Her feet are on a rung, clearly off the floor, making evident the fact that when she rocks she is not rocking herself, but is being rocked. In *Footfalls* May is discovered as she paces with her "disheveled grey hair, worn grey wrap hiding feet, trailing" (ibid.: 239). Whenever May comes to a halt in the midst of pacing, "facing front at R," (ibid.: 239), May and/or Woman's Voice speak about "The semblance" (ibid.: 242).

If and when they speak, these all-but-still figures are animated by the actor's energetic engagement with the musicality of Beckett's texts. Beckett crafts tempo-rhythm by arranging words and punctuation on the page with periods, question marks, commas, colons, semi-colons, and ". . ." He literally provides a performance score for each text. Words, punctuation, and stage directions orchestrate cadences, tones, and qualities demanded of the words as they are spoken. Beckett "produces language structures of unprecedented beauty" (Kalb 1989: 160).

At one extreme are the vocal scores for *Footfalls*, *Ohio Impromptu*, *Eh Joe*, and *Piece of Monologue* which possess a legato pace. The slow tempo makes it difficult for the actor to sustain an energetic and imaginative connection for the duration of phrases, much less an entire performance. At the other extreme are *Not I* and *Play* which must be precisely delivered at an almost impossible to achieve breakneck speed. For Whitelaw, "Working on *Play* was not unlike conducting music or having a music lesson" (1995: 78). She scored her original script with "musical notes" such as the "actual *stresses* of syllables" when saying, "Less confused, less confusing. At the same time I prefer this to . . . the other thing." For Whitelaw, the words did not carry "specific meanings," but were "*drum-beats*—a sort of Morse code*.*" When Beckett altered a single word or a punctuation mark at a rehearsal, it "altered the rhythm of a sentence" (ibid.: 78). As poet Anne Atik comments, "is it any wonder that so many composers were attracted to [Beckett's] work: Mihalovici, Dutilleux, Berio, Heinz Holliger, Philip Glass, Morton Feldman, John Beckett . . .?" (Atik 2005: 42).[4]

The musicality of Beckett's work is exemplified in comments actors have made who worked with Beckett as their director. Working with Beckett on *Footfalls*, Billie Whitelaw recalls how she

> felt like a moving, musical Edvard Munch painting . . . [H]e was not only using me to play the notes, but I almost felt that he did have the paint brush out and was painting, and, of course, what he always had in the other pocket is the rubber, because as fast as he draws a line in, he gets out that enormous India-rubber and rubs it out until it is only faintly there.
>
> (in Knowlson and Knowlson 2006: 170)

Working on *Endgame*, Alan Mandell was fascinated

> by Beckett's description of actions in musical terms. As a director, he seemed to conduct with both his hands raised like wings at about chest level, and to signify the end to a pause or silence he would raise the ring finger and the pinky on either hand. These for him were the equivalent of musical dynamics—a pause was a beat; a silence was a rest.
>
> (in Knowlson and Knowlson 2006: 201)

Similarly, Bud Thorpe noted how Beckett "was actually moving his hand up and down to the beat of the poetry. It was a symphony he was conducting" (in Knowlson and Knowlson 2006:

209). Perhaps also reflecting Beckett's love of chess, he crafted his scores with mathematical precision.

To actualize his carefully crafted "word-music" Beckett reiterated over and over again to the actors with whom he worked not to put "colour" in their delivery. Billie Whitelaw reports how Beckett constantly emphasized, "'No, no, that's too much colour, too much colour,' clearly a euphemism for 'Please don't act'" (1995: 80). Voicing Beckett's texts "without colour" means delivering the text without the contours of an everyday, behavioral, realist character-acting voice. Later in this chapter I provide examples of how the actor can access an energetics for delivering Beckett's texts by inhabiting vocal resonance and vibration in lieu of overt color.

States or conditions *in extremis*

As we have seen, Beckett locates his speakers in often stark, restricted environments where there is little if any overt movement, or even the possibility of movement. The "enclosed space from which there is no way out" originated with Beckett's work on *Imagination Dead Imagine* and *Lessness* for BBC Radio. Martin Esslin explains how *Imagination Dead Imagine*

> was all an enclosed space which is like a womb, you see, which is then broken open and now you have this wilderness in which there is only the little body standing up. That's the only thing that's still standing up. [. . .] Sam had an absolutely mystical obligation towards that poor, suffering, enclosed being that doesn't know there is a way out. But if you look through his work you find it confirmed over and over again.
>
> (in Knowlson and Knowlson 2006: 150–151)

In *Happy Days*, Winnie is buried in sand to her waist or neck. Mouth is static in *Not I*. Joe is immoveable once he sits on his bed and the Voice starts "in on him" in *Eh Joe*. Reader/Listener sit in virtual stillness in *Ohio Impromptu*. The 2 F and 1 M are entombed in their burial urns in *Play*. In *Piece of Monologue* the sole male figure stands in stillness within a room where he both recollects and describes the present moment, "now. This night" (Beckett 1984: 265).

Within these restricted environments, each figure's bodymind inhabits a state or condition *in extremis*.[5] In *Not I*, Mouth is all that exists and all that appears—a form of consciousness reduced to the act of gushing forth a constant stream. These situations help create part of what is unique about the Beckett form, and focus the actor's work on an embodiment of consciousness that revolves within those restricted environments.

What is meant by consciousness? On the basis of his numerous discussions with Beckett on the role of consciousness in his work, Patrick Bowles observes how consciousness in Beckett is "the consciousness of consciousness. Not merely the consciousness *of* some object, but the awareness of being *awake*, if you like" (in Knowlson and Knowlson 2006: 113).[6] When one inhabits this "consciousness of consciousness" where is one? "Where is this world? You're in it . . . that consciousness within ourselves of the movement of thought whose subject can be said to be that energy . . ." (in Knowlson and Knowlson 2006: 114). This "awareness of being awake" and therefore the awareness of one's thought as it happens is particularly relevant to the "world" Mouth inhabits in *Not I*, to the three players inhabiting their individual burial urns in *Play*, to May in *Footfalls*, as well as to *Piece of Monologue* and *Ohio Impromptu*. For example, in *Not I*, where words/thought are about to fail, the very failure of the thought process or the process of speaking becomes an act in itself. It is the struggle to get it (the thought; the word/s) out, or a specific act of perception per se that creates action. What is central to Patrick Bowles' summary of his discussion with Beckett is the notion of the "movement of thought."

The actor's work is to swim upstream against Cartesian dualism where thought or mind is understood as a phenomenon that only takes place in the head. The actor must allow thought as-it-happens to kinesthetically move. Psychophysical training sensitizes the actor to a point where she is able to feel the "consciousness of consciousness" at work within the bodymind.

A number of Beckett's texts shift between first person and third person, i.e., at one moment the actor's words describe the scene on stage in third person, and in the next moment one is acting in the first person as the figure *within* the state or condition described. The texts are also characterized by a continuous process of qualification of the state of being/thought/ condition in which the figure exists. The mind at-work in this state or condition is invoked and must be synaesthetically embodied. Therefore, an essential part of the rehearsal process is ensuring that the actor reaches clarity about each thought, its movement, and about how this *process of thought* is not something in the head, but the actor's own perceiving consciousness/awareness at work in the moment. The actor ideally enters and inhabits states of *active perception* where

1 one *is* the figure seeing/observing—as in *Footfalls* when May in the "Sequel" describes "The semblance" (herself) in movement (Beckett 1984: 242);
2 one *is* the figure hearing, sensing, feeling the saying of words as they are shaped in the mouth/consciousness—a process which activates the actor's inner resonance of associations through the sensory awareness of the act of speaking/voicing. (In *Eh Joe* Voice literally uses touch of tongue on teeth to voice the single and double "t" sounds: "Cut a long story short doesn't work . . . Gets up in the end sopping wet and back up to the house . . . Gets out the Gillette . . ." (ibid.: 206));
3 one *is* the figure sensing the resonance of overt and/or subtle movement-as-it-happens— such as May's sensory awareness of her feet as they "fall" with each sliding/wheeling action in *Footfalls*, most evident in the counting of her paces *"synchronous with steps. One two three four five six seven wheel . . ."* (ibid.: 239). The

counting takes place not simply in the mind, but the saying of the number is the "said" of the count in the feet as they are placed.

The actor must be clear about whether she inhabits the first-person or third-person mode of awareness, and be able to link and shape her energy and awareness appropriately in the transitions between these registers. The constant qualification of a thought, observation, or description is optimally sensed by the actor in each shift. For the actor, Beckett's pauses are not gaps of no-thought. Rather, pauses must be played. The actor actively engages the unsaid, the might-be-said, or the yet-to-be-said in these moments between. They are spaces to be inhabited fully without a gap in one's energy, awareness, or attentiveness—even if that moment is one of temporary suspension of any specific thought. Embodying a thought in a pause is an embodied activity even though this thought is not articulated as a specific idea. Thought does not land—it is in process.

With regard to these moments of stasis, Gay Gibson Cima usefully observes how

acting in Beckett, like acting in *noh*, may be "a matter of doing just enough to create the *ma* that is a blank space-time where nothing is done, and that *ma* is the core of the expression, where the true interest lies."

(1993: 200)

Both require a minimum of externally observable overt action; however, behind that apparent physical inaction is the blazing flame of an active, inner, vibratory energy and perception dialectically operating between inside and outside. Cima explains Zeami's views in the *Kakyo*:

"[N]o matter how slight a bodily action, if the motion is more restrained than the emotion behind it, the emotion will become the substance and the movements of the body its functions, thus moving the audience." A standard rule of acting, this dictum is carried

to its extreme in *noh* and in Beckett, until in fact "the times of action in *noh* [and in Beckett] exist for the sake of the times of stillness." May rarely walks and talks simultaneously . . . and her unwilling pacing serves in large part to highlight her parallel desire to stop "revolving it all," her wish to remain still.

(1993: 199–200)

When the actor's body is rendered virtually immovable in playing these Beckett roles, the requirement that an inner necessity be embodied becomes apparent to the actor. Blau describes acting in Beckett's plays as

realism in extremis. Which is to say that the realistic vision, its methodology, is taken about as far inside as it can go, interiorized so intensely that it seems to occur at the nerve ends.

(1994: 53)

The psychophysical training sensitizes and activates the actor's nerve ends for Beckett's "realism in extremis."

The impossible but necessary task of capturing the action of consciousness is reflected in a conversation between Beckett and Lawrence E. Harvey. Beckett is quoted as saying:

"Children build a snowman. Well, this is like trying to build a dustman." [. . .] [T]he point is that it [what he was trying to write] would not stay together. There was his sense of destruction and of the futility of words. And yet at the same time there was the need to make too.

(in Knowlson and Knowlson 2006: 137)

Beckett's work inhabits this liminal grey space of the "between." The urgency or need to make or express the impossible is constantly evident in the failure of any work to reach some or any kind of narrative conclusion. But the actor's work is to be aware of and sensitive to the urgent necessity of the attempt even as it fails.

Animating forces

Each force that animates the voicing of a text and its cadences within a specific restricted environment is unique. In *Play* it is the probing spotlight—what Whitelaw called "'the cow-poke'" (1995: 80)—that prompts the fragments of each of the three stories to "*immediately*" gush forth from each actor at break-neck speed. In *Not I* there is the "brain . . . raving away on its own . . . trying to make sense of it . . . or stop it . . ." [. . .] "keep on . . . not knowing what . . ." (Beckett 1984: 220, 222). In *Ohio Impromptu* Reader materializes and (re)appears "from time to time unheralded" at night to tell/read "the sad tale" through again "one last time" (ibid.: 287). In *Footfalls* whenever May comes to a temporary rest from the constant fall of her feet as she paces "back and forth"—she stands, "revolving it all" in her "poor mind" (ibid.: 243), trying to "tell how it was. [*Pause*] It all." (ibid.: 241). As *Rockaby* begins (Figure 7.1, p. 119), the Woman in her rocking-chair is momentarily poised/paused in the midst of a process of rocking. Her first voiced "More" (ibid.: 275) induces the act of being rocked once again, until she is

> done with that
> the rocker
> those arms at last
> rock her off
> stop her eyes
> fuck life
> stop her eyes
> rock her off
> rock her off
> [Together: echo of "rock her off," coming to rest of rock, slow fade out.]
> (Beckett 1984: 282)

The existential drive to keep on or go on in all these texts takes two primary forms. First is the compulsion or necessity that one *must* speak as in *Not I* or *Play*, that one *will be moved* as in *Act Without Words I*, or that one *must* listen as for Joe in *Eh Joe*. All these necessities are prompted by some unseen compelling force or consciousness.

Whether this compelling force or consciousness is outside or inside remains ambiguous. There is no clear conclusion to the *compulsion* prompting the figures to speak in *Not I* or *Play*. Both fade out, as does the light, but the implication is that the compulsion continues. Joe's image in *Eh Joe* literally dissolves as Voice dissolves with a final, open question, "*Eh Joe? . . .*" (Beckett 1984: 207). In *Act Without Words I*, the protagonist remains in stillness, looking at his hands—a gesture which itself is an open question mark.

A second form of existential drive is the desire to hear, speak, or listen again as in *Rockaby*'s plaintive "more"(s), or until that moment when "nothing is left to tell" and the "book" is closed (*Ohio Impromptu*, Beckett 1984: 288). In *A Piece of Monologue* the speaker inhabits the consciousness of the fact that there "Never were other matters. Never two matters. Never but the one matter. The dead and gone. The dying and the going. From the word go" (ibid.: 269). In these three plays the actor inhabits a gradual process of letting go, release, or diminishment to the point when all is extinguished, spent, or "gone" (ibid.: 269). The lights gradually fade out on a final moment of stasis, quietude, stillness—the resting of the rocker in *Rockaby* as W's "head slowly sinks, comes to rest, fade out spot" (ibid.: 273); Reader and Listener "*look at each other. Unblinking. Expressionless*" for the first time with a ten-second fade out to black; and in *Piece of Monologue* ten seconds of fade out to black as/after Speaker describes the fading: "The globe alone. Not the other. The unaccountable. From nowhere. On all sides nowhere. Unutterably faint. The globe alone. Alone gone" (ibid.: 269).

If Beckett's theatrical events require "*x* minus 5" or "*x* minus 25," how does the actor attain a state of "minus 5" or "*x* minus 25" and keep the audience's attention? In this process of reduction, Beckett appears to require the actor to overtly do less; however, what Beckett demands is that the actor does more. What is this more? Where is it located? How is it generated? What tools are available to and what tactics allow the actor the best possible of entering each state or condition? What images, actualized through an embodied act imagination, might enhance entry into a particular state or condition? How is it possible for Beckett's words to be made flesh, i.e., to be embodied so that the tempo-rhythm of his words conveys the underlying state or condition they describe? We turn now to the actor's dynamic process of filling out the special form and activating force(s) of Beckett's plays with a dynamic energetics of the bodymind as the actor "stands still while not standing still."

The Beckett Project in rehearsal and performance

In 1994 I began a nine-month project in which psychophysical training was applied to a diverse collection of Beckett's plays organized into two programs of plays performed in four locations within the same building: *Act Without Words I, Rough for Radio II, Footfalls, What Where, Eh Joe, Play, Ohio Impromptu,* and *Come and Go.*[7] In addition to the psychophysical training, our preparatory work was enhanced by a month-long pre-rehearsal residency with Billie Whitelaw, organized and facilitated by Karen Ryker and Patricia Boyette.[8] During the residency, Whitelaw took all of us on her "journey with Samuel Beckett" and generously shared her detailed personal notes on each text on which she worked with Beckett (see Whitelaw 1995).

It became clear how useful the training and ~~principles had been to working on Beckett's~~ ~~ng scores. Honing the actor's simple~~ ~~ship to breath, impulse, and action is~~ ~~by the necessity that each actor playing~~ ~~ns how to subtract whatever is~~ ~~vocally or physically from their acting~~ ~~the while keeping the flame of~~ ~~within. Maria DePalma (May in~~ ~~on how the preliminary work~~ ~~inced her that approaching~~ ~~her voice forced her to give~~

~~guity to Beckett's texts~~ ~~nterpretation for~~

the audience. For the first time in my life [I approached a performance without trying] to understand it at all . . . Instead of playing with interpretation, I played with pitch and speech using the words to guide me.

(Journal, 1995)

Karole Spangler (Voice in *Eh Joe*) noted the unrelenting nature of the requirement that she remain in the present throughout the thirty-five-minute performance:

If I slipped off . . . track [it was] invariably traced to moments when I tried to work from my head . . . manufacturing an effect, attempting to re-create something that worked in a previous rehearsal.

Like other actors, part of the difficulty for Spangler was adding nothing, since

the actor's psyche rebels. We exist, after all, as glorified interpreters—he who can invest the most of himself in a role and not lose touch with reality wins! Beckett wants investment, too. He wants more, but he wants it "pure." All past experience, all pain, all joy, with no opinion added . . . Beckett writes excruciating, concentrated stuff—plays full of the mind and body in agony. He lacks consideration for human limitations.

(Journal, 1995)

Peder Melhuse's encounter with Beckett (*Act Without Words I, Eh Joe,* and *Rough for Radio II*) led him to discover the "beauty in rhythm and sound and movement," and ultimately to "a much more open mind" about how to approach acting (Journal, 1995).

The project was so rewarding that Patricia Boyette and I made a long-term commitment to explore a psychophysical approach to Beckett's plays in performance that has continued to the present. We approach each play-in-production within the limitations Beckett sets for their performance, viewing these requirements as a challenge. In the formative years of the project, Billie Whitelaw continued to provide advice and shared her personal notes from her years of collaboration with Beckett.

We were not in a rush, taking the time necessary to problem-solve the demands of each text. We began with *Not I*. Boyette performed a work-in-progress showing I directed as part of a residency on psychophysical acting sponsored by the Centre for Performance Research (Aberystwyth, Wales) in 1997. We returned to the rehearsal room and premiered the first full evening of *The Beckett Project* at the Grove Theater Center, Los Angeles, on April 7, 2000. It included *Ohio Impromptu, Not I, Act Without Words I*, and *Rockaby*.[9]

Our work continued in 2003 with rehearsals of *Happy Days* toward a future performance. The third staging of *The Beckett Project* took place at the Granary Theatre, Cork, Ireland in May, 2004. To our original four plays, we added *Eh Joe, Footfalls*, and *Play*. Two evenings of seven plays were performed as follows:

> Programme 1: *Ohio Impromptu, Play*, and *Eh Joe*. Programme 2: *Not I, Footfalls, Act Without Words I*, and *Rockaby*.[10]

During the Beckett Centenary year (2006) *The Beckett Project* was performed in the US (Indiana and Wisconsin) and Singapore (Esplanade Theatres on the Bay, produced by Theatre Training and Research Programme).[11]

The remainder of this chapter focuses on the application of psychophysical process and principles to the specific acting problems of a few of Beckett's plays-in-performance.

Activating the actor with *ki*-awareness/energy

Practicing psychophysical disciplines, the actor coordinates and inhabits breath, focus, energy, awareness, and movement as a synaesthetic whole. This heightened *ki*-awareness and attentiveness are applied to Beckett's texts in three ways: (1) constantly inhabiting perceiving consciousness

and sensory awareness within the specific environment of a performance, (2) intuitively directing *ki*-awareness/energy to particular parts of the body to enhance the vibratory quality of inner engagement when enacting a performance score, and (3) applying *ki*-awareness to and through active images specific to the dramatic context.

These three modes of applying psychophysical work to Beckett operate simultaneously in performance. Patricia Boyette notes how Beckett requires the actor to

> work simultaneously on different "tracks." You have to choose one of those tracks as an initial point of departure. This particular track might be the physical score—prescribed physical gestures, i.e., physically where you are at each moment, what you are doing, where you are looking. Or, another track might concentrate on the vocal—finding the tone of the voice, the music and the pace, or the specificity of the words themselves. Or, yet another track might be the problem of myself in space, and the quality of the energy I am engaging, such as lightness or heaviness. All these different "tracks" must be simultaneously realized in performance, and layered with mathematical, geometrical precision. Given the structure of Beckett's plays, there is not a lot of "wiggle room" between or among these tracks or layers. Personally, performing Beckett is like playing chess on three levels simultaneously.
>
> (in Boyette and Zarrilli 2007: 74)

If performing Beckett is like "playing chess on three levels simultaneously," this phenomenon reflects the dialectical nature of the actor's chiasmatic deployment of her *ki*-awareness/energy (see pp. 59–60) as it responds to and is intuitively directed in the moment of "playing" between and among these tracks.

As one develops an ever more sensitive awareness of the poise and counter-poise in the spaces between each in- and out-breath and the subtle shifts of weight in the constant proprioceptive task of maintaining balance, the actor is working on how to embody awareness and consciousness within the space between—that place of possibility for the actor. In Beckett's texts these spaces/places of possibility "between" are marked by his use of punctuation, i.e., his use of "...," "—," or *pause* to mark what is happening to thought as it bodies forth from one moment to the next. Each bursts with possibility for the bodying/voicing-forth modulated *ki*-energy/awareness.

Jeff Morrison's description of his experience of this kind of "doubled up interiority" when acting "at the nerve ends" while performing *Play* in 1995 reflects this active, chiasmatic engagement of *ki*-energy/awareness to the specific tasks of his score:

> There has to be a score of energy, a seething something underneath, that drives an apparently immobile exterior and makes it compelling. The dilation of presence in a still body has to be enormous, because you don't have the advantage of movement to catch an audience's attention. That dilation comes through strong focus in a number of directions ... internal focus on the body, full awareness of every part of oneself; full awareness of the external world ... full awareness of the score and complete internalization of the score so that no energy need be wasted on keeping one's place ... and also an awareness of the quality of focus, some intuitive action that permits a mutable relationship between these other areas of focus. I managed to deal with all of these different points of focus by unifying them in my body and connecting them to the [spot]light. Conceptually, there was a continuous stream of energy that began at my feet and went straight up out my mouth and all the way over to the light ... I was not moving. I was completely still ... but I would be drenched in sweat at the end of each performance and by the second week, my entire body would shake with the effort of delivering each line. I was exerting maximum effort for maximum effect, but the outward manifestation of that effect was really quite minimal.
>
> (Journal, 1995)

Inhabiting active images and/or metaphors

It is clear from our work with Billie Whitelaw as well as published accounts of actors who worked closely with Beckett that he never explained the meaning of any of his texts. Rather, he chose to provide actors with "suggestions [that] were practical, detailed and down-to-earth [...] what they needed to speak their lines or perform their moves or gestures" (Haynes and Knowlson 2003: 8). Beckett often provided actors with what I describe as active images—images and/or metaphors that provide the actor with an active point of entry into inhabiting the moment through the modulation of their energy, attention, and perception. Horst Bollman who worked with Beckett on Clov in *Endgame* at the Schiller-Theater (Berlin) for the 1967 production noted how

> Every now and then Beckett would talk in particular about the silences, the long pauses. We asked him, "What does it mean? What are we supposed to do during the pauses?" He told us, "act as if you are in a boat with a hole in it and water is coming in and the boat is slowly sinking. You must think of things to do; then there is a pause; then you get the feeling you have to do something else and you work at it once more and the boat goes up again."
>
> (in Knowlson and Knowlson 2006: 181)

Not responding directly to the request about meaning, Beckett provided an extraordinarily useful and active task for the actor to engage—"thinking of things to do" while the boat sinks. If the actor follows Beckett's advice, works with this specific active image, and keeps his awareness/perception open within the engagement of the image, then he will literally "stand still while not standing still" while undertaking this activity. Since Beckett's figures existentially inhabit a state or condition of being-in-a-particular-world, as Beckett said to Ruby Cohn in a 1971 conversation, "Being is not syntactical" (in Knowlson and Knowlson 2006: 129). Explanations of meaning should not be expected.

Another active image Beckett conjured when directing is reported by Alan Mandell when he worked on Nagg in *Endgame*:

> I recall asking him if he could tell me something about Nagg's character, who he was and what had brought him to his current situation, on his stumps and in an ashcan. Beckett stared at me intensely and with a long sweep of his hand said, "He's greeeyy!" It wasn't the response I was expecting, but I jumped back into my ashcan thinking "Grey."
>
> (Knowlson and Knowlson 2006: 201).

What does Mandell mean when he says he was "thinking 'Grey'"? Is the term "thinking" appropriate to the actor's work in this instance? If Mandell means he jumped back into his ashcan and began to "inhabit a state of Grey," then he was actively entering into a state of being/doing informed by the qualities of greyness. Everything said and done would derive from the bodymind/awareness as it inhabits greyness. My hunch is that this is what Mandell probably meant. If he was actually thinking *about* Grey he would not be able to inhabit greyness as an active image/state.

Bud Thorpe who also worked with Beckett on *Endgame* provides a helpful clarification:

> I caught on very easily and very quickly over the fact that there are musical tones and canters to what we're doing in this. You don't have to play-act, but you do have to find it from the inside. And he kept on saying, "Tone, tone, tone, we have to hit the right tone."
>
> (in Knowlson and Knowlson 2006: 210)

Thorpe's reference to having "to find it from the inside" points to the necessity of the actor inhabiting a state or condition of being/doing where a tone or quality such as greyness is the actor's *modus operandi*—everything one says/does operates from/through/with greyness.

Also working on Nagg, Lawrence Held once innocently asked Beckett "what *Endgame* was about." Beckett replied with reference to the

world championship chess tournament then taking place: "'Well, it's like the last game between Karpov and Korchnoi. After the third move both knew that neither could win, but they kept on playing'" (in Knowlson and Knowlson 2006: 206). The image of playing *Endgame* as an absorbing if unwinnable chess match provides the actor with a clear point of tactical entry.

What is crucial is finding specific active images that allow an actor to gain an appropriate point of entry so that *ki*-awareness/energy is played between and among the various tracks of one's score and modes of embodied engagement.

The Beckett Project: general considerations

While our approach to Beckett's texts has been informed by the foregoing analysis, our studio-based work is pragmatic and focused on solving the specific problems present in each Beckett text. Given the clarity of Beckett's vision and scoring of each text, my directorial task is getting out of Beckett's way in order to focus exclusively on how actors meet the acting tasks demanded by each text.

These extraordinary demands are nowhere better exemplified than in the well-documented case of Billie Whitelaw's work with Beckett on *Not I* in 1973:

> She knew that it had to go fast, even if doing so produced sensory deprivation and a tension that made her feel that the top of her head would blow off. She broke down in rehearsal, leading [Samuel Beckett] to say, "Oh, Billie what have I done to you?" The performance was marked by a determination that became her hallmark: "If it is necessary, I will walk through brick walls . . . Later, I will collapse with broken bones, but if I've got to do it I will do it." This was not entirely hyperbole, as her efforts led to a damaged spine and a back "like a corkscrew."
>
> (Ackerley and Gontarski 2004: 643)

In her autobiography, Whitelaw explains:

> I didn't realise until much later that with the
> two seasons of *Not I*, I had inflamed an already
> damaged spine and neck. Performing in that
> play, all the tension that went to the back of my
> neck also aggravated the vertigo and nausea I'd
> had in my early twenties. I'd come to terms with
> this: the damage is something I'm stuck with.
> In fact, every play I did with Beckett left a little
> legacy behind in my state of ill-health, a price I
> have most willingly paid.
>
> (Whitelaw 1995: 131)

Part of our task in *The Beckett Project* has been to
address how it is possible for the actor to perform
plays like *Not I* and *Footfalls* without literally
being damaged when assuming extremely difficult
physical positions sustained for extended periods
of time.

Our strategy for meeting the rigors of Beckett's
plays is fourfold:

1   The actor's bodymind is prepared for the
    physical and mental demands of Beckett's plays
    by gaining strength and depth through ongoing
    psychophysical training.
2   The training process prepares the actor to meet
    the subtle demands of Beckett's texts for non-
    realistic, non-character-based performances
    by generating the actor's ability to engage
    and modulate one's *ki*-awareness/energy in
    engaging text "without colour." The actor
    simultaneously utilizes this energy to sustain
    active images for prolonged periods, such as in
    Footfalls and *Eh Joe*.
3   I work closely with Patricia Boyette and all
    involved in *The Beckett Project* to create simple
    technical solutions to potential problems,
    i.e., we make the environment and stage
    apparatus as safe as possible so that the actor
    can remain grounded with her energy and keep
    a lengthened spine while inhabiting difficult
    physical positions.
4   I develop a map and strategy for deployment of
    the actor's *ki*-awareness/energy specific to each

text so that the actor deploys and modulates
her energy and awareness as necessary to
specific tasks within the unique performance
environment.

The process of discovering and deploying *ki*-
energy/awareness is clearly *not* self-indulgent.
Rather than feeding the hungry ego and the actor's
narcissistic tendency for affirmation and/or self-
indulgence, this burns away the ego to a point
where the actor's overly subjective self is out of
the way. The actor's self as perceiving awareness is
present in the deployment of a focused awareness/
energy as it is shaped by each action/image with
simplicity and clarity. Once clarified, one's *ki*-
energy/awareness can better be shared with other
actors and with the audience in a process that
involves mutuality—the give-and-take of sharing
the energy appropriate to the dramaturgy and
tasks set for the acting ensemble.

One example of how we create such mutuality
is our approach to *Rockaby*. Woman is seated in
her rocking-chair throughout, listening to her
recorded voice, as she is being rocked. *Rockaby*
appears to be a solo performance, but the text
clearly communicates the fact that what is being
existentially explored is Woman's relationship to
"another creature like herself" (Beckett 1984: 275),
i.e., the *mutuality* of the self with [one's] Other.
The obvious way in which such mutuality is
created is via Woman's active act of listening to
her prerecorded voice as she is rocked. Who is she
calling to with each of her four calls for "More,"
until she is "done with that/the rocker" and finally
comes to "*rest of rock*" as her "head slowly sinks,
comes to rest, fade out spot" (ibid.: 282/273)?

We enhanced the means by which this act
of mutuality of self/Other might be accessed
for Patricia as actress. Beckett stipulates that
the rocking is "controlled mechanically without
assistance from W[oman]" (1984: 274). From
my perspective, if the rocking is controlled
mechanically, it *might* be experienced as
mechanical for the actress and audience. Instead
of a mechanical system, we developed a simple
means of having Patricia be rocked by another

actor. We attach a long black pole to the top of the rocking-chair with a hinged clamp. The pole extends through the upstage black curtain (or flat) and is of sufficient length (usually about 12–15 feet) to allow the actor rocking Patricia to remain unseen backstage. With careful placement of the rocking-chair in light, the pole remains invisible in the black that envelops Woman.

This simple technical solution allows Patricia-as-Voice to be rocked by an Other as she hears/absorbs her own voice/story. The act of being rocked is one which many Westerners may have experienced in childhood. Placing herself in "those arms at last" is an act of surrender and trust. Having an actor doing the rocking makes it possible for there to be "another living soul" (Beckett 1984: 277) with whom the actress communicates. Surrendering to "those arms at last" that rock her is one of the lynch-pins for the process of association and remembrance available to Patricia while being rocked.

The act of rocking is an important element in the success of a performance. Patricia as Woman is dependent on the actor rocking her. When I rock Patricia, it involves me in the familiar act of rocking another that one experiences as a parent. Standing with my left foot slightly forward, basically in the lion stance, so that my foot-awareness is strongly grounded, I loosely grasp the pole to rock Patricia. Keeping the connection from my lower *dantian* downward through my feet, and rising up through my palms holding the pole, I allow *ki*-awareness/energy to extend through the pole, just as one does in working with a long staff whether in form training or in more improvisatory staff exercises. The tempo-rhythm of each rock is initiated by and engages *both* actors' *ki*-energy/awareness. We are communicating with each other via the armature attached to the chair. As each line of the recorded text begins, this provides the impulse for me to draw back the rocking-chair on an inhalation in preparation for its forward motion on delivery of the line. The forward motion is on an exhalation, supported by my constant psychophysical connection to *ki*-energy from my palms through my feet as I rock Patricia forward

while silently "saying" each line of the text in time and in tune with Patricia's recorded voice. Since the lines of the text vary ever so slightly in length, there is a corresponding slight irregularity to the tempo-rhythm. Optimally, my act of rocking serves as an additional sensory vehicle stimulating Patricia while she is being rocked, and as she gives herself over into "these arms at last."

In addition to mutuality, two other general considerations guide our work in *The Beckett Project*: to create an overall dramaturgy for each program of plays, and to respect and provide a place for the unique dramaturgy, architecture, and musicality of each play. An audience's overall experience of a set of Beckett plays is naturally shaped by the order in which they are played. For our original programme of four plays— *Ohio Impromptu*, *Not I*, *Act Without Words I*, and *Rockaby*—we opened the evening with the meditative, legato *Ohio Impromptu*, followed by the up-tempo *Not I*, the physical play in *Act Without Words I*, and concluded with *Rockaby*.

In Ireland we created two programs organized so that the two most similar plays in terms of overall length (thirty minutes), tempo-rhythm, and texture—*Eh Joe* and *Footfalls*—were on different evenings. In Programme 1 the meditative *Ohio Impromptu* was followed by the up-tempo and lighter quality of *Play*, and we concluded with the excruciating journey of *Eh Joe*. In Programme 2 *Not I* began the program to capture the audience's immediate attention and was followed by the sustained energy of *Footfalls*. With its non-verbal physical score, *Act Without Words* provided a complete contrast with *Footfalls*, and *Rockaby* concluded the evening.

Just as important in our staging of programs of shorter plays is that we require the audience to leave the theater at the conclusion of each play. We do so in order to clear the audience's palate between each play. While the overall dramaturgy of the evening is important, the integrity of the audience's experience of each play as unique in its own right is paramount. Directorially, this strategy allows me to have the actors on stage as the audience enters the theater for each specific play, i.e., for *Ohio Impromptu* the audience enters the theater and discovers Reader and Listener already at the table. As the audience re-enters the theater for *Not I*, Auditor is visible as a shadowy presence in pre-set lighting.

I turn now to a discussion of our work on specific Beckett texts, beginning with the two pieces I have been performing since 2000—*Act Without Words I* and *Ohio Impromptu*.

At work on *Act Without Words I*[2]

Picking up my earlier discussion of Beckett's score for *Act Without Words I*, the actor engages a form of task-based acting in which perception and "attending to" are central as he responds to each stimulus in turn. What is being attended to in each of the actions within the score? Whether directing or acting in *Act Without Words I*, I make no attempt to develop a character-based subtext; rather, the score is taken at face-value. I work with the initiation of each action—such as "flung," "gets up," "dusts himself," "turns aside," or "reflects"— through an impulse, allowing the nuances of breath/*ki*-awareness/energy to fill each task/action in the score as it emerges in the moment.

What do I mean by impulse? Although from rehearsals I know the structure of actions in terms of their order and the cues that trigger each action, I cannot "know," in the pre-meditative sense, any action *before* it happens. It is my relationship to the known that is under examination. In enacting this score, I ideally enter the process of performance in a state of not-knowing and therefore am surprised by each task/action in *this* moment. I do not act surprised, but surprise is that state of optimal innocence within which I respond to each stimulus, or the shit, as it happens. Impulse is, therefore, the initiation of my embodied relationship to each action/task in the moment.

A psychophysical approach requires me to sustain and modulate a fully engaged *ki*-awareness in relation to each action, and between one moment of embodied attending to and the next. Off stage, before the first impulse arises, I prepare

to be "flung" by focusing on my breath through my feet. The house lights fade, the on-stage lights come to full, and I count three seconds through my bodymind. Sensing my feet . . . an impulse arises from lower *dantian*. I "am flung." Once flung on stage my feet are swept out from under me; therefore, I fall. Landing on the floor I sense my relationship to it, and "get up immediately." My awareness scans those places on my body that have made contact with the floor so that I "dust" those specific places. Having dusted, I sense the completion of the dusting so that the next action, "turns aside," is not anticipated. On a half-breath, I "turn aside." Each of these sequential actions must be knitted together without anticipation. I use *ki/*sensory awareness generated one moment to carry me into the next action, such as the linking action "turns aside" which carries me into "reflects." This awareness possesses a trace or resonance of the "where I just was" in the "where I am now." For example, if on the "turns aside" I have turned slightly to my left, on the "reflect" my one-quarter body turn to the right is sustained by keeping a residual sensory/kinesthetic awareness of where I was on the "turns aside."

There is an unremitting, mathematically precise logic to *Act Without Words I*. The seemingly unconnected elements that appear in turn within the environment—the tree, pair of scissors, carafe of water, three cubes, and rope—are eventually linked by this unremitting (and unseen) logic. Cumulative sequences of actions lead the protagonist to certain discoveries, such as his response to the third whistle from left wing, when, rather than exiting in response to the whistle as he did twice before, this time he "hesitates, thinks better of it, halts, turns aside, reflects" (Beckett 1984: 43). When the moment of hesitation and the resulting "thinks better of it, halts" is played in the moment, it generates a laugh because the audience sees this discovery as it happens. This is true of the "thinks better of it" actions in the score, such as the moment the protagonist is about to stack the large cube on the medium-sized cube for a second time when he "hesitates, thinks better of it, sets it [large cube] down, takes up small one and puts it on big one" (ibid.: 45). This time he does *not* repeat his earlier mistake in perception/logic—stacking the big cube on the smaller cube that led to his fall when trying to reach the water.

During the course of the approximately twenty minutes it takes to play *Act Without Words I*, the dynamic tension between the shit that happens, and the man to whom the shit happens cumulatively generates an increasingly dark dynamic. Once the carafe of water is revealed, what will happen each time the force activating the environment generates a new test for the man in relation to his attempts to reach or secure the carafe of water? The one (apparent) exception to the testing of the man is when he takes the length of rope left to him after he has cut the rope with the scissors and fallen (once again) to the ground. He "makes a lasso with which he tries to lasso the carafe" (Beckett 1984: 45) only for the carafe to "disappear in flies." Playing these moments is an actual test of focus, concentration, and perception for both actors, i.e., the actor playing man and the technician/stage-attendant who must ensure that the carafe literally disappears before it is lassoed.

Andy Crook's work as the stage attendant in activating and responding to my actions is as important a contribution to *Act Without Words I* as my own. It is our mutual awareness of the actions and reactions of each other that constitutes the warp and weft of the score as a whole. Since Andy initiates most of the sequences of action—the initial whistle, for example, and each subsequent whistle—his awareness must be hypersensitive to the particular way in which each audience responds to my reactive-actions. There must be sufficient space between actions/reactions for the audience's response. In this sense, although Beckett subtitles *Act Without Words I* "A mime for one player," in our playing it is a mime for two players—the man and the actor who manipulates the environment. If and when our playing works, it does so because of the triangulation of our energies—the subtle awareness of each other, and of the audience as the third actor.

A piece that usually begins with the laughter of recognition at what first appears to be a series of innocent Chaplinesque prat-falls, concludes on a much darker moment of absolute silence and stillness. In the final section of *Act Without Words I* the protagonist is on the floor, having been dumped there by the big cube as it is pulled out from under him. A set of five actions (*in italics below*) follow, the first four of which are in response to the continuing shit that happens:

> He remains lying on his side, his face towards auditorium, staring before him.
> The carafe descends from flies and comes to rest a few feet from his body.
> *He does not move.*
> Whistle from above.
> *He does not move.*
> The carafe descends further, dangles and plays about his face.
> *He does not move.*
> The carafe is pulled up and disappears in flies.
> The bough returns to horizontal, the palms open, the shadow returns.
> Whistle from above.
> *He does not move.*
> The tree is pulled up and disappears in flies.
> *He looks at hands.*
> (Beckett 1984: 46, italics added)

Each "does not move" must be enacted in response to a stimulus—the carafe descends and rests a few feet from his body, or it descends further, dangles, and plays about his face. To each stimulus, the actor responds by "not moving," "staring before him." When playing these moments, I follow each in- and out-breath, keeping an open awareness through my entire bodymind to the stimuli being presented. I must be in a state of not knowing what the next stimulus will be. In response to each stimulus—carafe, palm tree, whistle—my action is "does not move," an action embodied by allowing the resonance of the stimulus to move through me while actively not moving. The one action in the play which is not to a stimulus is the final action—"looks at hands." The final four "does not move" actions should be so fully felt through my body, and especially my palms which have come into contact with the floor when I fall off the cube, that the act of lifting them to look at them is filled with the *ki*-energy generated by actively not moving—attempting to *not* move generates inner vibration. The degree of vibration generated by maintaining a relationship between my lower abdomen, my palms, and the place ahead to which I have been looking becomes extremely activated during the "does not move" actions. Therefore, as I raise my hands so that my external focus shifts from an indeterminate place ahead to a specific place on one of my palms, and then shifts to the opposite palm, both my focus and palms are filled with the energy of the four earlier "does not move" actions, as well as the cumulative question mark that the hands have become—can they move? The act of looking is not a looking at the palms, but an act of seeing with my entire being—a world opens before me—a looking sustained with my entire bodymind until the lights gradually fade to black over a lengthy count. By this point in the process, my hands and entire bodymind are alive with *ki*-awareness/energy precipitated in part by the dialectic action between "does not move" and perceptually taking in each stimulus in the score—the descent of the carafe, the whistle, etc. It is the dynamic between not moving and inner movement of one's energy that creates an extraordinarily active amount of energy manifest as vibration. As Stanton Garner has perceptively observed, in this and other moments of apparent stillness in Beckett's work, for the live actor living "this condition of fixity . . . in the breathing and trembling [. . .] theatrical stillness is an impossibility" (1994: 81).[13] I am *not* standing still while apparently standing still.

The entire dramaturgy of *Act Without Words I* builds to this moment—a moment pregnant with the potential for resonance and meaning for the audience. If I have psychophysically created a score which links each moment through my use of energy/breath/focus to this final action without psychologically pointing to what it means, in the moment when I lift my palms to look at them, there is a palpable vibration shared in the act of looking and in the sensory awareness of the palms

being looked at that makes much available for the audience to absorb and experience.

With its precise, mathematical logic, *Act Without Words I* provides the actor with a highly structured score to be played through the modulated intensities of one's energetic *ki*-awareness as it engages each impulse/action. Unlike some other Beckett texts discussed below, I utilize no active images, nor do associations necessarily arise for me as I inhabit a particular action. If associations arise, I accept them, but they are not necessary here. Rather, as discussed with regard to the concluding set of actions, it is the connection between and intensities of my engagement within each moment that occupy my awareness and imagination throughout. For some in the audience, these intensities may be read or experienced as full of emotion or meaning, but if and when this is the case, these are a by-product of the modulation of the actor's *ki*-awareness within the immediate dramatic context.

At work on *Ohio Impromptu*[14]

[The] meticulously sculpted tableau remains nearly motionless the entire time, allowing spectators to meditate on its metaphoric significance while a flow of words emanates from the stage, guiding meditation.

(Kalb 1989: 49)

To emphasize "the meticulously sculpted tableau" of *Ohio Impromptu* for our performances, the audience enters the theater to discover the dimly but tightly pre-lit figures of Reader and Listener with their long white hair and long black coats seated as mirror images at the huge 4' × 8' white table and with "head[s] bowed propped on right hands[s]" (Beckett 1984: 285; Figure 3.1, p. 42). Open before Reader on the table is a "worn volume" and a single (shared?) wide-brimmed black hat. Inhabiting the stillness "as though turned to stone" (ibid.: 287), after the audience is seated and the pre-set lights intensify so that this still-life image is fully illuminated against the black void of the remainder of the stage, Reader initiates his reading, "Little is left to tell" (ibid.: 285).

With its "stone-like" almost *noh*-like sparseness and stillness, the only means for each actor's expressivity in *Ohio Impromptu* is the subtle engagement of one's *ki*-energy/awareness channeled through each specific task—the quality of Reader's modulation of his voice in reading the story "without colour"; Listener's act of listening to this particular repetition of the story; and both actors' engagement with the few physical actions/ gestures which animate the otherwise still image. Listener's knocks on the resonant wooden table signal each moment he wishes Reader to stop the reading in order to hear a particular section of the text repeated. He knocks again after the repetition to signal that Reader may continue the reading. Part way through the story, Reader has three overt actions quite near to one another. The first follows a pause in the reading, and is the subtle action of looking closer at the sentence he has just read—"After so long a lapse that as if never been" (Beckett 1984: 286). Reader adds a confirming "Yes" as he repeats the phrase. Reader's second action comes immediately after when he then attempts to "turn back" the book to "page forty, paragraph four" (ibid.: 286), but is checked by Listener's slightly raised left hand (ibid.: 286). As he returns to his reading, during the third line after being checked, he must turn a page to complete the story. When Reader finishes reading, "Nothing is left to tell" (ibid.: 288). Reader's closing of the book is signaled by Listener's penultimate knock. It is only after the book is closed, and on Listener's final knock that—after five seconds of silence— Reader and Listener "lower their right hands to table, raise their heads and look at each other. Unblinking. Expressionless" for a full ten seconds before the final fade out (ibid.: 288).

Against the stark non-movement of these two mirror-like figures, each of these seemingly simple actions takes on monumental proportion. Especially so the concluding act of allowing their heads to rise and become visible to the audience for the first time in the performance as they look (in)to the Other. It is the spareness and slow pace of these few actions-in-performance that allow *Ohio Impromptu* to become, as Jonathan Kalb expressed it above, an act of meditation. From my perspective on stage playing Reader, the performance is a meditative act for performers as well as audience. While the audience's act of meditation is necessarily somewhat passive, for Andy Crook and me, ours is an active form of meditation as we engage and direct our *ki*-awareness/energy and open our senses within each acting task. Performing *Ohio Impromptu* is very much a form of seated *taiqiquan* with words. In its non-movement, text, gesture, and environment must be suffused with the quality, modulation, and movement of *ki*-awareness/ energy. As illustrated in the opening of the text, the amount of white space to be filled is considerable, such as the numerous pauses that set off each section of the reading:

> Little is left to tell. In a last—
> [L knocks with left hand on table.]
> Little is left to tell.
> [Pause. Knock.]
> In a last attempt to obtain relief he moved
>   from where they had been so long together
>   to a single room on the far bank. From its
>   single window he could see the downstream
>   extremity of the Isle of Swans.
> [Pause.]
> Relief he had hoped would flow from
>   unfamiliarity . . .
>
> (Beckett 1984: 285)

The first white space is that prompted by Listener's initial knock for a repeat of the initial sentence. Then there are the white spaces of the two pauses. It is the actors' task to fill these white spaces without calling attention to that silent movement of energy/awareness with which these spaces are filled. In its subtle deployment of inner awareness/ energy *taiqi* explores the spaces between inhalation and exhalation. Psychophysically it is precisely this sense of inhabitation of the spaces between that is necessary in *Ohio Impromptu*.

The actors' tasks in *Ohio Impromptu* are made

particularly difficult by the physical position in which Reader and Listener are placed—with heads propped on right hands the actors are denied the possibility of utilizing the eyes or face as a medium of expression. Except for the concluding act of looking to each other, all actor-to-actor and actor-to-audience communication is indirect and/or peripheral. This means that the actors' awareness and deployment of their *ki*-energy must reach beyond their immediate kinesphere (the space your body takes up).

The training is particularly relevant to the type of energy and engagement necessary when delivering the melodic contours and inner resonance of the text in *Ohio Impromptu*. Work on awakening and activating one's vocal resonators while training is important in terms of finding a resonant pitch and tone through which to voice and "play" the text within a narrow range "without colour." In my own work on Reader, I utilize my chest resonator. When we warm up prior to a performance, we wake up all five resonators and access the particular pitch I find most resonant in the sternum. At the last moment before the house is open and the audience enters to discover Reader and Listener, I settle into my chair, ground my feet to the floor, re-sound and re-tune the pitch within the sternum resonator, and sound parts of the text. Given that Reader is looking down at the table to read the text before him, and that the head rests on the right hand, projection of the voice is technically difficult. I must engage and maintain throughout the performance a peripheral, sensory awareness of the top of my head in order to keep the spine lengthened and the sound going out to reach the back wall of the auditorium, as well as to pass through Andy/my Other beside me.

In *Ohio Impromptu* we encounter the problem of how consciousness of thought is to be actively inhabited and embodied by the actor. When acting, consciousness of thought does *not* mean that the actor takes the thought as an object of reflection; rather, consciousness of thought must be understood as an embodied process in which the actor is aware of the movement of thought in one's bodymind as it happens. How is this possible?

As in *Piece of Monologue* and *Footfalls*, in *Ohio Impromptu* the text moves between the third and first person, as in the following passage:

> One night as he sat trembling head in hands from head to foot a man appeared to him and said, I have been sent by—and here he named the dear name—to comfort you. Then drawing a worn volume from the pocket of his long black coat he sat and read till dawn. Then disappeared without a word.
>
> (Beckett 1984: 287)

Significantly, Beckett does *not* place quotation marks around the first person, "I have been sent by." This invites into the actor's reading an active dialectic between first and third person. I both am and am not the figure about whom I am reading, just as I am both this Other who listens, and my (identical) self.

Wherever we find this dialectic between first and third person in Beckett's texts, for the actor it invites deployment of the consciousness of thought *as it happens.* Part of my task is to engage the act of reading the text as both me and my Other beside me. In each moment of performance I *cannot* know whether my associations will be of my self as the I, of the text, or of the Other he whose story I am reading. It is the very openness of this mode of dialectical engagement that invites one form of inner movement, vibration, and awareness of the text in its said-ness. Kinesthetically following the thought as it moves between helps to create a felt sense of this movement of thought.

This awareness is enhanced in two other ways. First, in the act of saying/speaking I work with the feel of the words said as they are said. In the passage quoted immediately above, Beckett's use of so many "h's" and end "t's" gives the first sentence a particular shape in the mouth that provides the kinesthetic feel of trembling . Second, the movement of thought is enhanced by becoming Listener to the story as I read it. I must actually hear, and receive as Other what is said. This aural sense of literally hearing and absorbing the said allows me at times to inhabit not only the position of self/Reader, but also of my Other/Listener.

In contrast to playing *Act Without Words I* where I do not utilize an active image or associations, in *Ohio Impromptu* I work with one specific active image throughout and allow numerous associations to arise—giving the Other a warm, soothing sponge bath. Each sentence/thought becomes a tender, cleansing stroke with a warm sponge, soothing the Other. This image is reflected in the notion that Reader has "been sent by . . . the dear name—to comfort" (Beckett 1984: 287).

The meditative nature of *Ohio Impromptu* and this active image invite and call up various personal associations—my ninety-one-year-old father, my long-deceased but very "alive" mother, my partner, or Andy-as-present-Other, or my self as that Other. My performances in Madison, Wisconsin in September 2006 were informed by the fact that I was undergoing chemotherapy at the time for treatment of life-threatening cancer of the bladder. Particular associations are not planned, nor are they indulged. They pass in and out of my chiasmatic awareness, resonating with feeling and energy as I attend to the primary tasks of reading and listening. The most important among these is the presence of Andy/Listener-as-Other in the moment. The reading is always to/through both Andy and my Self as the I to be comforted.

The engagement of the active image of bathing the Other, and the range of associations it offers do not, however, constitute an interpretation per se. If sustained, the image and its attendant associations render a quality of engagement in action. Jonathan Kalb has put forward one particular interpretation of the story:

> Reader recites a story of a man who moves away from a place where he was "so long alone together" with a companion—probably a lover ("the dear name"), who may or may not have died—to a "single room on the far bank" from whose "single window he could see the downstream extremity of the Isle of Swans."

> Subsequently, the man is visited from time to time by a stranger, who may or may not have been "sent" by the lover.
>
> (Kalb 1989: 49)

However plausible Kalb's interpretation, as he himself says, "as soon as one attempts any explanation . . . its various levels of significance interconnect ironically and lead to a multiplicity of meanings" (1989: 49). For the actor as Reader or Listener, to fix any interpretation and the associations that arise in the act of reading and listening would foreclose the possibility of the active play of one's active imagination/association at the moment of reading, and therefore foreclose possibilities for the audience.

As in *Rockaby*, there is a dialectical engagement between the two actors as Self and Other with the difference that in *Rockaby* there is the single self on stage, and in *Ohio Impromptu* the actor's Other is literally present and available for engagement. These tactics create a feedback loop within the bodymind awareness of the actor which can heighten one's awareness of the said as-it-is-being-said. Behind the overt stillness of the piece must be the inner vibration and resonance of the relationship to the words, story, and its images as they are evoked. Reader and Listener are *not* frozen in the still-life image Beckett evokes, but *alive* in this stillness.

At work on *Not I*[5]

In this section my close and long-term collaborator Patricia Boyette and I reflect on our work on *Not I*. From the time of our first encounter with Billie Whitelaw in 1995, one of the main images she used to describe the delivery of the text was as an act of vomiting:

> . . . out . . . into this world . . . this world . . . tiny little thing . . . before its time . . . In a godfor—. . . what?. girl?. yes . . . tiny little girl . . . into this . . . out into this . . . Before her time . . . godforsaken hole called . . . called . . . no matter

... parents Unknown ... unheard of ...

(Beckett 1984: 216)

At the time of an initial reading of the text with Beckett and director Alan Schneider in Paris in 1972 in preparation for the world premiere at the Forum of Lincoln Center, Jessica Tandy recalls that while Beckett "didn't use the word 'vomited out,'" it is as though there is no control, the mouth is not controlling anything, the sound

> is just pouring out: "spewed out." If you look at one of those stone lions in a fountain; the water gushes out of its mouth. And it was a wonderful thing to keep in my head. I found that you must not think what you are saying; it just has to come out. The difference was that instead of, say, an exclamation mark, there would be nothing—or else there would be four dots. But it all makes perfectly good sense, musically [...] I found the less I thought about it and the more the mouth was working on its own, the righter it was.
>
> (in Knowlson and Knowlson 2006: 236)

In addition to the image of vomiting or spewing out the text, Billie Whitelaw has also described her experience of performing *Not I* as "like an athlete crashing through barriers, but also like a musical instrument playing notes" (in Knowlson and Knowlson 2006: 170). The actress encountering this convoluted, highly repetitious, tightly structured text and its demands is very much like a 100-metre Olympic sprinter who simultaneously must play notes while in a race for one's life.

The active images of vomiting and of an athlete crashing through barriers reflect the quality and experience of delivering what is without doubt one of the most difficult texts an actor could ever confront in terms of memorization if nothing else.

When we began work on *Not I*, one of our first concerns was technical. We wanted to design an apparatus that would allow Patricia to remain grounded while she ran this race. We wanted her to keep her lower abdomen supported, her spine lengthened, and her head still. Our solution was simple: a padded head-rest which supports Patricia's forehead, allowing her to keep her head still; a black megaphone-style cone through which Mouth appears when lit by a single tightly focused spotlight and through which her vocal delivery is amplified; a set of handle-bars for Patricia to grasp and a padded office chair set at a level which allows her to keep both hands and feet grounded, her lower abdomen supported, and her spine lengthened. The use of a cone megaphone allows Patricia's voice to project naturally, making it unnecessary to use an invisible microphone as indicated in the original text (Beckett 1984: 216).

Our early preparatory work focused on psychophysically preparing Patricia for the extraordinary difficulties of performing Mouth. Particularly important was working on Patricia's awareness of her lower abdomen and feet so that when seated she could generate support and energy from her lower body for delivery of the text and keep her voice from rising up in the body and constricting. In the box below, Patricia Boyette reflects at length on our approach to, and her experience of working on Mouth.

⊙ DVD-ROM: PATRICIA BOYETTE

Patricia Boyette reflects on *Not I* (Boyette and Zarrilli 2007: 76–79)

The Beckett roles on which I have worked—Mouth in *Not I*, Woman/Voice in *Rockaby*, Woman's Voice in *Eh Joe*, and most recently Winnie in *Happy Days*—get their energy from the act of striving to find answers to questions of life and death. It is not the answers to the questions that are important, but the compulsion to find a reason, or an "order" out of chaos. This is part of what propels things—finding a "yes" out of the world of "no."

When we started working on *Not I* in 1997, one of the problems was that if I went slowly with the text—which you have to do when you are learning it—it was hard to make any "connections." By connections, I mean whatever the journey is within the score I am developing. If I worked with my eyes open, it was very different from working with my eyes shut. Similarly, if I did it very still—staying in one place as it is done in performance—or if I allowed myself to move around, or if I did it at "speed," it would inform the work differently. The psychophysical connection would be different in each case. Part of the process with *Not I* was to allow myself to work in these different ways in order to discover these "layers" that might be present when performing the text, and therefore allow me to get the "sights" lined up. Just to be able to speak and think at the pace required by the piece was a huge challenge. Although it is always tremendously difficult to rehearse and perform *Not I*, it was fascinating to realize at some point that I *was* able to think and function on these different "tracks" simultaneously—to keep the mouth going, keep the words going, the breath centered, the tension controlled, the images separate and connected psychophysically, etc. I had to have a primary focus working along one track by being "in the moment" in the text, but at the same time I found that I was able to subtly be aware of and legislate, and to some degree control what was happening with regard to my breath, body, tension, and degree and flow of energy.

So eventually I was able to regulate, simultaneously, all of these "tracks" while still remaining focused on what was in the foreground—my connection with those images, text, and words. This is something that the psychophysical training helped me to do. First, by being aware of all the elements that go into the way the body communicates—internal focus and external focus, and to what degree external focus operates, to what degree internal focus works, where the energy is in the body, and if it's too high in the body. Is it going through the feet and hands, and is it being blocked along the way? I do not mean to make this sound as though I can do this all the time, but it was an important discovery for me that I could do this at all—especially under the extreme conditions that Beckett sets for his actors.

To some degree in the past before our collaboration began, I had also rehearsed by "layering" work on text and character, sometimes concentrating on text, sometimes on the physicalization of the character, sometimes on vocal issues, etc. And it was taken for granted that through rehearsal these various experiences would "line up," i.e., come together naturally where relevant and inform the work. What was new with this work was the continuous repetition of a set of psychophysical exercises that allowed me to discover with more depth and clarity how my own particular body, mind, emotions, thoughts connected to and informed each other. I focused and worked constantly on my energy by noticing "it is blocked here," or "at this point my energy is more external." I noticed how at particular moments I could "be more internal" in my relationship to an action, where I could relate in the moment to "what's happening to me in the space," and where my breath is "too high here" or "too shallow there." It is the conditioning brought about by the repetition, and constant focus on the psychophysical elements that is so different. Therefore, it becomes easier to know what is happening to me in the moment of performance and how to adjust things if and when necessary. These subtle adjustments become part of a practical psychophysical vocabulary. I think what the psychophysical work has done for me, and the overall value it has in training, is that it invites the actor to discover in a very practical way how their particular body, mind, breath, and emotions, "connect" and how that connection is fluid, and therefore can ideally be regulated and adjusted during performance.

Looking back at our earliest work together [performances of Franca Rame monologues in 1993], at that time I had a center that was much higher and wider than it is now. I was like a helium balloon! And through the psychophysical work [. . . I gradually . . .] settled into the earth. Just in terms of that basic centering, I know that my center has dropped and is more connected with my breath. I do not feel like this is a "heavy" grounding, but it is certainly *not* a high center. Overall, I believe I have become much more "centered" and therefore balanced. This allows for a greater range, depth, and clarity of psychophysical connections—how to recognize them and how to regulate them.

In my experience of *Not I*, the impulse is often equivalent to the action. There is an extreme physical need to tell all of this, to get it out, to purge herself. On top of this there is an urgent need for the character to tell all of this, i.e., to "get it right"—to be accurate—to "make sense of it." Billie Whitelaw used the image of all these words "vomiting" forth—nothing she can do about it—it's all coming out whether she wants it to or not—and in addition there is a "tormentor" (the brain god) that tortures her as with an electric cattle-prod each time there is the "buzzing" or the light that comes and goes. It is *very* physical. One reason for impulse and action being so close as to be almost one and the same in *Not I* is the speed at which the piece moves.

When we first rehearsed *Not I*, there was clearly this sense of vomiting forth, or a dam breaking and a tremendous surge of water rampaging forth. These are imagistic metaphors that seem to work to "trigger" the beginning for me. But this is not always an image that triggers a physical action. Sometimes the trigger for the action is something specifically sensory, such as an observation of her condition. For example, "feeling so dulled . . . she did not know . . . what position she was in . . . imagine! . . . what position she was in! . . ." (Beckett 1984: 217). Or, it might be an idea or discovery such as, " . . . that notion of punishment . . . which had first occurred to her . . . was perhaps not so foolish . . . after all . . ." (1984: 217). Yet another is the onset of a memory, such as " . . . sitting staring at her hand . . . where was it? Crocker's Acres . . ." (1984: 220). Then there might be a decision, such as, "try something else . . . think of something else . . ." (1984: 222). And sometimes impulse and action are almost the same thing. The impulse *is* the action here, such as when she says, "Imagine!"

Underneath all this of course I have to stay grounded from the psychophysical work so that the voice does not rise up. I need to keep it connected to the gut and the earth/floor, and then "fill" [. . .] the "negative" space behind and around me [see Chapter 3] so that I am not sucked into the vortex. So here I am using our psychophysical work to support and "ground" my impulses and actions.

There is also of course a tremendous personal journey involved in working on *Not I*. One of the questions is how the physical, emotional, psychological state of the actor affects the performing of *Not I*, and vice-versa, i.e., how doing *Not I* affects the state of the actor. Billie Whitelaw and other actresses have talked about the physical and emotional toll taken in performance of the piece. Some people think this is either an over-reaction or over-dramatization of the actress' experience. My own experience is that this is not at all an over-dramatization. By going to "the brink," edge or extreme required in *Not I*, in early rehearsals and the first few times I performed the piece, it took a decided physical as well as emotional toll.

During our first workshop rehearsals and performances of *Not I* in Aberystwyth, I made the decision to work without prompting. Although I got through the piece quite well during our rehearsal period, in the first performance I went "off" the text and got lost. I experienced this as like a "break-down." My mind was "short-circuiting," and I could not make the connections I had made in rehearsal. It was like a panic attack. It was extremely confusing. I did not know whether something was physically happening to me in terms of my mind not being able to memorize and remember this text the way it once did. I really wondered whether there was something "wrong" with me neuro-physiologically. It brought me into a state of dissociation. So, what the play is largely about was actually happening to me. And that was terrifying . . . actually terrifying. But what I learned from that experience is that if you go "too far" or too fast with the text for the mind and the body so that it is not physically and emotionally possible to be present, then there is "break-down." In retrospect, I do not think there was anything wrong with me, but at the time it did seem there might be something amiss. As a woman at that time I was actually going through hormonal shifts, and physiologically of course that may have had something to do with my entering this dissociative state.

When we opened the production in Los Angeles in 2000, we developed a cueing system which allowed me to have control over access to prompting if and when I needed or wanted it, and therefore allowed me to make more use of all the psychophysical work. This cueing system provided me with a safety-net. Doing the piece I am on a high-wire. Now I had the safety-net below me. This did not provide me with a sense of security or "rest," but it *was* there. Nevertheless, when we opened and performed *Not I* in Los Angeles, it still took its toll. There was still a sense of depression and fear resulting from performing *Not I*. In LA I physically got through it, even though I had a terrible flu!

When we remounted *Not I* for the limited UK tour in 2001, it did not take quite as much out of me personally as before. When I returned to *Not I* again in 2003 and 2006, the point was to get through the process without being quite so emotionally or physically beaten up while still finding the edge and walking that line between going to the extreme and not going far enough. And that is where the work lives and comes alive and is fully realized. The text itself and its images have, of course, become much more "familiar" to me with each set of performances, at least in the beginning part of performance of the text. That familiarity has allowed me to work in our most recent set of rehearsals in a subtler way on allowing the images to drop in psychophysically, and thereby allowing me to fine-tune some of the rhythmic demands of the text per se. This is a mixed blessing because the "edge" that personal panic can play for me in simply trying to remember the text may not be as sharp. So we have been exploring how the psychophysical work with kinesthetic awareness can help me to maintain an "edge" without having to remain in a state of personal panic.

Maintaining the "edge" when performing *Not I* comes in part from our continuing work on Patricia's experience of the consciousness of thought *as it happens*. When the text is operating in third person describing the state/condition in which the first person (actress) finds herself *now* in this moment of performance, the relationship between describing the present and inhabiting the present has the possibility of creating this edge. One such moment near the beginning of the text is when Mouth further qualifies the fact that she "found herself in the dark . . ." and where "she did not know . . . what position she was in . . . imagine! . . . what position she was in! . . . whether standing . . . or sitting . . ." (Beckett 1984: 217).

Then there are the moments when Mouth is describing how consciousness of thought becomes aware of itself in the act of speaking, mouthing specific words which have a certain feel in the act of saying, such as the following:

> . . . when suddenly she felt . . . gradually she felt . . . her lips moving . . . imagine!. Her lips moving! . . . as of course till then she had not . . . and not alone the lips . . . The cheeks . . . the jaws . . . the whole face . . . all those— . . . what? . . . the tongue? . . .? yes . . . the tongue in the mouth . . . all those contortions without which . . . no speech possible . . .
>
> (Beckett 1984: 219)

The act of speaking which is usually absent to us as and when we speak, is suddenly foregrounded within the actress' bodymind and creates a consciousness of thought as it is being felt in the act of saying. As such subtleties of performing the

text have revealed themselves they have provided a continuing "edge" for Patricia's work.

● DVD-ROM: *EH JOE*

At work on *Eh Joe*[16]

> [I]t is the live actor, the fact of life in the actor, that finally animates Beckett's stage pictures and amplifies the impact of their disturbing, melancholy beauty—even though that animation gains expression only through the most highly calculated sounds and movements. And every bit of psychological characterization, every hint of a complex, nonfictional life extending beyond the simple picture, weakens the effect of that sense of pure existence.
>
> (Kalb 1989: 66)

Nowhere is Kalb's statement more relevant than in the work I have undertaken to stage *Eh Joe* as a live but mediated televisual experience for an audience. I have directed and/or acted in three stage productions of this thirty-minute drama originally written for television. The premise of my approach has always been to provide the audience with an experience of the life in the actor juxtaposed with mediated images of the live. The 1995 production featured Peder Melhuse as Joe and Karole Spangler as Voice, and was staged in a fully equipped, professional television studio with three cameras. The 1999 Theater Asou production in Graz, Austria, with Christian Heuegger as Joe and Uschi Litschauer as Voice was staged as part of a city festival in a site-specific location—a part of a huge, old, wooden machine shed was adapted into a bed-sit. We used a single camera. For the production at the Granary Theatre in Cork, Ireland, in 2004 Patricia Boyette was Voice while I played Joe. Unlike the two earlier productions, our license for the 2004 performance stipulated that the audience view the production in the theater on television monitors; therefore, the live performance was staged in a small upstairs studio at the Granary Theatre with a live feed to large television monitors in the theater below. I focus my attention here on the 1995 and 2004 productions.

Each production and performance is a live broadcast of the television play—staged as written and following Beckett's precise stage directions for the movements of the camera as it dollies ever closer to Joe until the final position, in which Joe's face fills the entire screen and the image slowly dissolves. Each production creates a drab bed-sit with a single bed, door, window, and cupboard with curtains drawn closed. Along the back wall several television monitors are inserted into the surface. Although her voice is mediated by a microphone, the actress playing Voice delivers her devastating text from a perch located just above the set. Voice is draped in a head-covering shroud made of the same fabric as the walls. Dimly lit throughout, she remains a human presence, looking down on Joe from above as her mediated voice fills the studio via speakers. In the studio the audience watches a live performance juxtaposed with the mediated image of Joe. The audience in Cork, Ireland, watching the performance on television monitors, know that the actors are in a studio above them performing what they are seeing and hearing in the moment. In both the studio and in the theatre the live presence of the actors creates an additional layer of interiority not available when viewing a prerecorded television performance. Each production emphasizes this "now-ness."

As the audience enters, Joe is already seated on his single bed in an "intent pose" (Beckett 1984: 201), staring ahead. Joe slowly executes each of the initial five sets of actions described as follows in the script:

1 . . . getting up, going to windows, opening window, looking out, closing window, drawing curtain, standing intent.

2 . . . going from window to door, opening door, looking out, closing door, locking door, drawing hanging before door, standing intent.

3 . . . going from door to cupboard, opening cupboard, looking in, closing cupboard, locking cupboard, standing intent.

4 . . . going from cupboard to bed, kneeling down looking under bed, getting up, sitting down on edge of bed as when discovered, beginning to relax.

5 Joe seen from front sitting on edge of bed, relaxed, eyes closed. Hold, then dolly slowly in to close-up of face. First word of text stops this movement.

(Beckett 1984: 201)

Each of the first four sets of actions is concerned with what Joe perceives in the moment as he directs his consciousness/awareness to each place in the room. When playing Joe, I inhabit each action/moment with *ki*-awareness/energy shaped as a question to which there is no answer—"is there . . .?" By the fifth set of actions, when I sit on the edge of the bed with my hands on my thighs and allow my eyes to close, I release into each ensuing inhalation/exhalation sensing that, until now, there has been no response to this question.

Interrupting the ensuing silence, Voice begins its work on Joe—"low, distinct, remote, little colour, absolutely steady rhythm, slightly slower than normal" (Beckett 1984: 201–202):

Joe . . .
[Eyes open, resumption of intentness.]
Joe . . .
[Full intentness.]
Thought of everything? . . . Forgotten nothing? . . . You're all right now, eh? . . . No one can see you now . . . No one can get at you now . . . Why don't you put out that light? . . . There might be a louse watching you . . . Why don't you go to bed? . . . What's wrong with that bed,

Joe? . . . You changed it didn't you? . . . Made
no difference? . . . Or is the heart already? . . .
Crumbles when you lie down in the dark . . .
Dry rotten at last . . . Eh Joe?
[Camera move 1.]

(Beckett 1984: 202)

Woman's Voice activates Joe to open his eyes and
"resume intentness." The question, "is there?" has
been answered by the presence, once again in this
moment, of this voice in his head. Whenever Voice
is speaking, Beckett insists that Joe's eyes remain
"unblinking" and his face "impassive except in
so far as it reflects mounting tension of *listening*"
(1984: 202). When Voice momentarily stops
speaking, Joe relaxes his "intentness" thinking
that "perhaps voice has relented for the evening"
(Beckett 1984: 202).

In our approach, Joe's intentness derives
from the actor's listening to Voice and from Joe's
constant attempt to squeeze the voice out of his
head. Joe's effort to rid himself of this voice in
his head derives from the line, "That's right, Joe,
squeeze away . . ." (Beckett 1984: 205). Each time
Voice begins "in on him" again, when Joe hears
her first word he raises his head to eye level,
directs his external gaze into the camera, remains
unblinking, and literally attempts to squeeze the
voice out of his head. As Voice continues and does
not stop, he *must* hear it even as he attempts to
squeeze it out. It is important for the actor playing
Joe that he not know if or when Voice will or will
not stop speaking. It is only when he actually
senses that Voice has stopped, that he can relax
"intentness"—in the hope that Voice *has* stopped.

To prepare an actor for this incredibly difficult
act of squeezing, I use one of the preparatory
exercises of *kathakali* dance-drama intended to
develop plasticity in the facial muscles. In this
exercise, while keeping the eyes unblinking and
the upper lids open, the actor contracts his lower
lids by literally pushing "the [inner] wind" from
the lower abdominal region. This is used to help
create the expressive state of fury (*raudra*) in
kathakali. We use a simple, subtle version of this
state in the act of squeezing. Using this exercise

allows the actor to literally engage his entire
bodymind in the act of squeezing. It is exhausting
work. At a technical level it is next to impossible
for the actor to keep his upper eyelids open as
long as required for the delivery of each passage
of the text; however, it is the actor's literal struggle
with this extremely difficult psychophysical task
and the act of squeezing the voice away that help
create inner activation for the actor playing Joe.
During the approximately thirty minutes of the
performance the task becomes more and more
difficult. The weight of the stories he is *made* to
hear and absorb weighs on him. The actor inhabits
a torturous space-time *in extremis* as he is unable to
stop Voice from telling the story he does not want
to hear. Peder Melhuse concluded that playing Joe
was "exhausting physically and emotionally" (1995
journal entry).

The exhaustion of playing Joe derives from
being on the receiving end of the story Voice
tells and how the actress tells it. Billie Whitelaw
explained the primary active image she used as
Voice as a form of "Chinese water torture." Each
phrase is delivered without color as though a
drop of water is dripped into Joe's head.[17] Placing
the actress in the studio *above* Joe, looking down
from behind, allowed us to enhance the actress'
engagement in the image while delivering the text.
Maintaining this image is an extremely difficult
task for an actress. For the 2004 production,
Patricia Boyette and I added a second active image
to that of Chinese water torture—each phrase
delivered is a needle piercing the skin as she
stitched up Joe with her stories.

Using these two active images, Joe and Voice
are in a constant struggle as Voice drops a phrase
into his head or pierces his skin with a phrase. Joe
attempts to push out the drop of water or stop the
needle from piercing. This active struggle in the
moment produces, for Joe, an immense sense of
relief each time the Voice seems to stop.

In live performances of *Eh Joe*, the televised Joe
is present as the "thing-body" (*Körper*), juxtaposed
with the "body-alive-to-itself" (*Leib*) of the actor
playing Joe. This juxtaposition is evident from
the sweat on Joe's brow or the tears forming in his

unblinking eyes—both writ large on the television screen as the camera dollies ever closer, taking in the intimate details of Joe's intent face. This play between "thing-body" and "lived body" is further enhanced by the presence of the actress playing Voice. Her "lived body" present in the studio is juxtaposed against her "thing-like" voice as it is mediated/projected on the studio's speakers.

In addition to the use of active images, when developing the actress' work on Voice we utilized two additional tactics for accessing a fully lived embodiment of the text in its saidness: (1) the actress listens to each word/phrase as it is said in order to create an inner aural loop with what is said, and (2) the concomitant act of *feeling the words in the mouth* as they are shaped and said. Earlier in this case study (p. 157) I gave the example of *active perception* stimulated by Voice's articulation when delivering the conclusion of the story about "the green one, the narrow one." Voice is describing how "the green one" committed suicide. The constant use of "s" and "sh" sounds helps to create the sound of the tide as it is being described in the telling:

> Sees from the seaweed the tide is flowing . . .
> Goes on down to the edge and lies down with
> her face in the wash . . . Cut a long story short
> doesn't work . . . Gets up in the end sopping
> wet and back up to the house . . . Gets out the
> Gillette . . . The make you recommended for her
> body hair . . . Back down the garden and under
> the viaduct . . . Takes the blade from the holder
> and lies down at the edge on her side . . . Cut
> another long story short doesn't work either . . .
> You know how she always dreaded pain . . .
> (Beckett 1984: 206)

The "tt's" of "Gillette" and "cut" cut against the soft sound of the sea as it washes the stone with the tide. Throughout this lengthy speech, and the concluding section of Voice's text, the tension between *Körper* and *Leib* is especially evident.

> [Voice drops to whisper, almost inaudible
> except words in italics.] All right . . . You've had

the best . . . Now imagine . . . Before she goes . . .
Imagine . . . Face in the cup . . . Lips on a *stone* . . .
a stone . . .

(Beckett 1984: 206)[18]

In our performances as Patricia mouths the unvoiced (non-italicized) words in this lengthy ending speech the consonants click and clatter but are not fully heard. The voiced words emerge and force their way into consciousness above the background of the unheard:

> . . . imagine . . . imagine . . . stone . . . a stone . . .
> Joe Joe . . . stones . . . stones . . . lips . . . imagine
> . . . imagine . . . solitaire . . . stone . . . stone . . .
> eyes . . . the eyes . . . breasts . . . breasts . . . hands
> . . . imagine . . . imagine . . . . stones . . . . stones . . .

As Beckett requests in his stage directions, in the midst of this near-silent incantational materialization of the (immaterial) Woman's body (is it, was it, present?), Joe's image now begins to literally fade as a dissolve begins, and as Voice continues its occasionally audible recitation rising about the sound of the waves of consonants in the background:

> What are they fondling? . . . Till they go . . .
> There's love for you . . . Isn't it, Joe? . . . Wasn't it,
> Joe? Eh Joe? . . . Wouldn't you say? . . . Compared
> to us . . . Compared to Him . . . Eh Joe?
> (Beckett 1984: 207)[19]

On her final word, the monitors click out into blankness, the Voice stops, and Joe, with his "stinking mortality," remains visible to the studio audience sitting in the silence as the theatrical lights gradually close to complete blackness.

Engaging the performance of *Eh Joe* from her perch above the studio in 1995, Spangler made the following observation about her experience of performing *Eh Joe*:

> Beckett extracted pictures from his mind, along
> with their companion emotions, and placed
> them on stage . . . [so that] audiences respond

in primal, almost unvoicable ways. Every night of *Eh Joe* when the lights and monitors went out and the Voice stopped for the last time, the silence continued for what seemed to me a long time, then was broken by one person, then another, and then everyone, letting out the breath they'd been holding for who knows how long. None of them I talked to later could say, as none of them could remember, when they stopped breathing.

(Journal, 1995)

Why Beckett?

Each of the actors involved in *The Beckett Project* has discovered that there is a "necessary" to be found in acting Beckett which cannot be predetermined but must be discovered anew in each performance as the necessary becomes evident. Beckett demands this of the actors who engage his plays. Herbert Blau understood the presence of the "necessary" in both Beckett and the acting process. What can result from an encounter with the necessary in Beckett's plays is the "stink of mortality." This is not just the sweat of muscles working hard, but the sweat of the "heart"—Artaud's athlete as read through Blau's unremitting demand for "a deeper reverence of the mind's passion" (1976: 22). Here the actor-as-athlete begins to find what is necessary in Beckett, *and* in acting. As Jenny Kaminer explained,

> Throughout the rehearsal and performances of *Play*, my experiences ranged from elation to sheer terror to claustrophobia to utterly inexplainable emptiness . . . The terror I felt while in the urn was virtually all-consuming. One night I wanted to get out so bad I thought I would have to scream and stop the show, but somehow I just kept going: I opened my mouth and the right words poured out. Every night I lived in fear of forgetting my lines, and I dropped sweat as the light was on Karen or Jeff, paralyzed with panic.

(Journal, 1995)

8

The Water Station (*Mizu No Eki*) by Ōta Shōgo

[*The*] *Water Station* is an evocative antidote to our daily cacophony, offering quietude
as a way of theater . . . [using] the language of silence to contemplate man and his
relationship to natural elements.

(Gussow 1988: 17)[1]

[In *The Water Station*] . . . Ōta Shōgo breaks drama down . . . to its most basic elements . . .
We become systematically sensitized [to] the slow movements of the actors until we are
waiting with rapt attention for, say, Man A to . . . reach in for a drink of water. If drama can
be defined as waiting for something to happen, then a lot happens in *The Water Station*.

(Falkenstein 1998)[2]

Introduction

First created and performed in 1981 by Japanese
playwright/director Ōta Shōgo (1939–2006) and
the Theatre of Transformation (Tenkei Gekijo),
The Water Station is a remarkably suggestive,
poetic, non-verbal piece of theater. It has been
described as "visual poetry" (Neff 1998) and "'a
chamber piece that speaks in the rich language of
silence to the neglected part of the soul'" (quoted
in Montemayor 1998: 5). The published "'script as
document'" is a record of the psychophysical score
that resulted from the initial rehearsal process.[3]
The Water Station was devised and created from
a diverse set of source materials gathered from
plays, novels, paintings, poetry, film, as well as
some scripted dialogue initially authored and/or
selected by Ōta for possible use in some scenes
(Boyd 2006: 107–109).[4] The two main premises
guiding the company's development of the
performance score from these source materials

included "acting in silence, and to make that
silence living human time, acting at a very slow
tempo" (Ōta 1990: 150).[5]

The artistic process that crystallized for Ōta
while working on *The Water Station* has been
described by Mari Boyd as one of "divestiture"
(2006, *passim*), i.e., the discarding or paring away
of anything unnecessary from the performance
score and theatrical environment so that actors
and audience alike are taken out of their everyday
world and focus on the irreducible elements
of our shared existence—what Ōta calls "the
'unparaphrasable realm of experience'" (1990: 151).
As a result of this working method, Ōta's body
of work—especially his trilogy of non-verbal
"Station" plays (*The Water Station* (*Mizo no eki*,
1981), *The Earth Station* (*Chi no eki*, 1985), and *The
Wind Station* (*Kaze no eki*, 1986))—is "dominated
by silence, slow movement, and empty space"
(Boyd 2006: x).

When members of an audience enter a theater

for a performance of *The Water Station*, they immediately encounter the sound and sight of a constantly running, broken water faucet. As the thin stream of water from the spout hits the surface of the pool gathered in the basin, it creates a constant, base-line sound in an otherwise silent theater. To the audience's left and upstage of the broken faucet is a pathway—similar to that of the traditional *noh* stage—along which a series of travelers enter. The pathway leads them to a place near the "water station" center stage. Upstage center and behind the pathway is a huge pile of junk—shoes, tires, dishes, bicycles, birdcages, crates, etc. that have been discarded (or abandoned?). From the junk pile to the audience's right, the pathway continues—the way taken by each traveler as s/he departs.[6] In a series of nine scenes travelers enter the pathway from the audience's left alone, in pairs, or in a group:

Scene 1: A Girl [Figure 8.1];
Scene 2: Two Men (Man A with bedding or a
    futon on his back, Man B with a suitcase);
Scene 3: A Woman with a Parasol;
Scene 4: A Married Couple with an old baby
    carriage (filled with belongings);
Scene 5: An Old Woman wearing a single shoe
    (with a large basket on her back);
Scene 6: A Caravan including a Husband, Wife,
    three Daughters carrying laundry hung up to
    dry, two Young Men, and a Young Woman;
Scene 7: A Man and Woman;
Scene 8: A Man with a Huge Load on his Back;
Scene 9: A Girl.

First the Girl, and each traveler in turn, encounters and interacts with the water before continuing their journey and passing out of view.

Sometimes a traveler from one scene encounters those in another. In the transition from Scene 1 to Scene 2, when the Girl senses someone approaching, she sees two men approaching in the distance. Fascinated, she hides in the junk heap so that she can continue to observe them. When they discover and encounter the water, their two mouths lock together as they "fight for the slender

Figure 8.1 *The Water Station*: the Girl (Yoo Jeungsook) in Scene 1 "By the water [. . .] The girl watches the wind pass" (Ōta 1990: 157). (Photograph: Kimberly Tok, courtesy TTRP)

stream of water" (Ōta 1990: 161). Drawn toward them, the Girl stands to better see them. They sense her presence, turn, and discover her. When their eyes meet she is "pushed back by their gaze" so that she withdraws back into the junk heap (ibid.: 162). After the two men depart, as Scene 3 begins the Girl's attention is drawn to the Woman with a Parasol as she comes into view along the pathway: "The girl   trying to look away from the woman / Cannot   " (ibid.: 163).

During their moments of intense interaction, the Girl is so "pressured by the woman's dark eyes" that she cries out, "her open mouth [. . .] her wide open eyes" (Ōta 1990: 165). Avoiding the Woman, the Girl departs, leaving the Woman alone by the water clutching her broken parasol. During Scene 4 a Man emerges from the midst of the huge junk heap, brushes his teeth, reads an old newspaper, and observes the travelers and their interaction with the water station in Scenes 4, 5, 6, and 7 before disappearing as silently as he appeared during Scene 8.

For the duration of the approximately 100- to 120-minute performance the base-line sound created by the constantly running water is shaped into a dramatically variable soundscape in two ways. Each time a traveler interacts with the running water by touching it, taking a drink from the tap, filling a canteen, bathing, etc., the type of sound produced by the water changes. In Scene 7 when Man and Woman arrive at the water station, they gradually shed most of their clothes to bathe in the basin. When the water initially touches the Woman's skin, there is a period of absolute silence until the water begins to drip off her skin. The sound of individual drops of water dripping off the Woman's skin and hitting the pool creates an entirely different pitch, volume, and quality of sound from the base line of the constantly running stream. The sound shifts register according to both what the water hits and the mode, quality, and type of interaction of each surface with the water. The soundscape is also shaped by Ōta's strategic scoring of occasional incidental music, such as Erik Satie's *Three Gymnopédies*, No. 1, which is heard in the background in the transition between the Girl's encounter with the water at the end of Scene 1 and the entrance of the Two Men at the beginning of Scene 2, or the growing presence of Albinoni's Oboe Concerto during much of the Caravan scene.

While working on *The Water Station*, Ōta and his company were exploring the process of how to "stage living silence" (Ōta 1990: 151). In a program note to the 1985 Tokyo production, Ōta asked,

> Is it not possible to construct a drama from the nature of human existence itself rather than from elements of human behavior? I feel this question lies behind my search for appropriate dramatic experiences and my approach towards silence as a dramatic expression in itself . . . To me . . . silence is not so much a thing but a very

realistic situation. In the course of one day, I wonder how much time we spend uttering words (i.e., we are out of silence)? . . . [W]e spend almost 90% of our lives in silence . . . [S]ilence is not a kind of irregular behavior which belongs to special circumstances; rather it is the reality of our normal state. To exist, therefore, means to be mainly in silence . . . The silence may spring from the great amount of words that fills that human being's existence . . . The "Drama of Silence" which I am trying to construct is not designed to exalt human beings to some mystical height, but rather to root them in the fact of "being there." I want to explore the depths of the silence which occupies 90% of all our lives.

> (in Sarlos 1985: 137–138)

If, as Ōta states, silence is the human norm, then it can be argued that "verbalization does not deserve the prominence granted it by a drama of activity" (Boyd 1990: 153).

Ōta's "drama of silence" is first and foremost a divestiture of (unnecessary) words. Given the soundscape described above, Ōta's "living silence" is not the absence of any sound per se, but an attempt to turn down the volume of everyday life by abandoning the noise and clutter of our constantly wagging tongues and squirrel-like, busy minds. Ōta's theatrical silence is equally created by slowing the actors down so that each everyday action they perform is divested of anything unnecessary.[7] As reflected in *New York Times* critic Mel Gussow's response, the result is a performance score of minimal and monumental simplicity:

> [S]lowed . . . almost to a standstill . . . every second seems like a minute. Sometimes the movement is so minimal that it is imperceptible. Moving gracefully, but with glacial slowness, the people are like frozen figures . . . During those rare moments when there is a quick gesture by one of the actors, one is startled out of what has become a trancelike state.

> (1988: 17)

Along with divestiture, slowing actors down as well as slowing down their on-stage actions might also be described as a process of "decoction" for actors and audience alike—a lengthy process of "cooking" by which anything non-essential is taken away (see note 3 in Chapter 5). In each of his non-verbal "Station" plays, the *mise-en-scène* has been decocted to a point where only the essential elements of a particular environment remain on stage—in *The Water Station* the pathway, a running faucet, a junk heap. Removing anything unnecessary from the performance score and slowing down its performance decocts the audience's focus and concentration. Mel Gussow observed how *The Water Station* "tests a theatergoer's threshold of patience," resulting either in "rapt attention or in peaceful slumber." For Gussow himself the effect was "hypnotic and transporting" (1988: 17). Sid Smith of the *Chicago Tribune* found the work "hypnotic, compelling, challenging and exquisite, especially once one accepts Ōta's stringent demands on patience and concentration, only to gradually surrender to his unique capabilities as a stage innovator" (1988: 9).

Ōta's process of divestiture de-emphasizes "the functions of the playwright and director" and "return[s] the stage to the actor," i.e., "the physical presence of the actor in the here and now of the stage" becomes the focus (Boyd 2006: 97). Drawing inspiration from traditional *noh* acting during the 1970s and 1980s, Ōta and the Tenkei company evolved their own rigorous actor training process as a means of paring down the actor's overt modes of expression—"words, speech, gestures, and facial expressions" (Boyd 2006: 98–99)—to that fundamental relationship and confrontation in the moment between "the doer and done" (pp. 83–89 above). Tenkei's training regime eventually included four important elements: "(1) running to build endurance, (2) practicing Yoga *asana* to develop dynamic stillness, balance, and concentration [. . .], (3) doing Suzuki-method centering exercises to strengthen the lower body," and at many rehearsals (4) the repetition of "the slow walk" which forced the actors to work on "slowness, balance, and the preservation of the

natural arc of each step" (ibid.: 127). Similar to both the process and effect of the psychophysical training described in Chapter 4, the result of slowing down the actor's respiratory system through deep abdominal breathing is to distil the actor's relationship to each impulse and action so that this fundamental relationship becomes the focus of the audience's attention.[8] From the perspective of the actor, slowing down allows the actor to constantly maintain "the still centre of reality" (ibid.: 153) within oneself while embodying each state of being/doing that constitutes the score. The actor's dynamic inner energy (*ki*) thereby resonates with and between the actor qua actor and the actor's fictive body as one inhabits each action and state of being/doing. The actor must "exist purely in the here and now" (ibid.: 77).

Robert K. Sarlos describes the quality and affect of this process of divestiture or decoction with regard to the Girl's entrance during the 1985 production of *The Water Station* in Tokyo as follows:

> My body has hardly adjusted to the cramped space, my eyes to the dim light, when I grow aware of Young Girl [Tomoko Ando] . . . on the stage left walkway. Is she standing still? No, she is moving. Slower than I have ever seen a human being move, she lifts one foot, places it with control and grace in front of the other, and repeats this movement with her second foot. Her entire torso moves along almost imperceptibly. In about eight minutes, she traverses the dozen feet that brings her near enough to the tap to notice it.
>
> (Sarlos 1985: 131)[9]

In this slowed-down, non-verbal world, time itself slows down to a point where "silence breathes as living human time, not as form" (Ōta 1990: 150). Without the constant chatter of talking heads, for actors and audience alike the visual and auditory senses of observing and listening open up and are heightened. "[B]y reducing the tempo . . . Ōta breaks the dynamic propulsion of activity and enables the attention to linger on seemingly trivial events, leading to a new perception of life" (Boyd 1990: 153).

A simple, slowly performed, fully inhabited walk, look or gesture can "speak" volumes without literally speaking a single word. As one reviewer explained, *The Water Station* makes the audience notice the intricacies happening on the stage . . . Small movements and emotions which easily could have been forgotten in a "real-life-tempo" play, become grand and gorgeous in their simplicity—for example, the way the water falls from a hand into a basin, with light illuminating each drop.
(Reed 1998)

Given the stark, barren landscape and the length of time the audience has to observe each figure's relationship to each moment they inhabit that landscape, "stark images of divestiture, wandering, and bare survival are presented in their unrelenting entirety" (Boyd 1990: 153). Ōta has been quoted as saying the play is located "'anywhere and everywhere, [in] a place out of time . . . There are words here . . . you just can't hear them'" (Montemayor 1998: 5).[10] In his Station plays, and in particular in *The Water Station*, Ōta presents to audiences "in as pure terms as possible the human condition of *aru*, of being flung together, unmediated by socio-cultural forces," i.e., "what Heidegger calls the quality of 'thrownness-into-being' (*geworfenheit ins Dasein*)" (Boyd 2006: 82).

In contrast to the overt activity and conventions of realist drama which provide motivations and actions for individual characters within a narrative structure that guides an audience toward making a particular interpretation or gaining a specific meaning from what they observe, Ōta intentionally explores "the power of passivity" (Boyd 2006: 3). The audience is passive in that the stripped down *mise-en-scène* and the actors' engagement with the slowed-down performance score do not guide them to a specific interpretation, meaning, or conclusion;

rather, there is space and time to allow associations to arise as shaped by the actors' qualitative deployment of their inner energy to each action in the score.

The development of Ōta Shōgo's minimalism

Because of the development of his unique aesthetic of quietude achieved through divestiture, Ōta Shōgo is considered one of the most notable playwrights and directors to have emerged during the 1960s from the Japanese experimental little theater (*shogekijo*) movement. If, as Mari Boyd argues, *The Water Station* is the "play that best illustrates Ōta Shōgo's aesthetics of quietude" (2006: 167), both his aesthetic and work did not materialize overnight. Rather, there was a lengthy process of experimentation and gestation that eventually produced both. Ōta co-founded the Theatre of Transformation (Tenkei Theatre Company) in 1968 with Hodojima Takeo, Shinagawa Toru, and others in Akasaka, Tokyo. During the early years of the company Ōta served as playwright, assistant director, and then director. By 1970 Ōta was designated head of the company, and provided leadership as its director and resident playwright until the company was disbanded in 1988.[11] During the first decade of its existence, the company mainly produced works by Ōta as he and the company struggled to discover their own "alternative theatre code" (Boyd 2006: 73).

When Ōta and the Tenkei actors decided to stage their next project on a traditional *noh* stage in 1977, Ōta's search for a means of divesting everything unnecessary from a live performance crystallized, and the company reached a turning-point in its development. Drawing on the well-known Japanese legend of Komachi as well as Kan'ami's (1333–1384) *noh* play, *Sotoba Komachi*, based on the legend, Ōta authored *The Tale of Komachi Told by the Wind* (*Komachi fuden*).[12] Once rehearsals of the play began on the actual *noh* stage, Yasumi Akihito reports how Ōta and the cast felt that the space itself and its history rejected their contemporary language. Confronted with the cosmic quality of the time-space of the noh stage, Ōta was forced to strip the actors of their social attributes. The task of rewriting or deleting lines began. By the time the actors reached their final rehearsal, the Old woman (Komachi) had been silenced,

(2004: 217)

By the premiere, during the two-and-a-half-hour performance, no lines were spoken for approximately two-thirds of the time. In terms of Ōta's script, more than half of the dialogue was suppressed and not spoken on stage.

An unkempt Old Woman (Komachi) appears on the bridgeway "dressed in a bedraggled 'twelve-layered' court kimono" bleached and faded white "by the passing years" (Ōta 2004: 220–221). Shuffling along with "peculiar slow steps" (Akihiko 1997: 74), she enters "as if searching for the whereabouts of the breeze or as if abandoning herself to the whims of a gentle wind." It takes her five minutes to reach the stage proper where she comes to "a halt . . . sway[ing] as the wind penetrates her kimono and caresses her body" (Ōta 2004: 221). "We in the audience, pulled in by this slow method of movement, which surpasses any category of realism, seem to enter into an unreal, a dream world" (Akihiko 1997: 74).

With Vivaldi's Piccolo Concerto in A Minor playing quietly at half tempo, the other actors slowly cross the bridgeway "as though bearing some sort of magic objects." Each is carrying an element of the Old Woman's dilapidated apartment—"a shabby old dresser, a tea chest, a Japanese-style low dining table, torn sliding wall panels" (Akhiko 1997: 74). As the Old Woman silently observes to herself, the apartment in which she lives materializes before her very eyes: "Is it a wind? Who . . . what . . . it's a glass door. A glass door is sliding this way. A low dining table is crawling along the ground. It's a procession. Always, always a procession comes at the end of a dream . . ." (Ōta 2004: 222).

Komachi proceeds to cook and (eventually) eat her breakfast noodles on stage. Although in everyday life this process takes minutes, Komachi inhabits a world in which time is not clock time, but an alternative frame within which dream, fantasy, and reality intermingle. In her silence, she encounters the historic Lesser Captain of the past as well as those who people the world of her present—her landlord, the family next door (Father, Daughter, Son), an old granny, and the Doctor and Nurse. *The Tale of Komachi Told by the Wind* follows the aesthetic logic of the phantasmal type of *noh* play in which there is a "rereading of a past event through a dream" and where "multiple time-spaces" simultaneously exist (Akihito 2004: 218).

> "Fuden," in the original Japanese title, usually means "to be transmitted from somewhere, somehow," "fu" is wind (and can also refer to "inner landscape" or the "movement of the heart"). The fragments of the story, like leaves dancing in the wind, gather on the stage and then scatter.
>
> (Akihito 2004: 217)

Just as the elements of the apartment materialized on her arrival on stage, each element dematerializes in the wind and is carried away along the bridgeway before the fantastic dance duet between Komachi and the young Son-next-door about whom she fantasizes. With the center-stage completely empty, the Old Woman departs along the bridgeway "as if alone searching for the whereabouts of the wind or as if abandoning herself to the whims of the gentle breeze" (Ōta 2004: 243).

The well-known Japanese theater critic Senda Akihiko described the 1977 production, performed as it was on the traditional *noh* stage with its minimal dialogue, as a "totally new theatrical experience" (1997: 73). It was

> a kind of daring, silent drama. Those of us who have somehow forgotten the richness that silence can have can now experience it anew [. . .] The peculiar stateliness pervading every aspect of this play owes nothing to the style

of *noh* itself but flows rather from the skillful use of a device that, thanks to a rupture in the speed of everyday life, can pull forth a delicate sense of the things that can be located at the bottom of human consciousness, feelings that can be grasped only at a very slow speed.

(Akihiko 1997: 73–75)

The process of working on *The Tale of Komachi Told by the Wind* propelled Ōta and his Tenkei actors toward the full realization of Ōta's aesthetic of quietude achieved through divestiture in *The Water Station* and the company's subsequent work.[13] It also first called to the attention of critics and the international theater world Ōta's unique aesthetic.[14] Mari Boyd describes Ōta's body of work as a whole as expressing

an austere vision of the bittersweet fragility of life [. . .] : individuals traverse life alone—their paths may cross, some relationships may be stable, but essentially each person is alone. His quiescent theatre is carefully constructed through divestiture to engender in us a powerful affirmation of human life.

(2006: 163)

In workshop, rehearsals, and performance

What initially attracted me to *The Water Station* was Ōta's unremitting aesthetic attention to the divestment of anything unnecessary from a performance score. Here was an aesthetic with a minimalism similar to but different from those of either the traditional Japanese *noh* theater or the plays of Samuel Beckett—each in its own way requiring actors to "stand still while not standing still." In *The Water Station* the actor must inhabit and embody the states of being/doing which constitute each slowed-down, everyday action in a psychophysical score.

Like one's relationship to performing *taiqiquan*, minimizing and slowing down actions requires the actor to revisit the very basis of the art of acting—the type, quality, resonance, and duration

of the actor's sensory relationship to each impulse and action that constitutes a score. Every action is placed under the microscopic gaze of the spectator. Any break in the actor's energetic connection to and attentiveness within a specific action is magnified and becomes readily evident to the outside eye.[15]

In the remainder of this chapter, I focus on how I applied the psychophysical training and its principles to *The Water Station* in two contexts: an intensive training workshop hosted by Gardzienice Theatre Association in Poland March 2–7, 2004,[16] and a full production[17] of *The Water Station* directed in September 2004 for the Theatre Training and Research Programme (TTRP)[18] at the Esplanade Theatre Studio, Singapore. The Singapore production included a cast of eighteen: eight professionals and ten third-year TTRP acting students. Of the eight professionals five were recent TTRP graduates, one a member of staff, and two were actors (Klaus Seewald and Jeungsook Yoo) who had trained extensively with me, assisted me in teaching and/or demonstrations of the training, and applied the training to previous productions I had directed. Among the eighteen in the cast, sixteen were from Asia (Singapore, Korea, Taiwan, China, Philippines, Japan, and India) and two from Europe (Austria and Poland).[19]

⊙ DVD-ROM: *THE WATER STATION*

Ōta's published "script as document"

The published performance score is a "script as document" (Ōta 1990: 150) that retrospectively records many of the actions and movements of the travelers within the *mise-en-scène* originally devised and staged by Ōta and the Tenkei actors. Both the 1990 and 2006 translations of *The Water Station* by Mari Boyd are arranged in three categories of side-by-side columns: main action, minor action, stage directions. The stage directions column provides occasional specific notes on lighting, incidental music, the sound of the water, and the placement and movement of actors within the *mise-en-*

scène. For example, the pathway is described as stretching "from upstage left in front of the heap of junk to stage right" (Ōta 1990: 157). When and how loud to play prerecorded music such as Erik Satie's *Three Gymnopédies*, No. 1, is specifically indicated (Ōta 1990: 159).

Unlike these literal stage directions, as seen below, the Girl's main actions in Scene 1 are evocative, suggestive, and in some cases almost enigmatic.[20]

Scene 1: The Girl
Main action
A girl
Alone
In the dim light
Comes walking

On the way up the small incline
The girl unexpectedly stops

The back of the walking girl

The back of the walking girl

The neck twists around
Toward the way she came
Toward the far expanse
Her face turns

From the far expanse   her gaze drops to
    near her feet
Then to the direction she is heading

The profile of the girl
Walking

Fingers to the lips
Of the profile   walking

Stopping   the face turns   to the
    watering place
The finely running water
The delicate sound of water
The girl descends   to the watering place

By the water
She sits down   basket on her knees

The girl watches the wind pass [Figure 8.1]

In the girl's hand   a red cup from the basket

Toward the fine line of water
The red cup

The transparent line
Disappears into the red cup

In the gaze of her eyes
The red cup   fills with water

From the line of water   the red cup moves
To the girl's mouth

The girl drinking water
The water flowing through her body
The empty cup   the sky in the girl's eyes

The hand stretching to the basket   stops
The girl's eyes   turn to the old road.
                        (Ōta 1990: 156–159)

Ōta has explained that what is recorded in the published text can only suggest but cannot literally reproduce or represent "the inner state[s]" the Tenkei actors created during their rehearsal period (1990: 151).

What can we learn from an analysis of Ōta's text? The analysis that follows is neither a literary/critical reading of *The Water Station* for what it means, nor a realist actor's analysis of the text for objectives or motivations. Rather, it examines the script and its structure to discover how to guide actors through a psychophysical encounter with Ōta's aesthetic. The analysis which follows was therefore *not* shared with the actors prior to beginning work on their feet in the studio at either Gardzienice or Singapore. The actors encountered *The Water Station* not as a text to be read and analyzed, but as an extension of their engagement of *ki*/sensory awareness applied to structured improvisations.

Jo–ha–kyu: dramatic structure and movement in *The Water Station*

Expanding on my earlier discussion of the development of Ōta's minimalism, the first part of this analysis focuses on how reading *The Water Station* via *noh* theatre's tripartite progress—*jo* (initiation), *ha* (continuation), *kyu* (completion)—sheds light on the structure and tempo-rhythm of Ōta's score. Bethe and Brazell define this fundamental pattern and its progression with reference to dramatic structure as follows: "*jo* is a quiet, simple, introduction, *ha*, a development or exposition, where complexities appear, and *kyu*, a quick release or climax. The progression is cyclical: *kyu* returns to *jo*" (1982: 9–10).

This progression structures a *noh* drama as a whole, as well as sections within it, i.e., the *jo* section at the beginning of a drama is structured so that it too progresses from initiation (*jo*) through development (*ha*) to completion (*kyu*). The same is true of the *ha* and *kyu* sections of the drama as a whole.

Since the influence of *noh* on Ōta's work is indirect, the structure and dramaturgy of *The Water Station* reflects but does not slavishly reproduce all aspects of the *jo–ha–kyu* progression. Scene 1 in which the Girl appears, encounters the environment, and interacts with the water station clearly constitutes the *jo* section of *The Water Station*. As the house lights fade, the Girl's sustained entry initially captures and then dilates the audience's attention as the audience adjusts to the slowed-down tempo-rhythm and the relative silence of the constantly running water. The elaboration and complication (*ha*) of Scene 1 begins when the Girl senses and then sees the running water. As the water captures her attention and awareness, it complicates her relationship to the larger environment. A further dilation of focus and awareness comes with the Girl's encounter with the water, and again with the wider environment—the sky. The gradual completion (*kyu*) begins when the Girl senses the presence of, and then turns to see Man A and Man B as they begin their approach. This transition moment leads from the *kyu* of Scene 1 to the *jo* or initiation/introduction of Scene 2.

The further development (*ha*) of the performance score as a whole begins with Scene 2, and continues as the performance score gets progressively denser and more complex aurally, visually, and interpersonally as we move through Scenes 2, 3, 4, and 5. This gradual thickening of the score begins when the Girl stays on in Scenes 2 and 3 to respond to and interact with Man A and Man B and the Woman with a Parasol. It continues with the appearance and continued presence of the Man in the Junk Heap partway through Scene 4.

The densest and most complex development of the score—the *ha* of the *ha*—is Scene 6. When the Caravan of eight travelers arrives, ten actors are on stage simultaneously including the Old Woman in her basket and the Man in the Junk Heap. A highly complex set of interrelationships is psychophysically played out between the ten figures, their relationship to the place from which they have arrived, and their interactions with the water. The soundscape is also at its most varied and complex as (1) the three movements of Albinoni's Oboe Concerto pervade the scene with their themes and variations; (2) the gradual but highly significant shifts in the music's volume from low to loud(est) to low again; and (3) the sound generated by the different types of engagement of the water—the Young Woman bathing her legs, the Daughters fighting and laughing as they splash the water, Man A and Man B putting their heads in the water, and the Husband simply filling a cup with water. The degree of complexity of the scene as a whole is literally seen in Ōta's published text where main and minor actions are so complex as to require not just one, but two tightly spaced printed columns each to accommodate the text needed to describe all the actions (Ōta 1990: 174). In contrast to the single column of main actions needed for the Girl in Scene 1, the four columns needed here demonstrates just how thick the score is at this point.

The exit of the Caravan begins a gradual diminishment or thinning of the density of the score that continues through Scenes 7 and 8. By the beginning of Scene 8, the Man in the Junk Heap has hidden himself so that only the Man with a Heavy Load is on stage—"A lone figure" (Ōta 1990: 183). There is no clear concluding *kyu* section which brings *The Water Station* to completion or resolution. Rather, the cyclical pattern of returning to a new *jo*, present in *noh*, is literally played out in *The Water Station*. As the Man with a Huge Load departs, the Girl, walking backwards, re-appears on the pathway, "Alone" (Ōta 1990: 183). She enacts a score almost identical to that of the first part of Scene 1 up to the point where she begins to descend to the watering place. But this new *jo* is of course different from that played out in Scene 1. It is set in a new key. The Girl's relationship and response to the environment she encounters, and the inner states she experiences in response to that environment necessarily differ as she returns.

While Ōta's aesthetic of divestiture requires that the vast majority of main and minor actions be slowed down, this slowing down is relative to the progression of *jo–ha–kyu* within both the score as a whole, and each scene within the score. The *jo–ha–kyu* progression not only informs the structuring of action in *The Water Station*, but also serves as a practical tool for coaching actors on the relative tempo-rhythm of actions as we work on the development of the psychophysical score for each traveler.

Psychophysical stimuli for the sensory embodiment of actions

In the second part of my analysis I examine Ōta's text from the psychophysical actor's perspective, i.e., identifying cues about tempo-rhythm and points of entry for the sensory embodiment of action. From my perspective outside the original process that produced the published text, Ōta's selection and arrangement of main and minor actions on the page is a richly evocative form of visual poetry. Ōta's choice of specific words describing actions and his arrangement of words

on the page both function in a manner similar to the punctuation of Beckett's texts. In addition to *jo–ha–kyu*, their arrangement on the page provides a sense of the overall tempo-rhythm of the performance and serve to guide each actor's individual process of developing an individual score.

Ōta's text is also a source of non-psychologically based stimuli for the actors' sensory embodiment of specific action(s). A close analysis of a representative sample of main actions for the Girl in Scene 1 above reveals the following types of information and stimuli for developing the actor's psychophysical score:

1   *Movement/placement*: in addition to the specific stage directions, some of the main actions such as "On the way up the small incline," "The girl descends to the watering place," or "She sits down" at the water station provide specific directions for the placement of actions within the *mise-en-scène*. This information is self-evident and rather straightforward.

2   *Tempo-rhythm*: main actions such as "The girl unexpectedly stops," as well as the choice of particular words to suggest the actor's inner relationship to an action. The choice of the verb *descends* in the main action "descends to the watering place" guides both the tempo-rhythm of the action and the quality of the actor's relationship to an action.

3   *Sensory awareness within a particular part of the body*: "Comes walking" and "The back of the walking girl" direct the actress' sensory awareness and attention away from the visual and through a particular part of her body. "Comes walking" suggests that the actress direct her sensory awareness to her bare feet in the act of walking as they make contact with the pathway, here and now. "The back of the walking girl" directs the actress' sensory awareness specifically to her back—providing her with the opportunity to explore her relationship to the way from which she has come at this point in her journey along the pathway.

4   *Sensory awareness in relation to an object within the immediate environment*: actions such as "In the gaze of her eyes / The red cup fills with water" direct the actor to allow an object such as the red cup as it fills with water to fill up her sensory awareness of seeing. Therefore, the actress' focus here is drawn away from the wider environment into engagement with the cup as it fills, thus heightening awareness of her eyes as her gaze is literally filled with water as is the red cup.

5   *Sensing within the body*: "The water flowing through her body" directs the actor's sensory awareness away from anything in the immediate or wider environment to the water she has just taken in her mouth and swallowed, thereby heightening her sensory awareness and connection to the quality and feel of the water as it actually travels within her body.

6   *The quality of the sensory relationship to the wider environment*: actions such as "The girl watches the wind pass" and "the sky in the girl's eyes" shape and heighten the quality of the actor's visual engagement in what she is doing. Kneeling beside the water station, both actions invite the actor to be aware of her eyes as she engages with the passing wind and the sky—both constituting the larger, wider environment in which she now finds herself. "Watching" the wind pass and sensing the vast "sky" in her eyes suggest the Girl's relative smallness within this unfamiliar and vast environment that envelops her.

Each type of stimulus identified above provides a point of entry for the actor's immediate engagement of their sensory/*ki*-awareness while performing specific actions. As explained in detail below, when the actor fully embodies a particular action, such as "watching the wind pass" or "the sky in the girl's eyes," the actor enters a psychophysiological relationship to and through the action.

Performer Rachel Rosenthal has explained the difference between the process of creating a character and persona as follows:

In acting, or playing a character, you want to impersonate the personality of a person that is not yourself. A persona . . . corresponds to what you want to project from yourself, from within. It is like taking a facet, a fragment, and using that as a seed to elaborate on.

(quoted in Lampe 2002: 296–297)

Ōta's poetically suggestive text provides the psychophysical seeds which the actor's bodymind germinates as it engages them directly. The actor begins to discover the appropriate intensities and qualities of *ki*/sensory awareness through which to fill out each action from the inside. The contours of each inner state of being/doing are explored, and then the transitions from one action to another are joined. Like a spider weaving its web, the actor weaves a psychophysical score linking each action with her *ki*-awareness/energy, thus constituting a stage figure. As this figure begins to emerge, the actor's process of embodied, sensory engagement cumulatively shapes the overall aesthetic logic of the performance score for this specific role as a whole. The actor does not create a character from textually based analysis of motivations or objectives *prior* to rehearsals; rather, from this process of engaging sensory/*ki*-awareness in the rehearsal room, a particular figure-in-action such as The Girl begins to emerge.[21]

The preparatory process in the studio

During 2004, the one-week Gardzienice workshop and the initial week of work in Singapore followed parallel processes. The foundation was prepared by an initial three-day period of intensive psychophysical training and application of the principles to structured improvisations. As the actors started to discover and establish a sensory, psychophysical relationship to impulses and actions, the next step was to bring them into an initial encounter with elements of *The Water Station* without literally being told, "We are now going to apply the principles and psycho-dynamic quality of the engagement of your energy and sensory awareness to *The Water Station*."

The actors were taken through a progressive series of exercises further directing their awareness and the feel of the breath-in-action toward engagement of the types of inner states of being/doing in *The Water Station*:[22]

The actors are seated in chairs. Prior to the beginning of all the structures that follow, the actors collectively perform a series of repetitions of the opening *taiqi* movements in order to attune and sensitize themselves to each inhalation, exhalation, and the space between, as well as to the larger ensemble as a whole, thereby opening peripheral awareness.

1   *Shifting external focus between three points*: on the impulse of each half-breath (inhalation, exhalation), your external focus shifts between and among the following three points: directly ahead, slightly down and to the right, and slightly upward toward the space above, or the sky.

2   *Adding an awareness of the space behind*: while continuing the above, wherever the external gaze travels on each half-breath, sustain a very strong sensory awareness of your back, and through your back to the space behind. Allow this sense of the behind to become strong . . . and still stronger.

3   *Adding the awareness of a desire*: in addition to the strong sense of the back and the space behind, add the impulse of a desire to look back/behind; however, you are not actually allowed to turn and look back. This very strong desire should be sensed specifically in specific parts of your body . . . in the palms, in the feet . . . along the spine . . . etc. Allow this desire to look back to begin from and resonate in the lower *dantian* and from the *dantian* to radiate to specific parts of the body.

4   *Adding the impulse to look back . . . interrupted*: allow this very strong sensory awareness of the back, space behind, and desire to look back to become even stronger by degrees . . . Without anticipating when it will happen, sense the impulse in your lower *dantian* to look back, and start to look back . . . but STOP! You cannot look back. You are not allowed to look back.

5   *Adding another desire*: working between the three points of external focus, allow each shift in external focus to be informed by the desire to stay . . . you do not want to leave where you are . . . sense this desire to stay here, seated from the lower *dantian* . . . sense the feel of that desire to stay in the feet . . . the palms . . . behind your eyes . . .

6   *Adding a compulsion . . . a "must"*: as structure #5 above is continued, the following "must" is added. Sensing this strong desire to stay, you know that you must get up and leave, but you cannot get up. You do not wish to get up, but feel the compulsion that you know you must. Allow this compulsion, this must to inhabit each cycle of breath as it gathers in your *dantian*, as it travels . . . Now, you actually must stand up. You must get up and leave . . . you must leave . . . you must leave . . . "now" . . .

7   *Introduction to the slow walk*: at this moment in the progression we begin work on the kind of slow walk required in *The Water Station*. Keeping the strong sense of behind and the desire to stay and not leave, with your external gaze focused across the room through the wall at the far end, begin a slow, sustained walk toward the far expanse ahead. Walk as slowly as possible. It is not a mime walk, but your own, everyday walk, slowed down. From the outside, the walk should appear everyday, i.e., it should not call attention to the fact that it is slow. As you begin this slowed-down everyday walk, keep an awareness of your breath—of the in-breath as it travels to the lower *dantian*, and of the out-breath as it travels back up. Allow the awareness of and attentiveness to your in- and out-breath to help slow down your walk. As you continue to engage the

in- and out-breaths, allow the awareness *in* your breathing to reach to your feet. Allow the breath to be the activator of your sensory awareness in your feet as they touch the floor. Sense the *behind* in each foot as it makes contact with the floor, through the breath. What is the feel of the behind in the foot as it touches the floor?

This series of exercises further opened the actors' sensory engagement inward as well as outward to the environment. The inward relationship was sustained by keeping one's inner eye following each half-breath to and from the lower *dantian*, the intensification of awareness, and the addition of interrupted impulses—the desire to look. The outward relationship was the expansion and extension of one's awareness to and through external points.

The progression in task #1 above begins with the external focus shifting on each half-breath between three particular external points—the space ahead, slightly down right, and above to the sky. What is one's relationship to what might lie ahead, to the more reflective state embodied when the external focus is down to the ground, and the sense of expansiveness when one takes in the space above? The actor's relationship to the points ahead and above should not be restricted by the size of the room. Rather, the actor's engagement of her active imagination allows one to look beyond and through these surfaces to "what might be there." The addition of awareness of the back and the strong sense of the space behind in task #2, and then of the desire to look back in task #3 provide a set of relationships explored through interruption. The internal dialectic between the impulse of a desire to look, and the interruption of that desire, creates a strong psycho-dynamic engagement in the moment. Associations begin to arise that inform this emerging set of relationships.

As the actors at Gardzienice and Singapore were side-coached through each repetition and shift in the rules and qualities of engagement, their sensory awareness gradually opened outward as it deepened inward. After several repetitions, I divided the actors into two groups so that all could observe from the spectator's perspective the degree to which a clear and strong *ki*-awareness and energetic connection was or was not manifest. As they observed each other, they were able to see precisely when intention or pushing manufactured an inner relationship, rather than allowing such a relationship to arise psychophysically from breath and impulse; when an individual was self-conscious and trying to move slowly while walking, rather than *actually* slowing down their everyday movement; when the inner connection to an unfulfilled desire produced a simple, but deep connection, etc. The actors at the Gardzienice workshop and in the Singapore ensemble began to see that what works is when an individual inhabits a task as simply and un-selfconsciously as possible via an inner connection with breath. Then something happens.

Staying attentive to the connection of the breath from the *dantian* is not neutral. It initiates a relationship-in-action. This relationship is informed by the associations that arise as the actor establishes, maintains, and elaborates a "feeling-full" inner state of being/doing in relation to an action or task. The actor does not manufacture an emotion, but rather learns to be patient enough to allow the resonance of feeling-states to arise from the engagement of one's *ki*-energy/awareness in the psychophysical task at the moment.

Zeami's perspective can help us understand this process. In the *Kakyo* he identifies subtle distinctions in the types of internal qualities of energy that arise from the viscera. Movement and voice both arise from the viscera and are "colored by 'feeling tones'" (Nearman 1982: 363). Mark Nearman provides the following commentary on Zeami's perspective:

> to achieve the desired integrated effect of a "wondrous power," the actor would be expected to listen before he moves. What he listens to would not only be the sound of his own voice . . . and the inner "voice" of his tonal center . . . He now must learn also to listen to—that is, to be open and sensitive to—the whole environment

of "sound" in which he is performing. In other words, he must develop a sensitivity to the whole atmosphere in which he acts.

(Nearman 1982: 364)

The preliminary exercises above began to move the actors toward the type of heightened "sensitivity to the whole atmosphere"/environment necessary in staging *The Water Station*. With 99 percent of the action slowed down, it was the actor's inner engagement of states of being/doing that would potentially attract and hold the spectators' attention in performance.

Touching Ōta's source score

The next step in the process was to touch a few of the specific actions from the first scene of Ōta's text. I incorporated several of the main actions into the actors' repetition of the slowed-down, everyday walk. The description of my verbal instructions that follows is not my own, but that provided by a Korean actress Jeungsook Yoo who has worked with me extensively since 2000.[23] Since Jeungsook's first encounter with *The Water Station* was at Gardzienice her record of my basic instructions below is from the March workshop.

Touching Ōta's source score: Zarrilli's basic instructions

Walk slowly.
Not an exaggerated slow-motion but everyday movement slowed down.
Open your awareness toward the far expanse behind.
You must leave, but you don't want to leave.
Stronger sense of behind.
The back of the walking figure.
Sense behind from where you've started to leave.
Stop.
From where you are looking, turn your gaze toward where you've left.
Let the gaze drop near to your feet then back to forward.

Start walking again.
Your lips.
Your lips.
Sense your lips.
The mouth.
Bring your fingertips to your mouth.
To your lips.
Touch them.
Hear the sound of the water.

(Yoo 2007: 83–84)

(*Note:* the same basic instructions were given at this stage in the process in Singapore.)

Like the preliminary exercises above, I coached actors toward touching specific actions from Ōta's source score via a heightened sensory engagement, and concentration of their *ki*-awareness/energy through the back, the feet, the lips, the mouth, the fingertips, the ears, etc. Coaching actors through this progression of actions/awarenesses, I expanded or repeated key phrases. For "sense the behind" I invited actors to sense the subtler nuances of their awareness—"sense what is behind along the spine . . . sense that in the feet, the palms, along the spine and through the head . . ." Similarly I expanded on a phrase like "sense the lips" by asking the actors to "Sense the mouth behind the lips . . . the mouth behind the lips . . . bring the tips of the right hand to the lips . . . sense the fingers on the lips . . . the fingers on the lips."

Expansion and repetition are important for actors at such an early stage in their encounter with this type of psychophysical process. It is not sufficient for the actor to take their mind's eye to their mouth because I asked them to "sense your mouth." Rather, moving one's *ki*-awareness/attention into the mouth when I say "sense your mouth" should establish a psychophysiological connection that vibrates or radiates via the deployment of one's *ki*/sensory awareness.

Likewise, it is not sufficient for the actor's fingertips to merely touch their lips when I invite them to "bring your fingertips to your lips"; rather, what is crucial is that there is a heightened engagement or exchange in the act of touching.

Optimally informing this process of exchange is the actor's breath-in-action, i.e., the feel of the touch of the fingertips to the lips is accomplished as the breath travels from the *dantian* through the fingertips. The actor thereby senses or feels the quality and duration of the tips of the fingers as they come into contact with the skin of the lips. A contact is made; an exchange occurs. This is not neutral. The moment of contact makes itself available for the actor to explore and engage with their *ki*/sensory awareness via the breath. Slowing down such a simple, specific action as "Fingers to the lips" (Ōta 1990: 157) opens up a sensory world for the actor to explore with the perceiving awareness now . . . in this moment. It was via the specificity and nuances of the actor's sensory engagement in each specific task that a psychophysical score for *The Water Station* eventually began to emerge.

Jeungsook Yoo describes this initial moment of encountering *The Water Station* as "a meeting of three people, Ōta Shōgo, Phillip Zarrilli, and me" (2007: 84).

> *The Water Station* was given to me first as a set of concrete actions. The normative phase of understanding a literary text through reading was replaced by appreciating actions realized through my bodymind. Instructions such as "slow tempo," "looking back," "dropping gaze toward the feet," and "touching lips" were both practical, like instructions for yoga movements, and evocative, like a poem . . . [T]he actions generated strong sensations in me.
>
> (Yoo 2007: 84)

Commenting on my method of side-coaching, Jeungsook further observes how

> his way of delivering the instructions also "vibrated" me. When I listened to the instructions from the director, I perceived not only the words but also the quality of sound that his bodymind "radiated." It transmitted his understanding of the text by forming a field of particular *ki*, or an atmosphere. This process of

coaching is similar to his leading of the martial arts. For example, Zarrilli's instruction, "*Pun'i!*" for a jumping action in a *kalarippayattu* body exercise sequence triggers and supports my action with its specific quality of sound. In both cases, the materiality of the sound carried his knowledge about the actions so that it shaped the quality of my movements in an indirect way. I connected myself to the *ki* of actions and the director by being attentively aware of them, i.e., my *ki* was related to them, and appreciated what they offered to me

> (Yoo 2007: 84)

Using Ōta's terminology, the process of developing the actor's sensory awareness described above is more passive than active. As with structured improvisations, the actor works with breath and the quality of inhabitation of sensory awareness to see what arises in the moment and what relationships are established as the actor moves through subsequent shifts in focus/awareness. There is no prior definition of what it is that will or will not arise, i.e., an intention or motivation. In this process, the actor *becomes qualitatively active and attuned in relation to, not because of*. The actor does not analyze the text for beats, objectives, or motivations; rather, by trusting that something will happen if one's energy and awareness are available in the moment, associations, inner feeling states (or strong sensations) arise and one's active imagination is engaged in exploring one's relationship to the action. The sensations and associations that arise within one actor may be similar in some ways but also quite different to those of other actors.

The strong sensations generated within Jeungsook Yoo informed her relationship to actions such as looking back that might otherwise have been performed perfunctorily or neutrally. Jeungsook explains how

> The outer action, "looking back" has numerous potential meanings. At the moment of actualizing it, this action came to me as a vain longing accompanied with disappointment and confirmation of loss. The strong awareness of

the spatial far expanse behind was transformed for me into a temporal sense of the irreparable past which dragged at the back of my head. It was a sense of longing and regret. When I dropped my gaze near my feet, undeniable loneliness and despair visited me.

(Yoo 2007: 84)

The inner states of being/doing that emerged for Jeungsook during this part of our work at the Gardzienice workshop provided the basis for the development of a full psychophysical score for her performance of the Girl during later rehearsals in Singapore. The workshop at Gardzienice concluded at this point in the process.

In Singapore I expanded the actors' encounter with *The Water Station* by developing additional group exercises. Continuing work on the slow walk, I asked the actors to bring to rehearsal any personal object which was especially important to them. I asked them not to disclose why this object was important. Approximately two-thirds of the distance across the rehearsal space I placed a table against the wall. While performing the slowed-down walk across the space, I side-coached the actors with the following instructions:

Sense the object you are carrying—its feel . . . its weight . . . sense the past and the place behind in this object . . . Allow your breath as it travels to inhabit the object as you touch it, sensing its presence with you now . . . Stop . . . Sense the object . . . its presence to your touch . . . its relationship through your breath to the past behind . . . You must leave this object behind . . . here . . . now . . . Leave the object . . . Turn away, and continue your walk toward the way ahead . . . You cannot turn back . . . .

This particular exercise began to lay a psychophysical foundation for the actors' engagement with possessions and belongings, and to the memory and weight that such objects carry. But it was extremely important that each actor's relationship *not* become sentimentalized, or emotionally over-determined. We worked on

the simplicity of the engagement of touch via the breath as it reaches through the object to the space behind, and one's relationship to the act of leaving.

Developing specific psychophysical acting scores in rehearsal

In Singapore, after the initial week of training and preliminary exercises, each actor was given a copy of the text and a specific role. During the ensuing three-week period each actor developed their own specific two-part psychophysical score: (1) the physical part of the score including their figure's slow walk, all other overt movements or manipulation of objects, their overt physical interaction with other actors and with the water, and their interaction with and/or response to the environment or *mise-en-scène* per se; and (2) the inner states of being/doing through which the actor inhabited and shaped each action constituting the total physical score. With no text to speak, each actor faced the necessity of speaking without speaking, i.e., fully embodying and clearly communicating their inner state(s) of being/doing in relationship to their own inner world, the environment, and the other travelers. But as Ōta says, these "inner state(s)" are "wholly the actors' own" (1990: 151).

Our beginning point for developing each actor's physical score and tempo-rhythm was always Ōta's published text; however, a few actions were occasionally changed or slightly modified from Ōta's text. For example, in Scene 1 the Girl carried a rag doll rather than a basket, and, rather than using a red cup for her interaction with the water, she only used her tongue and mouth.

By the time we began our rehearsals of specific scenes in Singapore, we were fortunate to be able to work on the actual set—minus the junk heap and running water. Even for the highly complex Scene 6 with the Caravan and ten actors on stage at once, basic blocking and placement of actors on stage were quickly mapped out. We were able to focus on the subtle nuances and tempo-rhythm of each action within a physical score, and the actor's relationship to inhabiting each inner state informing the physical.

Consequently, the overall process of rehearsing was very much like that described above during our initial week of workshops—side-coaching actors through the physical score, ensuring that the actor was beginning to engage her *ki*-awareness/energy at it was becoming attuned to specific actions, allowing this relationship to gradually deepen and expand as associations emerged, and working on the dynamic tempo-rhythm between and among the travelers and within the scenic environment. In the remainder of this case study, I focus on how I worked with specific actors on developing their psychophysical scores for Scenes 1, 2, and 3.

> ⊙ DVD-ROM: *THE WATER STATION*: THE GIRL

Scene 1: The Girl

The initial set of strong sensations generated within Jeungsook Yoo at the Gardzienice workshop provided her with a beginning place from which to develop her unique psychophysical score for playing the Girl in Singapore. As documented by Jeungsook Yoo, during our rehearsals a few of Ōta Shōgo's directions for Scene 1 were slightly adapted or changed as follows [brackets indicate that an action in the source score is not performed]:

A girl
Alone
In the dim light
Comes walking

On the way up the small incline
The girl unexpectedly stops

The back of the walking girl

The back of the walking girl

The neck twists around
Toward the way she came
Toward the far expanse
Her face turns

From the far expanse   her gaze drops to near her feet
Then to the direction she is heading

The profile of the girl
Walking

Fingers to the lips
Of the profile   walking

Stopping   the face turns   to the watering place

The finely running water

instead of a basket
the girl carried a rag doll
with her right hand

The delicate sound of water
The girl descends   to the watering place

By the water
She sits down   [basket on her knees]   doll on her knees

The girl watches the wind pass

[In the girl's hand a red cup from the basket]   the girl approaches

Toward the fine line of water
[The red cup]   mouth open
                                                          tongue touches
The transparent line
[Disappears into the red cup]   the girl retreats

In the gaze of her eyes   the girl approaches again
[The red cup   fills with water]   the fine line of water

[From] the line of water [the red cup moves]
To the girl's mouth   mouth open
                                                          tongue feels water

The girl drinking water
The water flowing through her body
[The empty cup]   the sky in the girl's eyes [Figure 8.1, p. 145]

[The hand stretching to the basket   stops]
The girl's eyes   turn to the old road[24]

In rehearsals our focus was on the quality and nuances of Jeungsook's sensory relationship to specific actions. I provide on the next page, boxed, Jeungsook's published account of our detailed work on the Girl's entrance.

My directorial concern was solely with the quality and tempo-rhythm of Jeungsook's *ki*-awareness as she engaged each action. I did not state what specific associations/sensations Jeungsook should or should not have. What was important was that it was evident to me as the spectator that she was building a fully embodied sensory relationship to the inner state of being/doing informing each moment. Whatever specific associations, images, or feelings arose for her, my directorial concern was that they were simple, arose from the quality of her sensory engagement with an action, involved no form of indication, and were not over-determined or over-blown. It was clear to me throughout the rehearsal process that Jeungsook was gradually developing a very full and consistent relationship of inner states to outer score. When the type of connection Jeungsook was finding occasionally went missing, as noted above, I provided specific feedback to keep the inner state of her score full.

It was not until some months after the production was over when I read an early draft of Jeungsook's essay, that I learned about the specific associations—such as the ghost figure

Scene 1: an account of work on specific actions by Jeungsook Yoo (2007: 90–92)

"A girl alone in the dim light comes walking"

From the entrance of the Girl, the central instruction from the director was "awareness toward the far behind." It became the main psycho-score which dominated my physical action and emotion until the point where the Girl discovered the water faucet. When I entered, although I walked forward, my awareness of ahead was vague. There was no clear destination for the walking—no place to go and no expectation of the future. Instead I had a strong awareness toward the far behind. The director's instruction suggested one interpretation for this back awareness: "You must leave but you don't want to leave." For me this idea transformed into a strong past which haunted the Girl like a ghost—something that she was attached to once, but was permanently lost. Something she was dragging all the way through. This strong back awareness formed *ki* which was running toward the past or back space so that my steps slowed down even more. Another place of my awareness was the rag doll that I was carrying with my right hand. The doll was the only tangible thing from the Girl's past. The awareness of the presence of the doll, and my hand holding it continued throughout my acting. Sometimes, it was more emphasized and sometimes it became background awareness.

"The girl unexpectedly stops"

Then, I suddenly stop. I knew that I had to stop at some point. That was fixed in the text as part of the score. The problem was how to stop "unexpectedly" when I knew I had to stop. How could I create the impression of a sudden stop? The director suggested stopping without finishing one step completely; that is, stopping in the middle of a step. It solved the matter of the visible score. However, I still needed to decide when to stop. I knew the point where the stopping should happen according to the plan of my entire score. I decided to stop at a point without any specific reason. I just executed the action of stopping. Then, I enhanced the back awareness more than before.

After the unexpected stop, the text gave the line, "The back of the walking girl the back of the walking girl." It was clear that the stop was caused by something from behind. Rather than determining a reason in advance, I listened to, and focused on the back attentively to know what it was that made me stop. I felt that "thick" *ki* was formed around the area of the back of my head, neck, and upper back. It was pulling me backward. It was a feeling of fear combined with expectation. An association sprung into my awareness: was a ghost of someone that she loved behind me? Did the Girl want to see the person although that person is now a ghost? I let my neck twist toward the back following the attraction caused by *ki* on my back. The visible movement (Body) of the twist of the neck was a necessary result of the movement of invisible awareness (Mind) and *ki*.

"From the far expanse her gaze drops to near her feet"

When I looked back, my gaze followed the direction of my awareness and *ki*. At first it detected the area near to me. After seeing the empty space, it elongated more toward the far back expanse. Actually, in the rehearsal studio and theater, there was a wall blocking my gaze making it impossible to look at a far expanse toward the way she came. Therefore, I directed my focus inside which made my focus soft creating the effect of looking far away. This action brought me to the feeling of "discovering nothing." It was a kind of despair confirming the fact that I had no one to be with—even a ghost. In terms of the quality of *ki*, it was heavy and sank down toward the earth. Along with the movement of *ki*, my face and gaze turned and dropped near my feet. I then moved my gaze to the way ahead. Therefore, this score gained meaning within the relationship to the back as a resistance against the lingering attachment to the back that I maintained. As I began to walk again, the back awareness slowly weakened, but still without have a clear awareness of the space ahead. I was rather floating in the space. The awareness and *ki* was around my body.

Interestingly, although these awarenesses and *ki* are invisible, they are perceptible. While rehearsing, once, I experimented with reducing the back awareness when I entered before the unexpected stop to emphasize the back awareness after the stop even more. When I did this, the director immediately noticed the difference and asked for "more back awareness." It was clear that the direction, intensity, and quality of awareness and *ki* should be clearly rendered in this piece due to the calm and slow movement and atmosphere which allowed the audience more time to observe. Everything including the visible and invisible could be perceived by the audience. Especially, in this minimal performance, a different amount of awareness could cause a different effect. Whether it was mental or physical, what I did on stage should be under my control and "artifically" refined, because even unconscious use of awareness and *ki* could potentially be read and experienced by the spectator.

from her past—that constituted the inner life of her score. What was important for the audience was Jeungsook's manifest, palpable embodiment of an incredibly strong attachment to what she had left behind—to a place or a past that haunted her as the Girl. The ghost was and would remain Jeungsook's own.

As we worked on the next main action of the Girl's score, "Fingers to the lips," I picked up with Jeungsook the sensory work with the lips that was introduced in our initial workshop period. All of her attention and *ki*-awareness was directed to her lips. Having sensed her lips, she slowly brought her "Fingers to [her] lips," engaging the type of tactile sensation of the touch of her fingers noted earlier. Touching her lips, Jeungsook could also then sense the saliva in her mouth, thereby also engaging sensory awareness of her mouth.

In terms of the overall shape and texture of Ōta's physical score for the Girl, this is an extremely important moment. The Girl's sensory engagement shifts from the wider environment— "the far expanse" from which she has come and the "direction she is heading"—to her inner sensory environment. While her attention and awareness begin to focus within, she continues walking. The audience views the Girl's "Fingers to [her] lips" in profile as she continues along the pathway.

The next action is when the Girl stops. Working with Jeungsook on "stopping," the stimulus was that moment when she first actually heard the sound of the water. Just prior to this moment, her awareness had been focused on her lips, fingertips, and mouth. Obviously, the sound of the water was present throughout the scene. What

was important was that she actually remains so occupied with her lips, fingertips, and mouth that she did not know when her ears would open and hear. Optimally in performance, this moment of opening her auditory awareness actually surprised Jeungsook. It was only then that she stopped. Hearing the sound of the water, her "face turns to the watering place." She did not know what the source of the sound of the water was until she actually turned and saw the water running from the faucet for the first time.

Her encounter with the water in that moment optimally engaged Jeungsook's auditory and visual senses. The quality of her ongoing encounter with the water was further modulated by the following qualifiers in Ōta's score: "The *finely* running water / The *delicate* sound of water."

The qualifiers, "finely" and "delicate," provided Jeungsook with a clear sense of how to encounter the water in these subsequent moments. She saw the stream of water as "fine." She heard the sound of the water as "delicate." There is a clear progression from sensing something when the Girl first hears the water, to seeing the water and its source at the faucet as it runs, to experiencing the water as both fine and delicate. The Girl is attracted to the water, and then "descends to the watering place." If the actress' progression through this sequence is filled with an appropriately modulated *ki*-awareness, the spectators have been attracted to the actress' sensory journey from the general to this specific sensory engagement of the water as fine and delicate. Jeungsook's psychophysical encounter with the water thereby had a shape, progression, and tempo-rhythm that emerged from the direct engagement of her sensory perception alone, and not from motivations or objectives.

As Jeungsook explains below, her sensory engagement of the water now shifted from the auditory and visual to the tactile feel and taste of the water when, finally, she opened her mouth and her tongue first touched the water.

Jeungsook's literal psychophysical connection during this quick shift from the intimacy of the feel of the water inside of her to "the sky in the girl's eyes" was accomplished by ensuring that she kept a residual connection to her lower abdomen at the moment of the shift of awareness/focus from inside to outside. That is, when her focus changed from the indirect, soft, and blurred focus she inhabited as she felt the water moving inside to the "sky" in her eyes, it was important that each shift emanate from her lower *dantian*. The "sky in [her] eyes" had to be reflected all the way *through her bodymind* from her abdomen. This shift refocused the Girl's relationship from the water flowing within to the larger environment into which she had been thrust when she first appeared. It

---

Scene 1 (continued): an account of selected actions by Jeungsook Yoo (2007: 92–94)

"The sky in the girl's eyes"

Discovering the water, I approached the watering place and sat down by it. My awareness moved from the water to the open space above following the imaginary wind and back to the water again. When I drank the water, the awareness was on the sensation of my tongue, lips, and cheeks touching the cold water. After drinking, it was concentrated on the journey of the water flowing through my body. The mouth, throat, gullet, stomach. It was the most intimate, introverted moment in my entire acting scores for the Girl.

After the calm moment of swallowing water, a sudden change of *ki*'s quality happened: looking at the sky. My awareness and *ki* were directed outside from the water inside to the space above. The slightest change of physical score could cause crucial changes in psycho-scores. One day, when I was rehearsing the scores of the line, "the sky in the girl's eyes," the director suggested a change of physical score. What I was doing before was that after swallowing water from the faucet, I looked up to the sky slowly. This movement gave me a sense of rest and retrospective. My *ki* and gaze were soft from the initiation of the looking up. It was one psychophysical action until recognizing the traces of human beings at the beginning of the next scene.

The director's instruction was "to look up quickly." I discovered my reason or justification for the change immediately after executing this new action. After the introspective, still moment of swallowing water, this abrupt movement made my awareness, *ki*, and focus sharp and direct with a hint of surprise. It gave me an image of calling from the sky. From the Girl's past, maybe a lost mother, grandmother, a puppy which she was yearning after. My awareness was directed toward a certain point in the middle of the space above the auditorium. The images were not in my brain but there in the space. In this case, the site of my imagination, a function of mind was external; I projected associations into the space creating a relationship to it. It was a desperate search for something that she was longing for, something that seemed to be there just before. Following the awareness (Mind), my *ki* expanded toward where my eyes were looking. My breath also followed the direction so that it was almost out of my body. It stayed around my mouth, nose, and forehead.

Then, I realized my search was in vain. There was only a huge empty space in front of me. This produced a sense of despair. Because I was yearning for something with hope, the loneliness became even more poignant. This disappointment made my focus blur as I lost the specific point at which I was looking. My awareness became widespread without an object. The *ki* was withdrawn back toward my lower back and into the earth. The breath followed *ki* and sat around my tail bone. My body felt dragged down. Although the external score of my eyes was the same as before which was looking up at the sky, the invisible score changed and became more dynamic.

is precisely this contrast and tension between the inner sense and the outer environment that produced such a strong set of associations within Jeungsook's score, and that therefore produced such a potentially rich effect for the audience. Even if the audience could not precisely identify her inner state as "a desperate search for something that she was longing for . . . in vain," it was evident that the Girl embodied a profound sense of loss and loneliness—whatever its source.

In terms of the overall tempo-rhythm of Scene 1, most of the adjectives and adverbs Ōta uses throughout to describe and qualify the Girl's main actions suggest a sustained quality of engagement. This is appropriate to the scene as the initiation (*jo*) for the production as a whole. Variations within the overall sustained quality of the scene occur with such key actions as "The neck twists around," "her gaze drops," and the sudden shift in the Girl's awareness with "the sky in the girl's eyes." The subtle variations in Jeungsook's tempo-rhythm, in her inner states of being/doing, and her outer relationship to the environment shaped the contours of her acting score for the Girl into a complete journey for the audience to attend to.

Scene 2: Two Men

The Girl's relationship to the environment with "the sky in [her] eyes" shifts suddenly when she senses someone approaching. From the sky, her "eyes turn to the old road" (Ōta 1990: 159). She sees the backs of two men approaching slowly in the distance—one carrying bedding and the other a traveling case. They are coming along the same pathway she traveled. The audience's primary focus gradually shifts from the Girl to the two men as she becomes an observer, hiding herself away amidst the junk heap as she watches their approach. This transition is marked in part by Ōta's introduction of music for the first time—Erik Satie's *Three Gymnopédies*, No. 1—played at a low level.

Scene 2 is structured around a series of key encounters. I provide a brief description of these encounters and ask the types of questions posed

to Noushad Mohamed Kunju (Man A) and Pern Yiau Sim (Man B) as I coached them through the development of their outer and inner scores for the scene. As with Jeungsook Yoo, the associations and answers that arose for Naushad and Pern Yiau as they developed their inner scores in response to my questions were purely their own, and have remained unknown to me during and after the production.

The initial encounter in Scene 2 is between the two men and the place from which all the travelers arrive. With their backs to the audience as they enter, they are "Looking far away" (Ōta 1990: 159). What are they looking at? What *is* behind them, in the place from which they have come? Whatever is there in the distance behind has been experienced by the two men, the Girl, and the other travelers coming from the distant road. Once each of the two men shifts his gaze from "far away" to the "direction he's heading," what is their relationship to that past, to what lies ahead, to each other? What is the sensory feel and pull of that past? How does it relate to what lies ahead?

Their second encounter is with the water. When Man A and then Man B reach the water, each interacts with and savors it in his own way.

On Man A's fingertips   the line of water
Man B sees   Man A sitting by the
    watering place

Man B goes to the watering place
Into Man A's hands   the line of water

Down Man A's throat the flowing water

In Man B's hand   the line of water
Mouth savoring

Mouth to spout   Man B sucks water
In Man A's ears   the sound of water being
    sucked
<zzzzzz>

Facing each other
Staring at the faucet   the two men
                     (Ōta 1990: 161)

This moment of encountering and savoring the water contrasts strongly with whatever lies behind. As in the Girl's encounter with the water, it is an intimate moment in which their awareness is, for the most part, self- and inwardly directed.

But as each man encounters the water, the other man is present to him, watching—and therefore in his awareness. How aware is he of the other? What is the quality and feel of this other's presence? As they stare at the faucet, they are aware of the other, but what is the tone or color of that awareness? Are they wary of the other?

The men's third encounter begins at the point when it is clear that they are present to one another across the water. Note that they have not yet looked directly at each other. Their awareness has only been indirect. Keeping this indirect awareness of the other, their encounter takes an unexpected turn:

Man A   mouth to spout
<zzzzzz>

The faucet untaken

Man B brings his mouth near
Man A, thirst still unquenched, nears the
    faucet
Their mouths meet at the spout
Locked in a kiss   they fight for the slender
    stream of water
Their mouths   leave the faucet
Facing each other   the two men
                    (Ōta 1990: 161–162)

For the first time they look directly at each other with eye-to-eye contact. What do they see in the other's face at this moment? What is each man's inner relationship, now, as he looks into the other's eyes? How has it changed or shifted from the awareness of the other just moments before? This moment of face-to-face meeting is interrupted by the next main action in Ōta's score: "Their faces   turn to the sky" (Ōta 1990: 162).

What has attracted their attention in this moment, and shifted their focus from the other's gaze to the sky? As they look to the sky, what do they see there, now? Does each man still sense the presence of the other across the water?

Technically, the part of the sky to which Man A and Man B looked at this moment was different from the part of the sky to which the Girl looked in Scene 1. When Jeungsook looked to the sky, her look was more directly upward and above her, creating a sense of awe. In contrast, I directed Naushad and Pern Yiau to direct their gaze to that part of the sky on the horizon directly ahead of them and sufficiently above the audience so that it was clear they were not looking at the audience. The part of the sky in their gaze eventually turned ominous. Their gaze into this horizon was direct, and they absorbed from their interaction whatever association(s) vibrated within.

Following this initial gaze toward the horizon, the men's external focus and attention at least momentarily returned to the water.

Man B's finger   stretches to the line of
    water   the
                    fingertip wets cheek
Man A's finger   stretches to the line of
    water   the
                    Fingertip wets cheek

Turned to the sky
Their faces.
                    (Ōta 1990: 162)

Ōta sets up a dialectic tension within the men between the water, the other with whom he shares this environment in the moment, and the distant horizon of the sky. In my work with Naushad and Pern Yiau it was crucial that they execute each shift of focus/attention by keeping connected to their breath and ki-awareness from the lower dantian so as to maintain a residual awareness from one point of focus to the next. The shift for the two men here is from eye-to-eye contact to the sky. As each man's gaze is directed toward the sky, this act of looking/seeing is colored by the residue of the association(s) of the inner state each inhabited as they looked into each other's eyes.

Ōta then adds another encounter to this

equation—that between the two men and the Girl. Up to this point in the scene, the two men have only been aware of the place they have left behind, the water, the other, and the distant sky. The audience of course has been watching the Girl observe the men, and has witnessed how her curiosity has gradually drawn her out of her hiding-place in the junk heap. Jeungsook Yoo explains the inner dynamic with which she negotiated her relationship with the two men as follows:

> While I was sitting in front of the watering place, I noticed two men walking the way I had passed. My awareness was directed to the men. Both precaution and curiosity emerged as the basic elements of my response to them. The precaution came not only from the Girl's negative experiences with strangers that I imagined but also from my sensation of the *ki* of the two men which was heavy, dark, damp, and closed. It was understood as serious, depressed, tired, and remote. The *ki*-field with those qualities formed a closed boundary which pushed me away. It did not seem to welcome the other's presence. The two men had attraction as well, stimulating my curiosity—the fact that they were the first living human beings I encountered in this environment and the intensive actions that followed when they encountered the water. These elements form the repulsive and attractive forces in terms of the direction of the flow of *ki* between me and the two men.
>
> (2007: 94)

With the men's faces "Turned to the sky" for the second time, the concluding main and minor actions in Scene 2 follow:

Main actions	*Minor actions*
	From behind, she tries to peer into their faces
	Her head cocked to one side
Man B's face turns to Man A	Meeting the man's eyes
Man B sees the girl	The girl draws back
The two men's eyes	The girl is pushed back
Follow the girl	By their gaze
From the girl far away their gaze shifts	
Picking up their belongings they stand up	
The two men	
In the two men's eyes	The girl follows their gaze
The far expanse	From afar
To the far expanse they strain their eyes	
The two men	
Man B cranes his neck toward the road ahead	
Man A shifts his gaze to the running water	
The two departing men	The girl watches them leave.

(Ōta 1990: 162)

Another key transition is the moment at which Man B, just as he turns to look at Man A, sees the Girl, and both men turn to her. Who is this unexpected presence? Did this Girl see what just transpired—did she witness the moment when their mouths met at the spout? As the men push the girl back into the junk heap with the strength of their gaze, their attention is once again brought back to the far away horizon of the sky. What is there in the distant far expanse that continues to attract their attention now, and throughout the remainder of the scene? From the initial moment when their attention goes to the sky, the two men's focus is directed to the horizon five times. Constantly returning their gaze to that place on the horizon emphasizes an ominous and foreboding threat in the distance that vibrated psychophysically within both actors. What is *there*?

I worked with the two actors, Naushad and Pern Yiau, on their connection to breath, *ki*/sensory awareness, and points of focus. They constructed psychophysical scores that played chiasmatically between and among the place each had left behind, their encounter with water, the other, the Girl, and whatever lies on the horizon. They answered each question posed above with their own inner associations—known only to them. What was important was that these answers vibrated them qualitatively via their associations within.

Although Scene 2 has a tempo-rhythm that overall is sustained, structurally and in terms of complexity, it has a much denser (and darker) texture than Scene 1. This dark texture derives mainly from the men's relationship to the environment—whether the place they have left, or the ominous sense of foreboding on the far horizon—and to each other. This darkness is evident in Jeungsook Yoo's experience of the two men's *ki* as heavy, "dark, damp, and closed . . . serious, depressed, tired, and remote."

As the two men exit slowly along the pathway ahead, the Girl remains behind in the junk heap, watching them leave. The audience's attention passes from the two men to the Girl, and in the transition into Scene 3 to the approach of a Woman with a Parasol.

⊙ DVD-ROM: *THE WATER STATION— WOMAN WITH A PARASOL*

Scene 3: Woman with a Parasol

In contrast to the measured, sustained quality and tempo-rhythm shaping the actions throughout Scenes 1 and 2, the third scene has a different feel. Although the first three actions constituting the Woman with a Parasol's entrance are performed to a slowed-down pace, the subsequent section of her physical score is punctuated by intense inner psychophysical actions full of quick contrasts and sudden shifts, and the flurry of a wild dance along the pathway. Ōta's score for the Main and Minor Actions of the entire scene follows:

> Scene 3: Woman with a Parasol
> [I have added italics below to the actions which create the quick contrasts and sudden shifts within the Woman's score.]

Main actions		Minor actions
The heavily bent neck		
The woman's heavy eyes		Having watched the men leave
Turn from the way she has come	*suddenly*	The girl's eyes survey the area
to the sky		
The woman walks the air		
She walks the air	the woman's hand	The woman enters her range of vision
Crawls up her body		
From breast to neck	from neck to lips	

The woman's steps   The girl   trying to look away from the woman
Stop with the opening of the parasol   Cannot

Again her bare feet
Move wildly along the ground

The woman *stops*

Hugging the parasol   the woman shrinks into a crouch

In the woman's ear
The sound of water

The woman, attracted to the water,
Stoops down over the water

The trembling water surface
At the dissolving face   the woman peers

To the faucet   the approaching mouth
A fine line of water
Water flows into the woman's body

The woman's eyes open

The woman's neck   twists around
Her eyes turn toward peering eyes

The woman's dark eyes   moving toward the   Pressured   by the woman's dark eyes
peering eyes   The girl crawls up the heap
The woman pursues the peering eyes

The woman watches the peering face   The girl cries out
Her gaze relaxes   Her open mouth   her wide open eyes

Looking away from the girl   the woman sees   The girl's mouth
A human figure   Closes (slowly)

Looking at the approaching figure   Avoiding the woman the girl steps
The woman   smiles and grimaces   Toward the way ahead

The woman's face turns
Suddenly to the sky

The woman steps   to the road ahead.

(Ōta 1990: 163–165)

The Woman's relationship to what lies behind and what she has experienced *before* her arrival has produced an even heavier and denser inner quality for her entrance than that of the Girl and the two Men. I worked with Hiu Tuen Leung on how her inner connection to breath and *ki*-awareness were concentrated in her neck. Even though she is standing upright as she enters, she is literally weighed down. Her neck and shoulders bear this weight.

As she turns from the way she has come, lightness suddenly informs Tuen's impulse as well as the relative tempo-rhythm of her turn to the sky. There is no residual awareness of the heaviness of her relationship to the place behind, but a sudden contrast to the heaviness in her bent neck as she "walks the sky." Tuen's sky is different from that of both the Girl and the two men. She is suddenly borne upward toward and into the sky as she senses the sky in her entire body. She becomes lighter. She sees the earth below her. Here we used Tuen's work on the light quality of energy in her arms and upper body from *taiqiquan* as she began to "walk the air." Part of the wind in the air, she rides the clouds . . . she is the clouds she rides.

Another complete and quick shift in her awareness with no residual awareness takes place when Tuen senses the palm of her right hand. We used the image of her right hand becoming a huge black widow spider that, once a felt presence, begins very slowly to crawl up her leg.

> The spider presses itself against your body as it begins to crawl. It locks itself momentarily to your thigh. And then begins to move again. Sense your hand as the spider in your palm, and simultaneously sense your reaction to the spider as it is crawling up along your body, wherever it is touching. On your neck, it begins to choke you, until it is suddenly released!
>
> The right hand is no longer a spider. The parasol has opened into the wind, the wild wind of the sky, and it carries you into the wild dance as you "ride the wind."

We worked on Tuen "dancing the wind" as a fundamental problem of (im)balance. She was trying to keep her balance as she danced on her toes above the clouds, but the winds are wild and unpredictable. We worked on her not knowing where the parasol would move from moment to moment so that she was blown by the wind. She would reach a momentary point of balance, and then be blown in a different direction. Keeping the parasol away from her body, the wild dance became a semi-improvised series of moments between imbalance and momentary stasis. By the end of the dance, the parasol has been destroyed by the wind. In the moment when she suddenly stops the wild movement, and looks up to the parasol, she sees it now for the first time for what it is. And what is it? An infant? A child? What is it that she holds that is destroyed and in tatters? And when? When did this happen?

This initial part of the Woman with a Parasol's score is unlike the scores developed for the Girl and the two men. The Woman's score is a set of constant, sudden, and almost violent transformations—from the heavy weight of the place behind, she lightly dances the wind, experiences a terrifying spider crawling, is borne above the clouds into a wild wind, and finally sees destruction in her hands.

The remainder of the Woman's score begins when she hears the water. In this part of her score, her residual awareness of one action joins and knits together each moment to the next—unlike the previous section where the three major actions were not joined and where there was a complete shift and sudden juxtaposition of one moment to the next.

When the Woman arrives at the water, stoops down and sees in "the trembling water surface" a "dissolving face," whose face is it that she sees? Her own? A twin? An ancestor? A ghost? A husband? A child? Tuen's associations were again solely her own. Whoever's face appeared to her, Tuen's psychophysical connection to this association raised an extraordinarily strong inner *ki*/sensory vibration that terrifies the Girl when they make eye contact, and causes the Girl to open her mouth and eyes wide as she is pushed back further into the junk heap. When the Woman relaxes her gaze from the Girl, her attention is attracted to "a human figure" that begins to approach her from a distance. Is it the human figure whose face she saw? Or another? Whatever Tuen's association, this human presence vibrates Tuen-the-actress from her lower *dantian* through her entire bodymind. It vibrates the figure of the Woman within so profoundly that a small smile becomes gradually larger, and larger, and larger until it is distorted into a terrifying, grotesque grimace that melts her external focus from seeing this figure into a state of indirect, exhausted, blurred focus. We worked on this progressive transformation psychophysically by working on the subtleties of Tuen's relationship to the shaping of her breath within and the gradual blurring of her external focus. In the process of transformation, her breathing became more and more restricted/constricted and her focus increasingly blurred.

Summary of the process

The evocative, enigmatic actions of much of Ōta's text make no attempt to represent or define a particular inner state of being/doing; rather, they offer points of entry through which the actor's psychophysical engagement in the moment is activated. Any time that the actor is thus engaged, her active imagination is fully involved and engaged. In *The Water Station* the actor engages her sensory awareness and imagination fully in each moment. Sometimes this is a more literal engagement of the actor's senses with the touch or feel of the water, the fingertips to the lips, or the touch of a parasol, suitcase, canteen, sheet, etc. At other times the actor engages her *ki*/sensory awareness in sustaining the active imagination, as when the Girl "watches the wind pass" or the Woman with a Parasol sees the human figure. From both of these moments of imaginative engagement an inner, full sensory relationship develops for the actor.

It was important that the heightened quality

of the actor's engagement of inner states within the design of each acting score never became self-indulgent. Each actor's engagement was supported by the actor-qua-actor's wider, chiasmatic awareness. As Jeungsook Yoo explains, these

> other layers belong to the "pre-expressive level": the awareness of my whole body, the awareness of the whole theater space, the awareness of others including fellow actors and audience. It is developed through training ready to be used for each dramaturgy. These are "basic background awareness" which stays all the time during performance. Specific awareness which is planned according to the given character becomes a figure inside of this background awareness. For example, when I put my awareness on my internal organs while swallowing the water creating the most introverted use of *ki*, I had to keep my awareness of the whole theater space and the audience otherwise the score would become flat and too small. This multiple awareness is not a distraction but another task that an actor should execute.
>
> (Yoo 2007: 95–96)

In terms of the enactive account of acting discussed in Chapter 4, the performance score for *The Water Station* provides a remarkably literal and clear example of the actor-as-perceiver. Here the actor is clearly an *enactor* engaging and interacting with the first two of the three environments we inhabit—(1) the spatio-temporal environment of our immediate larger environment and (2) the inner spatio-temporal environment of sensations. The actor-qua-actor and the actor-as-traveler inhabit only these two environments, and not the third—the inner world of cognition. The actor does not try to reach conclusions or make decisions or judgments about the outer and inner environments. Rather, both actor and figure perceive, inhabit, and respond to these first two environments in the moment.[25] Once again, Mark Nearman's commentary on Zeami's *Kakyo* is useful in understanding this process:

[P]hysical expression (the gesture) derive[s] its impulse from the underlying energy of the actor. This outer expression, in turn, affects the flow of energy so that an interplay between outer expression and inner intent occurs. This mutuality would then permit for a particular kind of spontaneity in performance that would keep the achieved effect vital and immediate so that the acting does not fall into a mere execution of a set of prearranged gestures.

(Nearman 1982: 370)

Responding to *The Water Station*

One of Zeami's preoccupations throughout his texts is with how to create a specific relationship to the audience. Nearman provides a striking description of when an actor's performance is vibrating and full of tonal feeling:

the effect is analogous to the sea, whose surface alone is visible to the spectator on the shore. The actor's movement arises like waves, and when he ceases to move, it is like the sea's surface becoming calm. The spectator witnesses the play of movements and senses the forces that put such play in motion, although these forces remain "invisible," like the pull of the tides and the force of the wind whose presence is determined by the effects they create.

(Nearman 1982: 364)

In *The Water Station*, Ōta's divestment of spoken language and slowing down of everyday movement forces actors toward a level of restraint in their performance that is uncommon except in the *noh* theater, and occasionally in performances of a few of Beckett's later plays. If the actors are "standing still while not standing still" in a performance of *The Water Station*,

Spectators only see or hear what is explicitly expressed, but can sense the concentration and

energy that lie behind the expression. What the actor is demonstrating is not that he moves but his power to move.

(Nearman 1982: 370)

When this happens in a performance of *The Water Station*, the audience can take much away from a performance.

Mari Boyd describes the images of *The Water Station* as "abounding in . . . fragmentation and decay" (2006: 167). For Sid Smith *The Water Station* provoked an experience "almost universally dark . . . [where] human experience build[s] into a quiet, terrible beauty" (1988: 9). For Clarissa Oon (2004) the "silent chords" of *The Water Station* "struck notes of exile, loss and fraying endurance."[26]

The over-riding sense of fragmentation, decay, darkness, and loss that can affect an audience at a performance of *The Water Station* arises cumulatively from how the audience experiences each traveler as a figure or persona. Without the specific dialogue and conventions that provide sufficient information to define one's personal history and/or place that individual within a specific socio-political setting, the travelers in *The Water Station* are closer to the figures that populate the *noh* stage than realist characters. In Scene 3 after the Woman with a Parasol dances wildly across the pathway she suddenly stops her wild dance. When the impulse for her next action comes, the actress playing Woman returns to the glacial pace of her entrance as, "Hugging the parasol the woman shrinks into a crouch" (Ōta 1990: 163). Close to the ground, she cradles and embraces her closed, broken parasol.[27] A sense of pathos and loss pervade this moment. Something has happened to this Woman. She is a figure who psychophysically embodies and bears a certain weight, but the audience does not know the cause of the weight she carries.

The indefinable nature of such states of being/doing inhabited by the figures in *The Water Station* is reflected in Clarissa Oon's descriptions of the Girl and the Married Couple. She describes the Girl in Scene 1 as embodying "an expression of inscrutable regret," and the Married Couple in Scene 4 as conveying "frighteningly raw" emotions as they engaged in a "slow-motion fandango of almost unbearable lust and violence" (2004). Like the Woman with a Parasol, these figures all bear the weight of something more than any individual;[28] but what this more might be ultimately remains undefined and undefinable.

As Mari Boyd explains, Ōta does not want the spectator "to indulge in . . . facile identification" (Boyd 2006: 96–97) with these figures or the states of being they manifest and inhabit. To help achieve this, Ōta integrates into the *mise-en-scène* the Man in the Junk Heap. Between his initial emergence from the heap in Scene 4 and his re-immersion in Scene 8, like the audience he is a constant presence, and often an observer/voyeur. He inhabits his everyday world which includes watching but never interacting with the travelers who temporarily enter (t)his world and capture his attention. He both is inside the world of the performance, and stands slightly apart from it. His presence therefore prevents "facile identification with or pity for the wandering characters. He is

there to remind the audience that human suffering should not be consumed for entertainment purposes" (Boyd 2006: 137).

Divesting a performance of realist staging conventions, slowing down the overall tempo, creating figures rather than characters, and removing spoken language all invite the viewer into a "more sensuous than purposeful" (Boyd 2006: 134) relationship with and experience of the performance. It is an encounter that allows an open-ended, diverse set of associations and meanings to arise for members of an audience. Distanced from all the details and particularities of the behavior and socio-political beliefs of individual characters whose names one comes to know in conventional realist drama, Ōta's aesthetic "invites the viewer to a larger, cosmic outlook on human existence" (ibid.: 139). For at least one critic, the production itself serves "as a water station for the audience, a place for people to stop, drink in, and come away changed. It speaks to a place that is very personal. Each person who sees it is going to have an entirely different experience" (Neff 1998).

9

Speaking Stones

Images, voices, fragments . . . from that which comes after

with text by Kaite O'Reilly and German translation by Frank Heibert

Perhaps we are like stones . . . our own history and the history of the world embedded in us.

Susan Griffin, *A Chorus of Stones* (1992: 8)

Introduction

Speaking Stones was commissioned by Theater Asou[1] of Graz, Austria, as a response to the increasingly xenophobic and reactionary rhetoric and realities of contemporary Austrian politics—exemplified by Jörg Haider of the Freiheitliche Partei Österreichs (Austrian Freedom Party). It was commissioned as a response to the contemporary issue of the displacement of peoples within central Europe, but with an eye on an often unspoken past—the Holocaust as it was played out in Nazi-occupied Austria during World War II—an often unacknowledged, seldom discussed, and therefore hidden history. The play was devised and created with the company between Graz and my studio in Wales during three two-week periods of intensive work between April and September 2002, and premiered on September 12, 2002 at Theater im Palais (Graz). The original performance score was revised when the production was re-rehearsed for a second set of performances in an underground quarry in Aflenz (Austria) November 27–30, 2002. The

premiere in English of the revised performance score was performed in Wroclaw, Poland in 2003 by invitation of the Grotowski Centre. A fourth staging took place in the Aflenz quarry in 2004 as part of the first official exhibit of the history of the quarry.

Theater Asou invited me to direct and co-devise the project alongside playwright/dramaturg Kaite O'Reilly and the company.[2] The process was planned as a collaborative interrogation of a question, a dramaturgical possibility, and a performative premise.

- *The question*: in circumstances of the displacement and traumatizing of peoples, what fragments, images, and/or voices of the past(s) might be disclosed if the environment within which violence and trauma are propagated could speak, i.e., what would happen if stones could speak and hidden histories be revealed?
- *The dramaturgical possibility*: how might a fragmentary, non-narrative, psychophysical performance score be devised and assembled which could both evoke and provoke a synergy

between present realities in central Europe and historical memories?[3]

- *The performative premise*: how might the psychophysical process described earlier in this book be applied to a fragmentary, non-narrative, image-based performance score that would juxtapose quite different performance styles ranging from non-verbal psychophysical structures to those containing fragments of realist text?

This case study provides a description and analysis of the process used to answer these questions in practice through performance.

Two primary resources influenced our interrogation of issues of displacement and trauma as well as our creative process—Elaine Scarry's reflection on the phenomenology, experience, and problematic representation of torture and pain in her seminal book *The Body in Pain* (1985), and *A Chorus of Stones* (1992), Susan Griffin's often poetic reflection and uncovering of two parallel histories—the development of the nuclear industry in the US and the firebombing of Dresden during World War II—all the more horrible because these histories have remained hidden in personal and collective silence and/or denial. In keeping with the nature of the hidden histories she is unearthing, Griffin's writing strategy is indirect and suggestive—"I am not free of the condition I describe here. I cannot be certain how far back in human history the habit of denial can be traced" (1992: 3). Griffin asks her reader

How old is the habit of denial? We keep secrets from ourselves that all along we know . . . All history is taken in by stones . . . stones record history. The hard surface of the stone is impervious to nothing in the end. The heat of the sun leaves evidence of daylight. Each drop of rain changes the form; even the wind and the air itself, invisible to our eyes, etches its presence . . . I am beginning to believe that we know everything, that all history, including the history of each family, is part of us, such

that, when we hear any secret revealed, a secret about a grandfather, or an uncle . . . our lives are made suddenly clearer to us, as the unnatural heaviness of unspoken truth is dispersed. For perhaps we are like stones; our own history and the history of the world embedded in us, we hold a sorrow deep within and cannot weep until that history is sung . . . We forget that we are history. We have kept the left hand from knowing the right . . . We are not used to associating our private lives with public events. Yet the histories of families cannot be separated from the histories of nations. To divide them is part of our denial.

(Griffin 1992: 4, 6, 8, 11)

Griffin astutely observes how "by denying the truth of an event, one gains the illusion of control" (1992: 29). War produces events and realities often denied, some parts of which are intentionally kept "away from understanding" (ibid.: 32). We are all able to find ways "of standing outside ourselves in ignorance" (ibid.: 153). How might we attempt to give voice in performance to something long denied?

Forced displacement of a people inflicts direct physical pain and/or severe emotional trauma on its target. But as Scarry explains,

Physical pain has no voice, but when it at last finds a voice, it begins to tell a story . . . Physical pain does not simply resist language but actively destroys it, bringing about an immediate reversion to a state anterior to language, to the sounds and cries a human being makes before language is learned . . . Why pain should so centrally entail, require, this shattering of language [is made apparent] . . . by noticing the exceptional character of pain when compared to all . . . other interior states . . . [O]ur interior states of consciousness are regularly accompanied by objects in the external world . . . [W]e do not simply "have feelings" but have feelings for somebody or something, that love is love of x, fear is fear of y, ambivalence is ambivalence about z . . .

[M]oving through the human interior, one at last reache[s] physical pain [which], unlike any other state of consciousness—has no referential content. It is not of or for anything. It is precisely because it takes no object that it, more than any other phenomenon, resists objectification in language.

(1985: 3–5)

For Scarry, "physical pain . . . is language destroying," and is "made visible in the multiple and elaborate processes that evolve in producing it" (1985: 20, 52).

Given the often denied and/or hidden histories in which we are all complicit and the language-destroying nature of extreme states of pain and trauma, the dramaturgical possibility of the project is reflected in the subtitle of *Speaking Stones*: *"images . . . voices . . . fragments from that which comes after."* We did not set out to create a conventional modernist dramatic text or theater performance which addressed our question through a narrative that followed the journey of one or more specific characters within a specific set of historical circumstances. Rather, similar in some ways to Griffin's writing strategy in *A Chorus of Stones*, we set out to create an imagistic, impressionist, fragmentary performance score by creating a set of traces—like those in an etching. As Griffin observes,

> a story is told as much by silence as by speech. Like the white spaces in an etching, such silences render form. But unlike an etching in which the whole is grasped at once, the silence of a story must be understood over time

> (Griffin 1992: 172)

Offering not *a* story but fragments or traces of stories, the performance score required sufficient white spaces to create a montage and thereby render images and voices that might reflect denial, trauma, and/or pain's lack of referential content, and that might create resonances between socio-political realities and historical memories for a contemporary European audience. We decided to

assemble and shape the performance score from three types of sources/stimuli: (1) performance structures devised from non-verbal psychophysical work with states of being/doing, images, and music; (2) fragments of text and sign-language authored by Kaite O'Reilly and generated from her experience in former Yugoslavia during the war; and (3) additional found or authored text and music brought in by the ensemble or from our research.[4] These sources and strategies were shaped into a montage whose underlying aesthetic was to be textured as a weaving—the traces of an image or fragment of text in one structure might have resonances via juxtaposition and/or tension with the traces of another. From my directorial perspective, I wanted to provide a set of aesthetic and experientially stimulating traces and fragments of trauma and displacement that over the duration of the performance would create a journey through these disturbing realities. Associations arising during this journey could point to both the past and the present in central Europe.

The performative premise used to create the performance score is best phrased as a question. What happens when actors embody non-verbal traces of memory like those embedded in stone, i.e., the non-verbal white spaces of a performance etching? To address this question practically we made use of

1   the nuances of a heightened sensory awareness optimally embodied via immersion in the principles and techniques of psychophysical training;
2   work with structure improvisations (Chapter 6) as part of the devising process for the generation of performance structures;
3   inspiration drawn from two contemporary Japanese sources—the work of playwright/ director Ōta Shōgo's "Station Plays" with their non-verbal scores, "slowed-down everyday movement," and stories that are always present, but just not heard, and the image-based work of Japanese *butoh*, especially dancer/ choreographer Kazuo Ohno.

We intentionally did not want to limit the performance to one specific mode or style of performance. While there needed to be overall coherence both in dramaturgy and aesthetic, we were more concerned with what vortices of meaning and experience the audience might experience from traces created by figures or personas placed within performance structures animated by and resonating with tasks and stimuli. The six actors in the company would be expected to psychophysically transform from one figure/persona to another as required by the tasks of each structure in the score.

Before we began work, we knew that some structures would be non-verbal, emphasizing psychophysical engagement in tasks, while others gave voice to text—fragmentary memories, images, recollections, exchanges. Each structure and the etching as a whole would put into play many possible moments of resonance for the audience, but the impact and meaning would depend as much on what the audience brought as what we provided for them.

In rehearsal and performance

Initial work on devising and developing specific performance structures began during a two-week period in Graz in April 2002, continued in August in Wales, and concluded with a final set of rehearsals in Graz.[5] Our points of departure for the creation of a structure included: (1) embodiment of a psychophysical state of being/doing, (2) text authored by Kaite O'Reilly, and (3) pieces of found text. Whatever the beginning point, we elaborated and developed each structure by adding or juxtaposing that beginning point with music, additional images, embodiment of states, or other fragments of text. As with any devising process, there was a considerable amount of material that we tried out but eventually discarded. Decisions about which fledgling structures we kept was determined by the potential any particular scenario possessed on its own terms and in relation to the dramaturgy of the etching as a whole.

By the time of the initial set of performances at Theater im Palais in September 2002, we had developed a provisional performance score with twelve structures. After the first few performances it became clear that we should cut what was then the final structure ("Rubble"), and end the performance with "Why Did You Leave?"[6] "Rubble" provided much too literal an ending—suggesting a narrative closure and too closely mirroring the first lengthy structure with minimal dialogue, "Leaving." For the final performance in our initial run we tried out this change. Concluding the performance with "Why Did You Leave?" accentuated the failure of language central to our early conceptualization of the performance and provided a striking, distorted final image. Prior to the second staging of *Speaking Stones* in Aflenz November 27–30, 2002, we shifted some text and actions from "Rubble" to "Leaving," and made other minor adjustments to what became the definitive text and performance score with eleven structures (see box overleaf).

Structurally and aesthetically, *Speaking Stones* is post-psychological and therefore a post-dramatic performance score. The company of six actors engages specific psychophysical tasks and/or delivers fragments of text as they materialize and inhabit a series of figures and personas never named. Costumed in a generic assemblage of white/ivory colored pants, skirts, coats, shirts, vests, or waist-wraps with various types of black boots or heavy shoes, all were alike, but each was unique. The generic costumes allowed the actors to transform from structure to structure without the necessity of being defined as a specific character.

For "Internment" simple costume pieces were added which provided sufficient additional information for the figures to suggest but not become characters—the headscarves worn by the women suggest the women are eastern European, and the black belts of the three men identify them as soldiers. In "Internment" and "United Fucking Nations," the actors-as-soldiers come close to inhabiting conventional realist characters as they speak and act in response to the specific, material circumstances of the conflict in which they find

---

***Speaking Stones*: list of structures**

1   Preset/Song: out of the darkness, a lament . . . a mourning song is repeated . . .
2   Bewilderment of the dead: faces and palm turned upward . . . trying to see from/through the darkness . . .
3   Leaving: in the darkness, a bewildering laugh . . . suppressed . . . an arrival . . . anticipation . . . a violin . . . a couple dances . . . a slap . . . people departing . . . in the dark, a wall of stone collapses into a pile of rubble . . .
4   Footsteps of Dead: footsteps of the dead processing . . . "silent speaking" (in sign language) . . . then recessing . . .
5   Internment: internment with strangled syllables . . . watching *Dallas* . . . soldiers joke . . .
6   Marching: . . . marching feet . . . an Austrian folksong sings of the beautiful mountains . . .
7   United Fucking Nations: fragments of stories from "the United Fucking Nations" . . .
8   Semiotics of Zero: . . . a "lecture" . . . the semiotics of zero to a Bach cantata . . .
9   Chair Stones: . . . some bodies, compressed to stone, speak . . . others remain silent . . .
10 Interrogation: . . . questions are asked . . . no answers given . . .
11 Why Did you Leave?: . . . more questions are asked . . . a final sepia-orange image with faces/hands stopped . . . frozen in the act of speaking . . . "words destroyed" . . .

---

themselves. But in both cases these "almost characters" are juxtaposed with silent or silenced figures. In "Internment" the three women appear behind huge stones, attempting to speak, but their initial words catch in the throat—half-said and/or strangled in the act of speaking. At first, no words are articulated . . . only half-guttural sounds. When words eventually come, they are fragments of memory:

A: Her shoe, unlaced beneath the table.
B: When I saw him lying there, he was smiling.
C: It was a silly argument—some cross words.
B: Hands cold, skin thin like paper. Smiling.
A: Old dusty perfume bottles by the mirror.
B: My father never smiled.
A: Her engagement ring beside the sink.
C: The spoon was still in the bowl on the table.
B: His hat was sitting on the hook.
A: The smell of chrysanthemums.
C: We were the only ones to know.
B: The telephone bill came in his name.
C: Her last word was "no."

During the initial part of "United Fucking Nations" all six actors engage in repetitive simple tasks with various sizes, types, and shapes of stone—stacking, counting, balancing, listening—while two young men speak in turn directly to the audience without acknowledging the presence or activities of the other actors.

Young Man 1: There were four of us—O'Brien, Pavlovic and the Greek. They called us the United Fucking Nations. It was after the last time, that's when I—Four of us. Used kerosene. Old fashioned. Drag a mattress into the main room—horse hair—still burns—O'Brien splashing the stuff all over the bloody place, running down his arms. Singed the hair off, later. Said that'd teach him, he'd learn. Never fucking did. Smell of pork, burning. I left then. Nothing to it. Change of clothes, plenty on the road, nearly ended up in a collective center but carried on, due North. North West. Never had a compass, just walked, followed my nose, smelt my way. Easy. Could have passed as one of them. Often did. Any sign of trouble and I'd just open my mouth and they heard. "Oh." Good as a passport, better. Doesn't get wet when you swim.

Young Man 2: You help yourself to houses along the way. It's not stealing. I'm no thief. Nothing fucking left, anyway. Looted already, the lads before me. See them walking up the road with a telly on their head. Video. CD. Sometimes they'll take the cooker if they've wheels, don't bother with disconnecting, just rip it out, toss a match and there she blows.

Young Man 1: The things you find. Toys, potato mashers, football trophies. I spent an afternoon doing a jigsaw, sticking together these bits of paper. I would've fucking cried if I wasn't laughing. An afternoon doing that bollocks. That's when you know it's getting to you. Time to get out, boy, and no doubt. A birth certificate, a love letter and a fucking tax bill. Just that. No more.

Performances in the Roman quarry at Aflenz (Römersteinbruch)

While in rehearsals for the initial set of performances in Graz, members of Theater Asou heard about a vast underground quarry dating from the Roman period nearby, and that an official in Wagna, Walter Gluschitsch, had recently begun opening up the quarry as part of a new, regional cultural initiative. Theater Asou arranged for all of us to visit the quarry in Aflenz. It was a fortuitous moment. As we entered the space, there was no doubt that *all* of us immediately knew that *this* was the most appropriate space in which to perform *Speaking Stones*. What follows is a brief summary of the history of the Römersteinbruch, compiled by the company:

The underground quarry in Aflenz near Leibnitz has a long history. Within the district of Styria, located 35 miles from Austria's second largest city, Graz, and 6 miles from Leibnitz lies the quiet farming village of Aflenz. As one enters the village there is a rolling valley to one's right. No one would know that a massive (8,000 sq. metres) ancient underground quarry whose first use dates from the Roman period, lies hidden within the green hill to the left. Nothing has marked the presence of this quarry since at least the end of World War II. Until the

last few years the presence of the quarry, and its history, have been kept quiet. It is only when you are directed to walk around the hill along a gravel drive-way that you discover in the midst of a huge wall of rock, two old, massive wooden doors large enough to accommodate trucks capable of carrying quarried stone. The gravel drive-way leads into and through the maze of chambers that constitute the quarry. The chambers inside vary in size—some are immense (up to 10 metres high). When lit, there is a sense of caverns within caverns within caverns. The quiet within is profound. The space is alive to any sound made within its resonant walls and ceilings. The acoustics of the space are vibrant and clear—the stone an excellent transmitter of sound whether spoken/sung, or the sound of breath itself. Equally profound is the lack of light—when all electric lights, torches, or candles are extinguished, one enters a world of absolute darkness. Except inside the immediate entrance, the temperature in the space is a constant 8 degrees centigrade year-round.

When the Romans settled in the south and east of Styria, they dug tunnels into the mountain to extract limestone to build an amphitheatre, official buildings, and numerous houses in the nearby settlement, Flavia Solva. Due to the history of the quarry's use during World War II, any mention of the quarry was banished from the generally accepted Styrian historical registers. A brief summary of this lost history follows.

During the summer of 1943 as the first Allied war-planes coming from Italy dropped bombs onto strategically important targets throughout Styria, the Nazis began to transfer their war industry underground. In February 1944 the first transport of 201 prisoners from the concentration camp at Mauthausen to the labor camp at Aflenz took place. This was one of seven Styrian subordinate work-camps to which prisoners were distributed from the concentration camp at Mauthausen. Within a short time the halls of the quarry were changed into a modern machine-works factory. By July 1944 there were already 655 prisoners working underground in the quarry.

The mortality rate among prisoners was at times very high. Some deceased prisoners were taken back to Mauthausen for cremation, and later buried in a common grave near the camp. By late summer 1944 all the manufacturing equipment was fully installed, and from that time on the prisoners—most from the Soviet Union, Poland, and Yugoslavia—were used for the production of gear-wheels and crank shafts.

With the Allied advance through Italy the camp was liquidated on the 2nd of April 1945. 467 prisoners were marched off toward the camp at Ebensee. Eight prisoners were shot on the way because of weakness. 49 prisoners tried to escape near Judenburg, but most were caught and shot. On the 18th of April the remaining 407 prisoners arrived in Ebensee.

At the end of the war the Allies dismantled the underground factory. The only evidence of what transpired in the quarry during WWII today is a few rusty cable ends sticking out of some concrete.

A few years ago a cultural initiative was established in order to revisit and commemorate the history of the quarry through various cultural events. In 2002 and again in 2004 Theater Asou was invited by the artistic director of the quarry to present *Speaking Stones*.

When performed in the Aflenz quarry, *Speaking Stones* takes place deep within one of the large, central caverns of the quarry. For the performers and the audience alike, the space itself becomes an actor/activator—both physically and historically. This sense of activation begins with the ten-minute walk from the parking lot, and the journey into this cold, dark, underground environment. As discussed above, *Speaking Stones* was not created to literally tell the quarry's history, but locating the performance in the quarry allowed its images, voices, and fragments to resonate with that particular history—offering moments and glimpses backward and forward in time and creating a frisson not possible in a formal theatrical environment such as Theater im Palais.

Psychophysical work on specific structures

In the remainder of this case study, I discuss the application of the psychophysical training to the creation and performance of some of the specific structures in *Speaking Stones*. There were three quite different points of departure for our work on each structure, as follows:

- psychophysical states and/or image-based work was the beginning point for the development of "Bewilderment," "Leaving," "Footsteps," "Marching," and "Chair Stones";
- short sections of text authored by Kaite O'Reilly served as the beginning point for work on "Internment," "United Fucking Nations," "Interrogation," and "Why Did You Leave?";
- found text (Brian Rotman's *Signifying Nothing: The Semiotics of Zero*) was the beginning point for work on "The Semiotics of Zero."

● DVD-ROM: *SPEAKING STONES*

"Bewilderment"

"Bewilderment" was developed as a non-verbal, psychophysical score set to background music in which five of the six performers sustain a complex image and awareness throughout the structure—the dead searching for love. The primary psychophysical state of being/doing each actor inhabits is the mouth as a yawning chasm—a black hole reaching back inside one's own body (see cover photograph). As the actor allows the jaw to drop open, she senses the open mouth as a deep chasm, and then actively enters this chasm—in effect traveling back inside this black hole. The head is tilted slightly back, so that the eyes are turned upward toward the back beyond of space. But the actor does not focus on an external point; rather, the actor inhabits a dissociated state of awareness produced by indirect focus, i.e., the actor keeps the mind engaged on the task of entering the black hole of the yawning chasm and never focuses with the external gaze. The internal eye keeps traveling back inside. The actor also keeps attentive to the breath. With the jaw dropped open, the breath becomes audible—sounding as it draws in, and out, to and from the bottom of the black chasm below the navel. The actor actively listens to the breath as it sounds, and allows the breath to become the eyes that are looking for love. Through indirect focus and attentiveness to the breath, the actor senses her mouthlessness—a darkness reaching down through the entire body. With each cycle of breath the actor takes that journey of darkness through the body.

With the right hand held palm upward, each actor stands with one foot on the ground, and the other foot on a stone, creating a state of slight imbalance. This is intentional. In terms of balance, each actor senses their feet, and constantly attempts to slightly adjust position to find the balance point within the imbalance of the position between the feet. The result of this state of imbalance is the production of a subtle and at first almost imperceptible swaying movement like seaweed underwater moving with the current in a gentle sea. Using the chiasmatic multiple awareness discussed in Chapter 3, each actor's awareness circulates amongst and between several heightened states of awareness and/or images, i.e., each actor's awareness dialectically moves between and among (1) the primary image of continuously (re)entering the black hole of the yawning chasm, (2) making adjustment to one's balance while sensing the feet and thereby producing a subtle swaying, and (3) listening to and absorbing the sound of both the music and the breath as it moves inward and downward, and then outward again—looking . . . [again] looking . . . [again] looking—but never finding.

"Leaving"

The opening part of the third structure, "Leaving," was developed directly from work on structured improvisations discussed in Chapter 6. The initial score from which the structure as a whole eventually evolved began as follows (*note:* the actors' actual first names are used throughout the following description to identify specific acting tasks):

Five actors are seated next to each other—from audience left to right, Chris (holding a violin), Uschi, Gernot, Monika, and Laura. Klaus remains off-stage in the darkness behind the seated figures.

Psychophysical score for those seated: Focus ahead. Strong awareness of behind, and through ears/sound . . . Hear the sound of a clock ticking . . . absorb the sound of time passing . . . Keep an extremely strong sense of peripheral awareness of the others present, and of their presence . . . Add an additional point of focus up, shifting between ahead and up . . . Sense in the palm of the right hand the impulse to reach out and grasp with the right hand . . . But the impulse "fails" . . . There is nothing there to grasp . . . Sense the emptiness of the hand which has not touched . . . sense the "nothing" in the hand . . . At some point, if the impulse to look comes, look at the empty right palm.

On a musical cue, Klaus enters from off-stage: Looking to first seated figure, Laura, he crosses slowly and stands behind her . . . looking down to her before him.

Laura: keeping the very strong back awareness, she senses the presence of the standing figure behind her.

Klaus: keeping an extremely strong sense of awareness of the space behind, and of his palms, he places a hand on Laura's shoulder. He looks up, ahead. When his hand is placed on her shoulder, Laura absorbs the quality of his touch and senses this fully within.

Klaus senses the next seated figure, looks to Monika, crosses behind her, and places a hand on her shoulder. He looks ahead . . .
Repeated for Gernot and Uschi.

This simple series of points of external focus and actions was gradually elaborated. A young woman's laugh fills the darkness of the space, joined by a second woman's laughter until both abruptly stop. An internal element was added to the playing of the above psychophysical score—the extremely strong desire to stay and not to leave, even though all must eventually depart. In playing this structure, it was crucial for the actors to keep a residual awareness of each action as a new impulse shifts the point of focus, or the sensory awareness. Each moment was ideally knit into the fabric of the whole.

Eventually, "Leaving" was further elaborated with additional actions and text by Kaite O'Reilly that shaped the structure into a series of moments of departure:

Chris stands with his violin in hand, and steps forward. All look to Chris. He stops, starts to look back, and stops. Then he turns back, looking at Klaus and Uschi. He indicates the floor in front. Klaus and Uschi step forward, ready to dance. Before Chris can play, Laura stands, turns away, and takes a step. Chris stops . . . looks to her . . . pauses . . . looks back to Uschi and Klaus. He begins to play a single note as the couple dance.

Klaus: (As they dance) The one thing never to give is your name. There is power in knowing a name. They can call you then and when they do, there's no disobeying. You have to answer. No choice in it. (Chris stops playing. Turns and begins to exit.) No choice at all.

Uschi steps back. She slaps Klaus. She immediately crosses to pick up her bag. She pauses, looks at Gernot, who turns away. She crosses to Laura, places a hand on her shoulder, and they exit slowly together.

Klaus: (Looking downstage left, as the two women exit into the darkness upstage) My father cleared fields of stones for a penny a bucket. Flint blunted the plough blade—stones made the furrow crooked.

It was backbreaking work, dragging himself and the pails up and down the land to be ploughed. Each year he cleared it, shifting broken stones to the ditch. Every year they came back, rising through the soil as if to taunt him. The earth throwing up its seed from its belly. (Gernot stands, crosses to pick up his suitcase.)

My father always said a man was nothing unless he had land. (To Gernot)
All I have is the dirt beneath my fingernails. (Klaus crosses a few steps to a stone. He picks up a stone.) My father cleared stones for a penny a bucket. It was a good living.

My father hated stones. (He drops the stone, turns, picks up the suitcase. Klaus and Gernot exit together. Monica remains seated, looking ahead). Lights to black.

While there is one partial story here, it is told by only one speaker. The others present have their own stories, but they remain untold and unsaid. These unsaid silent stories, marked only by the psychophysical presence of the five actors not speaking, helped to create the white spaces within which the one story is told. There was much more that could have been said, but . . . at least at this moment, remains unsaid.

"Footsteps of the Dead"

Similar to "Bewilderment," "Footsteps" was developed as a non-verbal psychophysical score set to music—Pachelbel's Canon in D Major. But this all-too-familiar music was rendered different in an arrangement for traditional Korean plucked instruments. The performance score developed for this structure follows:

As lights fade up slowly, through haze the six actors are revealed as they begin to move . . . from far within the central cavern toward the audience.

Moving at a glacial pace, always ahead. When they reach the rubble, the rubble is part of the problem that must be solved in the slow progression forward—each footstep an effort.

Awareness and energy: working between awareness of the up through the top of the head, and down through the feet—the space below. Always modulating one's awareness between the up and the down, and maintaining a sense of the behind, and the before.

Palms slightly up, "carrying love" . . . In the act of carrying, always sensing the weight of what is being carried. When the weight is too much in one position, the weight being carried can be shifted.

On cue: mouths drop open wide. Entire body becomes the mouth. The footsteps always continuing across the space.

Then mouth closes. Jaw tight. Still keeping the sense of up.

Looking up, turning (some right, some left, wherever the impulse), but still, constantly moving forward, progressing, slowly.

Mouths open again.

FAST SHIFT: Look ahead . . . freeze, mouth open wide—

Figure 9.1 *Speaking Stones*, Christian Heuegger in "Footsteps of the Dead." (Photograph: Nina Herlitschka)

Sound out. Silence. In the silence:

All the images thus far inhabited are now allowed to gradually "melt" out of the actor's body. The "center" of awareness becomes clear—a fresh slate.

When completely "melted." Using sign-language, but remaining unspoken and unvoiced, in unison the actors "speak" with their hands: steps (focus out × 4 gestures, right/left/right/left) . . . dead (focus down, then coffin down with two fingers each side) . . . carry (left under right, coming up) . . . love (to heart, focus ahead). Slowly, all begin to step backward six steps . . . into darkness.

The embodiment of progressive psychophysical structures such as that described above is not intended to provide the audience with sufficiently detailed semiotic information for a definitive reading of what is witnessed or experienced. Rather, such structures are offered as part of the experience through which associations might arise for the audience. The audience need not know definitively that the actors are "carrying love." Nor do we expect the vast majority of the audience to be able to read the sign-language. Here the sign-language's primary purpose is not iconic meaning, but another task through which the actors are psychophysically engaged in shaping vectors of energy for the audience's experience.

"Semiotics of Zero"

This structure's point of departure was a set of short selections from Brian Rotman's (1993) provocative history of attempts to represent and signify "nothing," zero, or "the absent." I edited these into a lecture, delivered by Gernot Rieger into a microphone while standing at a podium with an overhead projector next to him. Gernot does not play the character of a lecturer, but rather is "one who lectures." In delivering the text, Gernot's task was to connect as simply as possible

to the words in the act of speaking, just as the actors did in their work with me on the Beckett texts. He was to convey the text not *to, but through* the actors engaged in psychophysically embodying images associated with the content of the lecture. He simultaneously listened to what he was saying as he spoke—thereby creating an interior loop of awareness resonating with the sense of what is said. This mode of speaking has more to do with engaging and modulating one's interior energy in a qualitative relationship to the act of speaking rather than to playing a character.

While the text of the lecture was our point of departure in this structure, I elaborated a simple, suggestive psychophysical score to work, point, and counter-point with the text, as both are set to music—Bach's Cantata #1 for altos. The image that becomes visible as the lights come up is of a woman (Monika), seated on the floor next to a man's body (Christian) on the audience side of the pile of rubble. Behind them, seated on three chairs facing different directions amidst the rubble, are two women (Uschi, Laura) and one man (Klaus). These three figures look off into the distance. They never look at Monika or the man on the floor. In silence, Monika lifts a flat stone in her hand, scoops water from a basin, and lets the water drip into the basin. We hear the drip of the water. The music begins. Absorbing the music, Monika begins to very slowly wash or cleanse the right hand and arm of the male actor (Christian) lying prone on the floor. Monika's acting tasks are two-fold: (1) to engage with her complete sensual awareness the tactile act of cleansing in which she is engaged—allowing this sensual awareness of the feel of the stone, the water, the holding of the hand to resonate within her; and (2) to simultaneously allow the music and text delivered in the lecture to pass through her, and to resonate with her embodied sensual awareness of her first task. She continues this cleansing through the structure. After she completes washing the body, she crosses the prone figure's arms across his chest. Throughout she serves as a vehicle for the text, absorbing the text into the act of washing, and finally in an act of silent repose.

The three seated actors were given the (necessarily impossible) primary task of attempting to embrace the absent. I worked with the actors on developing a very simple semi-improvised, repetitive psychophysical score: the impulse to initiate the first cycle of action was led by a shift in focus from the point ahead, to an unknown point in the space. As soon as they had connected to this new point with their external focus, then the impulse came to grasp, hold, or embrace—an impulse initiated from the lower *dantian*. As the embrace is embodied in each cycle, at some point in that psychophysical act of embracing there is a realization that *there is nothing there*. There is no one to embrace. At this moment the actor senses the absent s/he was about to embrace. The actor's relationship to the embrace is felt with full psychophysical/*ki*-awareness; however, there should be no display of any overt attitude projected onto this sense of absence —of nothing being there. At this point in the cycle, the actor stops or pauses sensing through the entire bodymind this void. When another impulse to find is generated, the actor looks to another point, initiating a new psychophysical cycle. Each cycle ends in failure to embrace. The position of the embrace changes with each impulse, becoming a choreography in space. The second task for these three actors, as for Monika in her acts of cleansing, was to absorb and become a vehicle for the text and music.

In silence.
Washer: hands in lap. Rock in right hand. Looking at crossed arms on body. Hold opening image. Count: 1,001 × 5. Right hand with rock to bowl of water, dip, let drip three times. When the stone is placed on the arm, ready to wash, the music fades in.

Speaker: What sort of mark is suitable to inscribe absence?
Three seated figures count 1,001 × 3, and begin first impulse. The actions continue except as noted.
Consider the mathematical, purely notational problem that zero addresses. It arises as a gap, an empty region, within the place of notation for individual numerals signifying, in the decimal case, the absence of 1, 2, 3, 4, 5, 6, 7, 8 and 9. An iconic, mimetic approach to the writing of this absence—take for example that of Babylonian mathematicians for nearly two millennia—might be the use of an empty space to signify it; so that, for instance:

11, 1 1, 1 1 (Writing on overhead projector, demonstrating the problem). One one. One space one. One space space one would notate eleven, one hundred and one, and one thousand and one, respectively.

But the scheme has an obvious defect: the right-hand space merges with the blank surface of writing, making 11 ambiguous between eleven, one hundred and ten, eleven hundred, and so on. Moreover, and for the same reason, an empty space is not transportable: unlike the other numerals it cannot be reproduced, written independently of its syntactical presentation with particular numerals, without it merging with the space used to separate words from each other. Signifying absence by absence is not, then, a stable and coherently interesting option for writing down zero.

What sort of mark is suitable to inscribe absence?

Movers and Washer pause . . . Movers freeze and Washer looks to Movers . . . then freezing . . . all listening . . .

Speaker places a glass bowl with water on the overhead projector, and continues: One can depict an absence through a signifier that contains a gap, by a space, an absence in its shape. The most elemental solution, the ur-mark of absence, is any instance of an iconographic hole; any simple enclosure, ring, circle, ovoid, loop, and the like, which surrounds an absence and divides space into an inside and an outside. Thus, presumably, the universal recognition of "o," "O" or "o" as symbols of zero. And thus a circle of associations linking zero and "nothing" . . . the absent.

What sort of mark is suitable to inscribe absence?

Movers: continue . . . three times . . . freezing at end . . . Washer dips once, washes three times, puts stone in bowl, taking hand they've been washing, and holds it in both hands.

What sort of mark is suitable to inscribe absence?

Monika places Chris' right hand on left. The four figures cross hands over chest, as when they began. Monika looks down. All freeze, suspending their actions as music fades out . . . Pause . . .

The "psycho" of the "psychophysical" in the enactment of a scenario like this is not "psychology," but rather the state of resonant awareness that is generated within one when one fully embodies this simple score and actually listens and is sensuous to the tasks in which one is engaged. During rehearsals, I had to work hard with Gernot *not* to put character into the delivery of the text and not to attempt to play a Lecturer, but rather to become a kind of sounding-box for the speaking of the words and ideas. For actors used to creating characters, it is often quite difficult to trust the fact that working without character, and with a simple relationship to energy and resonance in the act of speaking can create sufficient interest and experience for the audience, especially when spoken text is part of a qualitative montage. Here music, text, and task together create an inner frisson within the actor—optimally vibrating them in relation to their work.

"Why Did You Leave?"

The final structure began as a short four-line text authored by Kaite O'Reilly:

> Why did you leave?
> Why did you not want me?
> Why did you not want us?
> Words . . . destroyed.

We elaborated these four lines into a psychophysical score with progressive action. A still image opens the structure: three actors are seated amidst the rubble. Three other actors stand—each of these framed as a picture within the frame each holds. The image recalls that of "Leaving" with three empty picture frames seemingly suspended in the air behind the seated actors; however, rather than being empty, they now frame three faces. In silence, the three seated actors slowly begin to speak each line of the text, but in unvoiced sign language.[7] We worked the complete psychophysical connection of the actor to the saying of each sign with his entire bodymind. The actors were encouraged to take time with each word, keeping the other actors in their peripheral awareness so that, at least at the beginning of the structure, their signing was very close to unison. For the second repetition, the three actors continue signing the words, but also begin to silently mouth the words. For the third repetition, the three actors standing/holding picture frames join the delivery of the text as they drop the frames into the rubble. In the final cycle only "words . . . destroyed" are signed/said—their repetition over and again becomes a final chorus. The actors no longer repeat the words or gestures at the same time, but rather all six actors are part of a cacophony of flailing gestures and words— suddenly frozen in a final sepia image—"words . . . destroyed." Suspended in the midst of attempting to speak both with words and sign-language, each face and body is distorted in its own way and juxtaposed against the others.

Concluding discussion

The psychophysical work in *Speaking Stones* explored the inner action of vibration and resonance, not from a psychological/behavioral point of departure, but from a task-based, *ki*-awareness, or energetics point of departure. Akin to Artaud's vision of the ideal actor, in *Speaking Stones* the actors optimally became "athletes of the heart," creating and enacting a metaphysics "at the nerve ends ... through the[ir] skin" (1970: 237). The fragments of text played an extremely important part in the creation of the potential experience and meaning of *Speaking Stones*. What was crucial was that the actors possess a psychophysical understanding of each image they embodied so that they fully resonated with the text and music.

10

4:48 Psychosis by Sarah Kane

Introduction

4:48 Psychosis was the last play written by the
well-known British playwright, Sarah Kane
(1971–1999), in the fall and winter of 1998–1999
on commission by the Royal Court Theatre,
London, and first produced at the Royal Court
Jerwood Theatre Upstairs in 2000. *4:48 Psychosis*
is a highly poetic "open" text—a prime example of
postdramatic dramaturgy (Lehmann 2006: 18).[1]
There is no cast list. There are no character names.
There are no stage directions. The only marks that
help distinguish each of the twenty-four scenarios
or major units of text from another are a series of
dashes (— — —).[2] There are no indications of
who or how many people speak the words of the
text. There is no traditional arc of narrative action.
While working on the script Kane commented
that it "doesn't even have characters, all there is
are language and images" (quoted in Saunders
2002: 112).

Kane's text offers a relatively open set of
possibilities for how one might realize in
performance these images and the text's highly
suggestive/poetic language. But however "open"
the text appears to be, there is clearly a primary
"Figure" and/or "Speaker" whose state(s) of being
are elaborated throughout the play. There is also
one or more "Doctors" whom Figure interacts
with and struggles against. Figure's state of being
might be described as a prism; each shift or change
in the position of the prism reveals another facet
of a complex, mosaic set of deeply felt experiences
which collectively constitute "psychosis." In
November 1998, Kane wrote

> I'm writing a play called *4:48 Psychosis* . . .
> It's about a psychotic breakdown and what
> happens to *a person's* mind when the barriers
> which distinguish between reality and different
> forms of imagination completely disappear, so
> that you no longer know the difference between
> your waking life and your dream life. And also
> you no longer know where you stop, and the
> world starts. So, for example, if I were psychotic
> I would literally not know the difference
> between myself, this table and Dan . . . They
> would all somehow be part of a continuum, and
> various boundaries begin to collapse. Formally,
> I'm trying to collapse a few boundaries as well;
> to carry on with making form and content one.
> (Saunders 2002: 112, added italics)

Although the text explores what happens to the
boundaries within "a person's mind," *4:48 Psychosis*
is not about *an* individual character's mind.

I view the central Figure/Speaker as embodying *in extremis* our shared existential condition of "thrown-ness" into the world. Figure longs for the (absent) Other. This Other incorporates many Others—that part of one's self that is missing or incomplete, the Other as lover, partner, supporter, or the divine that might make us complete. Figure/Speaker is always searching for completion, but remains incomplete. She struggles against the limitations of the medical establishment's view and treatment of her within her condition. Release from the almost constant experience of fragmentation and dissociation is sought, and ultimately found in suicide.

The play's dramaturgy exposes various facets of this fragmented self in separation from itself and in response to the medical establishment. The Figure who suffers this condition is the collective "we" made explicit at times in Kane's text:

We are anathema
the pariahs of reason [. . .]

We are the abjects
who depose our leaders
and burn incense unto Baal.
(Kane 2001: 228–229)

From my directorial perspective I wanted to work on the performative actualization of this state so that it could *not* be reduced to, nor represented by, *an* individual/character.[3] I explored how to realize this state of psychosis in its "that it is-ness"—its inescapable if ever-shifting "realities" in the moment, and the inner strength of Figure's confrontation with and response to the medical establishment. The twenty-four scenarios cumulatively actualize this ever-shifting evocation of absence, longing, humour, and hurt within the human condition when it meets the limited response society offers to mental illness.

The issues of psychosis and suicide which Kane engages in *4:48 Psychosis* are complex and difficult, and have touched anyone who has had direct or indirect experience with mental illness among family or friends.[4] It is widely known that throughout her adult life Sarah Kane struggled with her own mental health and that she committed suicide on February 20, 1999. The text certainly draws on Kane's experience of the mental health system in the UK. However, just as the play should not be reduced to an individual character's psychosis, it is equally a mistake to reduce the suicide in the play to Kane's personal struggle with her mental health. I agree with Graham Saunders that "thinking of *4:48 Psychosis* as little more than a suicide note . . . risks impoverishing the play: moreover, such a commentary runs the risk of providing too reductive a reading, both of the play's content and its themes" (2002: 110).

Owing to Kane's death, the first production was postponed until June 2000. For the original production the director, James Macdonald, "split the play's voice into three: two women and one man" (Grieg 2001: xvii).

In rehearsal and performance

I initially worked on *4:48 Psychosis* in a studio-laboratory setting with an internationally diverse group of MFA/MA/BA actors at the University of Exeter (2004, 2007) and in a full production with a group of Korean actors at KNUA (Seoul, 2008).[5] I wanted to work on *4:48* because of its challenging content, structure, and dramatic form, as well as the relative openness of the text. Compared to most productions of *4:48 Psychosis*, I chose to work with a large group of actors (between twelve and twenty) so that the central Figure would be shared by many actors, and therefore the state of psychosis experienced by Figure could not be identified as belonging to an individual character. Using a large cast also allowed me to explore the choral potential of the poetic sections of the text in performance.

The point of departure for my work on *4:48 Psychosis* was Kane's observation that in a state of psychosis one does not "know the difference between myself, this table" and an-Other—a state in which one is "somehow part of a continuum" and "various boundaries begin to collapse" (Kane quote in Saunders 2002: 112). Among the twenty-four scenarios are four quite distinct types of material:

1   "I am" statements in which Figure describes or addresses in the first person her condition or state of being/doing, sometimes with a few lines of commentary or qualification.
2   Closely related journal or diary-like scenarios that are filled with highly evocative, poetic descriptions and/or images. These elaborate a context, experience, or internal state/condition for Figure. They are written (and spoken) in a narrative voice that describes some aspect of the condition or experience. They are either in the present, or reflect on a past memory. These states lend themselves to psychophysical embodiment.
3   A diverse set of short two-character dialogue scenes between Doctor(s) and the Figure, each of which explores the complexity of Figure's relationship with the medical establishment, and with one Doctor in particular.
4   Scenarios that materialize a state or condition on-stage—such as the scenario for which Kane offers the simple statement: "RSVP ASAP," or the two scenarios in which there is a voiced countdown in complete black from 100 toward zero, ending with 7 or 2, i.e., never reaching zero.

Each type of scenario offers a particular view, recollection, and/or experience of Figure within an ever-shifting state of psychosis—sometimes in the past, sometimes in the first-person present, and sometimes in dialogue with a Doctor. The "work" of the production is to materialize "Figure" and her state cumulatively between past/memory and present experience in response to the medical establishment represented by the Doctor(s).

Five points of entry were identified for the actors "playing" Figure: (1) speaking Figure's dialogue to a Doctor in the present; (2) delivering first-person, highly poetic, diary-like text to oneself as Figure; (3) speaking *for* Figure by delivering third-person text about her state, condition, or experience in the present; (4) speaking *about*

Figure's memory of a past experience by *entering into, and speaking back* to, that memory of her illness; and (5) psychophysical embodiment of a particular poetic image describing one or more aspects of Figure's state/condition. I scored Figure's text for delivery either as Figure (first-person voice) or as Speaker (third-person voice). When delivering Figure's lines, the following strategies were used:

•   delivering the poetic parts of the text as simply as possible by focusing on the "saidness" of the text, i.e., the texture of the words in the mouth as they are spoken;
•   kinesthetically locating an evocative, poetic image in a specific place within the body and sustaining that image through time while delivering text;
•   embodying the state or condition described in the text;
•   using an image or physical location to "enter" the condition of the Figure.

In a few scenarios Figure was played by an individual actor; however, in most scenarios Figure and Speaker were played by more than one actor.

In most scenarios in which Doctor(s) appear, they too were usually played by more than one actor. Using two or three sets of actors to play most Figure/Doctor scenes allowed the development of a choral delivery of the text—sometimes delivered in more than one language.[6] Points of entry for actors playing Doctor(s) were similar to those used for Figure: text spoken in first person as Doctor, text spoken in third person about the state/condition of Figure, and psychophysical embodiment of a particular poetic image based on Figure's experience of Doctor(s).

In addition to the image of a prism, work on *4:48* was guided by an image of weaving a rich, complex tapestry. One texture or colour is foregrounded in one moment, and shifts to another texture/colour in the next. The cumulative process of weaving renders the whole. When the actors inhabited states as Figure or Doctor(s), they existed on stage as texture rather than for dialogue or narrative. There is movement or flow, not of motivational action in the conventional realist sense, but rather of image/energy/focus/intensity—all modulated psychophysically. One of the important connective "threads" in this weaving was the near-constant "sound-scape" during the first-person/diary-like scenes—an ever-shifting musical underscore—sometimes overtly in the foreground, and sometimes in the background.

⊙ DVD-ROM: *4:48 PSYCHOSIS*

"I am . . ." statements: inhabiting, listening, absorbing, conveying

The third scenario consists of a lengthy series of "I am . . .," "I can't . . .," or I have . . . statements, followed by four observations:

> I am sad
> I feel that the future is hopeless and that things cannot improve
> I am bored and dissatisfied with everything
> I am a complete failure as a person
>
> [. . . concluding with]
>
> Some will call this self-indulgence
> (they are lucky not to know its truth)
> Some will know the simple fact of pain
> This is becoming my normality
> (Kane 2001: 206–207)

Played by the full ensemble, Figure's lines were distributed among the entire group, but were spoken as if one. The initial psychophysical state the actors were asked to inhabit in this scenario was one of being beyond tears—a state carrying a high degree of heaviness, weightiness, or cloudiness. All the actors were to maintain an extremely strong sensory awareness of the space behind—allowing that strong sense of behind to press on them. One group of actors were seated in a row of chairs with their elbows or forearms or hands resting on their knees, and focus slightly down toward the floor. Behind them sitting in chairs at a long table was the second group of actors with their hands/arms resting on the table. All the actors were to maintain a strong awareness of the weight of behind while listening to/following each cycle of inhalation/exhalation, i.e., breathing into the heaviness or cloudiness.

In this state, each actor spoke all the lines of the scenario silently. Each individual actor voiced those specific lines assigned. All maintained a constantly open state of auditory awareness. As with delivery of Beckett's texts, each actor was asked to maintain an internal/kinesthetic loop by allowing the resonance of each line voiced and/or heard to resonate within/along the spine, in their palms, in the soles of their feet, etc.

In speaking non-dialogue text such as these first-person statements (or third-person descriptions), I asked the actors to "feel the form" and shape of the words/images/thoughts as they are said. The "feeling of form" has to do not just with the body per se, but with the tactile, auditory relationship of the mouth, tongue, teeth, and lips as they are shaped to speak. In this way, words body-forth as they are spoken. A psychophysical approach invites the actor to inhabit a heightened embodied connection to the complex act of speaking. If the actor "feels" the shape of words in the mouth as they are being said, the "saidness" of the words-as-thought—as consciousness in action—is manifest. There need be no overt "motivation," but there must be inner resonation.

When the actors first worked on inhabiting the psychophysical state of being beyond tears, they began to discover what it felt like to inhabit such a state. However, it is always difficult to sustain the freshness of an initial psychophysical discovery and trust that working simply with breath and awareness is sufficient to sustain the state. It is easy for actors to fall into the trap of intentionally *trying* to play a state rather than discovering it through specific acting tasks. Korean actress Sunhee Kim described her work on this scenario as follows:

> In scenario three, the Figure describes the "simple facts" of the pain and emotions she

feels in short sentences such as, "I am sad," "I am bored and dissatisfied with everything," etc. The sentences reflect the emotional state and feelings of the Figure, i.e., depression, confusion, fear, desperation, etc . . . [When rehearsing this scene], Phillip said to us one day, "Don't be depressed!"—What did he mean by telling the actors performing a depressed character not to be depressed? Instead, he said, "Just listen to the lines the others speak—really listen, taking time . . . and listen to each of your own lines as you speak it."

When the actors "dropped in" to the specific psychophysical awareness described above—sensing the space behind along their backs, their weight on their elbows, attending to their own breath, and actually listening to and saying each line from this place of full-bodied awareness—the text was inhabited with a simple clarity that allowed the audience to experience each of the states conveyed by the "I am" statements—depression, confusion, etc. The actor/speaker serves as vehicle for the work of the text. As soon as any actor demonstrates an *intention*—trying to show depression, for example—rather than inhabiting the simple psychophysical state, the actor forecloses the possibility of being, in-this-moment of inhabitation, and cannot serve as an appropriate vehicle for the audience's experience.

The importance of listening in this approach cannot be overemphasized—a sensory awareness of listening allowed each actor to absorb each line as it was said, and to speak each line *even when not speaking*—similar to the actor's work in *The Water Station*. The lines formed an unbroken thread wherein each subsequent speaker absorbed the quality and energy of "the said" of the previous speaker. The image of the ensemble here was as if they were working as one weaver at a loom with twenty pairs of hands—all working intuitively together as one with an open peripheral awareness and energy.

To help prepare the group for the heightened quality of listening that this scenario and the dialogue scenes require, I utilized one simple

version of Meisner's repetition exercise that engages actors in both observation and listening.[7] In this version of the repetition exercises, Actor A observes Actor B, and when an impulse to speak comes initiates the exercise by observing, for example, "Your shirt is white." Actor B receives the observation, takes it in while continuing to observe Actor A, and then repeats the same phrase back to Actor A. Samata Russell reflected on the initial difficulties she experienced with such simple speaking, hearing, and listening:

> We began simply repeating simple sentences back and forth with a partner. We were instructed to notice the partner, take in every detail and when the partner spoke to allow what we noticed about the partner to affect how we repeated the line. We were to speak when the impulse to speak came, and were instructed not to attempt to "interpret" the lines. The words should simply come out. This was problematic for me. I could not speak without forcing meaning. I came to realize that my [. . .] limitations were self-imposed. Because I thought I might compare badly with others, I did [. . .] When I heard Phillip say to another performer, "really let go of your brain, release control," something clicked for me and I realized that I had been searching with my brain for "feeling"—an impossibility. This realization allowed me to "drop in" to saying the simple text. [. . . W]hen I held the sensation in my feet on the floor [. . .] I could speak without "thinking about" what I was saying. The words came out, surprising me each time in intonation and stress [. . . I stopped] trying to make the performance "mean" something.

". . . smelling the crippling failure oozing from my skin"

A much more complex set of acting scores was developed for the fifth scenario (Kane 2006: 208–210). Except for the last few lines of the scenario, the text consists of diary-like, first-person past-tense reflection on Figure's past experience of

Doctors—"Dr This and Dr That and Dr Whatsit." The diary-like text was delivered by two actresses as Speaker. Their acting score included three specific tasks: (1) to share the telling of Figure's story about her past experience of the medical establishment directly with the audience, (2) to maintain a constant awareness of each other as Speaker, and of Figure for whom they were speaking while telling the story, and (3) to actively step into and interact with the past memory about which they were communicating and the present reality of the impact this experience had on Figure.

Onstage with the two Speakers were one actress as Figure and the remainder of the acting ensemble as Doctors. The actress playing Figure was given the psychophysical task of embodying Figure's response to the experience described by Speakers: inhabiting a state of "aching shame" as she watches "crippling failure oozing from [her] skin" (Kane 2006: 209). Figure's embodiment of this "aching shame" takes place in the performative present. She focused all her attention on simply looking at her right palm, observing the crippling

failure as it begins to ooze out of the pores of her palm. As the scenario progresses, the effect of this crippling failure resonates her from within so that she would literally begin to tremble.

The actors playing Doctors psychophysically embodied a state of a small smile—that patronizing place where they are all "smiling and looking [at Figure] with secret knowledge of [her] aching shame" (Kane 2006: 209). The Doctors maintain their plastic, patronizing smile throughout the scenario as they gaze ahead, in a very slow walk along hospital corridors. They collectively created "a room of expressionless faces staring blankly at my pain, so devoid of meaning there must be evil intent" (Kane 2006: 209). Onstage, the Doctors embodied the "past" memory which the Speakers directly address. In playing these ever-smiling Doctors, the actors were never aware of each other, or of the Speakers if/when a Speaker addressed them directly. Each Doctor was to simply maintain their patronizing smile, look ahead and "see nothing."

The Speakers directly interact with the painful

[Note: lines are not assigned in Kane's text. The assignment of lines below, and the description of action in italics are to provide an understanding of production choices. The two Speakers are seated on chairs on platforms centre stage and stage left. Figure is seated on a third platform stage right. The two Speakers address their initial lines directly and simply to the audience, beginning to tell Figure's story. Figure's gaze is focused on her right palm. Scattered in the remainder of the playing space are the Doctors—each with a "small smile" pasted on their face—a self-satisfied smile. Their hands are either behind their backs, or clasped gently in front. As the lights come up and lines are spoken, the Doctors begin their very slow walking, unaware of Speakers, Figure or each other.]

Speaker 1: It wasn't for long.

Speaker 2: I wasn't there long.

Speaker 1: But drinking bitter black coffee I catch that medicinal smell in a cloud of ancient tobacco and something touches me in that still sobbing place and a wound from two years ago opens like a cadaver and a long buried shame roars its foul decaying grief.

Speaker 2: A room of expressionless faces staring blankly at my pain, so devoid of meaning there must be evil intent. (*Speakers become aware of, and then look at the "smiling" Doctors.*)

Speaker 1: (*Both Speakers, get up, and cross to a specific Doctor, addressing their lines to one of these patronizing smiles—speaking "back" to it.*) Dr This and Dr That and Dr Whatsit who's just passing and thought he'd pop in to take the piss as well. Burning in a hot tunnel of dismay, my humiliation complete as I shake without reason and stumble over words and have nothing to say about my "illness" which anyway amounts only to knowing that there's no point in anything because I'm going to die.

Speaker 2: And I am deadlocked by that smooth psychiatric voice of reason which tells me there is an objective reality in which my body and mind are one. But I am not there and never have been. Dr This writes it down and Dr That attempts a sympathetic murmur. Watching me, judging me. (*Speakers look to each other, then at Figure. They cross from the Doctors they have been addressing to Figure, and observe her gazing at her hand.*)

Speaker 1: Smelling the crippling failure oozing from my skin.

Speaker 2: My desperation clawing and all-consuming panic drenching me as I gape in horror at the world and wonder why everyone is

Speakers 1 and 2 smiling (Doctors stop slow-walking and slowly look directly to the audience as Speakers look to the Doctors.)

Speaker 1: And looking at me with secret knowledge of my aching shame.

(Doctors begin to whisper): Shame shame shame

Speaker 2: Drown in your fucking shame.

(Kane 2006: 208–209)

memory of hospitalization by addressing the Doctors, and then step to and beside Figure— observing the effect this experience was having on Figure as she trembles from the weight of shame. They speak to the audience *for* Figure, from out of her state of "aching shame" (Kane 2006: 209). At the conclusion of the scenario, the two Speakers return to stand beside Figure, placing a hand on her shoulders as the actress playing Figure gradually "melts" out of the state of psychophysically embodying "oozing failure." She now speaks the final line in first person directly to the audience in the present—"This is not a world in which I wish to live" (Kane 2006: 210).

For the actress playing Figure, embodying a constant state of "crippling failure" as it begins to ooze from her skin is an exhausting psychophysical task. Roberta Ensor described her process of actualizing this task as follows:

Thinking of the *taiqiquan* when going through this scene allowed me to [. . .] let go of all the tension in the muscles of my body . . . I could feel the energy coming from deep inside. It's important that I only project the energy from deep within my torso and not push it outward through every pore of my skin because that leads to loss of self-control—too much shaking. What worked best was lifting my head slightly, making sure my spine was aligned whilst my

knees were bent, and concentrating on my breath as it traveled down inside me, and not on the hand itself. This allowed me to be much more aware of the other actors behind and around me. Because the eyes have such an embodied power of their own, they are the last place I actually take into my awareness.

Embodying this psychophysical act of looking from deep inside, via her breath, allowed Roberta's relationship with looking to constantly shift and change. Roberta only emerged from this psychophysical state during the final few lines of the scenario—coming to a point of stillness from the trembling so that she quietly and directly addressed the audience with the final line of the scene.

"... scratch[ing] away at my skin": psychophysical symbiosis when delivering a monologue

In contrast to the third scenario in which the full ensemble shared the lines "as one" Figure, or the fifth scenario in which three actors shared Speaker/Figure's lines, for the ninth scenario, a single actor delivered Figure's text. Figure speaks in the first person, and/or direct address.

Sometimes I turn around and catch the smell of you and I cannot go on I cannot fucking go on without expressing this terrible so fucking awful physical aching fucking longing I have for you. And I cannot believe that I can feel this for you and you feel nothing. Do you feel nothing?

(Kane 2006: 214)

She speaks to herself as well as one or more Others—a hypothetic "you," as well as all those Others who "feels nothing" and have rejected her.

Fuck you. Fuck you. Fuck you for rejecting me by never being there, fuck you for making me feel shit about myself, fuck you for bleeding the fucking love and life out of me, fuck my father for fucking up my life for good and fuck my mother for not leaving him, but most of all fuck you God for making me love a person who does not exist, FUCK YOU FUCK YOU FUCK YOU.

(Kane 2006: 214)

The actor's task in this scenario was twofold: finding a psychophysical image that would provide an inner connection through which the speech would be delivered, and simultaneously being aware of and absorbing the energy of the ensemble as they engaged in a specific psychophysical task. The ensemble's task was to inhabit Figure's psychophysical "state" or condition of such rejection—a sense of being completely emptied. I used Kane's description from the second scenario as the basis for this image of being completely empty within:

a consolidated consciousness resides in a darkened banqueting hall near the ceiling of a mind whose floor shifts as ten thousand cockroaches when a shaft of light enters as all thoughts unite in an instant of accord body no longer expellant as cockroaches comprise a truth which no one ever utters . . .

(Kane 2006: 205)

I provided the ensemble inhabiting this state with the following progression:

standing still at the beginning of the scenario they begin to feel the ground moving under their feet. The ground begins to crack, and split apart. It is moving. You realize that the ground on which you are standing is actually composed of cockroaches. You feel each of the movements of the cockroaches in/through your feet. They are actually entering through your feet and beginning to fill you up, and "eat" you out from within . . . They are moving up through your legs, torso, shoulders, arms, hands, palms . . . and begin to burst out from all your orifices . . . through the mouth, ears, and through the skin . . . palms . . . are you being eaten out and emptied from within.

This is the material "truth" they "comprised" but which "no one ever utters." This series of active images produced trembling bodies, being emptied from within, some of which eventually collapse to their knees and/or onto the floor as Figure delivers her (devastating) text.

Claudia Palazzo, during the 2004 workshop, explained her process for working on Figure:

I chose to work with an image taken from the line, "physical aching fucking longing I have." It used this sense of longing for something so much that it becomes a physical ache that only gets worse and worse. This ache is generated in my gut, and thereby infects my entire body. Initially the ache is recognized in my breath . . . I was very conscious that I did not want to over-emotionalize this monologue. I was not "acting," but inhabiting a psychophysical image. I decided that the physical longing I had would not be something in the text, but a strong desire to look behind me. This meant that my back awareness was always open and the movement of others around me would affect me. It was not my intention to go into some kind of "trance-like" state of self-indulgent misery [. . .] Rather, I would let the very strong back awareness, and the movement of all the other actors that surrounded me affect me to a point where it would resonate inside my body, but without becoming melodramatic. I had never before performed like this . . . I "dropped in" to an image. I had never been able to remain so focused and aware of the smallest detail when performing . . . This process scratched away at my skin, and forced me to take a look inside at how I work as a person.

For the actor delivering this monologue, her awareness opened to the ensemble around her so that it created a synergy between the text and the image-based work of the ensemble.

In working with the ensemble on this process of emptying, I did *not* want the audience to literally see cockroaches coming out of the orifices of the actors. The image was developed to activate and modulate their inner psychophysical relationship to a state of becoming empty and hollowed out. What was important was that each actor embodied the progressive development of the active image with no gap in their awareness. Their inner relationship to the progressive image was to be informed by the powerful text as it was being delivered. For the actor delivering text, when she described her state as one in which, "I cannot go on I cannot fucking go on without expressing this terrible so fucking awful physical aching fucking longing . . ." the juxtaposition of her speech with the ensemble's embodiment of the psychophysical state evoked the condition of tremendous loss and emptiness which Figure experienced and embodied at this moment.

Irony on the edge of gallows humor

The exercises in listening noted above were also important in preparing the actors for the thirteenth and the fifteenth scenarios. In the thirteenth scenario listening played on the edge of gallows humour when twelve of the ensemble embodied the "fast/quick/lively" energy of a television game show, puzzling over and trying to find the right word to describe the state of mind Figure inhabited at that moment (Figure 10.1a–d). Having found what each thinks is the right answer,

Figure 10.1 *4:48 Psychosis*, Seoul, Korea, 2008: Lim Sung Mi as Figure (*a*) surrounded by three sets of actors trying to find the "right word" for Figure's state/condition (*b–d*). As each possible word is tried out, each individual actor in the background freezes, holding up their proposed word. (Photographs: Kim Hyun-Min, courtesy KNVA)

the actors located behind Figure each blurted out their word "brightly" *knowing* it must be correct! But none of the words are correct. No word is adequate to describe Figure's state. Inhabiting this state of the inadequacy of words, listening was equally important for the actor as Figure— listening to these voices within her head trying to figure it out—in this "sea of logic."

This scenario intentionally involved a strong juxtaposition between the stillness of Figure, seated center stage, and the exuberance of each of the twelve Speakers playing Figure's mind-game. All the words collectively create the "sea of logic"

(Note: These notes and the assignment of lines were not in Kane's original text and are present to provide the reader with a guide to how I worked on the text in performance. Figure is seated on a chair centre stage facing out. Twelve of the ensemble form three teams of four behind Figure. They are ready to play a game show. When lights come up, they are not as yet visible. The initial light is focused only on Figure who speaks directly and quietly to the audience.)

Figure: abstraction to the point of . . .

(Bright light snaps on, illuminating the twelve Speakers. Each in turn tried to "guess" the "right" word to describe Figure's state by holding up a white sheet of paper on which is printed each possible correct answer. As each word is held up and spoken brightly, the actor freezes in position with the word visible.)

Speaker 1: unpleasant
Speaker 2: unacceptable
Speaker 3: uninspiring
Speaker 4: impenetrable

Speaker 5: irrelevant
Speaker 6: irreverent
Speaker 7: irreligious
Speaker 8: unrepentant

Speaker 9: dislike
Speaker 10: dislocate
Speaker 11: disembody
Speaker 12: deconstruct

(All twelve speakers are each "frozen" in a different, almost grotesquely humorous position, holding up their words, as Figure continues to speak self-reflexively, to herself, reflecting on her state.)

Figure: I don't imagine
    (clearly)
        that a single soul
           could
              would
                should
                  or will

    and if they did
    I don't think
    (clearly)
that another soul
a soul like mine
    could
      would
        should
          or will

irrespective

(All Speakers allow the words on paper to fall to the floor as they maintain their frozen positions.)
(Kane 2006: 221–222)

in which Figure "drowns"—materialized in the form of pieces of paper with each answer printed on it. The final psychophysical positions of each of the actors in the chorus of words remained frozen in the "monstrous state of palsy" marked by the inability of language to solve anything. "[D]rowning in a sea of logic this monstrous state of palsy still ill" (Kane 2006: 223).

Here and at a few other places in our work, gallows humour played on the edge of irony.

"... black snow falls ..."

During the final scenario, three sets of three actors in turn shared Figure's highly poetic text. Each group of three constituted Figure. They shared physical contact—composed as one, and they shared Figure's voice—speaking the text simply and addressing the "you" of the text—anyone who might be there to listen. Supporting their simple, self-reflexive delivery of the text and its images, the remainder of the ensemble were scattered around the performance space, seated at first. Their task was to embody and elaborate a series of images-in-action drawn from the text: (1) looking up (inside Figure's mind); (2) snow begins to fall (you see, follow, and catch in the palm of your right hand one specific snowflake at a time, watching it melt in your palm); (3) the snowflakes become tears; (4) the snowflakes become black; (5) they turn to ash in the palm of the hand. The ensemble actors' task was to absorb

the images of the text as they were spoken and to allow the text to resonate with each image as it was embodied.

In speaking the text, the actor's task was to clearly understand each poetic image—allowing the image to be seen, heard, and to resonate within as it was delivered with simplicity. The scoring among the three actors once again created a quiet, choral-like echo—heightening the effect of the images as spoken.

For the actors involved in this psychophysical elaboration of Kane's text with its multiple dramaturgies, the work offered an opportunity to inhabit complex states or conditions in the delivery of text, and how to sustain over a considerable length of time a fully embodied psychophysical relationship to one or more images. The fragmentation of Figure and Doctor into pairs or multiples numbering up to twenty required the actors to maintain a wider awareness that extended beyond themselves and/or their specific partner, enhancing the psychophysical distance they needed to inhabit with their awareness. This was intentional. The use of multiple voices playing Figure as well as Doctor, and the judicious use of multiple voices within some scenarios created an intentional choral effect, producing a denser texture and tempo-rhythm as the shifting contours of specific images and/or patterns of speech were realized—from very dark, black, gallows humor, to bitter irony, to the poignancy of life always lived "on the edge" ... about to be lost.

11

Attempts on Her Life by Martin Crimp[1]

[O]nly a rejection of cynicism for its own sake can return art to its true social function.

(Dijkstra 2004: 60)

Introduction

Attempts on Her Life was first produced at the Royal Court Theatre Upstairs, London, on March 7, 1997 and quickly became an "international hit" (Sietz 2006: 55). Many subsequent productions include those in Munich (Bayerisches Staatsschauspiel 1998), Milan (Teatro Piccolo, 1999), New York (Soho Rep, 2002), San Francisco (Connecticut Theater, 2002), London's Battersea Arts Centre (2004), and the National Theatre (2007). *Attempts on Her Life* is subtitled "Seventeen Scenarios for The Theatre." The only clues to performance Crimp provides in the 2005 version of the script are scenario titles such as "Tragedy of Love and Ideology" (Scenario 2), a few stage directions for a pause or silence, dashes (— — —) indicating a change of speaker, and front-slashes (/) indicating interruption where dialogue overlaps between speakers.[2] Crimp provides no indication or description of the number of speakers or how to divide lines between speakers with the exception of Scenario 16 ("Porno"), where the principal speaker in the first half of the scenario is "a young woman."

Crimp supplies slightly more information for his more recent play, *Fewer Emergencies* (2005b). Each of the three subtitled sections ("Whole Blue Sky," "Face to the Wall," and "Fewer Emergencies") states the number of "actors required," time ("Blank"), and place ("Blank"):

"Whole Blue Sky": 1 (female), 2 and 3
"Face to the Wall": 1 (male), 2, 3, and 4
"Fewer Emergencies": 1, 2, and 3

The first two sections designate a specific gender for one of the three speakers, while for the third section no gender is specified for any of the three speakers.

Attempts on Her Life and *Fewer Emergencies* are both "open" scripts in that they do not identify place or time, and do not assign lines to specific characters. Productions of *Attempts on Her Life* vary according to the number and gender of the group of actors cast, and who among them is assigned lines within the scenarios.[3] Tim Albery's original production at the Royal Court utilized eight actors—four men and four women.[4] Gerhard Willer's 1998 Munich production cast three men and two women. Katie Mitchell's 1999 production at the Teatro Piccolo, Milan, had a cast of eight with four men and four women. The 2007 production also directed by Katie Mitchell at the National Theatre was performed by a cast of eleven—four men and seven women.

In each of the seventeen scenarios of *Attempts on Her Life*, attention is focused on the indefinable and unlocatable "her" of the title.[5] The scenarios taken together collectively create the primary, but absent character. But who is this "she"—this figure who seldom if ever appears on stage? Who is this "her" that the speakers in each scenario imagine, recollect, remember, talk to or about— each in their own way? In some scenarios this figure remains an ambiguous third-person "she" or "her"; in others, she is variously referred to as "Annie," "Anya," "Anushka," "Anne." Whoever she is, she materializes—all the theatrical language and signs point to her, indicating her presence. Possible exceptions to "her" non-appearance are Scenario 5, "The Camera Loves You," where the "you" addressed might be "her." And in Scenario 16, "Porno," the young woman who speaks at the beginning might be "her"; however, she remains nameless, unidentifiable. In the middle of the scenario she abandons her role by refusing to continue as the subject. The issue of "her" remains unsettled throughout *Attempts on Her Life*. Scenario by scenario, she is evoked and "appears," but always within quotation marks. Ultimately, who she is remains open. The materialization of these various manifestations of "her" constitutes the overriding aesthetic logic of *Attempts on Her Life*.

Inside the title page, Crimp provides a quotation from Baudrillard—"No one will have directly experienced the actual cause of such happenings, but everyone will have received an image of them" (2005a: 198). Crimp clearly puts into (theatrical) play on-stage the "play" of representation(s) and images that bombard us in our cosmopolitan, mediated culture today. *Attempts on Her Life* "plays" meta-theatrically with both the nature of (theatrical) representation per se, and with the "death of character"—the (non) character who constantly "appears" in various guises, even though "she" never appears. As David Edgar explains:

> Crimp's purpose is not only to question whether we can truly know another human being, but whether we can regard other people as existing at all independent of the models we construct of them. And he does this not by a bald statement, but by playing an elaborate and sophisticated game with the audience's expectations of how scenes connect with narrative.
>
> (Edgar 2006: 31)

Critical reaction to and readings of *Attempts on Her Life*

The first production of *Attempts on Her Life* at the Royal Court Upstairs in 1997 was controversial. The form and structure of the play were recognized as unconventional—a form of "anti-theatre" both "brilliant" and "radical" (Michael Coveney, *The Observer*, quoted in Luckhurst 2003: 48).[6] Mary Luckhurst summarized some of the critical responses to the 1997 production, noting how

> the overwhelming impression was that reviewers were unsure what to think, oscillating between admiration and condemnation. *The Independent's* Paul Taylor asked whether despite the play's "extraordinary flights of eloquence" it was "just cleverly knowing and darkly comic about its own ingenious futility"; Roger Foss in *What's On* argued that "artfully cryptic, deliberately inconclusive and depersonalized though it is, it stands completely alone as a coherent and poetic perspective on the underlying violence of late twentieth-century corporate global hegemony," but concluded that the piece never engages you at the human level of feelings or emotions; Nicholas de Jongh began his *Evening Standard* review with the "uneasy feeling that in *Attempts on Her Life* Martin Crimp has fired a warning shot to suggest what the brave new theatre of the twenty-first century will look like—both on stage and page," but ultimately judged that "the final impact is of a mannered cleverness, an arid imposition of a dramatic scheme which

casts no serious illumination, stirs no thought or induces any significant emotion," rounding off his review with the words: "Just heartfelt pretension."

(Luckhurst 2003: 48)

Many of the comments summarized above evaluate *not* the dramaturgy, structure, form, or language of the play per se, but rather the effect created by Tim Albery's production at the Royal Court. Nicholas de Jongh's experience of the production as "heartfelt pretension" is similar to Alastair Macauley's response in the *Financial Times*:

> To say that it is postmodern is like saying that the Pope is Catholic; it is also post-civilization, post-truth, post-art, post-feeling, post-teeth, post-everything ... Who cares? Not for a moment does the play suggest that its author does ... His [Crimp's] method is far more depersonalized than the depersonalized modernity on which he pretends to comment.
>
> (quoted in Luckhurst 2003: 47)

The play's post-dramatic structure allows us to confront certain characteristic forms of dispossession informing our contemporary reality, especially with reference to the construction/ imagination of women—the "her." Behind the openness of both the text and the "her" at its centre, there is an aesthetic logic operating behind the multiple perspectives. As Aleks Sierz argues,

> the piece has a satisfying symmetrical form, and [...] its kaleidoscope of scenes is based firmly on narrative. The whole play, Crimp has pointed out, is held together by the fact that people are "telling stories all the time."
>
> (Sierz 2006: 52)

The first question I wanted to address in my work on *Attempts on Her Life* is whether it is possible for a production to create an experience in which the audience encounters elements of the dystopic world we inhabit, not in a depersonalized way as

distant, cynical observers but rather as human beings who live with dispossession on a daily basis and who are thereby complicit in its creation. Following the highly evocative arguments of critic and theorist Jill Dolan in *Utopia in Performance* (2005: 1–3), my approach interrogated whether it was possible to move beyond the often inherent cynicism prompted by liberal responses to our postmodern condition. Is it possible to create in the inter-subjective act of theater-making a more transformative, human experience of this absent "her" at the center of Crimp's play?[7] The second question I wanted to address is whether a production could truly reflect in casting and use of language the "composition of the world beyond the theatre" which Crimp calls for.

In rehearsal and performance

I have worked on *Attempts on Her Life* several times because it resonates with the post-9/11 issue of terrorism, struggles with issues of representation raised by the absence of the primary character, and addresses the role that mediated images play in constructing our world today. In addition, it provides an opportunity to apply psychophysical training to a complex post-dramatic text and the embodiment of image-based psychophysical states.[8]

I conducted preliminary work on selected scenarios of *Attempts on Her Life* in 2005 with an international group of twelve MA/MFA and five BA actors from eight different countries in a laboratory setting at the University of Exeter.[9] I subsequently directed a full production in 2007 with an international cast of eleven hailing from ten different countries (Singapore, UK, USA, India, Hong Kong, Korea, Ireland, Spain, Mexico, Malaysia) at the Esplanade Theatre Studio in a TTRP production (Singapore).[10]

Of the eleven cast members in the Singapore production, eight were non-native English speakers. Their rich blend of various accents with which English was spoken reflects the "composition of the world beyond the theatre."

Crimp designates the use of two languages other than English for Scenario 7 ("The New Anny") and Scenario 16 ("Porno"). In "The New Anny" the primary speaker delivers text in her native language which is then translated into English. In "Porno" part of the text is delivered in English and is simultaneously translated into another language. In the Exeter workshop, Scenario 7 was delivered in Greek, while in Singapore it was delivered in Spanish. For "Porno," the primary text was simultaneously translated into Arabic in Exeter, while in Singapore it was translated into Korean.

To add to the linguistic mix, for the Singapore production we used languages other than English in three additional scenarios. Scenario 8 ("Particle Physics") was played in Cantonese and Korean with English sur-titles; Scenario 13 ("Communicating with Aliens") was played in Malayalam with sur-titles; and Scenario 12 ("The Statement") was played tri-lingually in English, Mandarin, and Korean. One of three actors performing the text in Scenario 9 ("The Threat of International Terrorism") spoke between Mandarin and "Sing-lish"—a local combination of Mandarin and English. These choices allowed the production to better reflect the multicultural, multilinguistic life encountered daily in Singapore beyond the theater.

My primary directorial concern was to actualize the text's aesthetic logic—the serious play of (theatrical/mediated) representation—but to do so in a way that would evoke and materialize for the audience this imagined "her"—a "her" with whom the audience might develop a relationship. This play of representation is evoked and materialized for the audience as each specific scenario produces its own imagined "her," and as each "her" contributes to the overall materialization of this indefinable "her" at the end of the evening. Each scenario actively generates a specific story about a "her." Each of these stories must have its own clarity and integrity. Nevertheless "she" remains a question mark. A dialectical tension exists—"Is she or isn't she?," "'Who' is this 'she'?" "What is my relationship to the 'her' created in this set of narratives?" By the final, seventeenth scenario in which there is a discussion amongst the whole ensemble of actors about this "her"—where she's living, if she's in a relationship, whether she's working or not—the audience ideally senses its complicity in the performance's creation of the various manifestations, narratives, and representations or "her." She is "present" as each of her manifestations in the first sixteen scenarios is echoed in the lines of this final scenario.

My second directorial concern had to do with one of the major attractions of *Attempts on Her Life*—its self-referential irony. What is irony? Especially with reference to postmodernism in its various guises, can irony only exist as a caricature of itself, endlessly calling attention to itself and its inability to settle? Or, can irony exist as an emergent experience for an audience?

Webster's Third International Dictionary, provides three definitions of irony: (1) "feigned ignorance," (2) "humor, ridicule, or light sarcasm that adopts a mode of speech the intended implication of which is the opposite of the literal sense of the words," and (3) "a state of affairs or events that is the reverse of what was or was to be expected: a result opposite to . . . the appropriate result" (1976: 1195). I would describe the first two definitions as surface performatives—they clearly show themselves as they are put on and performed. These types of irony call attention to their effect. To the observer both "feigned ignorance" and the adoption of a "mode of speech" which shows its intention as being "opposite" create distance, or surface irony. They can be experienced as knowingly funny. These types of irony can easily become caricatures of themselves.

The third definition of irony is very different. As a "state of affairs or events" it is not feigned and does not involve the adoption or putting on of a particular mode of speech to create an effect. Rather, it is based on action, discovery, and realization. Irony here is a result of a shift in action. Irony-in-action is felt and experienced as the opposite of what is an expected result. The action leads you to expect one thing, but there is a shift, change, or reversal that surprises. It is *not* what you expected. Irony-in-action is discovered. The observer does not stand outside, but is inside this process. The observer is surprised by, and therefore becomes complicit in, an emergent form of irony.

All types of irony are evident in *Attempts on Her Life*. The surface type of irony that points to itself is especially evident in Scenario 11, "Untitled (100 Words)," in which several critics are critiquing a work of art in a gallery setting. This type of irony is part of the fundamental premise of the scenario. Anne the artist takes self-performance beyond its logical extreme by documenting for artistic display her own attempts on her life. One of the critics launches into a highly self-referential critique of the process of meaning-making:

> With respect to you I think she'd [Anne, the artist] find the whole concept of "making a point" ludicrously outmoded. If any attempt is being made at all it's surely the point that the point that's being made is not the point and never has in fact been the point. It's surely the point that a search for a point is pointless and that the whole point of the exercise—i.e., these attempts on her own life—points to that.
> (Crimp 2005a: 251)

With its self-referential surface irony this scenario certainly "flirts skillfully with received postmodern clichés" (Luckhurst 2003: 47). When working with actors on this type of surface irony, we explored how to deliver the lines *on the edge* without falling into a full-blown caricature. To do so it is essential to ensure that the differences of opinion amongst the positions of the critics are clearly and fully developed so that there is a dramatic tension between critical perspectives.

But even more important to my directorial concern is irony that emerges when a series of actions results in the opposite of what was expected. As detailed in the analysis of specific scenarios below, the structure of action involves a discovery or surprise both for the actor and for the audience. Something unexpected occurs through a dialectical process of juxtaposition, reversal, and/or surprise. Unlike Scenario 11, this type of

irony is not a self-referential pose, attitude, or style. It is active and emergent; therefore, one feels complicit in the situation.[11] The audience exists in relationship to the object that initially produces laughter and irony. This type of irony is especially evident in scenarios 7, "The New Anny," 10, "Kinda Funny," 12, "Strangely," and 16, "Porno." I examine several examples in detail below.

Recognizing the vacuity of grand narratives, Crimp's *Attempts on Her Life* challenges audiences and critics alike to experience a post-dramatic text whose realization cannot be reduced to a few critical bullet points. While this may disarm some critics, it does not mean that the audience's experience of the play in performance is not felt or is devoid of all meaning. Central to the production of *Attempts on Her Life* described below was my attempt to utilize an emergent, action-based irony which structures the audience's experience so that their complicity in the condition and circumstances of "her" is not experienced at a distance, but is brought close to home.

◉ DVD-ROM: *ATTEMPTS ON HER LIFE*

The *mise-en-scène*: at play between "foreground," "background," and "environment"

To help actualize the irony in *Attempts on Her Life*, I created a dialectic between three uses of the space: foreground, background, and environment. When present, background was always in dynamic tension with the foreground. Scenarios played partially or fully within an environment suggest a specific settled location. The production began with the actors onstage dressed in black as the audience enters. Slow dance music plays. They are talking, smiling, drinking champagne, taking photographs of one another with digital cameras, dancing. Is it a party or a wake? We return to this same (party/wake?) environment in the final scenario ("Previously Frozen"). The large group of friends/acquaintances have stopped dancing. They sip their champagne and talk. They all seem to know "her," and are having a discussion about "her" life.

Foreground, background, and environment

were created through a series of eight mini acting areas. Five areas were defined by platforms of varying sizes and height, the two largest and highest platforms upstage. Both were extremely large wooden frames suspended from the ceiling. They created the effect of two massive picture frames behind which images were created or a few scenes were played. The three downstage areas closest to the audience included an area defined by a couch stage right, a stage left area with four chairs and a table, and a small area center stage around one or two stools. On the back wall was a framed projection screen, and far downstage right and left were two television monitors.

The framing devices—two large picture-frames, projection screen, and monitors—strategically put into play the Baudrillardian sense of how images and representations of events never directly experienced interpret those events for us. For some scenarios, live-camera projection mediated foreground text as it was being delivered. Prerecorded video footage was occasionally used, such as in Scenario 11 ("100 Words"). We imagined this scenario taking place in an art gallery where three critics are attending a private showing of what promises to be a controversial new installation. The critics discuss and argue about the work of this female artist as they view the exhibit (the entire area of the stage). The artist has "become her own victim" by making an attempt on her life. Traces of these attempts constitute the art work on display. Inside four chairs downstage left, marked off by blue and white police tape, is the artist's empty bed with its crumpled bed-clothes where she has had "intentionally unprotected sex." In the Singapore production, very short video clips punctuate delivery of the critics' text as "100 words" are delivered via video and simultaneously by three performers who engage in word-based tasks. They are part of the exhibit. The 100 words refer to these "attempts on her life."

Scenario 15 ("The Statement") began with a juxtaposition of foreground and background: two male officials bilingually (in English and Mandarin) interrogate a woman, asking questions from a statement taken from her about a female

who has raised their suspicions. The woman being interrogated is played bilingually (in English and Korean) by two actresses. As the interrogators conclude their questions, the female who was the subject of their interrogation is suddenly made visible in the background (upstage right picture-frame) as she literally rides a (stationary) bicycle against a video projection of her route to the market (in Singapore). Tomato plants are on the back of her bicycle. The two officials discover baskets beneath the women's seats. They each pick up a basket and examine them with suspicion. When bending over to pick up the two baskets, the interrogators put on Santa Claus hats. As they straighten up with baskets in hand and Santa Claus hats on their heads, romantic music by the Beijing Brothers begins to play, and the lights slowly illuminate the audience as the two interrogators shift their suspicious gaze to the audience. They cross to the audience with the baskets in hand, reach slowly inside, and then offer Christmas hard candy to the audience as they wish each person "Merry Christmas." Together they focus their attention on a bag at the feet of one of the audience members and begin to interrogate this person, demanding that s/he "open the bag!" The progression in this scenario is from the juxtaposition of foreground/background to an environment in which the audience is complicit.

The spatial movement within the production as a whole was designed to provide moments of direct address and complicity with the audience. This began just prior to the dimming of the lights at the end of the initial party/wake(?), with the entire ensemble on stage when all the actors look to the audience, and say nothing. This moment is replicated at the end of the final scenario, after the final line. Strategic scenarios were therefore directly addressed to the audience although the style of each mode of direct address was unique. In Scenario 5 ("The Camera Loves You"), two photographers in their studio address a member of the audience as their new model as they prepare for, and take, a digital photograph of the audience member. In Scenario 9 ("The Threat of International Terrorism"), three local politicians address a news conference. In Scenario 10 ("Kinda Funny") an American male tells a "down-home" story. In Scenario 12 ("Strangely"), a stylish television presenter reports live and on location from a strife-torn South American city. And in Scenario 15 ("Statement"), as noted above, the two interrogators interact directly with the audience. After the blackout that concludes the production, the photograph of the audience member, which was taken in "The Camera Loves You," is projected onto the screen and monitors as the audience leaves the theatre.

The actor's tasks in *Attempts on Her Life*

The challenges offered to actors in *Attempts on Her Life* are in some ways similar to those in Kane's *4:48 Psychosis*. Neither play has individual characters developed through a progressive narrative. Some of the actors I worked with had to confront their preconceptions about acting when faced with the very different tasks of the production—working with non-character-based text in which dramatic irony must be realized, and working with psychophysical states.

The delivery of Crimp's text depends on clarity about the context within which we imagine the lines in each scenario are said. Our first task in rehearsal was to determine the context within which each "she" is evoked or appears within a scenario. Because of the open nature of most of the text, only a few of the scenarios clearly identify who "she" might be, and identify the context within which the text is delivered. In Scenario 7, "Anny" is "The New Anny," i.e., a new car that "twists along the Mediterranean road," as "it hugs the bends between the picturesque hillside villages" with the sun gleaming "on the aerodynamic body" (Crimp 2005a: 238). The context is clearly a television advertisement for "The New Anny."

But in most scenarios, the speakers delivering the text must actively imagine, locate, and identify "her" through a form of mutual invention— either a collective act of the imagination or a form of interrogation and questioning. The key to the

actor's work lies in their active engagement either in telling a story about the "her" particular to a scenario, or in action/reaction with the other speakers as they collectively figure out who this "her" is. For example, Scenario 2 ("Tragedy of Love and Ideology") begins as follows:

> Summer. A river. Europe. These are the basic ingredients.
> And a river running through it.
> A river, exactly, running through a great European city and a couple at the water's edge. These are the basic ingredients.
> (Crimp 2005a: 208)

For this scenario three actors play a team of film writers who are collectively brain-storming the scenario for a new film they will pitch. "Anne" is the female lead. In playing the scenario the three writers constantly imagine and re-imagine, each from their own perspective, this "tragedy of love and ideology."

The initial speaker establishes a set of "basic ingredients" about the film scenario they are imagining: "Summer. A River. Europe." Building on the first speech, the second speaker absorbs these details and then adds, "And a river running through it." The third speaker adds even more detail to the unfolding scenario: "a couple at the water's edge." Active/actual listening in the moment is essential to Crimp's dramaturgy of discovery in the moment. Crimp's text comes alive for an audience to the degree that the actors engage their own imaginations as they discover, remember, or invent each specific detail that builds this film scenario. The engagement of the actor's active imagination in the moment is actualized through opening the auditory awareness and listening and receiving each idea/image offered, thus providing the impetus for each subsequent new image or idea as it emerges.

Once a context is set, the scenarios appear to have a settled narrative about its particular "her." But Crimp's dramaturgy unsettles the narrative at some point and creates a form of active irony. Crimp often provides a series of surprises that create the opposite of what is initially expected. In "The New Anny" the advertisement is undone by a series of darkly ironic, disturbing, and outrageously funny assertions about this new car: "No one ever packs the *Anny* with explosives to achieve a political objective" (Crimp 2005a: 238). For this type of irony to work in production, the actor delivering the text must never attempt to make their delivery of the text ironic or in some way self-knowing. Rather, the actor must take the context and text at face value.

The approach I took to working on text in *Attempts on Her Life* is summarized by the lines Crimp himself puts in the mouth of the young woman at the beginning of Scenario 16 ("Porno"):

> Of course there's no story to speak of . . . or characters. Certainly not in the conventional sense. [. . .] It isn't just acting. It's actually far more exacting than acting—for the simple reason that it's really happening.
>
> (Crimp 2005a: 270)

The performer's task when delivering text was clearly not character-based. The actor's task was to be present in the moment while engaging the active imagination in each discovery, each statement of fact, or each moment of telling. Jordanian actress Miriam Hilmi Abdul-Baqi explained how this absence of conventional characters meant she "was faced with only myself as a resource of representation. Thus my challenge . . . was to 'inhabit a state,' i.e., 'be present,' 'remain attentive' and 'listen.'"

In addition to work on Crimp's text, I also utilized psychophysical scores as part of the background for specific scenes. I focus the remainder of this chapter on the approach taken to two specific scenarios.

Scenario 9: "The Threat of International Terrorism™"

Three actors shared the lines in Scenario 9.[12] During the initial workshop and devising period, we tried a number of possible contexts for delivery of the lines. The following context offered the most compelling situation: three outraged local politicians have been asked to speak at a live televised press conference about a terrorist event in the heart of their city. Individually and collectively they express their moral outrage at what has happened, and their shock that the individual (Anne) who has apparently perpetrated this outrage has been known to them since she was a child.

Framed for the audience as a picture upstage left on the raised platform, the three politicians sit at a table, each with a microphone and a plastic bottle of water. They speak their lines directly to the members of the community gathered at this press conference, to the camera located slightly below them, or to each other across the table.

The background to delivery of the text included a dimly lit male figure standing upstage right behind a microphone inside the second large frame and, downstage left front, a child's playpen created by four chairs and emergency plastic tape. Inside the playpen was an actress dressed as the young child, Anne, in her "pink gingham dress and a straw hat" who is playing with her two favourite dolls—"Fantasy Barbie" and "Fantasy Ken."

The actors delivering the text remain unaware of both Anne's presence playing downstage, and of the insertion of the single line of commentary, "Trade Mark™" after each "trade-marked" item in Crimp's text—"Fantasy Barbie™," "Fantasy Ken™," "God™," "Minnie Mouse™," "Diet Pepsi™," "*Vogue*™." As each of the politicians speaks, a live-camera extreme close-up of each face is projected onto the screen upstage right. The scenario was played so that the audience was simultaneously (1) part of a live studio broadcast to whom the politicians were speaking, (2) observers of the televised news conference, (3) aware of the commentary ("trade mark"), and (4) witnesses to the perpetrator of the terrorist act as a child at play.

As indicated in Crimp's text, once set in motion all of the speeches longer than one word or a single phrase overlap with the previous speech so that the tempo-rhythm is decidedly fast and up-beat. Each longer speech ended with a front-slash so

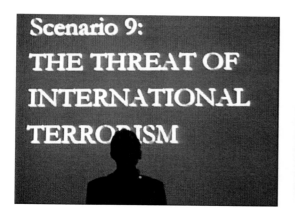

Figure 11.1 *Attempts on Her Life*: Scenario 9 (Singapore production, 2007). "The Threat of International Terrorism™": Top left, standing at microphone: Zachary Ho Tze Siang (Singapore). Top right, seated at table and bottom left, on live camera: (left to right) Hye Ok Kim (Korea), Heidi Love (Ireland), Seng Soo Ming (Malaysia). Bottom right, seated on floor in foreground: (left to right) Claire Lindsay (UK) as Barbie, Tam ka Man (Hong Kong) as the young Annie, Alberto Ruiz Lopez (Mexico) as Ken. (Photographs: Choon Hun of PhotoUnique)

that the actors collectively picked up and pushed forward each idea/impulse. The scenario begins as follows:

> She doesn't seem to care. She has no conscience. She expresses no remorse. She says, "I do not recognize your authority." "I do not recognize your authority." Just what does she mean by that?
>
> (Crimp 2005a: 241)

Each speech drives forward the politicians' collective creation of "this . . . Anne." There is a relentless and urgent search to understand what "this" Anne has done, and why.

The tempo-rhythm of the scenario was tightly choreographed and required the actors to have a strong sense of the collective maintenance of the up-tempo delivery of their lines. The actors' primary tasks were quite simple:

- to hear each image/idea as it is formulated and expressed—allowing this hearing to resonate internally through their entire body, and from that hearing to generate the impulse for the next idea;
- to keep a simple and direct connection to each idea as it is expressed, hearing the idea while saying it, and keeping a psychophysical connection to the sense of its "said-ness";

- to keep awareness of the two other actors, the cameraman, and the audience all constantly open so that the text as delivered was reaching all.

Given its fast tempo-rhythm, playing the text required quick releases of energy most evident, actress Heidi Love remarked, in the quality and type of energy released when doing *kalarippayattu* kicks (Love 2005).

The overall effect of the scenario was to activate Crimp's emergent irony created by both the text itself and the interplay between foreground and background. At the beginning of the scenario it is clear to the audience that something unspeakably awful and terrifying has happened. It soon becomes clear that this act has been unexpectedly perpetrated by a grown woman who possesses "Not one spark—that's right—of human feeling or any sense of shame" (Crimp 2005a: 241). Outrage and disbelief are expressed:

> Is this the same child, is this the same child who once wore a pink gingham dress and a straw hat and went with the daughters of doctors, dentists, TV presenters and property developers to the school on the hill with the polished brass plate and the teacher in strict tartan skirts?
>
> (Crimp 2005a: 241)

Disbelief and moral outrage color the delivery of the text, including the aftermath of Anne's terrorist act where physical evidence of the crime takes the form of "pieces of human flesh, false passports, lists of names, traces of explosives" (Crimp 2005a: 242). The images are increasingly horrific, callous, and outrageous—Annie appears "twice on the cover of / *Vogue*™ magazine" and settles "the film rights for two and a half million / US dollars" (Crimp 2005: 244). Was this (supposed) act of violence real, or was it imagined, produced by the hysteria of those who are morally outraged? An almost unimaginable act of violence and its aftermath are juxtaposed uncomfortably with childhood innocence. The self-righteous attitude

of moral outrage that accompanies the search for the cause and/or meaning behind this violent act creates paranoia and suspicion.

Scenario 10: "Kinda Funny"

Scenario 10 is the only scenario in which there is a single speaker:

> It's kinda funny and it's kinda sad.
> I guess it's kinda bittersweet.
> I guess it's one of these kinda bittersweet things, one of these laughing through *tears* things.
> After so much time, after so many years, he finally comes back to his mom.
> And at first, y'know, like "Who *is* this?" Then there's the moment of realization: "Oh *God*: it's my very own son."
>
> (Crimp 2005: 245)

The text is written in American vernacular for a male voice. It was probably inspired by the period during which Crimp lived in the United States.[13] The story told is of an American prodigal son who, having left home years earlier, unexpectedly returns one day in his pickup truck to his Mom, whom he has not seen for years. With him are some special "surprise(s)"—two "strong and innocent children" and his good wife, Annie.

> She's like real tall and fair and strong-limbed with these clear blue eyes that look right into your heart, and she's like—well I guess she's like every man's dream of what a good woman should be, and every mother's dream of the wife she would choose for her boy.
>
> (Crimp 2005a: 246)

In sharp contrast to the up-tempo Scenario 9, I worked with the actor delivering the text on using a simple, direct, understated, homespun, American story-telling style. While telling the story the actor inhabits a constant psychophysical state of a small, self-satisfied smile—a sense of sincere self-satisfaction should inform the telling. Each image and sentence in the story is said with a friendly, knowing smile to a specific member of the audience, optimally drawing the audience into complicity. Only later in the narrative is the frisson revealed between the honesty with which the words are spoken, and the bigotry and hate that inform the speaker's view of the world.

Juxtaposed with the tale were two upstage framed images. In the stage right frame is Annie—played by multiple actresses in identical blond wigs with the Annie in front holding the hands of their two "tiny tiny children" (a boy doll and a girl doll). The Annies embody a constant state of a small smile, radiating their (all-American) happiness and love.

In contrast to the ever-happy, smiling Annie, Mom sits at her kitchen table staring out of the window in the stage left frame. She remains unblinking throughout as she absorbs the story her son delivers about this young man who returns home. Using a live-camera close-up, Mom's unblinking, staring face is projected onto the upstage screen immediately behind Annie and the children. The *mise-en-scène* put into play the down-home foreground story, the ever-smiling Annie with their two fine children, and the effect the story has on Mom.

> ⦿ DVD-ROM: *ATTEMPTS ON HER LIFE*—
> "KINDA FUNNY"

And they're [mother and son] hugging each other right there in the kitchen and y'know that is so moving.
I mean that is just so moving to see that he has found that thing, that strength, to forgive his Mom.
That he has forgiven her her alcoholism.
That he has forgiven her for running round with other men.
That he has forgiven her for destroying his father's faith in himself and driving him to suicide.
And they're both kinda crying and laughing and crying again all at the same time in

the same kitchen he sat in as a little boy witnessing his parents' terrible arguments. His Dad in tears pouring her liquor down the sink at ten o'clock in the morning while she screams how if he was a real man with one iota of self-respect she wouldn't need to booze herself to death, would she. And there are these tiny scratches in the table which he recalls having made secretly with a fork. And you're aware, y'know, like of the continuity of things, of the bittersweetness of things.
(Crimp 2005a: 245–246)

When the actor says, "And you're aware, y'know, like of the *continuity* of things . . ." a stage-assistant who is standing (back to the audience) to the actor's right and slightly upstage throughout the scenario, raises her right hand. She holds a small child's fork. The teller looks at the fork, takes it in his hand, looks back to the audience, and continues to tell the story. This is his fork; this is *his* story. As the actor talks about the new life he, Annie, and the kids have been living—a life "away from the city" where they live off the land, grow and trap "stuff," and bore "under the earth for clean pure water . . ." (Crimp 2005a: 246), it becomes clear that they have been part of an American group often known as "survivalists."

And over lunch—which is basically a kind of chicken salad with mayonnaise—we learn how he is in fact the commanding officer of a whole group of like-minded individuals who have armed themselves not out of any thirst for blood, but out of necessity because it is war. "War?" says Mom. "How d'you mean, war?"
(Crimp 2005a: 246)

The actor continues to tell the story with casual ease and pleasure, explaining how

they don't believe in taxes or welfare or any of that shit. How the war is a war against a government that takes the bread out of the working man's mouth and gives it to the pornographers and abortionists of this world.

Is a war against the God-forsaken faggots.
Is a war against the crack dealers and the Blacks.
(Crimp 2005a: 246–247)

In the middle of the story, he casually takes off his trousers and puts on a pair of camouflage pants. This survivalist solder—this "big guy in camouflage"—does "all that caring, domestic stuff. 'Cos family is at the heart of things, I guess" (Crimp 2005a: 247).

Crimp structures the story so that by its conclusion the audience experiences the dramatic opposite of the apparently happy family story being narrated. In our production, as the mother hears her prodigal son telling this story of his new life, tears begin to fall down her cheeks from her unblinking eyes—projected large on the video screen.

> And one of the tiny tiny children looks up from his chicken and says, "Daddy, why is she crying?"
> And it's true.
> His mother is crying.
> As she sits there at the family table gazing on this family she never knew she had—the son and his fine young wife, their strong and innocent children with their whole lives ahead of them—she is, yes indeed, crying her eyes out like a tiny child herself.
> And Annie strokes the boy's hair—which is clipped real short, y'know—like a real young soldier—and says, "Because she is so happy, son. Because she is so happy."
> (Crimp 2005a: 247–248)

Action-based irony results from the realization that Mom's tears are *not* because she is "so happy, son . . . so happy," but the reverse.

In working with the actors playing the Teller/Son and his Mom, I wanted to create as strong a juxtaposition as possible between the Son's state of self-satisfaction and the Mom's disbelief in what he is saying. The difficulty the actor telling the story faces is how to consistently embody the simple psychophysical state from which he maintains

an honest, self-satisfied sincerity without it becoming a caricature of itself. I worked with the actors playing Teller/Son on how to possess, like his wife Annie, an "inner light." This "inner light" is a congratulatory, self-satisfied, American self-righteousness. He knows that he possesses a god-given right as an individual and as a group to hold the views that he does and to be satisfied and happy with his worldview. Psychophysically, we worked on the actor allowing his self-satisfied smile to radiate from lower *dantian* so that each line was suffused with a self-knowing satisfaction that his view is . . . well . . . "right."

Beginning to tell the story while seated on a stool—isolated in a pool of light—Teller/Son addresses specific members of the audience as a neighbor or friend, enjoying that moment of person-to-person communication. It's a story that makes him feel good, and gives him a warm inner-glow—the glow of the "inner light" that both Annie and the Son possess. He is completely self-satisfied with his new life.

For the actress playing Mom, sitting on the raised upstage platform at the kitchen table, staring transfixed out of the window, her tasks were psychophysical and auditory: (1) to constantly engage in staring ahead, unblinkingly, at her son, with disbelief at his return, and in extreme disbelief that he could be saying what he says; (2) to grasp the edges of the table with her hands and to feel this disbelief in her palms as they contact the table; and (3) to absorb each detail of the Son's story even though she does *not* want to hear it. Drawing on the psychophysical training in awareness through stillness-in-motion, on her own previous work as a dancer and physical theater performer, and the inspiration provided by Japanese *noh* theatre, Jo Shapland reflected on her inhabitation of the mother as follows:

> I was trying to embody the room. [In *noh* acting, one's work] "is based on the continuous, profound concentration of the actor, who is supposed never to relax his inner tension [. . .] The moments of non-action, as well as those before and after, are all rooted in the

same reality, the *kokoro* (spirit) of all things, which provides the profound continuity to the apparent non-continuity of action" (Ortolani: 113). It felt like I was moving inside a great deal, while outside I was relatively still. When the eyes are kept open without, or even rarely, blinking for a period of time, tears are released. When this is done with awareness, focus and openness to what is happening, to the text, there can be a change in consciousness . . . e.g. release of tears, flow of energy through the body, change in quality and rate of breathing. These shifts are occurring in time with what is being said [. . . This touched] such intense sadness and darkness.

(Shapland 2006)

The object of our work throughout this scenario was to consistently produce the possibility that the audience would experience this moment as deeply but sadly ironic. Such irony does not produce laughter, as in some other scenarios in *Attempts on Her Life*. The possibility of experiencing this irony of loss cannot be produced if the actor telling the story does so with an overt cynicism, or somehow makes a mockery of the reality of the survivalist mentality that prompts and creates isolation, fear, and a deeply felt racism and homophobia. From my directorial perspective, the Teller here must enter and inhabit the state of sincerity at the heart of America's socio-political, narcissistic malaise—

its *real* belief in its own untouchable sense of rightness, and its belief in itself and its inhabitation of a complete state of innocent, wholesome goodness. Perhaps one wonders, retrospectively, how can someone who is so nice, be so despicable?

It is this subtler type of action-based irony that shaped my work with the actors on *Attempts on Her Life*. Perhaps audiences who experienced this approach to Crimp's play developed a relationship to this indefinable "her" in her many manifestations.

The final scenario ends with what appears to be an inane question. It is asked amidst a failed attempt to locate and define this "her." Among the series of things "she might've missed" is "That thing about the fresh salmon," i.e., the question of whether the word "fresh" can mean "'previously frozen'" with reference to salmon (Crimp 2005a: 283–284). The apparent inanity of the question is, I would argue, precisely what makes the non-presence of the "her" so strong. Crimp does not let us pretend that life is constituted by a series of profound questions or grand narratives; however, this fact does not mean that the lives lived amidst small questions are insignificant. Just as the text ends on a question mark, "And *can* it . . . mean 'previously frozen'?" (Crimp 2005: 284), so did "she" remain an ever-present question mark— unanswerable, but nevertheless very much there? We are all complicit in the creation of these Annies.

Afterword

I am occasionally asked by those who work with me whether the practice of the psychophysical disciplines I teach is spiritual or has changed me in some way. Given the highly problematic Western assumptions that usually surround the use of the word spiritual I can think of no better definition of the term than that provided by His Holiness the Dalai Lama:

> when I say "spiritual" I do not necessarily mean any kind of religious faith. When I use the word "spiritual" I mean basic human good qualities. These are: human affection, a sense of involvement, honesty, discipline and human intelligence properly guided by good motivation.
>
> (Dalai Lama 2002: 15)

Attempting to create and maintain an atmosphere in the studio and rehearsal room where practice is guided by affection, involvement, honesty, discipline, human intelligence, and good motivation is an ideal to which we might all constantly aspire.

With regard to the question of whether I have been changed by the disciplines I teach, my answer is a simple one—yes, of course. Any long-term psychophysical discipline practiced assiduously and with appropriate attentiveness will fundamentally change the relationship between one's body and one's mind. Indeed, change is an ongoing part of the subtle process of engagement with psychophysical practices over time. Precisely what constitutes change and the specific entailments of any manifestation of change are specific to each individual and to the context within which each person lives and practices in the moment.

"the body becomes all eyes . . ."

What, precisely, is acquired or brought to accomplishment through long-term bodymind training? To become accomplished is to achieve an optimal level and quality of relationship between the doer and the done where the "body(mind) becomes all eyes." Body and mind have been attuned to each other so that they constitute a gestalt beyond dualism. One manifests in practice a full and complete (internal and external) relationship to the specific act/tasks at hand: the object of meditation for the meditator, the target for the martial artist, the performance score for the actor. One is able to comfortably inhabit a state of readiness—that creative state of possibility between. Becoming accomplished means that one enters into a state of being/doing in which one is constantly at play in the moment.

Appendix 1
A. C. Scott and the
Asian Experimental Theater Program

A. C. Scott (1909–1985) founded the Asian Experimental Theater Program in 1963 and served as its director until 1979–1980. When A. C. Scott approached retirement age, Phillip Zarrilli was invited to take over direction of the program. Scott and Zarrilli co-directed and taught the program during 1979–1980, allowing Zarrilli to work side-by-side with Scott and to learn *taiqiquan* directly from Scott. The program was highly unusual in that it had its studio set aside for its work.

Like other Westerners of his generation, A. C. Scott first encountered the theaters of East Asia in the immediate post-World War II period while serving as an officer for the British Council in China (from 1946). Fluent in Chinese and Japanese, Scott subsequently spent some fifteen years in Asia researching theater and dance styles. In 1955 Scott began a prodigious output of books on the theater and acting practices of Japan and China. A partial list of his most notable books includes *The Kabuki Theatre of Japan* (1955), *The Classical Theatre of China* (1957), and *Actors are Madmen* (1982). Scott also published three distinguished volumes of *Traditional Chinese Plays* (Vols I, II, and III [1967, 1969, 1975]) in translation with extensive notes on acting styles appropriate to each set of plays. Remarkably, in 1956 Scott was given permission by the Chinese government to visit Beijing and interview Mei Lan-Fang, the internationally known Beijing Opera actor who so influenced Bertolt Brecht. Originally trained as an artist, Scott illustrated his books throughout with fluid, expressive line drawings that capture actors in movement and illustrate the intricacies of costuming and stage conventions, or the flavor of daily life.

While in Hong Kong between 1947 and 1952 Scott became a student of the Wu school of *taiqiquan* and trained under Master Cheng Yung-kuang, thus laying the foundation for his visionary work in using *taiqiquan* as a basis for the psychophysical training of the contemporary actor.

The Asian Experimental Theater Program was initiated at the University of Wisconsin-Madison in the fall of 1963 under the direction of A. C. Scott and became active in 1964 as the nucleus of a newly established International Theatre Program, in its turn the result of an increased concentration on International Studies within the university as a whole. Initial support for development of the program was provided by grants from the Rockefeller Foundation and the Ford Foundation.

The activities of the program benefited from numerous additional grants supporting the regular presence of guest artists from throughout Asia. Grants were awarded by the Brittingham Foundation, the Japan Foundation, the Fulbright

Program, the National Endowment for the Humanities, among others. The program was a pioneer of its kind in the US in that it combined theory with intensive daily practice of Asian martial arts in the studio as a prelude to work on an annual production project.

While Director of the Asian Experimental Theater Program, Scott directed a number of brilliant productions, including Beckett's *Waiting for Godot*, which was performed by invitation in the gallery space at the Walker Art Center, Minneapolis, designed by Isamu Noguchi.

Appendix 2
Yuasa Yasuo's body-scheme

Yuasa Yasuo proposes a body-scheme comprised of four interrelated experiential circuits in order to account for both how we live our bodies from within, and how these experiential circuits correlate with neuro-physiological structures of the body—the object-body. Yuasa's scheme offers a careful and insightful analysis of the lived body since it explicates "the inseparability and the oneness of the lived body-mind as it is *achieved*" through embodied, self-cultivating modes of psychophysical practice (Nagatomo 1992b: 59). The entire scheme operates as a multilayered system. The four experiential circuits are:

- *The external sensory-motor circuit*: this is the circuit that connects the body to the external world through the sensory organs. When we receive experience through this circuit, there is an active motor response via the central nervous system.
- The circuit of coenesthesis: this is the circuit of the internal sensations of the body, consisting (in Yuasa's scheme) of two subdivisions. (1) The "circuit of kinesthesis" operates in close connection with the motor-nerves of the external sensory-motor circuit such as the sensory-motor nerves attached to the muscles and tendons of the limbs. These are clearly locatable motor sensations constituting an often

invisible awareness that allows us to engage the external world and environment through perception and action, allowing us to do many physical activities unthinkingly—word processing at a computer, or playing the piano, etc. This circuit always stands "ready to activate the body toward an action in the external world" (Nagatomo 1992a: 50). (2) The second subdivision of the circuit of coenesthesis is the "circuit of somesthesis" concerned with the internal organs, and the even less recognizable set of sensations experienced via the splanchnic nerves attached to these internal organs. In normal health, these sensations recede into the background of awareness. For Yuasa, these sensations form a kind of background awareness of the body. Most importantly, behind our consciousness, there is clearly what Yuasa calls an "automatic memory system" achieved through a training which does not require the conscious effort of recall, i.e., "the body learns and knows" (ibid.: 51–52).

- The emotion–instinct circuit: for Yuasa this circuit accounts for our experience of emotion and instinct—those non-localized, whole-body experiences. This circuit is "correlated with the autonomic nervous system, which controls and regulates the function of the various internal organs such as the respiratory organs (lungs), the circulatory organ (heart), and the digestive organs (stomach and colon)" (Nagatomo 1992a: 52). As noted above, we do not usually have a conscious awareness of the functioning, under normal circumstances, of the internal organs; however, the "centrifugal path sends out to the distal internal organs those stimuli which the brain receives from the external world vis-à-vis the sensory organs, converting them into an emotional response (i.e., pleasure or pain), which may turn into stress or a stressful response" (ibid.: 53).

- *The circuit of unconscious quasi-body*: this circuit corresponds to the *ki*-meridian system or network beneath the skin covering the entire body as used in acupuncture, and is roughly equivalent to the subtle body of yoga. This body-circuit "does not conform to either the subject or object bodies," "defies our ordinary understanding," is invisible anatomically, and cannot be perceived via external perception. However, through the practice of various methods of self-cultivation, this invisible circuit can be made visible, i.e., it is brought into awareness and utilized. The *ki*-meridian system and the *nadi* of the yogic subtle body are both understood as networks through which energy (*ki* in the East Asian system; *prana* and/or *kundalini sakti* in South Asia) is understood to flow. (Although yet to be fully explained biomedically, the existence and efficacy of this circuit are now fully recognized.) The experience of this quasi-body takes the form of sensations of flow, heat, and/or vibrations, but is quite different from the experience of nerve-impulses. (Yoshio Nagahama's experimental tests reveal that "the vibration of *ki*-energy is measured as 15–50 cm/sec. while nerve-impulses travel 5–80 m/sec." (Nagatomo 1992b: 269).)

This summary of Yuasa's body-scheme is based on Nagatomo's two summaries (1992a, 1992b), and on Yuasa's detailed account (1993, especially 99–128).

Notes

Preface in three voices

1 As the culminating point in my ongoing training, Gurukkal Govindankutty Nayar gifted me the traditional *pitham* (stool) representing mastery in 1988. I was the first non-Malayali to receive this honor and the entitlement that goes with it. The honorific plural of the "guru" is the title, "gurukkal." It is plural because the teacher embodies and represents the lineage of all the masters before him. My years of training and practical research also culminated in my ethnographic study, *When the Body Becomes All Eyes* (Zarrilli 1998a).

2 A. C. Scott founded the Asian Experimental Theater Program at the University of Wisconsin-Madison in 1963. I learned Wu style of *taiqiquan* from Scott, and also absorbed from Scott an uncompromising attitude toward the importance of daily training in the studio. See Appendix 1.

1 Historical context

1 Sharon Carnicke explains that the terminology of Stanislavski's original Russian texts assumed a monistic rather than a dualistic view of the mind–body relationship. The Russian noun *chuvstva* applies "equally to the five physical 'senses' and to emotional 'feelings,' while the *chuvstvovat'* means to feel, 'to have sensation,' 'to be aware of,' 'to understand.' ... [T]he simultaneous physical and emotional associations implicit in *chuvstva* invariably get lost in English translations. Indeed, the classic versions of Stanislavski's books generally privilege emotional layers in the word, supporting the Americanization of the System" (Carnicke 1998: 139). The fact that physical sensation, feeling, and awareness are all implicit in Russian terminology is similar to the monism of non-Western terminologies rather than the dualism of mind/body in English.

Later in her book Carnicke concludes that Stanislavski remained tied to language with "deeply dualistic assumptions" (1998: 144). In spite of himself, "Stanislavski creates an almost endless series of oppositional concepts: inner/outer, emotion memory/muscle memory, mind/body ... etc. ... [H]e unwittingly betrays hidden Cartesian elements of his thinking" (ibid.: 144).

2 The earliest English publication to seriously discuss yoga in Stanislavski's work is Wegner's 1976 essay. More recent publications by

Carnicke (1998, especially 138–145; and 2000) and White (2006) address the historical problem of yoga and Stanislavski. White argues that "a full understanding of Stanislavski's technique is impossible without knowledge of the intersections between his system and Yoga" (2006: 73).

3 As R. Andrew White reports, Stanislavski's library included three books by Ramacharaka—the American "lawyer-turned-metaphysician William Walker Atkinson (1862–1932)" (2006: 82). Since Stanislavski did not speak or read English, he relied on Russian translations of Atkinson's books—*Hatha Yoga; or, The Yogi Philosophy of Physical Well-being, Raja Yoga or Mental Development*, and *Teachings of Yoga about the Mental World of the Person*. Helena Roerich "observes [. . . how] Ramacharaka books themselves [. . .] offer secondhand information and present a diluted version of Yoga aimed at a curious but largely uninformed readership" (in White 2006: 83).

4 White describes Stanislavski as adapting "specific Yogic exercises in order to help actors transcend the limitations of the physical senses and tap into higher levels of creative consciousness" (White 2006: 73). White's description is historically correct since it reflects the highly problematic Western understanding of yoga present at the time as it was absorbed into often generic notions of spiritualism. The occult-spiritualism of the period displays an inherent orientalism since books such as those by Ramacharaka did not seek to explain classical yoga in the Indian context. As White explains, yoga was not being studied or written about as a "system in and of itself; rather, followers frequently combined it with other ideologies as they constructed their own occult systems" (2006: 77). As discussed in detail in Chapters 2, 3, and 4, considerable confusion arises when this type of generic spiritualism pervades discussions of acting. Indian yoga per se does not carry the burden of spirituality and the occult that has often been projected onto its practices

or its philosophy, especially during the early twentieth century. My representation of Stanislavski's use of yoga exercises as attuning and heightening the actor's sensory awareness rather than as transcending the limitations of the physical senses points to a much less loaded and hopefully a much clearer articulation and understanding of the internal experience of acting than was possible at the time Stanislavski lived. While historically it is extremely important for scholars such as Carnicke and White to recover the spiritual element present in Stanislavski's thinking and writing, to do so practically in the studio will only continue to unnecessarily obfuscate the practical, material usefulness of selected yoga-based techniques and principles.

5 As explained in detail in Chapter 3, *prana-vayu* is a central principle and material reality in the two major paradigms informing how one experiences the bodymind and their relationship throughout South Asia—Ayurveda and yoga philosophy.

6 White provides an extended discussion of the subconscious and superconscious, comparing Ramacharaka's source text with Stanislavski's understanding (2006: 86–87). From my own practical perspective, Stanislavski's use of "superconscious" and "subconscious" are both highly speculative and therefore problematic. In my experience the use of such imprecise terminology only serves to muddy the conceptual and practical specificity necessary to keep the actors focused and clear about their work.

7 From as early as 1918 Chekhov reacted "against Stanislavski's use of personal experience and emotion, arguing that this, in effect, binds the actor to the habits of the everyday self" (Chamberlain 2000: 81). Chekhov's approach emphasizes psychophysical integration via work on psychological gesture, radiation, and the imagination (Chekhov 2002, 1991, 1985; see also Chamberlain 2004).

8 Regarding the problems with Hapgood's English translations, see Carnicke (1998,

1994, 1993) and Benedetti (1999, 1993, 1990). Benedetti observes how "Stanislavski tried to use simple, everyday words when describing the 'system,' what he called his 'home-grown' vocabulary. He divided the play up into bits, and for each bit he found a task. Elizabeth Hapgood translated these words as units and objectives, which are rather more technical in tone. There is also a difference in meaning between a task, which is here and now, facing me, and an objective which is a project, something to work towards. Stanislavski often refers to a 'goal' (*tsel*) which corresponds more closely to 'objective.' More important, perhaps Elizabeth Hapgood sometimes confuses 'objective' with 'action,' the means by which the objective is achieved" (Benedetti 1999: 367). See also the comparison between the Hapgood and Benedetti translations of one section of Stanislavski's text (Benedetti 1993). Most importantly, see Jean Benedetti's long awaited new translation (2008). It encompasses a full two-year program of training: Year 1 is devoted to "Experiencing" and Year 2 to "Embodiment." The new translation makes clear how problematic versions of Stanislavski's work have been when they are limited to such controversial techniques as "emotion memory" and when they do not take account of Stanislavski's emphasis on embodiment.

9 The physical inactivity of *The Blind* foreshadows Gertrude Stein's "landscape" plays (Stein 1995 [1949]), and the highly restrictive physical situations in which Beckett's plays often placed their speakers to create "landscapes" of consciousness. Along with the development of the historical avant-garde and neo-avant-garde of the 1950s/1960s new forms of dramatic texts have long possessed modes of narration and reality which are present "only in distorted and rudimentary shape" (Lehmann 2006: 49).

10 Shomit Mitter explains that Stanislavski's early work on developing a system by identification of "objectives" and "superobjectives," etc., led to "a crippling self-consciousness . . . When he looked back on this [early] period Stanislavski realized that the more self-consciously an actor works out what a character is about, the more self-conscious he becomes—and the less able he is to perform. In response to this problem Stanislavski instituted the so-called 'Method of Physical Actions.' This was a system of work which was diametrically opposed to the 'system' in that it took as its starting point the assumption that a role is most effectively inhabited when approached not through the mind (through research and analysis), but through the body (through gait, for instance, or make-up) . . . Stanislavski repeatedly emphasized that '[w]hen the actor starts to reason the . . . will is weakened. Don't discuss, just do it'" (Mitter and Shevtsova 2005: 14–15).

11 In its narrower usage, psychology refers to Western psychologies of the self as developed since the inception of the field in the nineteenth century. A relatively recent development has been the field of cross-cultural psychology which considers how specific cultures have developed social, linguistic, and cultural ways of accounting for the types of individual and social experiences marked by Western notions of mind, self, and emotion. One of the earliest and most important collections of essays was that edited by Shweder and LeVine (1984).

12 As discussed in Chapter 4, this inner feeling has often been confused in contemporary Western acting with subjective, everyday, personal emotions.

2 Beginning with the breath

1 I returned for more advanced training with Govindankutty Nayar in 1980, 1983, 1985, 1988, 1989, 1993, 1995, and 1998. Gurukkal Govindankutty Nayar gave me permission to teach what I had learned as early as 1977. In 1989 I also studied with C. Mohammed Sherif and Sreejayan Gurukkal at the Kerala Kalarippayattu Academy, Kannur. In 1989

I began training in yoga with Chandran Gurukkal of Azhicode, Kannur District, and in 1993 I continued yoga training with Dhayanidhi in Thiruvananthapuram.

2 *Aikido* is a generic term for a set of contemporary Japanese martial arts that developed in the early twentieth century. The individual most noted for the development of *aikido* and most often cited as its founder is Morihei Ueshiba (1883–1969). Ueshiba brought together elements of a number of styles of jujusu, as well as elements of fencing and spear fighting, as he developed his version of *aikido*. See Stevens (1987); Reed (1986: 105–128); Draeger (1979: 137–162); Westbrook and Ratti (1970).

3 An enactive approach to acting and embodiment

1 The first and second parts of this chapter were originally published separately in *Theatre Journal* (Zarrilli 2008a, 2004).

2 A complete phenomenology of performance would necessarily articulate not only the phenomenology of the actor's perception and experience, but also that of the spectator.

3 There is not sufficient space to address here many of the issues raised by phenomenological approaches to embodiment and experience. Since most phenomenological accounts focus on everyday, normative experience, this account moves beyond the everyday by providing an account of extra-daily embodiment and experience through which awareness is cultivated. A full phenomenological account of embodiment and experience is only possible when both ordinary and non-ordinary modes are considered together. For a history of phenomenology from Edmund Husserl (1859–1938) to the present, and for a discussion of its limitations and possibilities, see Moran (2000).

4 As Stanton Garner explains, "Phenomenology offers to supplement the semiotic (or materialist) body with the phenomenal (and phenomenalizing) body—to counter the signifying body in its dephysicalized readability with what we might call the 'embodied' body in its material resistance. By addressing issues of embodiment, phenomenology opens up the dimension of 'livedness,' of which objectifying theory can give no account and which it must bracket in order to maintain its analytic stance. The phenomenal body resists the epistemological model of a corporeal object yielding its meanings to a decorporealized observer" (1994: 50). Sandahl (2002) addresses the potential for a phenomenological perspective to consider issues of disability experience and performance. Camp provides an extensive critique of Husserl and States, finally proposing "concentration on the sensory aspects of performance considered separately from their status as signifiers" (2004: 93). As evident throughout this study, the "sensory aspects of performance" are at the center of both my approach to acting and how we think about acting.

5 The reader should be alert to the two uses of the term "acting" in the discussion which follows. In the title for this section, "Acting as a Process of 'I can,'" I am using the term "acting" to refer to the work of the stage actor. In the philosophical discussion that follows, "acting" is used more generically with reference to how, as human beings, we act in the world. The more generic use of the term "acting" includes within it, of course, stage acting.

6 Leder trained as a physician and received his MD before turning to philosophy. His phenomenological account is therefore informed by biomedical models of physiology, anatomy, etc. His account is also culturally sensitive, recognizing that any insight about the construction of human experience "involves an ambiguous set of possibilities and tendencies that take on definite shape only with a cultural context . . . The body's practices and self-interpretations are always already

shaped by culture" (1990: 151), and I would add also by gender and ethnicity.

7 Since my discussion focuses on acting, I have chosen to use the term "extra-daily" to mark the type of non-ordinary, voluntary modes of engagement described here. The pursuit of non-ordinary modes of experience can of course be applied to the practice of everyday living as is the ideal in certain forms of Buddhist engagement in the everyday world, or as evident in the legacy of Elsa Gindler and body awareness training for everyday life (see, for example, Rebecca Loukes 2003).

8 Leder explains that "Such schemas are meant to have not only explanatory but phenomenological power, charting experiences open to the ordinary person or to those who engage in spiritual practices. These energetic portrayals may capture the subtle and shifting quality of inner experience better than an image of fixed, massy organs" (1990: 182–183). The aesthetic inner body corresponds to Yasuo's fourth circuit—the "circuit of unconscious quasi-body" which mediates between the other experiential circuits (Nagatomo 1992: 59).

9 I use the term "character" from conventional Western drama to temporarily mark the actor's body when offered to the gaze and for the experience of the audience even when there is no dramatic character present on stage. In conventional genres of theater the performer's body is clearly a fictive body; however, in some forms of postdramatic theater/performance the performer's body becomes the site of dynamic play between the fictive and the real (see Lehmann 2006: 99–104). The fictive body may appear as character, figure, persona, or the active embodiment of images.

4 The source traditions

1 Some of the most esoteric aspects of these traditions are not addressed here, such as the alchemical dimensions of Taoist and Siddha yoga traditions. Radical forms of Taoist and Indian tantric practice ultimately aim to literally reverse the aging process.

2 For more complete information on the history and diversity of classical yoga practices and philosophy see Flood (1996: 75–102), White (1996), Filliozat (1991), and Varenne (1976).

3 For further discussions of yoga see the translations by Aranya (1983) or Reiker (1971), and the historical, philosophical, and ethnographic studies by Varenne (1976), Feuerstein (1980), Filliozat (1991), and especially White's exhaustive study of the Siddha yoga traditions of medieval India (1996, *passim*). For the best study of modern yoga to date, see De Michelis (2005).

4 See Zarrilli (1998a) for a complete account of *kalarippayattu* in cultural context.

5 As André Padoux explains, energy (*sakti*) "is at the same time Word (*vac*), consciousness (*cit*, *samvid*), breath, and vital or vibrative energy (*prana*): there are no absolute distinctions, no discontinuity between the human and the cosmic, the vital, the psychic, or the spiritual" (1990: xi). Whatever phenomena occur on the macrocosmic level are mirrored at the human level.

6 For more complete discussions of the history of Chinese martial arts in general, and of *taiqiquan* and the philosophical dimensions of Taoism and Neo-Confucianism that inform its practice see Kennedy and Guo (2005), Liao (2000), Schipper (1993), Yuasa (1987, 1993), Draeger and Smith (1980), Wong (1978), Huard and Wong (1977), and Moore (1967). On the underlying principles of Chinese medicine that inform the martial arts see Needham's ground-breaking series of publications (1954).

7 *Hsing-i* is a system of practice based on observation of animal and bird movements. Similar to *kalarippayattu's* animal poses, *hsing-i* techniques only take the underlying idea or principle (*i*) of the movements (*hsing*) and are not literally imitative. *Baqua* emphasizes constant circular, evasive movements. It is

based on the eight trigrams of traditional Chinese thought, and is derived from the *Book of Changes (I Ching)*. For basic discussions of both see Reid and Croucher 1983: 90–102.

8 Two key terms used for the Chinese martial arts in general are *wushu* and *kunfu*. *Wushu* derives from the Mandarin for "martial methods" or "war arts." *Kunfu* (kung fu) simply means "skill," "proficiency," or "effort" and can be used to refer to the effort taken to successfully pass an examination or a chef who is good at cooking. Only recently has the term "kung fu" been widely used to refer to some of the external Chinese martial arts.

9 Having learned *taiqiquan* from A. C. Scott, his teacher in Hong Kong was a member of the Wu Tang sect. The founder of this lineage was the Taoist philosopher, Chang San-feng, who is said to have retreated to Wu Tang mountain during the Sung period (1127–1278).

5   The psychophysical actor's "I can"

1 Yoshi Oida trained in Japanese *noh* and subsequently worked closely with Peter Brook. His series of books on acting (authored with Lorna Marshall: 1997, 1992) provide insightful observations on transposing principles from his traditional training into contemporary acting practices.

2 These elements/principles are similar to those identified by Eugenio Barba in his life-long exploration of the art of the actor, East and West (Barba and Savarese 2005).

3 "Decoction" comes from the Latin *de* = down and *coquere* = to cook. Many traditional medical preparations, such as the range of specialist oils utilized in Ayurvedic treatments in Kerala, India, are prepared through a process of decoction in which each recipe with its particular set of ingredients is boiled over, and over, and over again until only the essence remains. The same process is used to extract the essence of fragrances when making perfumes.

4 Unlike the approach to training through martial arts and yoga described here where *ki*-awareness is always a dialectic between the inward and one's relation to the environment, in some forms of meditation practice the outward/external environment is disregarded or intentionally shut out in order to focus entirely within.

6   Exercises for "playing" in-between

1 All productions used multiple casts and stages to emphasize the underlying meta-theatricality and hyper-reality of Genet's script evident in the *première version éditée* and in Bernard Frechtman's 1953 English translation. The Asian Experimental Theatre production of 1980 utilized three stages including one Japanese *bunraku*-style puppet stage. The 1989 Madison production had three casts performing on three stages. The 2003 Trinity College, Dublin, production used three main stages with one all-female, one all-male, one mixed cast, plus a tenth actor who played all the roles on a dress-up stage and moved freely between stages. For the 2005 production with Theater Asou I worked with a company of five—one Madame and two sets of actors playing Claire and Solange.

2 During rehearsals we explore each shift in role register. When is Solange speaking as Solange, as Solange-the-maid, as Claire, or as Madame? The actor(s) playing Madame are located on stage, above Madame's bedroom, as an observer throughout the production. Does she know the game the two maids are playing or not?

3 In production, the dressing-table mirror is never a real mirror—but rather imagined, or simply an empty, oval frame.

7   *The Beckett Project*

1 Whitelaw reflects on the fact that her lack of formal actor-training, rather than being a

minus when working with Beckett, "became a plus for me" (1995: 82).

2 As Jonathan Kalb remarks, accepting that "ambiguity [is] a positive value . . . is no guarantee of success, especially in works such as *Rockaby* and *Ohio Impromptu*" (1989: 48).

3 Jonathan Kalb quotes Michael Goldman's analysis of subtext: "It is the combination of subtexts, then, that produces the effect, with one important proviso: *that no subject be treated as privileged.* This is in sharp contrast to the standard convention of modern subtexts before Beckett, in which the subtext is understood to represent the authentic score of the text . . . [O]ur engagement with the actors, though it can be intense, must not be confidently located. We must not be allowed to feel, 'Yes, I can get behind these appearances.'" (1989: 38).

4 See also Mary Bryden's book-length study, *Samuel Beckett and Music* (1998).

5 Whitelaw describes Beckett's plays as "hooks on which to hang a specific human condition. They are not plays *about* anything, they represent emotional states of mind. In the case of *Play* it was the mind exploding in chaos and confusion—often expressed with humour" (1995: 76). The state or condition *in extremis* in which Beckett's speakers find themselves can be viewed and experienced by an audience as emotional, but as Whitelaw clearly recognized, this is not the actor's work.

6 On the "consciousness of consciousness" in Beckett see the entry on "consciousness" in Ackerley and Gontarski (2004: 108–109) and Hesla (1971).

7 The project was the annual production of the Asian/Experimental Theatre Program at the University of Wisconsin-Madison. There were thirteen MFA and BA actors and five directors who were MA/PhD students. I directed three of the plays myself and coordinated the two sets of plays.

8 Patricia Boyette is a professional actress and acting teacher. She has played major roles on stages throughout the United States including the American Conservatory Theatre, the California Actors Theatre, the Magic Theatre, Michigan Ensemble Theatre, Madison Repertory Theatre and many others. Patricia was personally cast and directed by Tennessee Williams as Claire in the West Coast premiere of his *Two Character Play* and as Laura in *The Glass Menagerie*. In addition to her acting career, Patricia is Head of Acting at the University of Wisconsin-Madison. Karen Ryker is a master voice teacher at the University of Connecticut.

9 Casting included: *Ohio Impromptu*: Phillip Zarrilli (Reader), Peader Kirk (Listener); *Not I*: Patricia Boyette (Mouth), Peader Kirk (Auditor); *Act Without Words I*: Phillip Zarrilli (Protagonist), Peader Kirk (Stage Attendant); *Rockaby*: Patricia Boyette. The evening received critical acclaim and two major Orange County theater awards: Boyette for "Best Actress," and "*Huevos Más Grandes*" award for courageous producing. See reviews by Hodgins (2000) and McCulloh (2000). The production had a limited UK tour in 2001 to Leicester Haymarket Theatre, Charter Theatre (Preston), Exeter Phoenix, Cochrane Theatre (London), Chapter Arts Centre (Cardiff). In 1999 I directed an evening of Beckett plays with Theater Asou in Graz (Austria) entitled, *Was? Wer? Ohio Impromptu, Spiel, Eh Joe, 3 Stücke 3 Raume.*

10 Casting included: *Ohio Impromptu*: Phillip Zarrilli (Reader), Andy Crook (Listener); *Play*: Bernadette Cronin (Woman 1), Regina Crowley (Woman 2), Andy Crook (Man); *Eh Joe*: Phillip Zarrilli (Joe), Patricia Boyette (Voice); *Not I*: Patricia Boyette (Mouth), Regina Crowley (Auditor); *Footfalls*: Bernadette Cronin (May), Mairin Prendergast (Voice); *Act Without Words I*: Phillip Zarrilli (Protagonist), Andy Crook (Stage Attendant); *Rockaby*: Patricia Boyette. See Daboo (2004), Heyley (2004), Leeland (2004), McMullan (2004), and Sheridan (2004).

11 The Singapore production included: *Not I, Footfalls, Play, Rockaby*. Due to ill-health, I

could not travel to Singapore to co-direct. Patricia Boyette directed in my absence. Performances in Greencastle, Indiana, and Madison, Wisconsin, included *Ohio Impromptu*, *Not I*, *Act Without Words I*, and *Rockaby*, performed by Phillip Zarrilli, Andy Crook, and Patricia Boyette.

12 *Act Without Words I* was written in French in 1956 for dancer Deryk Mendel. The premiere was at the Royal Court Theatre, London, April 3, 1957. *Acte sans paroles I* was published with *Fin de Partie* (Minuit) in 1957, and the English translation with *Endgame* (Grove and Faber) in 1958.

13 This is equally true of the stillness of Reader/Listener in *Ohio Impromptu*, Mouth in *Not I*, Joe in *Eh Joe*, and W1, W2, and M in *Play*.

14 Beckett wrote *Ohio Impromptu* for a symposium at Ohio State University honoring his seventy-fifth birthday. With David Warrilow as Reader and Rand Mitchell as Listener, it premiered on May 9, 1981. Alan Schneider directed.

15 Written in 1972, *Not I* premiered as part of the Samuel Beckett Festival by the Repertory Theater of Lincoln Center, New York November 22, directed by Alan Schneider. Jessica Tandy played Mouth and Henderson Forsythe Auditor. The first London performance with Bille Whitelaw as Mouth and Brian Miller as Auditor was at the Royal Court Theatre, January 16, 1973.

16 Beckett's first play for television, *Eh Joe* was written in 1965. The first broadcast was in German with Deryk Mendel as Joe and Nancy Illig as Voice. The first production in English was for BBC 2 (July 4, 1966) directed by Alan Gibson with Jack MacGowran as Joe and Sîan Phillips as Voice. Billie Whitelaw conducted preliminary work for her performance of Voice with Beckett in 1988 for the production directed by Walter Asmus with Klaus Hern as Joe (RM Productions).

17 Whitelaw describes her rehearsals with Beckett in Paris for the 1988 film for television production with Klaus Herm as Joe as follows:

"We read it together. I found it unbearably moving but we read it [. . .] and we read it through and he kept on saying as always, 'No colour, no colour' and 'slow,' I mean slower than *Footfalls* . . ." (in Knowlson and Knowlson 2006: 174).

18 A quotation from Whitelaw's copy of the published script with additions by Beckett.

19 Among Beckett's friends in Paris were the well-known painter Avigdor Arikha and the poet Anne Atik. In a memoir of time spent with Beckett, Atik tells the story of how after a rehearsal Beckett had with Billie Whitelaw for *Eh Joe*, Billie returned to their flat and recited the final part of the text on which they had worked: "What we heard [. . .] was a voice which no longer seemed that of a woman, but rather of waves beating against the shore, something that was part of nature, rising, falling, murmuring. We heard shingles in the shshshs, the swish of water, rocks, the pull of the tide, a rumble, Billie's arms lifting and turning as though she were thrashing in the water, ourselves on the shore, overwhelmed" (2005: 58–59).

8 *The Water Station (Mizu No Eki)* by Ōta Shōgo

1 Mel Gussow of *The New York Times* reviews Ōta's 1988 production at the Japan Society, New York.

2 Falkenstein's discussion of the type of drama which takes place in performances of *The Water Station* is from a review of the 1998 Madison, Wisconsin, production which I directed.

3 The English translation by Mari Boyd of the original version of *The Water Station* was first published in *Asian Theatre Journal* (1990). Boyd's translation is based in the 1988 Japanese script. For a production record of *The Water Station* between its premiere in 1981 and 1988, see Boyd (2006: 167–168). The 1990 English translation includes a note from Ōta Shōgo, and an introduction by the translator. Ōta

and the company later developed two more versions of *The Water Station*: *The Water Station 2* (1995) and *The Water Station 3* (1998). I focus my discussion on the first (published) version. Mari Boyd has completed a draft English translation of *The Water Station 3* as yet unpublished.

Between 1997, when *The Water Station* first came to my attention, and my production of 2004 in Singapore, my knowledge of Ōta's work and the principles informing his work was limited to the few sources in English available during that period (Akihiko, 1997; Ōta, 1993, 1990, 1985; Boyd, 1990; Sarlos, 1985). As will be made clear in the following discussion, there are parallels between the psychophysical work-process I had been developing during the 1970s and 1980s and that being developed by Ōta and his company during the same period. The following analysis is informed in particular by Mari Boyd's recent (2006) in-depth, book-length study of Ōta Shōgo's body of work and its underlying aesthetic principles of quietude and divestiture, *The Aesthetics of Quietude: Ōta Shōgo and the Theatre of Divestiture*. The book includes translations of three plays: the non-verbal score for the original version of *The Water Station* based on the 1988 script, and two of Ōta's plays with text, *Afternoon Light* and *Elements*. Some slight differences exist between the 1990 and 2006 published English versions of *The Water Station*. Also see the astute analysis of Ōta's developing body of work in *The Voyage of Contemporary Japanese Theatre* by Senda Akihiko (1997).

4 Among the key sources listed by Boyd (2006: 109) are the plays and novels of Fernando Arrabal, Betsuyaku Minoru, Ishizawa Tomiko, and Ogata Kamenosuke; the paintings of Egon Schiele and Eugène Delacroix; and a Greek film by Theo Angelopoulos.

5 According to Ōta, it should take an actor five minutes to walk a distance of two meters (Shōgo 1990: 151).

6 In the *noh* theater all actors exit by the same bridgeway on which they entered to the audience's left. Having all travelers exit to the audience's right extends their world out into and through that of the audience, suggesting the necessity of having to continue their travels.

7 As indicated in the subtitle to Boyd's detailed analysis of Ōta's body of work, divestiture is one of the key principles informing the development of his theater aesthetic and its practice (2006, *passim*, especially 18, 86–88, 96–100).

8 Given the centrality of yoga to Tenkei's training regime, it is not surprising that Ōta emphasized "the importance of the spine" and verticality in the development of his actors (Boyd 2006: 99–100). "On the level of practice, Ōta notes that our sensitivity to the outer world depends partly on the condition of the spine as a metaphoric antenna, and wants acting to be done on the highest level of receptivity" (ibid.: 100). I would argue that the kind of heightened *ki/* sensory awareness required of the actor to fully sustain slowed-down actions is a result of deep psychophysical training which engages the spine and thereby the lower *dantian*— such as that developed by Ōta and discussed throughout this book. Boyd also provides a description of Ōta's process for working with new actors after the disbanding of the Tenkei company in 1988 (ibid.: 127–128).

9 According to Sarlos, the production of *The Water Station* on which he reports at length was produced for a ten-day run at the small Theatre of Transformation space in an alley near Akasaka Station in Tokyo. Sarlos states that an audience of approximately 120 squeezed into the small theater. According to Boyd the 1985 performances were at the T2 Studio.

10 Since the unspoken words provide neither detailed information about the (nameless) figures (Girl, Man A, Man B, etc.) nor an overarching narrative, members of the

audience are relatively free within a wider horizon of possibilities to allow their own associations, images, and/or narratives to shape their experience of *The Water Station*.

11   For a chronology and complete discussion of Ōta's life and career, see Boyd (2006: 67–80; 255).

12   According to the legend, Komachi both was beautiful and possessed superb skill as a poet. While young she had numerous suitors, but she was heartless and mocked the pain they all suffered. Shii no Shosho, one of her many lovers, traveled a great distance to win her favor. Responding, she said she would not listen until he had made the trip from his house to hers for one hundred nights without interruption. Accepting the challenge, he made the long journey each day. On the last night before reaching her, Shii no Shosho died. Growing old, Komachi became a beggar and went mad as she was possessed by the spirit of Shii no Shosho. Kan'ami's *Sotoba Komachi* is one of a number of *noh* plays based on the legend. (For an early English translation see Waley 1976: 114–124.) In *Sotoba Komachi*, Komachi is a restless spirit unable to die until Shosho's spirit is exorcized by a Buddhist priest.

13   It is important to emphasize that even while Ōta was developing his aesthetic of quietude and process of divestiture he continued to write plays with dialogue. Boyd's full-length study of Ōta's work provides a description and analysis of his plays with dialogue (2006, *passim*).

14   *The Tale of Komachi Told by the Wind* (1977) received the Kishida Drama Prize in 1978 and toured Europe. In 1983 *The Water Station* toured throughout Europe. In 1984 Tenkei received the Kinokuiya Theatre Award (group category) for *The Water Station* and other work. In 1985 Tenkei moved to the T2 Studio in Tokyo—a somewhat larger space in a renovated warehouse. Between 1985 and the disbanding of the company in 1988 the company staged four new plays by Ōta, restaged those in their repertory, and toured France, the US, Canada, and Korea (Boyd 1990: 152). After 1988 Ōta continued his work as playwright and director with such new works as *Sarachi* (1991), *The Sand Station* (1993), *Elements* (1994), *The Water Station 2* (1995), and *The Water Station 3* (1998). Between 1990 and 1999 he served as artistic director of the Fujisawa Civic Theatre in Kanagawa, and in 2000 he was appointed Chair of the Theatre Department at the Kyoto University of Art and Design.

15   Similar to the performance of structured improvisations discussed in Chapter 6, when actors observe other actors from outside a structure or score, these breaks or gaps in focus, concentration, *ki*-awareness, attention, etc., are immediately evident.

16   Gardzienice Theatre Association was founded in 1977 by Wlodzimierz Staniewski. For a discussion of the principles and practices of the company's work and its history, see Staniewski (2004). Gardzienice recently founded an Academy for the training of young Polish theater practitioners. The March 2–7, 2004 workshop was part of the fourth Academy. This and other workshops I have conducted at Gardzienice are for students of the Academy as well as permanent company members. In a workshop setting participants can only begin to learn how to apply the awareness and energy generated through the training to the problem of inhabiting this non-verbal score of slowed-down everyday actions. The most important result of working on *The Water Station* in a workshop setting is that participants begin to gain an understanding of how to engage the sensory awareness of the entire bodymind in the embodiment of an action. There is not time, as when working on a full production, to bring the work on sensory awareness to a full realization.

17   *The Water Station* was first brought to my attention while conducting an intensive training workshop with MA students at the University of Wales, Aberystwyth

in 1998. Undergoing the psychophysical training described in Chapters 4–5, Michael Stubblefield suggested that the principles of the training might fruitfully be applied to selected scenes from *The Water Station*. My first full production of *The Water Station* was with an ethnically diverse cast of eighteen MFA/BA acting students at the University of Wisconsin-Madison in 1998. I directed a second production with MA/BA Theatre Practice students at the University of Exeter in 2000.

18 The Theatre Training and Research Programme was founded in 2000 by the internationally known and respected playwright, director, and father of contemporary Singaporean theater, Kuo Pao Kun, and T. Sasitharan. TTRP runs a three-year professional actor training program dedicated to integrating traditional training conducted by master teachers of specific Asian genres of performance with contemporary Western training in voice, movement, and acting. As part of their core training program, TTRP actors study both contemporary Western approaches to movement, voice, and acting, as well as traditional modes of Asian psychophysical training. TTRP training today includes daily practice of *taiqiquan* and meditation. There are extended periods of intensive immersion in traditional Asian performing arts with master teachers of *kutiyattam* (Kerala, India), *noh* (Japan), *Wayangwong* or Balinese dance (Indonesia), and Beijing Opera (China). For further information on TTRP see www.ttrp.edu.sg.

19 The Singapore cast included: Scene 1: Girl (Jeungsook Yoo, Korea); Scene 2: Man A (Noushad Mohamed Kunju, India) and Man B (Pern Yiau Sim, Singapore); Scene 3: Woman with Parasol (Hiu Tuen Leung, Hong Kong); Scene 4: Married Couple (Miyuki Kamimura, Japan and Yann Yann Yeo, Malaysia) with Man in Garbage Heap (Jia Liang Sau, Singapore); Scene 5: Old Woman (Adrianna Koralewska, Poland); Scene 6: Caravan with Husband (Wai Shek Ng, Hong Kong), Wife (Jing Hong Kuo, Singapore), Daughters (Pei Ching Hung, Taiwan, and Nog Chao Au, Macau), Young Man A (Ban Loong Lee, Singapore), Young Man B (Xiao Jian, China), and Additional Man (Klaus Seewald, Austria); Scene 7: Man and Woman (Yeun Kwon Leung, Hong Kong and Pei ann Lin, Taiwan); Scene 8: Man with Heavy Load (Filemon Blanco, Philippines). The design and production staff included: lighting by Dorothy Png; costumes by Hella Chan; and Assistant Director, Klaus Seewald.

20 Scene 1 includes no minor actions because the Girl is alone on stage. In subsequent scenes, the main actions are those of the primary figures within a scene, such as Man A and Man B in Scene 2 or the Woman with a Parasol in Scene 3. Minor actions are those of the secondary figure(s) in a specific scene, such as the Girl in Scenes 2 and 3. As explained below, the scene with the most complicated set of main and minor actions is the Caravan in Scene 6 when ten actors are on stage at the same time.

21 This process is emergent in that it begins and evolves from one's psychophysical engagement with specific actions/tasks and *not* from analytical engagement with the text. The arc of this process mirrors the entire process of psychophysical training and development described in Chapters 5–6.

22 The ordering of the exercises listed here is from the Singapore production. The sequence and set of instructions at the earlier Gardzienice workshop were similar to, but not necessarily the same in all specifics as, that described here. Whenever and wherever this process is utilized there are always changes and adjustments made both for the context and as a response to individuals and/or group dynamic.

23 Through the remainder of this chapter I occasionally quote at length from Jeungsook's published reflection and analysis of "acting process in *The Water Station*" authored from her perspective inside the process (2007: 81).

Jeungsook has trained with me since 2000, assisted me in teaching and leading workshops (including the week-long session during March 2004 at Gardzienice), acted in productions I directed of *Eftermale: That Which Comes After* (2000) and *The Bald Soprano* (2003), and played the role of the Girl in the 2004 Singapore production.

24 See Yoo 2007: 89–90 for her version of the score. I have slightly changed the formatting. The actions cut from Ōta's source score are those involving the basket and red cup. The actions added involve the Girl's direct engagement and interaction with the water with her tongue and mouth rather than the cup.

25 Even when acting a conventionally realist drama in which a character reaches and makes conclusions or expresses a thought, the actor should not have the thought in his head before it arrives.

26 These responses suggest parallels between the effect on the audience of *The Water Station* and many Japanese *butoh* performances. (Boyd and Smith are responding to Ōta's performances, and Oon to the 2004 Singapore production directed by me.)

27 My description of the playing of Scene 3 is with reference to the 2004 Singapore production discussed above.

28 Mari Boyd explains that Ōta "aims to demolish the assumption of psychological portrayal of character by actor, and . . . he aims to reinvent the aspects of the actor's body that are taken for granted in realism" (2006: 97).

9 **Speaking Stones: Images, voices, fragments . . . from that which comes after**

1 Theater Asou was founded in 1994. It is a free, independent company receiving partial subsidies from the city of Graz and the Styrian government. (See http://www.theaterasou. at for further information on Theater Asou.) I began working with the company when they participated in the psychophysical training at intensive workshops hosted by Passe Partout in Utrecht, the Netherlands in 1998. My first production with Theater Asou was the 1999 production of three Beckett plays: *Was Wer?* 3 *Stucke* 3 *Raume*. In 2002 when we began work on *Speaking Stones*, the six members of the company were Christian Heuegger, Gernot Rieger, Uschi Litschauer, Monika Zöhrer, Sandra Urbans, and Klaus Seewald. For the 2003–2004 productions, Sandra was replaced by Laura Dannequin. The accompanying DVD-ROM excerpts and photographs are from the most recent (2004) production in Aflenz. All quotations from *Speaking Stones* are from the definitive English version by Kaite O'Reilly for the November 2002 performances in Aflenz. The German translation is by Frank Heibert with the exception of fragments of text used in "The Semiotics of Zero" which was edited from Brian Rotman's *Signifying Nothing: The Semiotics of Zero* (1993) and translated by George Fischer.

2 Kaite O'Reilly is a well-known, award-winning UK-based playwright and dramaturg. *Yard* won the 1998 Peggy Ramsay Award and premiered at the Bush Theatre, London. In a translation by Frank Heibert, *Schlacthaus* was in repertory at the Maxim Gorki Theater, Berlin, from 2000 to 2002. *Belonging* was commissioned and produced by the Birmingham Rep in 2000. *Perfect* was commissioned and produced by Contact Theatre, Manchester, in 2004. *Peeling* was commissioned and produced by Graeae Theatre, London in 2002 for national tour, and received a second staging as part of the British Council showcase at the Edinburgh Festival, 2003. Kaite O'Reilly is a co-founder of The Fingersmiths, Ltd, whose production *In Praise of Fallen Women* premiered in London, 2006. I directed the premiere of *The Almond and the Seahorse* for Sherman Cymru (Cardiff, on tour) in 2008. For further information see www.kaiteoreilly.com.

3 The performance score we developed can be described, following the publication of

the English translation of Lehmann's *Post-Dramatic Theatre* (2006), as post-dramatic in its design and implementation. We worked against creating any over-arching narrative. There were to be no fully rounded characters taking an individual journey, but rather figures or personas with the cast of six constantly transforming from one figure/persona to another. (See Lampe (2002) for a discussion of figures and personas.) We utilized multiple approaches and styles of performance appropriate to specific structures as they were developed. The audience's associations and responses to the score were intentionally left relatively open.

4 "The Semiotics of Zero," was edited by Phillip Zarrilli from Brian Rotman's provocative history of the mathematical concept of zero (1993). In addition, Kaite O'Reilly edited short contributions from company member Gernot Rieger, a poem by L. L. Zarrilli senior, and a few short fragments of text from Griffin's *A Chorus of Stones* (1992) for use in other structures.

5 Our sessions began with intensive psychophysical training.

6 The titles for the structures are simple, descriptive, and mnemonic devices for use in rehearsals only. None of these titles or the descriptions provided below was made available to the audience. It was important for the audience *not* to be led in their experience of the performance by the associations that these titles and descriptions might generate.

7 Kaite O'Reilly worked with the cast on their performance of the unvoiced signs for this part of the text. For a discussion of her early work in sign-dance theater, see O'Reilly (2001).

10 *4:48 Psychosis* by Sarah Kane

1 Graham Saunders notes the influence of Martin Crimp's work, especially *Attempts on Her Life*, on the formal development of Kane's plays, *Crave* and *4:48 Psychosis*, including

the "move away from formal methods of characterization" (2002: 111). *Attempts on Her Life* is discussed in Chapter 11.

2 All quotations are from *4:48 Psychosis* in Kane (2001). The assignment of speakers indicated in quotations is specific to the work described below. If we accept Kane's dashes as indicating specific units of action, then there are twenty-four scenarios or "scenes," some of which are as brief and sketchy as simply "RSVP ASAP."

3 The materialization of this state of mind through non-representational, non-character-based means is similar to the materialization of the absent "her" [Annie, Anne, etc.] in Crimp's *Attempts on Her Life*. As discussed in Chapter 11, the "her" in *Attempts* is never literally present, while Figure in *4:48* is present in that actors speak her text. The work of both texts is to materialize the Annie or Figure as more than an individual, a character, etc.

4 Part of my interest in Kane's play is the fact that my own family, like many others, had to deal with issues of mental health. They are inescapable when they arise. For an intelligent discussion of Kane's relationship to her work, see Singer (2004).

5 The 2004 Exeter workshop included ten MA/MFA and ten BA students from Greece (Tina Alexopoulou, Makis Kyrlis), Israel (Shulamit Druckman), Korea (Hye-Ok Kim, Sunhee Kim), Wales (Teifi Vaughan, Sian Rees), Guernsey (Samata Russell), England (Angela Bradley, William Dickie, Roberta Ensor, Sophie Harris, Alex Kaye, Laura Marshall, Merlyn Perez-Silva, Claudia Palazzo, Benjamin Shelley), Jordan (Beisan Elias), Ireland (Heidi Love), and Taiwan (Ya-Ruei Han). The 2007 workshop in Exeter included an international group of 12 MA/MFA/PhD students from the USA (Thorvald Aagaard, Emily Kreider), Korea (Kyounghee An), Singapore (Kuo Jing Hong), Taiwan (Ma Ying-Ni), Anirudh Nair (India), Greece (Maria Kapsali), and the UK (Lindsay Gear, Liz Pennington, Hannah Silva, Simon Strain, Duncan Jamieson). The workshops culminated with

a closed work-in-progress showing of my psychophysical approach to selected scenarios of Kane's text. The Korean cast included Yoo Jeungsook, An Kyounghee, Kim Hyeok, Kim Sunhee, An Kyounghee, Change Sehoon, Lee Sang Min, Lim Jong Wan, Shin Jae Hwan, Yang Don Tak, Shin Moon Young, Kim So Jin, Lee Hannim, Woo Hyo Jung, Kim Mo Eun, Kim Ji Young, Kho Ae Ri, Yun So Hee, Choi Mi Hyang, Lim Sung Mi, Noh Susanna. The 2008 production in Seoul, Korea, included twenty actors: fifteen women and five men. There were six public performances.

6 In Exeter in 2007 one Doctor–Figure scenario was played by two pairs—one speaking English, and the second speaking Korean and Mandarin. Another was played with three sets working in English, Taiwanese, and Greek. In Korea one scene was played between English and Korean with two pairs of Doctor–Figure.

7 See for example Krasner (in Hodge 2000: 142–147).

11 *Attempts On Her Life* by Martin Crimp

1 Martin Crimp was born in 1956. Among his many other plays are *Definitely the Bahamas* (1987), *Dealing with Claire* (1988), *No One Sees the Video* (1990), *The Treatment* (winner of the 1993 John Whiting Award), *The Country* (2000), and *Cruel and Tender* (2004). He has also translated plays by Ionesco, Genet, and Molière.
   Martin Crimp: Plays 1 and *Plays 2* are published by Faber and Faber (2001 and 2005 respectively). The most complete and balanced account and analysis of his life and work is *The Theatre of Martin Crimp* (Sierz, 2006). It includes interviews with three directors of *Attempts on Her Life:* Tim Albery (Royal Court, London, production), Katie Mitchell (Milan, Italy, production), and Gerhard Willert (German premiere in Munich).

2 In the version of the text published at the time of the first production, Crimp asks that "each

scenario in words—the dialogue—unfold against a distinct world—a design—which best exposes its irony" (1997: ii). These stage directions do not appear in the 2005 edition.

3 Scenario 10 ("Kinda Funny") is the only scenario that is clearly a monologue with all the text spoken by one actor.

4 For a brief description of Tim Albery's production see Sierz (2006: 51).

5 In Samuel Beckett's *Waiting for Godot* Vladimir and Estragon perpetually occupy themselves in a barren landscape while waiting for Godot. Godot remains an absence, never arriving. Similar in some ways to the "her" in *Attempts,* Godot is "materialized" while remaining an ever-present absence. In *Attempts*, the absent "her" is a plurality, and the various scenarios do not occur in the same landscape.

6 The 2007 National Theatre production by Katie Mitchell was equally controversial, but for different reasons. By 2007 the text and its international reputation were well known to UK critics. With the exception of Charles Spencer writing for the *Daily Telegraph* (2007), those who were critical focused on the directorial choices made by Katie Mitchell rather than Crimp's play per se. For example, Michael Billington of the *Guardian* began his review by noting how "Crimp's postmodernist piece has been translated into twenty languages; and it's not hard to see why. In denying the idea of fixed identity or linear narrative, it speaks to the modern age. But much as I admire Crimp's text, I'm not sure it is helped by Katie Mitchell's hi-tech revival" (2007). With the exception of the book-ending of the production with the cast onstage talking to each other and the audience (Scenarios 2 and 17), the cast of eleven played the production at break-neck speed as each scenario was set up as a mediated event. For some critics, such as Billington, the production was "restlessly busy" in its "self-conscious media satire" and therefore lacked "moral anger" (2007). In contrast Kate Bassett of *The Independent* found the production a "new,

riveting, experimental take on Martin Crimp's radically fragmented anti-play" (2007). See also Benedict Nightingale's review in *The Times* (2007).

7 I disagree with Mary Luckhurst's conclusion that "a weakness of the play is that, crudely, its politics might be summarized as: men are wicked and brutal, women are less wicked and brutal but may be partially to blame for their own victimhood" (2003: 60). This statement oversimplifies the complex construction of "her" throughout the play and provides no sense of the potential for realization in performance of a collective (male/female) socio-political complicity in the at times brutal constructions and representations of "her" central to *Attempts on Her Life*.

8 Thanks to Peader Kirk for suggesting that I work on *Attempts on Her Life*.

9 This international group ranged in age from nineteen to early forties and included actors from Korea (Seok ha Hwang, Hye Ok Kim), Greece (Christina Chatzivasileiou, Efrosini Mastrokalou), Ireland (Heidi Love), USA (Nathan Mitchell, Jane Rosenbaum), New Zealand (James McLaughlin), Taiwan (Tzu-I Tung), Jordan (Miriam Hilmi Abdul-Baqi), Wales (Jo Shapland), and England (Sarah Goldingay, James Hedges, Martha King, Lucy Mitchell, Lara Pearce, Rachel Southern).

10 The cast of eleven in Singapore included Soledad Garre-Rubio (Spain), Michael Stubblefield (USA), Claire Lindsay (UK), Hye Ok Kim (Korea), Heidi Love (Ireland), and six TTRP actors, including Alberto Ruiz Lopez (Mexico), Seng Soo Ming (Malaysia), Sajeev Purushothama Kurup (India), Sreejith Ramanan (India), Zachary Ho Tze Siang (Singapore), and Tam ka Man (Hong Kong).

11 As indicated in note 2, the issue of irony is clearly central to Crimp's own understanding of *Attempts on Her Life*. Although Crimp's statement "Let each scenario in words—the dialogue—unfold against a distinct world—a design—which best exposes its irony" (1997: ii) is invitingly cryptic, I interpret irony here as of the second, action-based, structural type.

12 In the Exeter workshop the three actors were Sarah Goldingay (England), Heidi Love (Ireland), and Hye-Ok Kim (Korea). For the Singapore production, the three actors were Heidi Love, Hye-Ok Kim, and Seng Soo Ming (Malaysia).

13 The text in "Kinda Funny" was delivered by two Americans: Nathan Mitchell for the Exeter workshop and Michael Stubblefield in Singapore. In Exeter the Mom was played by Jo Shapland, and in Singapore by Soledad Garre-Rubio.

Bibliography

Ackerley, C. J. and S. E. Gontarski, 2004. *The Faber Companion to Samuel Beckett*. London: Faber and Faber.

Akihiko, Senda, 1997. *The Voyage of Contemporary Japanese Theatre*, translated by J. Thomas Rimer. Honolulu: University of Hawaii Press.

Akihito, Yasumi, 2004. "Introduction" to *The Tale of Komachi Told by the Wind* by Ōta Shōgo, translated by Mari Boyd in *Half a Century of Japanese Theater 1960s* Part I, Volume VI. Tokyo: Kinokuniya Company, pp. 216–219.

Alter, Joseph S., 1992. *The Wrestler's Body*. Berkeley: University of California Press.

Aranya, Swami Hariharananda, 1983. *Yoga Philosophy of Patanjali*. Albany: State University of New York Press.

Artaud, Antonin, 1970. "Athlete of the Heart," in *Actors on Acting*, edited by Toby Cole and Helen Crich Chinoy. New York: Crown Publishing, pp. 235–240.

Atik, Anne, 2005. *How It Was: A Memoir of Samuel Beckett*. London: Shoemaker Hoard.

Austin, James H., 1998. *Zen and the Brain: Toward an Understanding of Meditation and Consciousness*. Cambridge, MA: MIT Press.

Barba, Eugenio, 2004. "The House of My Origins— and My Return," *The Drama Review*, 48, 1: 6–10.

—— 2002. "The Essence of Theatre," *The Drama Review*, 46, 3: 12–30.

—— 2000. "Tacit Knowledge: Heritage and Waste," in *Odin Teatret 2000*, edited by John Andreasen and Annelis Kuhlmann. Arhus: Arhus University Press, 13–29.

—— 1995. *The Paper Canoe*. London: Routledge.

—— 1985. *The Dilated Body*. Rome: Zeami Libri.

—— 1972. "Words or Presence," *The Drama Review*, 16, 1: 47–54.

Barba, Eugenio and Nicola Savarese, 1991. *A Dictionary of Theatre Anthropology*. London: Routledge.

Bartow, Arthur, ed., 2006. *Training of the American Actor*. New York: Theatre Communications Group.

Bassett, Kate, 2007. "Attempts on Her Life," *The Independent*, March 18.

Beckett, Samuel, 1984. *The Collected Shorter Plays*. New York: Grove Press.

Benedetti, Jean, 2008. "Translator's Foreword," *An Actor's Work* by Konstantin Stanislavski. London: Routledge.

—— 1999 (1988). *Stanislavski: His Life and Art*. London: Methuen.

—— 1993. "From *The Actor: Work on Oneself*," *The Drama Review* 37, 1: 38–42.

—— 1990. "A History of Stanislavski in Translation," *New Theatre Quarterly*, 23: 266–278.

—— 1982. *Stanislavski: An Introduction*. New York: Theatre Arts Books.

Benedetti, Robert L., 1973. "What We Need to Learn from the Asian Actor," *Educational Theatre Journal* 25: 463–468.

Berberich, Junko Sakaba, 1984. "Some Observations on Movement in Nō," *Asian Theatre Journal* 1, 2: 207–216.

Bethe, Monida and Karen Brazell, 1982. *Dance in the Nō Theater*: Volume I, *Dance Analysis*. Ithaca, NY: Cornell University China-Japan Program, East Asian Papers 29.

Billington, Michael, 2007. "Attempts on Her Life," *The Guardian*, March 15.

Blau, Herbert, 2004. "The Theatre Journal Auto/ Archive," *Theatre Journal*, 56: 733–744.

—— 1994. "Herbert Blau," in *Directing Beckett*, edited by Lois Oppenheim. Ann Arbor: University of Michigan Press.

—— 1982a. *Take Up the Bodies*. Urbana: University of Illinois Press.

—— 1982b. *Blooded Thought: Occasions of Theatre*. New York: PAJ Press.

—— 1976. "Seeming, Seeming: The Disappearing Act," *Drama Review*, 20, 4: 7–24.

Bloch, Susana, 2006. *The Alba of Emotions: Managing Emotions through Breathing*. Santiago, Chile: Ediciones Ultramarinos PSE.

—— 1993. "Alba Emoting: A Psychophysiological Technique to Help Actors Create Real Emotions," *Theatre Topics* 3, 2: 121–138.

Bloch, Susana, Pedro Orthous and Guy Santibañez-H., 2002. (1987) "Effector Patterns of Basic Emotions: A Psychophysiological Method for Training Actors," in *Acting Reconsidered*, edited by Phillip B. Zarrilli. London: Routledge, 219–238.

Boleslavsky, Richard, 1949. *Acting: The First Six Lessons*. New York: Theatre Arts Books.

Boyd, Mari, 2006. *The Aesthetics of Quietude: Ōta Shōgo and the Theatre of Divestiture*. Tokyo: Sophia University Press.

—— 1990. "Translator's Introduction," *The Water Station (Mizu no Eki)*, *Asian Theatre Journal*, 7, 2: 151–153.

Boyette, Patricia, 2007. "Psychophysical Training and Its Application to Performance of Beckett's Later Plays," in *Samuel Beckett and the World*

Stage: Textuality and Performativity, edited by Mari Boyd. Tokyo: Institute of Comparative Culture, Sophia University, 30–39.

Boyette, Patricia and Phillip Zarrilli, 2007. "Psychophysical Training, Physical Actions, and Performing Beckett: 'Playing Chess on Three Levels Simultaneously,'" *Contemporary Theatre Review*, 17, 1: 70–80.

Brandon, James R., ed., 1997. *Nō and Kyogen in the Contemporary World*. Honolulu: University of Hawaii Press.

—— 1985. "Time and Tradition in Modern Japanese Theatre," *Asian Theatre Journal*, 2, 1: 71–79.

—— 1978. "Training at the Waseda Little Theatre: the Suzuki Method," in *The Drama Review*, 22, 4: 29–42.

Braun, Edward, 1969. *Meyerhold on Theatre*. New York: Hill and Wang.

Bryden, Mary, 1998. *Samuel Beckett and Music*. Oxford, Clarendon Press.

Byckling, Liisa, 2005. Unpublished printed notes in lecture handout, "Theatre of the Future? Michael Chekhov and 21st Century Performance," delivered at a conference convened at Dartington Hall, UK, November 11–13.

Camp, Pannill, 2004. "The Trouble with Phenomenology," *Journal of Dramatic Theory and Criticism*, 19, 1: 79–100.

Carnicke, Sharon M., 2000. "The Life of the Human Spirit: Stanislavski's Eastern Self," *Teatr: Russian Theatre Past and Present* 1: 3–14.

—— 1998. *Stanislavski in Focus*. Amsterdam: Harwood.

—— 1994. "*An Actor Prepares/Rabota aktera nad soboi, Chast'I*: A Comparison of the English with the Russian Stanislavski," *Theatre Journal* 36, 4: 481–494.

—— 1993. "Stanislavski Uncensored and Unabridged," *The Drama Review* 37, 1: 22–37.

Caruthers, Ian and Takahashi Yasunari, 2004. *The Theatre of Suzuki Tadashi*. Cambridge: Cambridge University Press.

Chamberlain, Franc, 2004. *Michael Chekhov*. London: Routledge.

—— 2000. "Michael Chekhov on the Technique of Acting," in *Twentieth-century Actor Training*, edited by Alison Hodge. London: Routledge, 79–97.

Chekhov, Michael, 2002. *To the Actor*. London: Routledge.

—— 1991. *On the Techniques of Acting*. New York: Harper Perennial.

—— 1985. *Lessons for the Professional Actor*. New York: Performing Arts Journal Publications.

Cima, Gay Gibson, 1993. *Performing Women: Female Characters, Male Playwrights, and the Modern Stage*. Ithaca, NY: Cornell University Press.

Classen, Constance, 1993. *Worlds of Sense: Exploring the Senses in History and across Cultures*. London: Routledge.

Clifford, James, 1988. *The Predicament of Culture*. Cambridge, MA: Harvard University Press.

Cole, Toby and Helen Krich Chinoy, eds., 1970. *Actors on Acting*. New York: Crown.

Connerton, Paul, 1989. *How Societies Remember*. Cambridge: Cambridge University Press.

Cooper, David E., 2003. *World Philosophies*. Oxford: Blackwell.

Crimp, Martin, 2005a. *Martin Crimp Plays 2*. London: Faber and Faber.

—— 2005b. *Fewer Emergencies*. London: Faber and Faber.

—— 2000. *Martin Crimp Plays 1*. London: Faber and Faber.

—— 1997. *Attempts on Her Life*. London: Faber and Faber.

Csordas, Thomas, 1993. "Somatic Modes of Attention," *Cultural Anthropology*, 8, 2: 135–156.

Czikszentmihali, Mihaly, 1990. *The Psychology of Optimal Experience*. New York: Harper and Row.

Czikszentmihali, Mihaly and Isabella Selega Csikzentmihali, eds., 1988. *Optimal Experience: Psychological Studies of Flow in Consciousness*, Cambridge: Cambridge University Press.

Daboo, Jerri, 2004. "Standing Still While Not Standing Still," *Total Theatre*, 16, 3/4: 16–17.

Dalai Lama, 2002. *The Dalai Lama's Little Book of Wisdom*. London: HarperCollins.

Dasgupta, Gautam, 1993. "Dhanur Veda," chapters 249–252 in *Agni Purana*, unpublished translation from *Agnipurana of Maharsi Vedavyasa*. Varanasi: Chowkhambra Sanskrit Series, 1966.

Decroux, Etienne, 1978. *Mime Journal*, 7/8 (Etienne Decroux Eightieth Birthday Issue).

De Michelis, Elizabeth, 2005. *A History of Modern Yoga: Patanjali and Western Esotericism*. London: Continuum.

Dijkstra, Bram, 2004. "The Dialectics of Hope versus the Politics of Stasis in Art," *Tikkun*, November–December, 60–62.

Dolan, Jill, 2005. *Utopia in Performance*. Ann Arbor: University of Michigan Press.

Draeger, Donn F., 1979. *Modern Bujutsu and Budo*. New York: Weatherhill.

Draeger, Donn F. and Robert W. Smith, 1980. *Comprehensive Asian Fighting Arts*. Tokyo: Kodansha International.

Durham, Kim, 2004. "Acting On and Off: Sanford Meisner Reconsidered," *Studies in Theatre and Performance*, 23, 3: 151–163.

Dyczkowski, Mark S. G., 1987. *The Doctrine of Vibration*. Albany: State University of New York Press.

Edgar, David, 1999. *State of Play: Playwrights on Playwriting*. London: Faber and Faber.

Ekman, Paul, ed., 1984. "Expression and the Nature of Emotion," in *Approaches to Emotion*, edited by Klaus R. Scherer and Paul Ekman. Hillsdale, NJ: Lawrence Erlbaum Associates, 319–343.

—— 1982. *Emotions in the Human Face*, 2nd edition. Cambridge: Cambridge University Press.

Eliade, Mircea, 1958. *Yoga, Immortality, and Freedom*. Princeton: Princeton University Press.

Falkenstein, Linda, 1998. "The Water Station," *Isthmus*, November 20.

Feld, Steven, 1990 (1982). *Sound and Sentiment*. Philadelphia: University of Pennsylvania Press.

—— 2005. "Places Sensed, Senses Placed: Toward a Sensuous Epistemology of Environments," in *Empire of the Senses*, edited by David Howes. New York: Berg, 175–191.

Feuerstein, Georg, 1980. *The Philosophy of Classical Yoga*. Manchester: Manchester University Press.

Filliozat, Jean, 1991. *Religion, Philosophy and Yoga*. New Delhi: Motilal.

—— 1964. *The Classical Doctrine of Indian Medicine*. Delhi: Munshiram Manoharlal.

Fischer-Lichte, Erika, 1983. *Semiotics of Theater*. Bloomington: Indiana University Press.

—— 1989. "Theatre and the Civilizing Process: An Approach to the History of Acting," in Bruce McConachie and Tom Postelwait, eds., *Interpreting the Theatrical Past: Essays in the Historiography of Performance*. Iowa City: University of Iowa Press, 19–36.

Flood, Gavin, 1996. *An Introduction to Hinduism*. Cambridge: Cambridge University Press.

Fuchs, Elinor, 1996. *The Death of Character: Perspectives on Theater after Modernism*. Bloomington: Indiana University Press.

Gangadharan, N., trans., 1985. *Agni Purana*, Part II. *Ancient Indian Tradition and Mythology*, edited by J. L. Shastri, vol. 28. Delhi: Motilal Banarsidass.

Gantar, Jure, 1996. "Catching the Wind in a Net: The Shortcomings of Existing Methods for the Analysis of Performance," *Modern Drama*, 39, 4: 537–545.

Garner, Stanton, 1994. *Bodied Spaces: Phenomenology and Performance in Contemporary Drama*. Ithaca, NY: Cornell University Press.

Gaynesford, Maximilian de, 2003. "Corporeal Objects and the Interdependence of Perception and Action," in *The Philosophy of the Body*, edited by Mike Proudfoot. Malden, MA: Blackwell, 21–39.

Genet, Jean, 1954. *The Maids*, translation by Bernard Frechtman. New York: Grove Press.

George, David E. R., 1996. "Performance Epistemology," *Performance Research*, 1, 1: 16–31.

Gibson, J. J., 1979. *The Ecological Approach to Visual Perception*. Hillsdale, NJ: Lawrence Erlbaum.

Gordon, Robert, 2006. *The Purpose of Playing: Modern Acting Theories in Perspective*. Ann Arbor: University of Michigan Press.

Grieg, David, 2001. "Introduction," in *Kane: Complete Plays* by Sarah Kane. London: Methuen.

Griffin, Susan, 1992. *A Chorus of Stones*. New York: Anchor Books.

Grotowski, Jerzy, 1997. "Towards a Poor Theatre," in *The Grotowski Sourcebook*, edited by Lisa Wolford and Richard Schechner. London: Routledge, 26–35.

—— 1995. "From the Theatre Company to Art as Vehicle," in *At Work with Grotowski on Physical Actions*, edited by Thomas Richards. London: Routledge, 115–135.

—— 1992. Interview in *Les Dossiers H*. Paris: L'Age d'Homme et Bruno de Panafieu, 102–103.

Guerts, Kathryn Linn, 2005. "Consciousness as 'Feeling in the Body,'" in *Empire of the Senses*, edited by David Howes. Oxford: Berg, 164–178.

—— 2002. *Culture and the Senses: Bodily Ways of Knowing in an African Community*. Berkeley: University of California Press.

Gussow, Mel, 1988. "Man and the Elements in a Mystical Drama." *New York Times*, June 21: 17.

Hamilton, James R., 2000, "Theatrical Enactment." *Journal of Aesthetics and Art Criticism*, 58, 1: 23–35.

Haynes, John and James Knowlson, 2003. *Images of Beckett*. Cambridge: Cambridge University Press.

Hesla, David, 1971. *The Shape of Chaos: An Interpretation of the Art of Samuel Beckett*. Minneapolis: University of Minnesota Press.

Heyley, Liam, 2004. "The Beckett Project Beckons," *Cork Evening Echo*, Tuesday, May 25, 2004, "Beckett: Genius or Trickster?" *Cork Evening Echo*, Tuesday, May 25, 2004: 26.

Hodge, Alison, ed., 2000. *Twentieth-century Performer Training*. London: Routledge.

Hodgins, Paul, 2000. "An Evening of the Absurd," *Orange County Register*, April 10: 21.

Hornby, Richard, 1992. *The End of Acting: A Radical View*. New York: Applause Books.

Howes, David, ed., 2005. *Empire of the Senses: The Sensual Culture Reader*. Oxford: Berg.

Huang, Wen-Shan, 1979. *Fundamentals of T'ai Chi Ch'uan*. Hong Kong: South Sky Book Company.

Huard, Pierre and Ming Wong, 1977. *Oriental Methods of Mental and Physical Fitness*. New York: Funk and Wagnalls.

Huston, Hollis, 1995. "The Secret Life of a Theoretician," *Theatre Topics*, 5, 2: 123–132.

—— 1992. *The Actor's Instrument*. Ann Arbor: University of Michigan Press.

Ingold, Tim, 2000. *The Perception of the Environment*. London: Routledge.

Johnson, Don Hanlon, ed., 1995. *Bone, Breath, and Gestures: Practices of Embodiment*. Berkeley, CA: North Atlantic Books.

Johnson, Mark, 1987. *The Body in the Mind: The Bodily Basis of Meaning, Imagination, and Reason*. Chicago: University of Chicago Press.

Kalb, Jonathan, 1989. *Beckett in Performance*. Cambridge: Cambridge University Press.

Kane, Sarah, 2001. *Kane: Complete Plays*. London: Methuen.

Kantor, Tadeusz, 1993. *A Journey through Other Spaces: Essays and Manifestos, 1944–1990*. Edited and translated by Michal Kobialka. Berkeley: University of California Press.

Kaptchuk, Ted J., 1983. *The Web That Has No Weaver: Understanding Chinese Medicine*. New York: Congdon and Weed.

Keene, Donald, 1973 (1966). *Nō: The Classical Theater of Japan*. Tokyo: Kodansha International.

Kelly, Sean D., 2003a. "Edmund Husserl and Phenomenology," in *The Blackwell Guide to Continental Philosophy*, edited by Robert C. Solomon and David Sherman. Oxford: Blackwell, 112–142.

—— 2003b. "Merleau-Ponty on the Body," in *The Philosophy of the Body*, edited by Mike Proudfoot. Malden, MA: Blackwell, 62–76.

Kennedy, Brian and Elizabeth Guo, 2005. *Chinese Martial Arts Training Manuals: A Historical Survey*. Berkeley, CA: North Atlantic Books.

Knowlson, James and Elizabeth, 2006. *Beckett Remembering Remembering Beckett*. New York Arcade Publishing.

Konijn, Elly, 2000. *Acting Emotions*. Amsterdam: University of Amsterdam Press.

—— 1995. "Actors and Emotions: A Psychological Perspective," *Theatre Research International*, 20, 2, 132–140.

Krasner, David, ed., 2000a. *Method Acting Reconsidered*. New York: St. Martin's Press.

—— 2000b. "Strasberg, Adler and Meisner: Method Acting," in *Twentieth-century Actor Training*, edited by Alison Hodge. London: Routledge, 129–150.

Lakoff, George and Mark Johnson, 1999. *Philosophy in the Flesh*. New York: Basic Books.

—— 1980. *Metaphors We Live By*. Chicago: University of Chicago Press.

Lampe, Eelke, 2002. "Rachel Rosenthal Creating Her Selves," in *Acting (Re)Considered*, edited by Phillip B. Zarrilli. 2nd edition, London: Routledge, 291–304.

Leach, Robert, 1989. *Vsevolod Meyerhold*. Cambridge: Cambridge University Press.

Leder, Drew, 1998 (1992). "A Tale of Two Bodies: The Cartesian Corpse and the Lived Body," in *Body and Flesh: A Philosophical Reader*, edited by Donn Welton. Oxford: Blackwell, 117–129.

—— 1990. *The Absent Body*. Chicago: University of Chicago Press.

Leeland, Mary, 2004. "The Beckett Project Granary Theatre, Cork," *The Irish Times*, Wednesday May 26, 2004: 14 and Thursday, May 27, 2004: 31.

Lehmann, Hans-Thies, 2006. *Postdramatic Theatre*, translated by Karen Jürs-Munby. London: Routledge.

Lendra, I Wayan, 2002. "Bali and Grotowski," in *Acting Reconsidered*, edited by Phillip Zarrilli. London: Routledge, 148–162.

Levine, David Michael, 1999. "The Ontological Dimension of Embodiment: Heidegger's Thinking of Being," in *The Body*, edited by Donn Welton. Oxford: Blackwell, 122–149.

—— 1985. *The Body's Recollection of Being*. London: Routledge.

Liao, Waysun, 2000 (1977). *T'ai Chi Classics*. Boston: Shambhala.

Loukes, Rebecca, 2003. "Body Awareness Training: The Legacy of Elsa Gindler." Unpublished PhD thesis, Department of Drama, University of Exeter.

Luckhurst, Mary, 2003. "Political Point-Scoring: Martin Crimp's *Attempts on Her Life*," *Contemporary Theatre Review*, 13, 1: 47–60.

Lutz, Catherine A., 1988. *Unnatural Emotions*. Chicago: University of Chicago Press.

Lyons, William, 1980. *Emotion*. Cambridge: Cambridge University Press.

Marks, Joel and Roger T. Ames, eds., 1995. *Emotions in Asian Thought*. Albany: State University of New York Press.

Maund, Barry, 2003. *Perception*. Chesham: Acumen Publishing.

McCulloh, T. H., 2000. "Dreamlike Appeal of Beckett's Work Evident at Grove," *Los Angeles Times* April 10: B8–B9.

McDaniel, June, 1995. "Emotion in Bengali Religious Thought: Substance and Metaphor," in *Emotions in Asian Thought*, edited by Joel Marks and Roger T. Ames. Albany: State University of New York Press, 39–63.

McMullan, Anna, 2004. "*The Beckett Project*; The Disciplined Body," *Irish Theatre Magazine*, 54–56.

McTeague, James H., 1993. *Before Stanislavski: American Professional Acting Schools and Acting Theory 1875–1925*. Metuchen, NJ: Scarecrow Press, Inc.

Meisner, Sanford and D. Longwell, 1987. *Meisner on Acting*. New York: Vintage.

Merleau-Ponty, Maurice, 1968. *The Visible and the Invisible*, translated by Alphonso Lingus. Evanston, IL: Northwestern University Press.

—— 1964. *The Primacy of Perception*, edited by James J. Edie. Evanston, IL: Northwestern University Press.

—— 1962. *Phenomenology of Perception*. London: Routledge and Kegan Paul.

Merlin, Bella, 2007. *The Complete Stanislavski Toolkit*. London: Nick Hern Books.

—— 2003. *Konstantin Stanislavski*. London: Routledge.

—— 2001. *Beyond Stanislavski: The Psycho-Physical Approach to Actor Training*. New York: Routledge.

Mitter, Shomit and Maria Shevtsova, eds., 2005. *Fifty Key Theatre Directors*. London: Routledge.

Monier-Williams, Monier, 1963 (1899). *A Sanskrit–English Dictionary*. Delhi: Motilal Banarsidass.

Montemayor, Karen, 1998. "Notes on Ōta Shōgo and *The Water Station*," program for *The Water Station*. Madison: University of Wisconsin, University Theatre, 1–8.

Moore, Charles A., ed., 1967. *The Chinese Mind: Essentials of Chinese Philosophy and Culture*. Honolulu: University of Hawaii Press.

Moore, Sonia, 1979 (1968). *Training an Actor: The Stanislavski System in Class*. New York: Penguin Books.

—— 1967. *The Stanislavsky System*. New York: Viking.

Moran, Dermot, 2000. *Introduction to Phenomenology*. London: Routledge.

Morley, James, 2001. "Inspiration and Expiration: Yoga Practice through Merleau-Ponty's Phenomenology of the Body," *Philosophy East and West*, 51, 1: 73–82.

Nagatomo, Shigenori, 2006. "In Praise of Non-Performance in the Performing Arts," unpublished keynote address, "The Changing Body" Symposium, Department of Drama, University of Exeter, January 6–8.

—— 1992a. "An Eastern Concept of the Body: Yuasa's Body-Scheme." In *Giving the Body Its Due*, edited by Maxine Sheets-Johnstone. Albany: State University of New York Press, 48–68.

—— 1992b. *Attunement through the Body*. Albany: State University of New York Press.

Nagatomo, Shigenori and Monte S. Hull, 1993. "Translator's Introduction," in *The Body, Self-Cultivation, and Ki-energy*, by Yuasa Yasuo. Albany: State University of New York Press, ix–xxxvii.

Napier, Mark, 1986. *Mask, Transformation, and Paradox*. Berkeley: University of California Press.

Nearman, Mark, 1984a. "Feeling in Relation to Acting: An Outline of Zeami's Views," *Asian Theatre Journal*, 1, 1: 40–51.

—— 1984b. "Behind the Mask of Noh," *Mime Journal* 4: 20–64.

—— 1983. "*Kakyo*—Zeami's Fundamental

Principles of Acting," *Monumenta Nipponica*, 38, 1: 49–70.

—— 1982. "*Kakyo*—Zeami's Fundamental Principles of Acting," *Monumenta Nipponica*, 37, 3: 333–374; 4: 459–496.

—— 1980. "*Kyakuraika:* Zeami's Final Legacy for the Master Actor," *Monumenta Nipponica*, 35, 2: 153–198.

—— 1978. "Zeami's *Kyui*, A Pedagogical Guide for Teachers of Acting," *Monumenta Nipponica*, 33, 3: 299–332.

Needham, Joseph, 1954. *Science and Civilization in China*, Vols. 1–5. Cambridge: Cambridge University Press.

Neff, Debra, 1998. "The Water Station," *The Capital Times*, November 16.

Nightingale, Benedict, 2007. "Attempts on Her Life," *The Times*, March 16.

Noë, Alva, 2004. *Action in Perception*. Cambridge, MA: MIT Press.

Oida, Yoshi with Lorna Marshall, 1997. *The Invisible Actor*. London: Methuen.

—— 1992. *An Actor Adrift*. London: Methuen.

Onians, R. B., 1988 (1951). *The Origins of European Thought*. Cambridge: Cambridge University Press.

Oon, Clarissa, 2004. "Noh man's land," *The Straits Times*, September 20: L5.

O'Reilly, Kaite, 2001. "What Words Look Like in the Air," *Contemporary Theatre Review*, 11, 3/4: 41–44, 47.

Ortolani, Benito, 1995. *The Japanese Theatre: From Shamanistic Ritual to Contemporary Pluralism*. Princeton: Princeton University Press.

Ōta Shōgo, 2004. *The Tale of Komachi Told by the Wind*, translated by Mari Boyd in *Half A Century of Japanese Theater 1960s*, Part I, Volume VI, edited by Japan Playwrights Association. Tokyo: Kinokuniya Company, 209–244.

—— 1993. "*Sarachi*: A Play by Ōta Shōgo," translated by Robert Rolf. *Asian Theatre Journal*, 10, 2: 133–162.

—— 1990. *Mizo no Eki* (*The Water Station*), translated by Mari Boyd. *Asian Theatre Journal* 7, 2: 150–184.

—— 1985. "From Water Station's Program: 'Silence As a Means of Expression,'" in Robert K. Sarlos, "Tenkei Gekijo (Tokyo): *Water Station*," *The Drama Review*, 29, 1: 137–138.

—— 1978. *Komachi fuden* (*The Tale of Komachi Told by the Wind*), unpublished English translation by Mari Boyd. Original Japanese version in *Komachi Fuden: Ōta Shōgo gikyokushu*, 87–143. Tokyo: Hakusuisha.

Padoux, André, 1990. *Vac: The Concept of the Word in Selected Hindu Tantras*. Albany: State University of New York Press.

Pant, G. N., 1978. *Indian Archery*. Delhi: Agam Kala.

Pavis, Patrice, 2006. *Analyzing Performance*. Ann Arbor: University of Michigan Press.

—— 2003. *Analyzing Performance*. Ann Arbor: University of Michigan Press.

Pfister, Joel, 1997. "On Conceptualizing the Cultural History of Emotional and Psychological Life in America," in *Inventing the Psychological*, edited by Joel Pfister and Nancy Schnog. New Haven, CT: Yale University Press, 17–59.

—— 1995. *Staging Depth: Eugene O'Neill and the Politics of Psychological Discourse*. Chapel Hill: University of North Carolina Press.

Pfister, Joel and Nancy Schnog, eds., 1997. *Inventing the Psychological: Toward a Cultural History of Emotional Life in America*. New Haven, CT: Yale University Press.

Pisk, Litz, 1975. *The Actor and His Body*. New York: Theatre Arts Books.

Pitches, Jonathan, 2006. *Science and the Stanislavski Tradition of Acting*. London: Routledge.

Poggi, Jack, 1973. "The Stanislavski System in Russia," *Drama Review*, 17, 1: 124–133.

Polyakova, Elena, 1982. *Stanislavski*. Moscow: Progress Publishers.

Quick, Andrew, 2006. "The Gift of Play: *Ubung* and the Secret Signal of Gesture," in *Contemporary Theatres in Europe*, edited by Joe Kelleher and Nicholas Ridout. London: Routledge, 149–162.

Rafferty, Ellen, ed., 1989. *Putu Wijaya in Performance: A Script and Study of Indonesian*

Theatre. Madison: University of Wisconsin Center for Southeast Asian Studies, Monograph 5.

Rayner, Alice, 1994. *To Act, to Do, to Perform: Drama and the Phenomenology of Action.* Ann Arbor: University of Michigan Press.

Reed, Gregory, 1998. "The Water Station," *The Daily Cardinal,* November 23.

Reed, William, 1986. *Ki: A Practical Guide for Westerners.* Tokyo: Japan Publications.

Reid, H. and M. Croucher, 1983. *The Fighting Arts,* New York: Simon and Schuster.

Reiker, Hans-Ulrich, 1971. *The Yoga of Light: Hatha Yoga Pradipika,* translated by Elsy Becherer. Los Angeles: Dawn Horse Press.

Reinelt, Janelle G. and Joseph R. Roach, eds., 1992. *Critical Theory and Performance.* Ann Arbor: University of Michigan Press.

Richards, Thomas, 1995. *At Work with Grotowski on Physical Actions.* London: Routledge.

Riley, Jo, 1997. *Chinese Theatre and the Actor in Performance.* Cambridge: Cambridge University Press.

Roach, Joseph, 1993. *The Player's Passion: Studies in the Science of Acting.* Ann Arbor: University of Michigan Press.

Rotman, Brian, 1993. *Signifying Nothing: The Semiotics of Zero.* Stanford, CA: Stanford University Press.

Sandahl, Carrie, 2002. "Considering Disability: Disability Phenomenology's Role in Revolutionizing Theatrical Space," *Journal of Dramatic Theory and Criticism,* 16, 2: 17–32.

Sarlos, Robert K., 1985. "Tenkei Gekijo (Tokyo): Water Station." *The Drama Review,* 29, 1: 131–138.

Sartre, Jean-Paul, 1954. "Introduction," in *The Maids and Deathwatch* by Jean Genet. New York: Grove Press, 7–31.

Saunders, Graham, 2002. "*Love Me or Kill Me*": *Sarah Kane and the Theatre of Extremes.* Manchester: University of Manchester Press.

Scarry, Elaine, 1985. *The Body in Pain.* New York: Oxford University Press.

Schechner, Richard, 2007. "Rasaesthetics," in *The Senses in Performance,* edited by Sally Banes and André Lepecki. London: Routledge, 10–28.

—— 1988. *Performance Theory,* revised edition. London: Routledge.

—— 1985. *Between Theater and Anthropology.* Philadelphia: University of Pennsylvania Press.

—— 1977. *Essays on Performance Theory.* New York: Drama Book Specialists.

—— 1976. "From Ritual to Theatre and Back," in *Ritual, Play, and Performance: Readings in the Social Sciences/Theatre,* edited by Richard Schechner and Mady Schuman. New York: Seabury Press, 196–222.

—— 1973. *Environmental Theatre.* New York: Hawthorn Books.

Schechner, Richard and Mady Schuman, eds., 1976. *Ritual, Play, and Performance.* New York: The Seabury Press.

Scherer, Klaus R. and Paul Ekman, eds., 1984. *Approaches to Emotion.* Hillsdale, NJ: Lawrence Erlbaum Associates.

Schipper, Kristofer, 1993. *The Taoist Body.* Berkeley: University of California Press.

Schmitt, Natalie Crohn, 1990a. *Actors and Onlookers: Theatre and Twentieth-Century Scientific Views of Nature.* Evanston, IL: Northwestern University Press.

—— 1990b. "Theorizing about Performance: Why Now?" *New Theatre Quarterly* 7, 23: 231.

Schrag, Calvin O., 1969. *Experience and Being.* Evanston, IL: Northwestern University Press.

Scott, A. C., 1993. "Underneath the Stew Pot, There's the Flame . . . *T'ai Chi Ch'uan* and the Asian/Experimental Theatre Program," in *Asian Martial Arts in Actor Training,* edited by Phillip Zarrilli. Madison: Center for South Asia, University of Wisconsin-Madison, 48–61.

—— 1982. *Actors Are Madmen.* Madison: University of Wisconsin Press.

—— 1979. Unpublished class lecture. University of Wisconsin-Madison, October 10.

—— 1975. *Traditional Chinese Plays,* Vol. III, Madison: University of Wisconsin Press.

—— 1969. *Traditional Chinese Plays,* Vol. II, Madison: University of Wisconsin Press.

—— 1967. *Traditional Chinese Plays,* Vol. I, Madison: University of Wisconsin Press.

—— 1957. *The Classical Theatre of China*, London: George Allen and Unwin.

—— 1955. *The Kabuki Theatre of Japan*, New York: Collier Books.

Shaner, David Edward, 1985. *The Bodymind Experience in Japanese Buddhism*. Albany: State University of New York Press.

Shastri, Manmatha Nath Dutt, 1967. *Agni Puranam*. Varanasi: Chowkhamba Sanskrit Series.

Sheridan, Collette, 2004. "Beckett Project," *The Irish Examiner*, June 1.

Shweder, Richard A. and Robert A. LeVine, 1984. *Culture Theory: Essays on Mind, Self, and Emotion*. London: Cambridge University Press.

Sierz, Aleks, 2006. *The Theatre of Martin Crimp*. London: Methuen.

Singer, Annabelle, 2004. "Don't Want to Be This: The Elusive Sarah Kane," *The Drama Review*, 48, 2: 139–171.

Sklar, Deidre, 2007. "Unearthing Kinesthesia," in *The Senses in Performance*, edited by Sally Banes and André Lepecki. London: Routledge, 38–46.

Smith, Sid, 1988. "'Water Station' Can Be Hypnotic," *Chicago Tribune*, June 30: Zone C, 9.

Smith, Wendy, 1990. *Real Life Drama: The Group Theater and America*. New York: Alfred A. Knopf.

Sonenberg, Janet, ed., 1996. *The Actor Speaks*. New York: Random House.

Spencer, Charles, 2007. "Is the Heroine a Woman or a Brand of Car? If the Author Doesn't Know How Can We?" *Daily Telegraph*. March 16: 34.

Staniewski, Wlodzimierz with Alison Hodge, 2004. *Hidden Territories: The Theatre of Gardzienice*. London: Routledge.

Stanislavski, Konstantin, 2008. *An Actor's Work*, translated by Jean Benedetti. London: Routledge.

—— 1961. *Creating a Role*, translated by Elizabeth Reyholds Hapgood. New York: Theatre Arts Books.

—— 1949. *Building a Character*, translated by Elizabeth Reyholds Hapgood. New York: Theatre Arts Books.

—— 1948 (1924). *My Life in Art*, translated by J. J. Robbins. New York: Theatre Arts Books.

—— 1936. *An Actor Prepares*, translated by Elizabeth Reyholds Hapgood. New York: Theatre Arts Books.

States, Bert O., 1996. "Performance as Metaphor," *Theatre Journal*, 48, 1: 1–26.

—— 1971. *Great Reckonings in Little Rooms: On Phenomenology of Theatre*. Ithaca, NY: Cornell University Press.

Stein, Gertrude, 1995 (1949). *Last Operas and Plays*, edited by Carol Van Vechten. Baltimore, MD: Johns Hopkins University Press.

Steiner, George, 1967. *Language and Silence*. Harmondsworth: Penguin.

Stevens, John, 1987. *Abundant Peace: The Biography of Morihei Ueshiba*. Boston: Shambala.

Stinespring, Louise M., 2000. "Just Be Yourself: Derrida, Difference, and the Meisner Technique," in *Method Acting Reconsidered*, edited by David Krasner. New York: St. Martin's Press, 97–109.

Sutherland, Lorraine, 2007. "Knowing, Perceiving and Believing." Unpublished MA dissertation, Department of Drama, University of Exeter.

Suzuki Tadashi, 1986. *The Way of Acting*. New York: Theatre Communications Group.

Tachelet, Koen, 2000. "Displaced Consciousness: Tracing the Blind Spot of Our Perception," *Performance Research*, 5, 1: 83–90.

Torzecka, Marzena, 1992. "Running to Touch the Horizon: Ryszard Cieslak interviewed by Marzena Torzecka," *New Theatre Quarterly* 8, 31: 261–263.

Urban, Ken, 2001. "An Ethics of Catastrophe: The Theatre of Sarah Kane," *PAJ: A Journal of Performance and Art*, 69: 56–66.

Varela, Francisco, J. Evan Thompson and Eleanor Rosch, 1991. *The Embodied Mind: Cognitive Science and Human Experience*. Cambridge, MA: MIT Press.

Varenne, Jean, 1976. *Yoga and the Hindu Tradition*. Chicago: University of Chicago Press.

Varryar, Unnayi, 1975. *Nala Caritam Attakatha*, translated and introduced by V. Subramanya Iyer, edited by Farley Richmond. *Journal of South Asian Literature*, 10, 2–4: 211–248.

Vasu, Rai Bahadur Srisa Chandran, ed. and trans., 1975. *The Siva Samhita*. New Delhi: Oriental Books Reprint Corporation.

Waley, Arthur, 1976. *The Nō Plays of Japan*. Rutland, VT: Charles E. Tuttle Company.

Wangh, Stephen, 2000. *An Acrobat of the Heart: A Physical Approach to Acting*. New York: Vintage.

Webster's Third International Dictionary, 1976. Chicago: Encyclopedia Britannica, Inc.

Wegner, William H., 1976. "The Creative Circle: Stanislavski and Yoga," *Educational Theatre Journal* 28, 1: 85–89.

Welton, Donn, ed., 1999. *The Body*. Oxford: Blackwell Publishers.

Westbrook, A. and O. Ratti, 1970. *Aikido and the Dynamic Sphere*. Rutland, Vermont: Charles E. Tuttle.

White, David Gordon, 1996. *The Alchemical Body: Siddha Traditions in Medieval India*. Chicago: University of Chicago Press.

White, R. Andrew, 2006. "Stanislavski and Ramacharaka: The Influence of Yoga and Turn-of-the-Century Occultism on The System," *Theatre Survey*, 47, 1: 73–92.

Whitelaw, Billie, 1995. *Billie Whitelaw . . . Who He?* New York: St. Martin's Press.

Wilshire, Bruce, 1982. *Role Playing and Identity: The Limits of Theatre as Metaphor*. Bloomington: Indiana University Press.

Winnicott, D. W., 1989 (1971). *Playing and Reality*. London: Tavistock/Routledge.

Wolford, Lisa, 2000. "Grotowski's Vision of the Actor," in *Twentieth-century Actor Training*, edited by Alison Hodge. London: Routledge, 193–208.

Wolford, Lisa and Richard Schechner, eds., 1997. *The Grotowski Sourcebook*. London: Routledge.

Wong James I, 1978. *A Sourcebook in the Chinese Martial Arts*. Stockton, CA: Koinonia Productions.

Woodward, Kathleen, 1990–1991. "Introduction," *Discourse*, 13, 1: 3–11.

Wylie-Marques, Kathryn, 2003. "Opening the Actor's Spiritual Heart: The Zen Influence on *Nō* Training and Performance," *Journal of Dramatic Theory and Criticism*, 18, 1: 131–160.

Yoo Jeungsook 2007. "Moving *ki* in Inner and Outer Space—A Korean Perspective on Acting Process in *The Water Station*," *Contemporary Theatre Review*, 17, 1: 81–96.

Yuasa Yasuo, 1993. *The Body, Self-Cultivation, and Ki-energy*. Albany: State University of New York Press.

—— 1987. *The Body*. Albany: State University of New York Press.

Zarrilli, Phillip B., 2008a. "Embodying, Imagining, and Performing Displacement and Trauma in Central Europe Today," *New Theatre Quarterly*, 24: 1, 24–40.

—— 2008b. "An Enactive Approach to Understanding Acting," *Theatre Journal*, 59, 5: 635–647.

—— 2007. "Senses and Silence in Actor Training and Performance," in *The Senses in Performance*, edited by Sally Banes and André Lepecki. London: Routledge, 47–70.

—— 2004. "Toward a Phenomenological Model of the Actor's Embodied Modes of Experience," *Theatre Journal*, 56: 653–666.

—— ed., 2002a. *Acting (Re)Considered*, 2nd edition. London: Routledge.

—— 2002b. "Action, Structure, Task, and Emotion: Theories of Acting, Emotion, and Performer Training from a Performance Studies Perspective," in *Teaching Performance Studies*, edited by Nathan Stucky and Cynthia Winner. Carbondale: Southern Illinois University Press, 145–160.

—— 2002c. "The Metaphysical Studio," *The Drama Review*, 46, 2: 157–170.

—— 2001. "Negotiating Performance Epistemologies: Knowledges About, For and In," *Studies in Theatre and Performance*, 21, 1: 31–46.

—— 2000a. *Kathakali Dance Drama: Where Gods and Demons Come to Play*. London: Routledge.

—— 2000b. "Embodying the Lion's Fury: Ambivalent Animals, Activation, and Representation," *Performance Research*, 5, 2: 41–54.

—— 1998a. *When the Body Becomes All Eyes: Paradigms, Practices, and Discourses of Power*

in Kalarippayattu, A South Indian Martial Art.
New Delhi: Oxford University Press.

—— 1998b. "From Kalarippayattu to Beckett,"
video by Peter Hulton. Exeter: Arts Archives,
the Fourth Archive 1998/99.

—— 1997. "Acting 'at the nerve ends': Beckett,
Blau and the Necessary," *Theatre Topics,* 7,
2: 103–116.

—— 1995. "Between Theories and Practices:
Dichotomies or Dialogue?" *Theatre Topics,* 5,
2: 111–122.

—— ed., 1993. *Asian Martial Arts in Actor Training.*
Madison: Center for South Asia, University of
Wisconsin-Madison.

—— 1990. "What Does It Mean to 'Become
the Character?'" in *By Means of Performance,*
edited by Willa Appel and Richard Schechner.
Cambridge: Cambridge University Press,
132–148.

—— 1989. "Three Bodies of Practice in a
Traditional Indian Martial Art," *Social Science
and Medicine,* 28, 12: 1,289–1,310.

—— 1987a. "Where the hand is . . ." *Asian Theatre
Journal,* 4, 2: 205–214.

—— 1987b. "From Martial Art to Performance,
Part II," *Sangeet Natak,* 83, 14–45.

—— 1986. "From Martial Art to Performance,
Part I," *Sangeet Natak,* 81–82, 5–41.

—— 1984a. "'Doing the Exercise': The In-body
Transmission of Performance Knowledge in a
Traditional Martial Art," *Asian Theatre Journal,*
1, 2: 191–206.

—— 1984b. *The Kathakali Complex: Actor,
Structure, Performance.* New Delhi: Abhinav.

Zeami, Motokiyo, 2006. *The Flowering Spirit:
Classic Teachings on the Art of Nō,* translated
by William Scott Wilson. Tokyo: Kodansha
International.

—— 1984. *On the Art of the Nō Drama: The
Major Treatises of Zeami,* translation and
introduction by J. Thomas Rimer and Yamasaki
Masakazu, Princeton: Princeton University
Press.

Zinder, David, 2007. "'The Actor Imagines
with His Body'—Michael Chekhov:
An Examination of the Phenomenon,"
Contemporary Theatre Review, 17, 1: 7–14.

—— 2002. *Body Voice Imagination: A Training for
the Actor.* London: Routledge.

Unpublished journals/portfolios/personal communication

Abdul-Baqui, Miriam Hilmi, 2005.

Balakrishnan, Kallada, interview, 1983, Kerala.

Barbe, Fran, 2007 (in workshop).

DePalma, Maria, 1995, University of Wisconsin-
Madison.

Dietchman, Sherry, 1990, University of Wisconsin-
Madison.

Ensor, Roberta, 2004.

Goldingay, Sarah, 2006, University of Exeter.

Kaminer, Jenny, 1995.

Kaye, Alex, 2004.

Lanier, Dora, 1990.

Love, Heidi, 2005.

Marshall, Laura, 2004.

Melhuse, Peder, 1995, University of Wisconsin-
Madison.

Mitchell, Nathan, 2006, University of Exeter.

Morrison, Jeff, 1995, University of Wisconsin-
Madison.

Nustad, Brooke, 1990, University of Wisconsin-
Madison.

Palazzo, Claudia, 2004.

Russell, Samata, 2004.

Shapland, Jo, 2005, University of Exeter.

Spangler, Karole, 1995.

Sunhee Kim, 2004 and 2008.

Index

Page numbers in *italics* denote an illustration;
n signifies note

Abdul-Baqi, Miriam Hilmi 206
absent body 51, 60
acting: approaches to contemporary Western 41–42; as enquiry 5–6; theories and meta-theories of 41–46; transposing key elements of traditional training into contemporary 81–83
action: and perception 46
activating phrases: and utilization of residual awareness 90–92
"active analysis" process 18
active images 89–90; and *The Beckett Project* 126–127, 135, 141
acupuncture 75
Adler, Stella 16
aesthetic inner bodymind 50–51, 52, 55–57
aesthetic outer body 51, 52, 58
affective memory 16
Aflenz: Roman quarry at 179–180
Agni Purana 66–67
aikido, Japanese 27, 222n
Akihiko, Senda 149–150
Akihito, Yasumi 148–149
Albery, Tim 199, 201
American Laboratory Theater 15, 16
Amritabindu Upanisad 70

anthropological ecology 42, 45, 47
Arikha, Avigdor 226n
Artaud, Antonin 4, 8, 34–35, 40, 63
Asan, Raju 25
asana 28, 66, *66*, 91
Asian Experimental Theater Program 24, 116, 215–216, 219n, 224n
Asian perspectives: on mind, body and emotion 76–80
Atik, Anne 120, 226n
Atkinson, William Walker 220n
Attempts on Her Life 199–211, 231n; actors' tasks in 205–206; aesthetic logic and actualization of 200, 201, 202; critical reaction to and readings of 200–201, 232–233n; dialectic between foreground, background and environment 203–204; irony in 202–203, 206, 208, 211, 233n; issue of "her" 200, 202; "Kinda Funny" scenario 208–211; languages in 202; open nature of text 199, 205; productions of 199; in rehearsal and performance 201–205; scenarios 200; "The Threat of International Terrorism" scenario 206–211, *207*
attunement: of bodymind 78, 83, 84, 85, 87
auditory awareness 97, 163
Austin, James 45
Austrian Freedom Party 174
Ayurvedic medicine 37, 67, 70, 224n

Balakrishnan, Kallada 69
balance 84
baqua 73, 223–224n
Barba, Eugenio 4, 5, 8, 30, 39, 50, 81, 98, 101, 224n
Barbe, Fran 56
Bassett, Kate 232–233n
Baudrillard, Jean 200
Beckett, Samuel 40, 88, 221n; *Act Without Words I* 116–117, 123, 125, 130–132; animating forces 123–124; architecture and musicality in scores of 118–120; and consciousness 121, 123; *Eh Joe* 118, 119, 120, 121, 123, 124, 125, 139–143; *Endgame* 120, 126, 127; *Footfalls* 115–116, 119, 120, 121, 123, 124, 125; *Happy Days* 120, 125; *Imagination Dead Imagine* 120; interpretive indeterminacy of 117–118; iterative ambiguity of plays 115–116; *Not I* 116, 118–119, 120, 121, 123, 125, 127–128, 135–139; *Ohio Impromptu* 42–44, 42, 45, 48, 58, 60, 118, 119, 120–121, 123, 125, 132–135; *Piece of Monologue* 118, 119, 121, 123; places of possibility "between" in texts 126; *Play* 116, 117, 118, 119–120, 121, 123, 125, 126, 143; *Rockaby* 116, 118, 119, *119*, 123, 125, 128–129, 135; shifting between first and third person 121–122, 134; and simplification of action by acting scores 117, 118; states or conditions *in extremis* 120–122; *Waiting for Godot* 232
Beckett Project, The 124–143; activating the actor with *ki*-awareness/energy 125–126, 128; active images 126–127, 135, 141; casting for plays 225n; creation of mutuality 128–129; general considerations 127–130; leaving of audience at conclusion of each play 129–130; ordering of plays 129; strategies for meeting rigors of plays 128; work on *Act Without Words* 130–132; work on *Eh Joe* 139–143; work on *Not I* 135–139; work on *Ohio Impromptu* 132–135
Beijing opera 82
Benedetti, Jean 5–6, 15, 16, 221n
Benedetti, Robert 22, 24
Berberich, Junko 38
Bethe, Monide and Brazell, Karen 152
Bhagavad-Gita 70
bhava 23, 69, 70, 79
Billington, Michael 232n
biomechanics 4, 20–21, 57
Blau, Herbert 8, 31, 39–40, 115, 122, 143

Blind, The 15, 221n
Blue Bird, The 15
"body becomes all eyes" 1, 24, 60, 86–87, 91, 99, 213
body–mind dualism 13, 17, 18, 32, 39, 44–46, 76, 85
body–mind relationship 1, 4–5; Asian perspectives 76–78; and male culture 23; rediscovering through practice 22–24
body schema 51
bodymind 4–5, 31–32, 64; aesthetic inner 50–51, 52, 55–57; attunement of 78, 83, 84, 85, 87; as a gestalt 58–59; preliminary psychophysical training as form of preparation for 83–85
bodymind awareness 38; and breath/breathing 25; first-order 32, 38; modes of 32, 33; second-order 32, 33–34, 38, 76, 90–91; strategies to develop 89–97; third-order 32, 33, 38
Bogart, Anne 8
Boleslavsky, Richard 15, 16
Bollman, Horst 126
Bowles, Patrick 121
Boyd, Mari 144, 148, 150, 172, 173, 226n, 227n
Boyette, Patricia 43, *119*, 124, 125, 128–129, 135, 136–139, 140, 225n
breath/breathing 19, 21, 25–28, 29, 55; and aesthetic inner bodymind 55, 56–57; and auditory awareness 97; and awakening of energy 83; and bodymind awareness 25; cultivating "emotion in body" through training of 35; and emotional states of *kathakali* dance-drama 35, 36, 37, 77–78; focusing "inner eye" on 25–26, 27, 28, 31, 56, 89, 92; and *noh* actor 38; and structured improvisations 103; and *taiqiquan* 74
breath-in-action 158
breathing exercises 28, 56–57, 72, 74, 103; and structured improvisations 101, 103
Brecht, Berthold 8
Brook, Peter 224n
Buddhists 56
butoh 7, 57, 58, 176
Byckling, Liisa 20

cakras 70, 71, 72, 86
Carnicke, Sharon 14, 15, 219n
centering 84

Centre for Performance Research 125
Chandran Gurukkal 5, 222n
characterization 38–39
Chekhov, Michael 5, 8, 15, 20, 39, 220n
Chekhov Theatre Studio (Dartington Hall) 15
chiasmatic model 59–61, 83, 89, 181
Cieslak, Ryszard 4
Cima, Gay Gibson 122
cinta bhava 77
circuit of unconscious quasi-body 218, 223n
cittam 77, 78
Clurman, Harold 16
coenesthesis, circuit of 217
cognitive science 42, 45
Cohn, Ruby 126
consciousness 2, 38, 40; and Beckett 121; structured improvisation and double/multiple 107
consciousness of thought 134
Cooper, David 76
Copeau, Jacques 1, 8, 25, 33, 34, 38, 39, 85
corporeal absence 50
Crawford, Cheryl 16
Crimp, Martin 8, 231n, 232n; and *Attempts on Her Life* 199–211; *Fewer Emergencies* 199
Crook, Andy 44, 131, 133
cross-cultural psychology 221n

Dalai Lama 213
Dannequin, Laura 230n
dantian 89, 92, 93, 94, 96, 156, 164
Dasgupta, Gautam 67
de Jongh, Nicholas 200, 201
decoction 87, 147, 224n
Decroux, Etienne 21
DePalma, Maria 124
Descartes, René 13, 46
desire: introducing of in structured improvisations 107–108
Dhanur Veda 66
Dhayanidhi 5, 25, 222n
Dietchman, Sherry 17
divestiture: Ōta Shōgo's aesthetic of 144, 146–147, 148, 150, 153
Dolan, Jill: *Utopia in Performance* 201
dramaturgy, actor's 113
Dullin, Charles 25

Edgar, David 200
embodied modes of experience 50–60; aesthetic inner bodymind body 50–51, 52, 55–57; aesthetic outer body 51, 52, 58; recessive body 50, 52, 54–55; surface body 50, 51, 52, 53–54
embodiment: chiasmatic model of 60–61; enactive approach 41–60; and *Ohio Impromptu* 42–44, 45; and phenomenology 45, 222n
emotion–instinct circuit 39, 88, 93, 217–218
emotion memory 16
emotion(s): Asian perspectives on relationship with mind and body 76–80; controlling of 88; separation from body 76
empty space: filling 91–92
enactive approach 41–60; implications of enactive view of acting 48–50; towards perception 47–50; views actor as a sentient perceptual being 42, 44, 46–50; and *The Water Station* 171
energy *see* inner energy
energy vectors 93–95, 95
enquiry, acting as 5–6
Ensor, Roberta 194
Esplanade Theatre Studio (Singapore) 150
Esslin, Martin 120
experience: and cognition 46
external sensory-motor circuit 217
exteroception 51, 54, 58

Falkenstein, Linda 144
faqi (radiate presence) 19
feet: enhancing awareness of tactile sensation through 91
first-order bodymind awareness 32, 38
fish pose 64
Forced Entertainment 7
forgetfullness of body 53
Forsythe, Henderson 226n
Fort, Paul 15
Foss, Roger 200
4:48 Psychosis 188–198, 205; embodying images-in-action drawn from the text 198; embodying state of "crippling failure" 193–194; entry points for actors "playing" Figure and Doctor 190; guiding of work by image of weaving a tapestry 190–191; "I am . . ." statements 191–192; importance of listening and exercises

in 192, 196–197; and irony 196–198; issues of suicide and psychosis 189; as "open text" 188; psychophysical symbiosis when delivering a monologue 194–196, *196*; types of scenarios 190; use of large cast 189, 231–232n; use of multiple voices 198

Gardzienice Theatre Association 53, 150, 228n
Garen, Erast 4
Garner, Stanton 45, 50, 58, 222n
Garre-Rubio, Soledad *64*
Garrick, David 113
Gaynesford, Maximilian de 46
Genet, Jean 109; *The Maids* 109–111, 112, 224n
gestalt 49, 50, 58–59, 67, 83, 87
Gibson, Alan 226n
Gibson, James: *The Ecological Approach to Visual Perception* 46, 47, 49
Gluschitsch, Walter 179
Goffman, Erving 109
Goldman, Michael 225n
Gordon, Robert 13; *The Purpose of Playing* 41–42
Govindankutty Nayar, Gurukkal 3, 4, 23, 24, *24*, 25, 63, 69, 72
Granary Theatre (Cork) 140
Griffin, Susan 1–2, 174; *A Chorus of Stones* 175, 176
Grotowski, Jerzy 4, 5, 8, 20, 82, 86
Group Theater 16
Gussow, Mel 144, 146, 147

ha 152
Haider, Jörg 174
hands-on work 92–93, *92*, 94
Hapgood, Elizabeth 15, 220–221n
Harris, Rosemary 117
Harvey, Lawrence E. 122
hatha yoga 5, 25, 28–29, 65, 67, 68
Heibert, Frank 230n
Heidegger, Martin 148
Held, Lawrence 118, 127
Heuegger, Christian 139, *183*, 230n
Hindus 20, 56
Ho Tze Siang, Zachary 207
hsing-i 73, 223n
Huston, Hollis 2–3
Hye Ok Kim 207

"I can" of the body 45–46, 81–98
ida 71, 72
imagination 20, 39, 87
improvisations, structured 100–112, 176; basic rules guiding beginning work 105; and breathing exercises 103; creating psychophysical scores and reduction 103; and desire to speak 109; double/multiple consciousness in 107; introducing a desire 107–108; introducing objects 108–109; and *The Maids* 109–111; reduction exercise 101–102; repetition of opening *taiqiquan* and breathing 101; and residual awareness 104; seating structures 104–107
in-between: exercises for "playing" 99–112
Ingold, Tim 45, 46, 47
"inner action" 14
inner energy 19–21, 77; awakening of 21, 83, 84, 85–87; circulation of in *kalarippayattu* 69–70, 72; cultivation of 87–88; exercises to engage in *The Water Station* 155–156, 160; Meyerhold's use of scientific metaphor to describe 20–21; modulating of in *noh* acting 38; and *taiqiquan* 74–75; *see also* ki/qi; prana-vayu
"inner eye": focusing of on breathing 25–26, 27, 28, 31, 56, 89, 92
intellectual knowledge 59
inter-subjectivity 95–96
International School for Theatre Anthropology (Denmark) 101
interoception 54, 58
Intruder, The 15
irony 202–203; in *Attempts on Her Life* 202–203, 205–206, 208, 211, 233n; in *4:48 Psychosis* 196–198

jing-luo 75
jo–ha–kyu: and *The Water Station* 152–153
Johnson, Mark 45
Jouvet, Louis 25
Juan, Deane 92

kabuki 65
Kadensho 34
kalarippayattu 4, 5, 22, 23, 29, 38, 40, 48, 55, 63, 64–72, 80, 85; body(ies) in 67–72; breathing

exercises 56, 72; circulation of vital energy 69–70, 72; exercises and poses 67–68; lion pose 24, *24*, 53, 54, 59, 63, 89, 90, 91, 93, 94, 95; and long staff 68, *68*, 95–97; massage 68–69, *69*; possessing knowledge of the body 67; roots of 66; subtle body and vital energy 70, *71*, 72; transposing to contemporary acting from 82; and weapons 68, *68*, 95–96; and yogic paradigm 66–67

kalaris 22

Kalb, Jonathan 115, 132, 133, 135, 139, 225n

Kaminer, Jenny 143

Kane, Sarah 8, 188–198

Kantor, Tadeusz 8, 87

karma yoga 65

kathakali dance-drama 4, 5, 8, 19, 22, 23, 35–38, *36*, 65, 69, 77–79, 141; and centered groundedness 37; emotional states and breathing 35, *36*, 37; hand-gestures 37

Kerala 22, 81–82

Kerala Kalamandalam 23

Kerala State School of Arts 4

ki-awareness 57, 86, 87, 108, 154, 224n; activating of in *The Beckett Project* 125–126

ki-meridian system 75, 218

ki-sensitive person 39

ki/qi 19–21, 39, 55, 56, 73, 74–75, 86, 87–88

King Nala's Law 77–78, 80

Knebel, Maria Osipovna 14

Knowlson, James 118

Komachi, legend of 148, 228n

KRAKEN 39

ksatriyas 66

Kuo Pao Kun 229n

kyu 152

Lakoff, George 45

Lan-Fang, Mei 215

"landscape" plays 221n

Lanier, Dora 31

Lao Tsu 115

Leach, Robert 20–21

LeCoq 57

Leder, Drew 45, 50, 53–55, 59, 222–223n; *The Absent Body* 51

Lehmann, Hans-Thies 7

Levine, David Michael 50

Lindsay, Claire *207*

lion pose 24, *24*, 53, 54, 59, 63, 89, 90, 91, 93, 94, 95

listening exercises 196–197

Litschauer, Uschi 139, 230n

"livedness" 45, 222n

Lopez, Alberto Ruiz *207*

Love, Heidi *64*, 102, *207*, 208

Luckhurst, Mary 200–201, 233n

Lyotard, Jean-François 21

Macauley, Alastair 201

Macdonald, James 189

MacGowran, Jack 226n

Maeterlinck, Maurice 15, 16; *The Blind* 15; *The Blue Bird* 15; *The Intruder* 15

Maids, The 109–111, 112, 224n

male culture: and body–mind relationship 23

mana 76, 77

manasa 79

Mandell, Alan 120, 127

martial arts 1, 8, 55, *64*, 65, 73, 81, 224n

Matsui, Akira 5

maya yoga 65

Meisner, Sanford 16–17

meiyou qi (no presence) 19

Melhuse, Peder 118, 124, 139, 141

Mencius 74

Mendel, Derek 226n

meridian system *see ki*-meridian system

Merleau-Ponty, Maurice 45–46, 51, 59

Merlin, Bella 18, 20

meta-theory 42

method acting 16, 17

Meyerhold, Vsevolod 4, 5, 8, 15, 20–21, 57

mind: Chinese word for 76; Japanese word 76; *see also* body–mind dualism; body–mind relationship; bodymind

mind-aspect 31, 32

Mitchell, Kate 199, 232n

Mitchell, Rand 226n

Mitter, Shomit 221n

Mnouchkine, Ariane 8

Mohamedunni Gurukkal, Sakhav P. 25, 26

"moming" 29

Moore, Sonia 18; *Training an Actor* 17

Moran, Dermot 45
Morrison, Jeff 126
Moscow Art Theatre 15–16; First Studio 14
motionlessness 25

nadi 70, 71, 72, 86
Nagatomo, Shigenori 45, 59, 85
Namboodiri, M. P. Sankaran 4, 5, 23, 37
Nearman, Mark 38, 101, 102, 108, 156–157, 171–172
neikong 75
nirvana yoga 65
"no-mind" state 74, 76, 90
Noë, Alva 44, 45, 47, 48, 49
noh 5, 8, 18, 37–38, 57, 65, 116, 227n
Noushad Mohamed Kunju 165, 166, 168
Nustad, Brooke 31

objects: introducing of in structured
    improvisations 108–109
occultism 13
Ohno, Kazuo 176
Oida, Yoshi 8, 224n
onkan 38
Oon, Clarissa 172–173
O'Reilly, Kaite 174, 182, 186, 230n
Ōta Shōgo 144–173, 227n; aesthetics of quietude
    148, 150; co-founding of Tenkei Theatre
    Company 148; development of minimalism
    148–150; divesiture process 144, 146–147, 148,
    150, 153; and importance of the spine 227n; new
    works 228n; Station plays 144, 147, 148, 176; *The
    Tale of Komachi Told by the Wind* 148–150, 228n;
    training regime 147; *see also Water Station, The*
otta 3, 68
Ouspenskaya, Maria 15, 16

Padoux, André 223n
pain 54
Palazzo, Claudia 195
perception 46–50; and action 46–47; ecological
    approach to 47, 49; enactive approach to 47–50;
    types of understanding of 47–48
perceptual awareness: attunement of actor's 49, 50
performance score 39, 40, 58, 79–80, 84, 88, 89,
    113
Pern Yiau Sim 165, 166, 168

Pfister, Joel: *Inventing the Psychological* 19
phenomenology 42, 45–46, 51
Phillips, Stan 226n
pingala 71, 72
play/playing 99–100
"playing" inbetween, exercises for 99–112
prana/prana-vayu 14, 15, 19, 20, 21, 35, 55, 72, 78,
    220n
"pre-expressive" territory 5
proprioception 54, 58
psyche 18, 19, 87
psychological gesture 20, 39
psychology 13, 18–19, 221n
psychophysical integration 85
psychophysical paradigm 5, 29

qi see ki/qi
qigong 74
Quick, Andrew 99

Rajeshekharan Nayar 3
Ramacharaka *see* Atkinson, William Walker
Rayner, Alice 45
recessive body 50, 52, 54–55
reduction 101–102, 103, 108
rehearsal process 30
Reparatory Theater of Lincoln Center (New York)
    226
repetition exercises 192
residual awareness: and structured improvisations
    104; utilization of by activating phrases 90–92
Ribot, Théodule Armand 8, 13, 14
Rieger, Gernot 184, 230n
Rig Veda 65
Roach, Joseph: *The Player's Passion* 19
Roerich, Helena 220n
Römersteinbruch 179–180
Rosenthal, Rachel 154
Rotman, Brian 184
Royal Court Theatre 188, 199, 200
Ryker, Karen 124

San-Feng, Chang 75, 91, 92, 224n
Sandahl, Carrie 222n
Sarlos, Robert K. 147
Sartre, Jean-Paul 109

Sasitharan, T. 229n
Saunders, Graham 189, 231n
Scarry, Elaine: *The Body in Pain* 175–176
Schechner, Richard 30, 31
Schipper, Kristofer 74
Schneider, Alan 136, 226n
Scott, A. C. 5, 22, 24–25, 40, 84–85, 215–216
second-order bodymind awareness 32, 33–34, 76, 90–91
Seewald, Klaus 64, 150, 230n
self 18–19
self-consciousness 18, 221n
Seng Soo Ming 207
sense memory 16
sensitization 87
sensorimotor knowledge 47–48, 49–50
Shaner, David Edward 32, 33
Shapland, Jo 64, 210–211
Sherif, C. Mohammed 25, 221n
"Shooting a bow" *étude* 4
Sierz, Aleks 201
Smith, Sid 147, 172
Soloviovo, Vera 14
somatic knowledge 58–59
Sotoba Komachi 148
source traditions 63–80 *see also kalarippayattu; taiqiquan; yoga*
Spangler, Karole 124, 139, 142–143
Speaking Stones 88, 174–187; "Bewilderment" structure 180–181; commissioning of 174; costumes 177; developing of performance structures 177, 178; displacement and trauma issues 175–176; dramaturgical possibility of 174–175; "Footsteps of the Dead" structure 182–184, *183*; "Leaving" structure 181–182; performances in Aflenz Roman quarry 179–180; performances of 174; performative premise 176–177; in rehearsal and performance 177–179; resources/stimuli for performance score 176, 230–231n; "Semiotics of Zero" structure 184–186; "Why Did You Leave" structure 186
Spencer, Charles 232n
spiritualism 13, 220n
squeezing exercise 141
Sreejayan Gurrukal 25, 221n
staff, and *kalarippayattu* training 68, *68*, 95–97

"standing still while not standing still" 22, 24, 25, 38, 115, 124, 150
Staniewski, Wlodzimierz 228n
Stanislavski, Konstantin 1, 5, 8, 13–18, 117; and acting as enquiry 5; "active analysis" process 18; American versions of 15–18; and *The Blue Bird* 15; and forgetfulness of body 51; legacy of 14–15; and Maeterlinck 15; and "Method of Physical Actions" 221; and *A Month in the Country* 14; moving beyond 18; *My Life in Art* 14; psychophysical theory and sources of 8, 13–14; Soviet censorship of interest in yoga 15; translation of work 15, 220–221n; and yoga 14, 220n
States, Bert O. 45
"static theatre" 15
Stein, Gertrude 221n
Stephens, Robert 117
"stillness at the center" 22, 24, 25
Stoppard, Tom 116
Strasberg, Lee 16
structured improvisations *see* improvisations, structured
Stubblefield, Michael 229n
subconscious: and superconscious 14, 220n
subtext 225n
subtle body 70, 71, 72
Sulerzhitsky, Leopold Antonovich 14
Sunhee Kim 191–192
superconscious: and subconscious 14, 220n
surface body 50, 51, 52, 53–4
Suzuki training 57
sweat, mental dimension of 63
symbolism 15

tactile awareness: opening of through the skin 91, 93
Tadashi, Suzuki 7, 8, 81
taiqiquan 5, 25, 29, 38, 63, 72–76, 80; and breathing techniques 74; form of training 73; name 73; origin of as martial arts practice 73; *qi* and ways of cultivating 74–75; and state of non-mindedness 74; and structured improvisations 101, 104–109; transposing to contemporary acting from 82; yin–yang symbol 72–74, *74*
Takeo, Hodojima 148

Tam ka Man 207
Tandy, Jessica 136, 226n
tanjamppayattu 63
tantric practice 223n
Taoist practices 56, 73, 75, 223n
Taylor, Paul 200
Tenkei Theatre Company 144, 147, 148, 228n
thang-ta 66
Theater Asou 174, 179, 224n, 230n
Theatre Arts Monthly 16
Theatre Training and Research Programme
    (TTRP) 82, 150, 229n
Theatre of Transformation *see* Tenkei Theatre
    Company
theories of acting 41–46
third-order bodymind awareness 32, 33, 38
Thorpe, Bud 120, 127
thought, physicalization of 38–40
Toporkov, Vasily Osipovich 14–15
Toru, Shinagawa 148
training 24–34; and atmosphere 29; and body–
    mind relationship 31; breathing exercises 25–26,
    28; complementary strategies to help attune
    and activate the actor 89–97; and Copeau 25;
    and development of internal state of awareness
    25, 31–32; and energy vectors 93–95; *hatha yoga*
    exercises 28–29; and personal justification 30;
    as pre-performative 29, 83; as process of self-
    definition 30; psycho-dynamic elements/
    principles of 83; separation of preparation
    from rehearsal 31; through repetition 29, 30,
    31; and time 31; transposing of elements of
    traditional training into contemporary acting
    81–83
Tsung-yueh, Wang 73, 74
Tuen Leung, Hiu 170–171

Ueshiba, Morihei 222n
unbendable arm exercise 27–28
unconscious quasi-body 57, 218, 223n
United States: approaches to Stanislavski's work
    15–18
University of Exeter 189, 201, 231n, 233n
University of Wales 228–229n
Upanishads 65
Urbans, Sandra 230n

Varela, Francisco 45, 46
Variyar, Unnayi 77
vocal resonators, work on 134

Warrier, G. S. 78
Warrilow, David 226n
Water Station, The 40, 144–173, 145; acting in
    silence and slow movement as premises for
    144, 146–147, 150, 172; audience's relationship
    with performance 172–173; and decoction 147;
    developing specific psychophysical acting
    scores in rehearsal 159–171; divestiture principle
    146, 147, 150, 172, 227n; dramatic structure and
    movement in 152–153; exercises to engage inner
    awareness and energy 155–156, 160; Man in the
    Junk Heap 173; preparatory process in studio
    154–157; psychophysical stimuli for sensory
    embodiment of actions 153–154; relationship
    between The Girl and Two Men 167–168;
    scenes in 145–146; "script as document" 150–151;
    slow walk work 155–156, 159; slowing down of
    actions by actor 150; soundscape and music 146,
    152; source materials 144, 227n; staging of living
    silence 146; and The Girl 160–165; touching
    Ōta's source score 157–159; and Two Men
    165–168; and Woman with a Parasol 168–171
Wegner, William H. 221n
White, R. Andrew 220n
"white spaces" 1–2
Whitelaw, Billie 116, 117, 119–120, 123, 124, 125,
    127–128, 136, 138, 141, 224–225n, 226n
Willer, Gerhard 199
Wilshire, Bruce 45
Wilson, Robert 7
Winnicott, D. W. 99
Wong, James I. 72–73, 74
Wooster Group 7

Yen Lu Wong 22
yin–yang 72–74, 74, 75
yoga 1, 8, 13, 14, 20, 28–29, 38, 40, 55, 63, 65–66, 80,
    86; *asana* 28, 66, 66, 91; and *cakras* 70, 71, 72, 86;
    and occult-spiritualism 220n; origin of term 65;
    philosophy of 65–66; and Stanislavski 14, 220n;
    transposing to contemporary acting from 82;
    varieties of 65; *see also hatha yoga*

Jeungsook Yoo 145, 150, 157, 158–159, 160, 161–165, 167, 171, 223–224n

Yuasa Yasuo 29, 33–34, 34, 39, 45, 51, 56–57, 58, 74, 75, 80, 88, 217–218

Zarrilli, Phillip B., *Acting (Re)Considered* 41

Zeami, Motokiyo 5, 26, 34, 38, 40, 108; *Kakyo* 90, 101, 102, 108, 122, 156–157, 171–172

Zinder, David 20

Zöhrer, Monika 230n

About the DVD-ROM

This product is designed primarily to run in a Windows Operating System on a PC or in Apple Mac OSX. It will load automatically onto a Windows PC. Mac users who do not have access to a Windows Operating System should go to the disk's directory and double click on the Director file – Zarrilli.osx. A dedicated Mac application will then load.

The minimum specifications for the successful operation of this DVD-ROM are:

- Pentium 4 2.8 GHz
- QuickTime 7 player installed (available as a free download for Windows from www.apple.com)
- 4 × DVD-ROM
- Graphics card min. 32 Mb
- Sound card
- 512 Mb RAM
- Minimum resolution 1024 × 768
- Windows XP +
- Media Player (available as a free download from www.microsoft.com)
- Mac OSX

Please close down other applications while running this DVD-ROM.